VISUAL QUICKSTART GUIDE

ADOBE FLASH CS4
PROFESSIONAL

FOR WINDOWS AND MACINTOSH

Katherine Ulrich

 Peachpit Press

Visual QuickStart Guide

Adobe Flash CS4 Professional for Windows and Macintosh

Katherine Ulrich

Peachpit Press

1249 Eighth Street
Berkeley, CA 94710
510/524-2178
510/524-2221 (fax)

Find us on the Web at: www.peachpit.com
To report errors, please send a note to errata@peachpit.com
Peachpit Press is a division of Pearson Education

Project Editor: Wendy Sharp
Production Editor: Danielle Foster
Contributor: Andreas Heim
Copy Editor: Jacqueline Aaron
Tech Editor: Andreas Heim
Compositor: WolfsonDesign
Indexer: FireCrystal Communications
Cover design: Peachpit Press

Notice of Rights

Notice of Liability

Trademarks

ISBN 13: 978-0-321-59192-0
ISBN 10: 0-321-59192-5

9 8 7 6 5 4 3

Printed and bound in the United States of America

*To Perry Whittle, whose support,
both moral and technical, helps me
keep it all in perspective, and who
downplays my failings and promotes
my successes shamelessly.*

Thank You

Special thanks to the editor of this edition, Wendy Sharp, Senior Acquisitions Editor, for her helpful editorial direction, words of encouragement, and perseverance throughout the process of creating this book. A huge thank you to Jen deHaan, Adobe Senior Software Quality Engineer, for guiding me through the mysteries of the new motion-tweening model; for answering my questions with good humor and good advice; and for reviewing the animation chapters of this book and providing generous, useful feedback and tips. Continued thanks to Andreas Heim, Director of Technology, Smashing Ideas; for writing Chapter 15 (originally for the CS3 edition of this book); and for once again taking on the role of technical reader/technical resource for this edition. A round of applause for copy editor Jacqueline Aaron; it's been wonderful having her eagle eye watching my back for errors of spelling, grammar, logic, and style. Kudos to Production Editor Danielle Foster and compositor WolfsonDesign for making these pages clean and clear. Thanks also to Emily Glossbrenner for expert indexing on a tight time line and to Michael J. Ulrich for help in testing import of Adobe Illustrator artwork.

A tip of the hat to those whose various forms of assistance in past editions still echo in this one: Brad Bechtel, Lisa Brazieal, Erika Burback, Jeremy Clark, Cliff Colby, Pat Christenson, Peter Alan Davy, Jane DeKoven, Jonathan Duran, Lupe Edgar, Victor Gavenda, Suki Gear, Connie Jeung-Mills, Mark R. Jonkman, Becky Morgan, Erica Norton, Christi Payne, Janice Pearce, Nancy Reinhardt, Sharon Selden, Kathy Simpson, James Talbot, Tiffany Taylor, Bentley Wolfe, and Lisa Young.

And finally, a special note of thanks in memory to Marjorie Baer, who brought me to this project in the first place and who has been so often in my thoughts as I worked on this revision.

CONTENTS AT A GLANCE

TABLE OF CONTENTS

TABLE OF CONTENTS

INTRODUCTION

Adobe Flash Professional CS4 is the latest version of the enormously popular Web design tool. In its original incarnation, Flash gave Web designers an efficient way to send artwork and animation over limited-bandwidth connections. Flash's claim to fame was its ability to deliver vector images over the Web, making download times shorter. Flash's use of progressive downloading and streaming allowed some elements of a Web site to display immediately, making sites more responsive.

Today Flash is a robust toolkit for creating anything from simple animations to full-fledged Web sites and complex Web applications. To the simple tools for creating and animating artwork and interface elements and writing the HTML necessary to display all those elements in a Web page via a browser, Flash adds a full-fledged object-oriented scripting language, the ability to display video, and ever-more sophisticated graphics and animation tools.

In Flash CS4, new tools enable users to manipulate and animate symbols in 3D, work with animation segments as objects, and create and animate puppet-like inverse-kinematics structures. Plus Flash offers import features for working with Adobe Photoshop and Adobe Illustrator artwork, tools for importing and displaying encoded video files, user-interface and data-handling components, and ActionScript 3.0 for scripting complex interactivity.

About Flash Player

In Flash's early days, the need to use a player to view Flash content was considered a drawback to creating Web content with Flash. Designers feared that users would be reluctant to spend time downloading another helper application for their browsers. But Flash has become the de facto standard for delivering Web rich-media content—especially interactive vector art, animation, and video—and Flash Player is now widely distributed. At the time this book was published, Adobe estimated that roughly 97 percent of viewers in the United States, Canada, the United Kingdom, Germany, France, and Japan had already adopted Flash Player 9.

How Flash animates

Flash allows you to use standard animation techniques to create the illusion of movement. You create a series of still images, each slightly different from the next. By displaying the images rapidly, one after another, you simulate continuous movement. Flash CS4 also provides some new animation techniques and tools: An object-oriented tweening technique (*motion tweening*) and a new panel for working with such animations (the Motion Editor) give animators a great deal of control in animating the properties of objects. Inverse kinematics tools enable animators to create skeleton-like structures that help to animate characters or mechanisms with naturalistic movement. Flash's animation tools help you create, organize, and synchronize the animation of multiple graphic elements, sounds, and video clips.

Flash interactivity

Over time, Flash's tools for creating interactivity have become more robust. Flash CS4 contains a full-fledged object-oriented scripting language, in two versions: ActionScript 2.0 and 3.0. Both are compliant with the ECMA-262 specification, which is also the foundation for JavaScript, so they should feel familiar to anyone who already knows JavaScript. With ActionScript, Flash has become a toolkit for creating what have come to be called Rich Internet Applications (RIAs). An RIA might be anything from an online store to a corporate training module to a video-clip-display site to a snazzy promotional piece describing this year's hottest new car, complete with customizable virtual test-drives.

Flash file formats

Flash provides both an authoring environment for creating content and a playback system for making that content viewable on a local computer or in a Web browser. You create artwork, animation, and interactivity in Flash-format files. These files have the extension .fla and are often referred to as *FLAs*. To make that content viewable on the Web, you convert the FLA files to Flash Player format; Flash Player files have the extension .swf. Another name for the playable format is *SWF* (pronounced *swif*).

How Flash delivers

Flash's publishing feature creates the necessary HTML code to display your Flash content in a Web browser. You can also choose alternate methods of delivering Flash content—as animated GIF images, for example. Flash creates the alternate files during the publishing process.

Figure i.1 The Tools panel is now resizable and customizable.

A

B

C

Figure i.2 You can't see it in this gray-scale image, but the X value, 138.9, is highlighted in blue like a live link (A). Known as hot text, this number actually contains a hidden value-entry system. A double-arrow pointer appears when you move the mouse over a hot text area (B). Click the text to activate a text box (C); drag the text to activate a slider.

Flash CS4: What's New?

This version of Flash offers significant new tools for designers and animators. Adobe also continues to integrate Flash with other Adobe products, especially those in the Adobe Creative Suite. Let's look at some highlights of Flash CS4.

Interface enhancements

Application frame. Flash CS4's interface more closely matches that of other applications in Adobe's Creative Suite. Pieces of the Flash application dock to a resizable window called the *application frame.*

Panel control. More panels are resizable, including the Property inspector (which now has a vertical layout) and the Tools panel. You can make the Tools panel any width you like (**Figure i.1**). You can also customize the Tools panel, reconfiguring tool locations and submenus, even excluding items you don't use.

Hot text. CS4 introduces a new interface element: *hot text* (**Figure i.2**). Where previously you might have entered a value by typing in a text field or dragging a slider, in Flash CS4 you'll frequently find values highlighted in blue. Dragging within the highlighted text area activates an invisible slider for entering values interactively; clicking the blue text activates a text box for entering a new value.

Library enhancements. Additions to the Library panel include the ability to apply the same property settings to multiple symbols, a search function, and a direct connection to the symbol-creation dialogs (as you create a new symbol, you can place it in a specific folder in the library).

Design enhancements

Pattern makers. Flash CS4 comes with two new tools that make patterns. The *spray-brush* tool lays down a random pattern of elements. The *deco* tool lays down pattern elements in three styles: connected by lines in a vine pattern, arranged in a grid, and arranged symmetrically—around a point, for example (**Figure i.3**). The pattern elements are editable, and you can substitute your own symbols for the default elements.

Added dimensions. There are 3D tools for manipulating 2D symbols in 3D space. The tools enable you to move symbols along the z-axis to simulate changes in depth for static graphic elements and for animation.

Colorful themes. Adobe's Kuler Web site comes directly into the Flash workspace through the new Kuler panel. You can use the panel to connect to the Kuler Web site and browse color palettes (called *themes*) online, or use the panel to create and save your own Kuler themes.

Fonts on parade. Flash now previews fonts directly in the font menu (**Figure i.4**). Using menu and keyboard commands to apply bold and italic styling to selected text brings in the appropriate bold and italic characters of the font family when those fonts are installed on the Flash developer's system.

Created with the spray-brush tool

Created with the deco tool

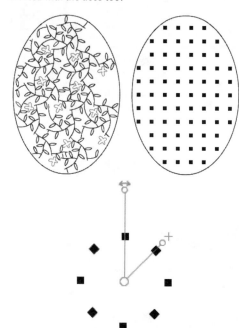

Figure i.3 The spray-brush tool works like a spray can to create a swath of randomly placed pattern elements; the default element is a dot (top). The deco tool creates more structured patterns: a vine pattern, a grid pattern, or a symmetrical pattern (bottom).

T Kailasa		...
M Kepler MM		Sample
O Kino MT		**Sample**
T Kokonor		...
T Krungthep		**Sample**
T Lucida Blackletter		Sample
T Lucida Bright		Sample
T Lucida Calligraphy		*Sample*

Figure i.4 Flash's font menus now include a sample of each font right in the menu.

Tween span

Motion Editor

Motion path —

Resized motion path

Figure i.5 Flash's new motion tween is an object-based form of tweening. The changes to the position of the tweened item are captured in an editable Bézier motion path that appears on the Stage. The tween span in the Timeline is also an editable object. You can edit the tween's properties in the Motion Editor.

Animation enhancements

Object-oriented tweening. Flash CS4 introduces a new method of animating with an old name: *motion tweening*. (For those familiar with earlier Flash versions, the old-style motion tweening is still available; it's called *classic tweening*.) New-style motion tweening works with symbol instances and text fields, and treats each segment of animation as an object. All of the property changes that animate the tweened object reside within the motion tween itself. Changes to a tweened object's position appear on the Stage as a Bézier path. You can edit the animation by editing the path; for example, you can change where the animation takes place on the Stage by dragging the motion path with the selection tool. You can change the duration of the animation by dragging the span containing the tween in the Timeline. You can save a motion tween as a preset and apply it to other symbols. A Preset panel comes with presets that create a number of common animation segments, such as fly-ins and bounces. A Motion Editor panel provides graphs and controls for editing motion-tween properties at any frame (**Figure i.5**).

continues on next page

Inverse kinematics. Flash CS4 also introduces tools for creating animation via inverse kinematics (IK). The new bone tool enables you to create a skeleton-like structure called an *IK armature,* which controls the relationships between connected symbol instances as you position them to create animation. IK armatures can also control changes to the outline of a shape to create animation (**Figure i.6**). A bind tool lets you adjust which bones affect different portions of the shape's outline.

Collaboration, cross-pollination, and more

Flash CS4 opens XFL files created in Adobe InDesign and Adobe After Effects, making it easier for designers to collaborate using these applications. If Adobe Soundbooth is installed on your system, you can open sounds in Flash and go directly to Soundbooth to edit them. A new File Info panel provides a place to store information about the Flash document as XMP metadata. When you publish the file, you can make that data available to search engines. Other new publishing capabilities include the option to remove some artifacts of JPEG compression; to improve playback speed and quality by using hardware acceleration; and to publish Flash movies as Adobe AIR applications.

Figure i.6 Flash CS4's bone tool enables you to add inverse kinematic (IK) structures to a collection of symbols. Here, a rag doll has an IK structure that governs how all the body parts move together. (You can also use the bone tool to create an IK structure within a single shape.)

How to Use This Book

Like all the books in the *Visual QuickStart Guide* series, this one seeks to take you out of passive reading mode and help you get started working in the program. The tasks in the book teach you to use Flash's features. The book is suitable for beginners who are just starting to use Flash and for intermediate-level Flash designers. The initial chapters cover the basics of creating graphic elements by using Flash's unique set of drawing tools. Next, you learn how to turn graphic elements into animations. After that, you learn to create basic user-interface elements, such as rollover buttons. To make your content interactive, you'll work with the Actions panel to create ActionScript for basic interactivity. You'll also learn about importing and working with various non-Flash content: artwork from other applications, sounds, and video. Finally, you'll learn to use Flash's Publish feature to create HTML for putting your Flash creations on the Web.

What you should already know

In order to get you started quickly, this book makes a few assumptions:

◆ Adobe Flash CS4 is already installed on your computer.

◆ You're familiar with the workings of your operating system.

◆ You can carry out basic tasks, such as opening, closing, and saving documents; opening, closing, resizing, collapsing, and expanding document windows and dialogs; using hierarchical menus, pop-up menus, radio buttons, and check boxes; and carrying out standard application commands such as copy, cut, paste, delete, and undo.

Cross-platform issues

The Flash authoring environment has a very similar interface on the Macintosh and Windows platforms. Still, differences exist where the user interfaces of the platforms diverge. When these differences are substantial, this book describes the procedures for both platforms.

Originally, Macintosh computers required Macintosh keyboards, and some key names were unique to that keyboard: for example, Return (instead of Enter) and Delete (instead of Backspace). This book generally uses Enter and Delete for these two key names.

Keyboard shortcuts

Most of Flash's menu-based commands have a keyboard equivalent. That equivalent appears in the menu next to the command name. When this book introduces a command, it also describes the keyboard shortcut. In subsequent mentions of the command, however, the keyboard shortcut usually is omitted.

Contextual menus

Both the Macintosh and Windows platforms offer contextual menus. To access one of these contextual menus, Control-click (Mac) or right-click (Windows) an element in the Flash movie. You'll see a menu of commands that are appropriate for working with that element. For the most part, these commands duplicate commands in the main menu; therefore, this book doesn't generally note them as alternatives for the commands described in the book. The book does point out when using the contextual menu is particularly handy or when a contextual menu contains a command that is unavailable in the main menu bar.

Artwork, scripts, and more

The Flash graphics in this book are easy to draw. In most cases the examples are based on simple geometric shapes, which means you can spend your time seeing the Flash features in action instead of re-creating fancy artwork. To make it even easier, Flash files containing the graphic elements that you need for each task are available on Peachpit Press's companion Web site for this book. In Chapter 15, you'll learn to create scripts for basic interactivity, and Flash files containing the completed scripts for these tasks are also available. In addition, the site offers some bonus tasks that we just couldn't squeeze into the pages of this book.

To access the files, you must register at www.peachpit.com. Click the Account Sign In button to create an account (or log in to your existing account). Click the "Register your products here" link and enter the book's ISBN (0321591925) in the text field that appears. A link to the supplemental content will appear on your account page.

THE FLASH AUTHORING TOOL

1

Before you start working in Adobe Flash CS4 Professional, it's helpful to familiarize yourself with the authoring environment. On first opening Flash, you'll see the default workspace in an *application frame*. The application frame holds pieces of the Flash application in a resizable window. At the top of the frame lies the application bar, which offers maximize, minimize, and quit buttons; a menu for choosing workspace layouts, and a text field where you can enter terms for searching Flash's Help system. Various docked panels appear around the edges of the window.

By default, the center of the application frame holds any open Flash documents; if no documents are open, a Welcome screen with options for creating new documents or opening recent ones appears in the middle of the workspace. You can choose to make documents and panels float over the workspace instead of docking to the application frame.

Working with Flash Documents

Most of the basic document operations in Flash—opening, closing, and saving files—are straightforward to experienced computer users. Creating new documents may be a little different than in other programs, because Flash creates a variety of document types. Flash's Welcome screen assists you in opening and creating these various Flash documents.

To set launch preferences:

1. From the Flash application menu (Mac) or Edit menu (Windows), choose Preferences.

   The Preferences dialog appears. The General category is selected by default.

2. From the On Launch menu, choose one of the following (**Figure 1.1**):

   ▲ No Document. Flash's menu bar, application frame, and panels appear at launch, but no document opens.

   ▲ New Document. Flash opens a new document at launch.

   ▲ Last Documents Open. Flash opens the documents that were open when you ended the previous work session.

   ▲ Welcome Screen. (The default setting.) Flash displays the Welcome screen at launch and anytime you have closed all the documents during a work session.

3. Click OK.

✔ Tip

■ To change launch preferences to the New Document option quickly, click the Don't Show Again button in the lower-left corner of the Welcome screen. A dialog appears to remind you that you must change the launch settings in the General tab of the Preferences dialog to see the Welcome screen again.

Figure 1.1 The On Launch options in the General category of the Preferences dialog tell Flash what type of document(s), if any, to open on when you launch Flash.

About Preferences

To see, or not to see, the Welcome screen is just one of many preference settings in Flash. To choose new settings, you open the Preferences dialog. From the Flash menu (Mac) or Edit menu (Windows), choose Preferences, and select a category from the list in the left-hand pane. Choose settings for that category in the main window. Preferences fall into ten categories: General, ActionScript, Auto Format, Clipboard, Drawing, Text, Warnings, Workspace, PSD File Importer, and AI File Importer. You'll learn about specific Preferences settings as they relate to specific tasks throughout this book.

Touring the Welcome Screen

Flash's default setting opens the Welcome screen when you launch. The Welcome screen contains active links that let you open documents quickly. You can open a new document, a document that you worked on recently, or a template document. You can link to Flash tutorials or to the Flash Exchange site, where you can download third-party extensions, such as new components, as they become available (**Figure 1.2**).

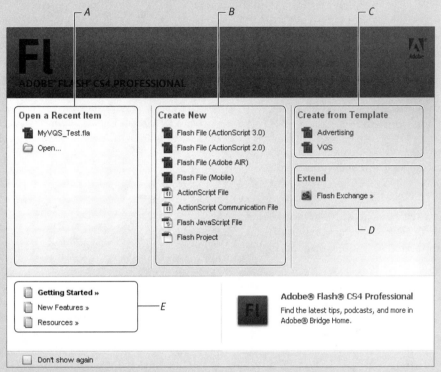

Figure 1.2 The Welcome screen presents common operations you might want to carry out at the beginning of a work session: opening a document you worked on recently (A), creating a new Flash document (B), or creating documents from templates (C). There are also links for browsing the Flash Exchange site, to find third-party extensions (D). For new users, there are links to the tutorials that come with Flash as well as other training resources (E).

To create a new Flash document:

1. From the Welcome screen, in the Create New section, click the Flash File (ActionScript 3.0) link.

   Flash opens a new blank document.

   or

   Choose File > New, or press ⌘-N (Mac) or Ctrl-N (Windows).

   Flash opens the New Document dialog (**Figure 1.3**). This dialog has two views: General and Templates. General is selected by default.

2. In the General view, select Flash File (ActionScript 3.0).

3. Click OK.

   Flash opens a new blank document.

✔ Tip

- To switch views in the New Document dialog, click the appropriate button (Mac) or tab (Windows) at the top of the dialog.

Figure 1.3 To create a new document in Flash, choose File > New. The New Document dialog opens, with the General view and Flash File (ActionScript 3.0) selected by default. Click OK to create a new document.

WORKING WITH FLASH DOCUMENTS

Which Flash File Type to Create?

The Create New section of the Welcome screen lists eight types of files; which one is right for you? In this book, we'll work exclusively with Flash files, but you still have two choices: ActionScript 3.0 or ActionScript 2.0. For many of the graphics, text, and animation tasks you'll do, either choice is fine. The difference becomes important when you start scripting. (You'll learn about scripting in Chapter 15.) The scripting options and features available to you depend on which version of ActionScript you use. This book deals with ActionScript 3.0. When an exercise asks you to create a new file, choose Flash File (ActionScript 3.0) unless instructed otherwise. If you decide to use a different version of ActionScript later, you can change the file type to ActionScript 2.0 (or 1.0) in the Publish Settings dialog. (You'll learn about publishing in Flash in Chapter 18.)

Open a Recent Item

📄 UsingSymbols_cs4.fla

📄 ChgStackOrder_cs4.fla

📄 FlameTweenReverse.fla

📁 Open...

Figure 1.4 The Open a Recent Item section of the Welcome screen allows you to view links to the last eight documents you worked on. Clicking a filename opens the document.

Click to close document   *Click to view document*

Figure 1.5 Viewing multiple open documents as tabs in a single window is the default setting for Flash CS4. Click an inactive title tab to bring that document to the front. To close the active document, click the close button in the tab.

To open an existing document:

1. From the Welcome screen, in the Open a Recent Item section, click the name of a recent file (**Figure 1.4**). Flash opens that file directly.

   or

   From the Welcome screen, in the Open a Recent Item section, click the Open link.

   or

   Choose File > Open.

   The Open dialog appears.

2. Navigate to the file you want to open.

3. Select the file.

4. Click Open.

✔ Tips

■ In Flash's default environment, multiple open documents appear as tabs within the application frame. Tabs for inactive documents are a darker gray. Click a tab to bring that document to the front (**Figure 1.5**).

continues on next page

WORKING WITH FLASH DOCUMENTS

- You can change the order of the tabs for open documents by dragging a tab to a new position (**Figure 1.6**).

- When you've been working with a document—adding and deleting graphic materials, sounds, video, and so on— the file size builds up because data about the deleted items remains in the file. Choosing File > Save and Compact reduces the file size. When you begin editing the file, it again bulks up quickly. You may wish to compact the file only at the end of the authoring process or when file size is crucial—for example, if you need to email the file to a colleague.

Figure 1.6 To change the tab position for open documents, click the name area of a tab and drag to the right (or left). The current document stays selected, but the tab position changes (bottom).

A Note about Help

Adobe provides two versions of Help: Local Help consists of files that install on your system with Flash); Web Help contains additional and updated materials. To access Help, choose Help > Flash Help. Flash opens Help in your system's default browser. You can also access Help by entering a word or phrase in the Search field at the right side of the Application bar and pressing Enter. When Flash is set to use Local help, searches are restricted to the local files. When Flash is set to use Web Help, searches also access Adobe's Community Help site, which offers various resources for information about Flash and other Adobe products. To access Web Help, you must allow Adobe Services to work online; to access Local Help you must restrict Adobe Services to working offline. Access the Connections panel (if it's not open, choose Window > Extensions > Connections). From the panel menu, choose Offline Options, in the window that appears, deselect (for Web Help) or select (for Local Help) the Keep Me Offline checkbox, and click OK. Note that the offline setting affects your ability to use any of Adobe's other online services, such as browsing Kuler themes, during your Flash work session.

Figure 1.7 To turn a Flash file into a template that can be the basis of future documents, chose File > Save As Template.

Figure 1.8 The Save As Template command lets you save Flash documents for reuse. You can create your own template categories and provide a brief description of the template file you're saving in the Save As Template dialog.

✔ Tip

■ Once you've completed the template, close the document. You may think that after saving the document as a template you're working in a copy made from the template, but you're not. You're still working in the master template document until you close it.

Working with Template Documents

If you work repeatedly with one type of Flash document—for example, you create banner ads of a specific size with a consistent background or elements—you can save that basic document as a template.

To create a template document:

1. Open the document that you want to turn into a template.

2. Choose File > Save As Template (**Figure 1.7**).

   The Save As Template dialog appears, showing a preview of your document (**Figure 1.8**).

3. In the Name field, type a name for the template.

4. To specify a category, do either of the following:

   ▲ To select an existing category, from the Category pop-up menu, choose the desired category.

   ▲ To create a new category, in the Category field, type a name.

5. In the Description field, type a brief summary or reminder of what the template is for.

   Although you can enter as much text as you like in this field, once you click Save, Flash limits the description that accompanies the actual template to the first 255 characters. Still, it's a good idea to give some indication of the intended uses for the template or what its special features are.

6. Click Save.

   Flash saves the file as a master template document in a folder named Templates within the Configuration folder (see "The Mystery of the Configuration Folder," later in this chapter).

To open a new document from a template document:

1. From the Welcome screen, in the Create from Template section, click a template-category link (**Figure 1.9**). The New from Template dialog appears.

   or

   Choose File > New.

   The New Document/New from Template dialog appears (**Figure 1.10**). The New Document and New from Template dialogs are identical except for their names. Both display two views: General and Templates. The dialog's name changes to reflect the active view. When you click a template folder in the Welcome screen, the Templates view is selected by default in the dialog.

2. From the Category list, choose the appropriate category.

   The folder you select in step 1 is selected by default and its contents appear in the Templates list. To view other templates, select another category.

3. From the Templates list, choose the template you want to use.

   The dialog previews the selected template's first frame and provides a brief description of the template, if one is available.

4. Click OK.

   Flash opens a new document with all the contents of the template.

✔ Tip

■ When you choose File > New, Flash displays the document-creation dialog based on the type of file you created previously. The New Document dialog appears if the last file you created was a document. The New from Template dialog appears if the last file was a template.

Figure 1.9 Choose a template-category link in the Welcome screen to access the New from Template dialog.

Figure 1.10 The Templates view of the New from Template (or New Document) dialog displays a preview and a description (when available) for the item selected in the Category and Templates lists.

The Mystery of the Configuration Folder

The operating systems that run Flash CS4 can be configured for multiple users, storing each user's files and special settings separately. To handle customized settings, Flash uses different types of Configuration folders. At the application level, Configuration folders govern settings for everyone who uses Flash on the computer. At this level, there are language-specific Configuration folders (which handle settings for each specific language installation of Flash on the system) and a Common configuration folder (which handles settings common to all the languages installed on the system). You must have administrative privileges to make changes to folders at this level.

At the user level, the Configuration folder contains the files that each user has customized while working with Flash on this computer. When you create a template document, for example, Flash stores it in a Templates folder inside your user-level Configuration folder. The templates that come with Flash are stored in one of the application-level Configuration folders.

To add, delete, or rename items in a Configuration folder manually, you must have the required access privileges and navigate the hierarchy of nested folders on your hard drive to open the folder. The folder that most individual Flash users need to work with is the user-level Configuration folder for the specific language version he or she uses. The first part of its folder hierarchy is slightly different in each operating system:

Windows XP/2000: *BootDrive\Documents and Settings\userName\Local Settings\ Application Data*

Windows Vista: *BootDrive\Users\userName\AppData\Local*

Mac OS X: *HardDriveName:Users:userName:Library:Application Support:*

From there on, the hierarchy of folders is always the same. For those using the English version of Flash, it's *Adobe\Flash CS4\en\Configuration*. Users of localized versions will see their language code instead of *en* in the folder hierarchy.

About the Flash Authoring Environment

Flash CS4 introduces a new user interface for the authoring environment: the *application frame*. This frame holds Flash's panels and documents in a resizable window. The frame keeps elements together, making the most efficient use of space and creating a Flash "desktop" that hides elements of other open applications. (In the Mac OS, such elements would otherwise show through any spaces between panels and documents, creating a distracting visual field.) A menu bar containing the Flash commands appears at the top of the screen, above the application frame.

Touring the Workspace

The layout of elements within the application frame is called the *workspace*. Flash comes with five preset workspaces: Classic, Debug, Designer, Developer, and Essentials. Each one uses a different set of docked panels (**Figure 1.11**). The workspace is customizable. You can open and close documents and panels, docking them where you prefer within the frame. Or you can undock panels and documents and float them anywhere on the desktop. You can save these configurations in new workspaces. Flash remembers the current workspace setup from one work session to the next.

Figure 1.11 Flash offers five preset workspaces, each with a different configuration of open panels and docking locations. Two workspaces are pictured here: Essentials (left), a bare-bones setup, and Designer (right), a layout of panels commonly used while creating artwork in Flash.

Figure 1.12 Choose Window > Workspace > New Workspace (top) to access the New Workspace dialog (bottom). Enter a name for your current desktop configuration and click OK.

Figure 1.13 The Workspace pop-up menu in the Application bar gives you quick access to preset and custom workspaces as well as workspace-management commands.

To save a custom workspace:

1. Configure panels in the application frame and/or in floating windows, using the techniques you'll learn later in this chapter.

2. Choose Window > Workspace > New Workspace.

   The New Workspace dialog appears (**Figure 1.12**).

3. In the Name field, enter a title for this workspace.

4. Click OK.

   Flash saves that configuration and adds the name to the Workspace menu.

To restore a workspace:

1. Choose Window > Workspace.

2. From the submenu that appears, choose one of the following:

   Classic opens a minimal set of panels, similar to those opened in the default workspace in earlier versions of Flash.

   Debug opens just the panels needed to troubleshoot ActionScript.

   Designer opens panels commonly used in creating artwork.

   Developer opens panels commonly used in creating ActionScript.

   Essentials opens a very minimal panel set.

   If you've created a custom workspace, you can choose it from the submenu as well.

✔ Tips

- You can also save and choose workspaces from the Workspace pop-up menu at the right side of the Application bar that forms the top of the application frame (**Figure 1.13**).

- To restore a workspace, choose it by name from the Window > Workspace submenu or from the Workspace pop-up menu in the Application bar.

Touring a Document

Each Flash document consists of a tab (or Title bar if the document is in a floating window), with a close button; an Edit bar, which displays identifying text and menus for choosing symbols and scenes; a Stage, the area in which your movie displays; and a Pasteboard, extra space around the Stage (**Figure 1.14**). By default, open documents are docked, filling the middle of the application frame; you can undock them and let them float over the workspace if you prefer. Floating document windows sit above the application frame, and therefore obscure any docked panels below. Floating panels sit above floating documents.

Touring the Timeline

The Timeline (**Figure 1.15**) visually represents every element of a movie, and is the framework for building projects. In Flash CS4, the Timeline appears in an independent panel that displays information about the open and active document. You'll use this panel extensively when you create animations.

Figure 1.14 A Flash document consists of the Title tab (or Title bar if the document is in a floating window), the Edit bar, the Stage, and the Pasteboard.

Figure 1.15 The Timeline is the complete record of your movie. It represents all the scenes, frames, and layers that make up the movie. Frames appear in chronological order. Clicking any frame in the Timeline takes you directly to that frame and displays its contents on the Stage.

Using Panels

Flash organizes drawing and authoring tools as *panels*. Some panels contain tools for creating or modifying graphic elements. Others help you organize and navigate your Flash document. You can dock panels within the application frame or have them float independently. You'll learn to work with specific panels in later chapters of this book. For now, you'll learn general features of panels and how to manage them in the workspace.

Accessing Panels

An open panel appears as a tab inside a panel frame; the frame may appear inside a dock in Flash's application frame or inside a floating window. You can group multiple panels within one panel frame; they appear as horizontal tabs. Clicking a tab in a group activates that panel, making it visible in the frame. You can also stack frames vertically within a dock or floating window. To manipulate panels, use the interface elements shown in **Figure 1.16**.

Figure 1.16 Common panel-interface elements help you work efficiently with panels. Whether panels are in floating windows or docked, you can group them, stack them, and collapse them to icons to save space.

To open (or close) panels:

◆ From the Window menu, select the desired panel—for example, Color (**Figure 1.17**).

One of the following actions takes place:

▲ If the selected panel is closed, a frame containing that panel opens. The frame may appear in a dock or in a floating window, depending on the selected workspace and any modifications you've made to it.

▲ If the selected panel is minimized (to the Tab bar) or collapsed (to an icon), it expands.

▲ If the selected panel is obscured behind other tabs in the same frame or other floating panel windows, the selected panel moves to the front.

▲ If the selected panel is the only tab—or the front tab—in a frame in a floating window that is already open, expanded, and in front, the entire window closes.

▲ If the selected panel is the only tab—or the front tab—in a docked frame that is already open and expanded, the frame containing that panel (including all its tabs) closes. Other frames stacked within the dock remain open.

✔ Tips

■ To remove one panel from a panel frame, from the panel menu (located at the right side of the Tab bar), choose Close; the active panel closes. To remove all the panels from that frame, choose Close Group; the panel frame (and all the panel tabs in it) closes; any panel frames stacked above or below that frame stay open (**Figure 1.18**).

■ To close all the panels in a floating window quickly, click the window's close button. The window closes, along with all the panel frames within it (**Figure 1.19**).

Figure 1.17
The Window menu contains a list of the panels in Flash.

Figure 1.18 You can close panels individually or as groups (whether docked or floating). In the Tab bar of the frame containing the panel (or panels) you want to close, click the panel menu and choose Close or Close Group.

Figure 1.19 Clicking the close button on a floating panel window closes the window and all its panels, including stacked panels.

USING PANELS

Figure 1.20 Clicking an empty area of the Tab bar (above) minimizes a panel frame so that all you see is the tabs (below).

Sizing Panels

To reduce workspace clutter, you can reduce a panel frame to its Tab bar, or put panels into icon mode. A single click restores full-size panels. You can also change the dimensions of some panels by dragging.

To minimize (or maximize) a panel frame:

◆ Click the Tab bar (**Figure 1.20**).

The frame toggles between a minimized state (showing only panel tabs) and the maximized state (showing the full panel frame).

✔ Tip

■ Another way to minimize or maximize an open panel window is to Ctrl-click (Mac) or right-click (Windows) the panel's Title bar, and choose Minimize Group(s)/Restore Group(s) from the contextual menu.

Tab Bar vs. Tab

The Flash documentation doesn't have a name for the area of a panel frame that holds a panel's tabs. But it is an important element. Dragging the gray area to the right of the tabs moves the frame with all its panels. Dragging a tab moves that panel individually. For the tasks in this book, the gray area to the right of the tabs is called the *Tab bar*.

Saving Space with Panel Icons

To make efficient use of screen real estate, you can collapse most panels to icons that expand when clicked on. (Panels that are docked at the top or bottom of the application frame don't collapse to icons, but you can minimize them to show just tabs.) To switch between icon and full-size view, click the Collapse to Icons button (the double triangle) at the right side of the Title bar of a window or dock (**Figure 1.21**). Click an icon to open its panel in a full-size frame; if the panel is grouped with other panels, the icon view reflects that and the complete group opens.

Click to collapse/expand

Click to collapse/expand

Figure 1.21 The double-triangle at the right side of the Title bar (the Collapse to Icons button) toggles between an expanded view with full-size panels (left) and a collapsed view with icons (right). The icons can be in floating windows, or docked to the application frame.

There are two styles for closing expanded panel icons. By default, clicking outside the expanded panel closes it to icon form. To prevent Flash from closing the panel automatically, you must change preference settings. To do this quickly, Ctrl-click (Mac) or right-click (Windows) a panel icon or the Title bar of a floating panel window or dock, then deselect Auto-Collapse Icon Panels in the contextual menu that appears (**Figure 1.22**). That setting changes accordingly in the General section of the Preferences dialog. To access the dialog, choose Preferences from the same contextual menu or choose Flash (Mac) or Edit (Windows) > Preferences. When Auto-Collapse Icon Panels is inactive, to close an open panel you must click the Collapse to Icons button.

Figure 1.22 To change the AutoCollapse setting for panels quickly, Ctrl-click (Mac) or right-click (Windows) any panel icon or the Title bar of any floating panel window or dock. Choose the desired setting from the pop-up menu.

Docked panels in icon form lack close buttons, and their contextual menu has no Close option. To remove a docked panel icon from the workspace, first expand the panel to full size, then choose Close from its panel menu. You can also drag the icon from the dock into a floating window and click its close button.

Pointer ready to resize horizontally

*Pointer ready to resize —
horizontally and vertically*

Figure 1.23 You can change the size of many floating panel windows. Position the pointer over the lower-right corner of the window; when the pointer changes to a double-headed arrow, drag the corner to resize the window vertically and horizontally at the same time. To resize the window in one direction, position the pointer over the left, bottom, or right side of the window; when the resize pointer appears, drag that side.

To resize a floating panel window:

Do any of the following:

◆ To resize a panel window vertically and/or horizontally, position the pointer over the bottom-right corner of the panel. When the resize pointer (a double-headed arrow) appears, click and drag the lower-right corner of the window (**Figure 1.23**).

◆ To resize a panel window vertically, position the pointer over the bottom edge of the panel. When the resize pointer appears, drag up or down to lengthen or shorten the panel.

◆ To resize a window panel horizontally, position the pointer over the left or right edge of the panel. When the resize pointer appears, drag the edge left or right to narrow or widen the panel.

✔ Tips

■ Some panels can't be resized. For fixed-size panels, the double-headed arrow fails to appear when you position the pointer over the edges of a panel window. If a panel frame mixes resizable and fixed-size panels, the resize arrow appears only when a resizable panel is active.

■ Most panels must display all their content; you can't make them so small that some elements disappear. You can resize a few panels, such as Swatches, to hide some content, but scroll bars appear, indicating that there's more to see. An exception is the Tools panel. You can make it small enough to hide some of its tools, and no scroll bars appear. If you see fewer tools than you need, try resizing the Tools panel.

■ By default, panels in icon mode include the panel name. To save the most space, resize them horizontally to show just icons.

USING PANELS

Placing and Combining Panels

You can position floating panels anywhere on the desktop. You can combine panels into groups (multiple panel tabs within one frame) and stacks (multiple panel frames linked vertically). The techniques for combining panels are the same whether you're working with panels in floating windows or in docks.

To position floating panel windows:

◆ Click the panel's Title bar, and drag the window to a new location (**Figure 1.24**).

The panel window becomes transparent as you drag, allowing you to position it among other items on the desktop.

To group panels as tabs in one frame:

1. With two or more panels open, click a tab directly on the panel name.

On the Mac, Flash highlights the tab in gray.

2. Drag that tab out of its current frame and over another panel frame (the target frame).

The panel being dragged becomes transparent (**Figure 1.25**). As the pointer touches various parts of the target frame, Flash highlights *drop zones* in blue, indicating how the panels will combine.

3. Position the pointer over the target frame's Tab bar.

Flash highlights the perimeter of the target frame in blue, indicating the drop zone for creating a group of tabbed panels.

4. Release the mouse button.

The panel you dragged appears as a tab in the target frame.

Figure 1.24 Drag a floating panel window by its Title bar to reposition it in the workspace. The panel becomes transparent as you drag it.

Figure 1.25 When you drag a panel tab from one panel frame (top) to the Tab bar of another panel frame, the perimeter of the target frame highlights (middle). Releasing the panel into this drop zone creates a group of tabbed panels in the target frame (bottom).

Drop zone, stack

Figure 1.26 To stack panel fames vertically, drag one panel frame by its Tab bar to the top or bottom edge of another frame. Releasing the dragged frame over the drop zone at the bottom edge of the target frame (top) stacks the panel frames with the target frame on top (bottom).

✔ Tip

■ In the preceding task you dragged a single panel to create a group. You can also drag a panel group. In step 1, for a panel frame containing a group of tabs, click the Tab bar. Dragging now moves all the tabs together. When the perimeter of the target frame highlights, release the mouse button. The tabs you dragged appear in the Tab bar of the target frame, together with the target's original tab(s).

To stack panel frames vertically:

1. With two or more panel frames open, click one panel's Tab bar.

2. To stack the first panel frame above the second, with the mouse button still down, drag to position the pointer at the top edge of the target frame.

   or

   To stack the first panel frame below the second, position the pointer along the bottom edge of the target frame.

   Flash highlights the target frame's drop zone for stacking with a blue line (**Figure 1.26**).

3. Release the mouse button.

   The first panel frame is now stacked above or below the target frame.

USING PANELS

To separate grouped panel tabs:

1. To remove one panel from a group, click the panel's tab.

   On the Mac, Flash highlights the tab in gray.

2. Drag the tab away from the panel window.

   The panel being dragged becomes transparent, and its spot in the original window turns gray (**Figure 1.27**).

3. Position the pointer over the workspace, away from any docks or panel windows, and release the mouse button.

   Flash places the panel in a floating window.

✔ Tip

   If you position the pointer over a window or a dock, you can highlight drop zones for adding a panel to that window or dock.

To separate stacked panel frames:

1. To separate one panel frame from a stack, click the frame's Tab bar and drag away from the stack.

   The frame being dragged becomes transparent, and its location in the original stack turns gray (**Figure 1.28**).

2. Release the mouse button.

   Flash creates a floating window for the dragged frame. This technique works for frames with one panel and frames with grouped panels.

Figure 1.27 Dragging a panel by its tab lets you move that panel individually—for example, to remove it from a group.

Figure 1.28 Dragging a panel frame by its Tab bar lets you move the entire panel frame with all its grouped tabs. Use this method to remove a panel frame from a stack.

Drop zone, dock

Figure 1.29 Dragging a floating panel window to the edge of Flash's application frame activates a dock. When the blue drop-zone highlight appears (top), release the mouse button and Flash adds all the panel frames from the window to the dock (bottom).

Docking Panels

The methods for docking and undocking panels are similar to those in the preceding tasks. To manipulate all the frames in a floating window, drag the Title bar; to manipulate a single panel, drag its tab; to manipulate grouped panels, drag their Tab bar.

To create a "new" dock:

1. Click the Title bar of any floating panel window.

   The window may contain a single panel frame (containing one tab or a group of tabs) or a stack of panel frames.

2. Drag the Title bar to the right, left, bottom, or top edge of the application frame.

   A gray rectangle edged with a blue line appears (**Figure 1.29**). The rectangle is the border of the dock, and the blue line is the dock's drop zone. When a dock is empty, it stays hidden, waiting in the wings until you drag a panel to it.

3. Release the mouse button.

   Flash adds the panel(s) to the dock.

✔ Tips

- You can also use an individual panel, or a frame containing a panel group, to create a dock. In step 1 of the preceding task, drag a single panel by its tab, or drag the panel frame by the Tab bar.

- You can relocate a dock by dragging its Title bar to a different edge of the application frame. When the dock drop zone appears, release the mouse button.

- You can resize most docked panels. Position the pointer over the edge of the dock closest to the Stage. When the resize pointer (a double-headed arrow) appears, drag in the direction the arrows point (horizontally or vertically) to make the dock smaller or larger.

To move all panels from a floating window to an existing dock:

1. Click the Title bar of a floating panel window.

   The window may contain a single panel frame (with one tab or a group of tabs) or a stack of panel frames.

2. Drag the Title bar to an existing dock.

   The window being dragged becomes transparent. As the pointer touches various areas of the dock, drop zones highlight in blue.

3. To position the panel frame(s) inside the dock, do the following:

   ▲ To put the panel frame(s) above a frame in the dock, position the pointer along the top edge of the docked frame; to add the new frame(s) below a frame in the dock, position the pointer along the bottom edge of the docked frame (**Figure 1.30**).

   ▲ Release the mouse button.

   Flash moves the panel frame(s) from the floating window, into the dock.

To create panel groups in the dock:

1. Click an individual tab in a panel frame in the floating window and drag the tab to an existing dock.

2. To create a new panel group in the dock or add to an existing group, do the following:

   ▲ Position the pointer over the Tab bar of an existing panel frame; the drop zone highlights the perimeter of that frame.

   ▲ Release the mouse button.

   Flash adds the panel's tab to the target frame within the dock (**Figure 1.31**).

Drop zone

Figure 1.30 When you drag panels from a floating window to the top or bottom edge of a panel frame in a dock, the drop zone highlights in blue. Release the mouse button when the drop zone appears in the location you want (top); Flash adds the panel frame(s) to the dock (bottom).

Figure 1.31 Dragging a panel frame over the Tab bar of a frame in the dock highlights the drop zone for creating a group (top). Release the mouse button to add the panel tab to the docked frame.

✔ Tips

■ You can also add a group of panels to a frame in the dock. Follow the steps in the preceding task, but in step 1, click and drag the Tab bar of the group in the floating window.

■ When you drag a panel stack into a dock, the panel frames lose their connection. You can only drag them out of the dock individually.

■ You can create double docks. Dragging a panel frame to the edge of an existing dock activates a drop zone along the left or right edge of the dock. Release the mouse button when one of these drop zones appears, to create another layer of dock (**Figure 1.32**).

Drop zone

Figure 1.32 Double-docking can be useful. Drag a panel window to either side of an existing dock till the drop zone appears (left), then release the mouse button to add another layer of dock (right).

USING PANELS

To convert docked panels to floating windows:

1. To convert docked panels to floating windows, do one of the following:

   ▲ To create a single-panel window, click the docked panel's tab and drag away from the dock.

   ▲ To create a panel group, click the Tab bar of the docked group's frame and drag away from the dock.

2. When the panel (or group's) place in the dock turns gray, release the mouse button.

   Flash creates a floating window containing the panel or panel group.

The Mystery of Hot Text

Flash CS4 introduces a new interface element for entering numeric values, called *hot text*. When a number in a panel appears in blue (as if it were an active link), that number is hot text. A pointing-finger icon with a double arrow appears when you position the pointer over hot text. Once the hot-text pointer appears, you can enter new values in different ways. You can drag the hot text, as if using an invisible slider (**Figure 1.33**). After you enter a new value, a dark blue box highlights the hot text. When this highlight is present, you can use the up- or down-arrow keys to change the hot-text value incrementally: up-arrow increases the hot-text value by 1, Shift–up-arrow increases the value by 10, down-arrow reduces the value by 1, and Shift–down-arrow reduces the value by 10. You can also click hot text to activate a text-entry field (**Figure 1.34**).

Ready to drag   *Drag right to increase value*

Figure 1.33 When the hot-text pointer appears, you can click and drag to change the values of that hot-text item. To increase the value, drag upward or to the right; to decrease the value, drag downward or to the left. The number changes as you drag. In many panels, entering new values by dragging the hot text is interactive; the changes you make directly affect elements on the Stage, for example.

Figure 1.34 To enter precise hot-text values, click the hot text once. Flash activates a text field and highlights the current value; you can enter a new value immediately. (Double-clicking the hot text activates the text field and places an I-beam pointer at the end of the current value; you can then delete or select the old value and enter a new one.) To confirm the new value, press Enter or click outside the text field.

USING PANELS

The Property Inspector: A Special Panel

Think of the Property inspector as a context-sensitive super panel—a panel that changes to reflect whatever item you have selected. The Property inspector displays information about the active Flash document or a selected tool, frame, or graphic element (a merge shape, drawing-object, primitive shape, grouped shape, symbol, text field, bitmap, or video clip). The Property inspector is also the place for choosing many tools' settings and for changing the attributes of selected elements.

Select the line tool, for example, and the Property inspector becomes the Line Tool Property inspector (**Figure 1.35**). In this incarnation, the panel presents all the line tool's attributes for you to set: color, thickness, and style. Select a merge-shape line on the Stage, however, and the panel becomes the Shape Property inspector. When the selected shape is a line, the panel displays attributes similar to those shown in the Line Tool Property inspector; change the settings in the panel now, and Flash changes the selected line to match.

Click a blank area of the Stage, and you'll see the Document Property inspector, which gives you access to various document settings. Select a symbol instance on the Stage, and the Property inspector reveals the instance's heritage (which master symbol it came from), as well as other properties of the symbol. For example, the Position and Size section of the Property inspector shows the symbol's current *x*- and *y*- coordinates, height, and width. Change the settings in the panel and Flash applies those changes to the selected symbol instance.

For some items, the Property inspector holds a lot of information. To make this data easier to work with, Flash divides the properties into sections. You can hide or show a section's information by clicking the collapse/expand triangle to the left of the section name (**Figure 1.36**).

You can access the Property inspector from the Window menu, as you would any other panel (choose Window > Properties), or you can press ⌘-F3 (Mac) or Ctrl-F3 (Windows).

Figure 1.35 The Property inspector displays information about selected items and allows you to modify them. The Line Tool Property inspector, for example, lets you set the color, thickness, and style for lines that the line tool creates.

Click to collapse

Click to expand

Figure 1.36 To view fewer properties in the Property inspector, collapse a section by clicking the downward-pointing triangle. To view more properties, expand a section by clicking the right-facing triangle.

About Document Properties

The Document Properties dialog lets you define the Stage (its dimensions, the color of the background on which your artwork appears, and the units of measure for rulers and grids) and set a frame rate for playing your movie. Frames are the lifeblood of your animation, and the frame rate is the heart that keeps that blood flowing at a certain speed. Flash CS4's default setting is 24 frames per second (fps)—a reasonable setting for animations viewed over the Web, and the standard frame rate for film movies. You'll learn more about how frame rates affect animation in Chapter 8. You can also use the Document Property inspector to set some document properties.

To open the Document Properties dialog:

◆ Choose Modify > Document; or press ⌘-J (Mac) or Ctrl-J (Windows).

The Document Properties dialog appears (**Figure 1.37**).

✔ Tip

■ When the Stage has focus, the Document Property inspector's Properties section contains a shortcut to the Document Properties dialog. In the Size section, click the Edit button.

Set Stage dimensions — *Set background color* — *Set frame rate* — *Select a unit of measure* — *Set default* — *Restore default*

Figure 1.37 The Document Properties dialog is where you set all the parameters for viewing the Stage. Selecting a unit of measure for rulers resets the unit measurement for all the Stage's parameters. Clicking the color control pops up the current set of colors and lets you choose one for the background. Clicking the Make Default button sets the parameters for all new documents you create.

Dimensions: [550 px] (width) x [400 px] (height)

Figure 1.38 To assign new proportions to your Stage, type a width and height in the Dimensions section of the Document Properties dialog.

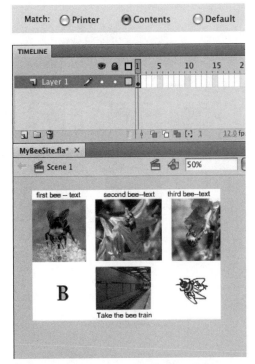

Figure 1.39 To make the Stage just big enough to enclose the elements in your movie, select the Contents radio button in the Match section of the Document Properties dialog (top). Flash creates a Stage that's just big enough to show all the objects you've created and placed at the time you select the radio button (bottom). (If you've placed an object on the Pasteboard, Flash sizes the Stage to include that object.)

To set the size of the Stage:

1. Open the Document Properties dialog, and do one of the following:

   ▲ To set the Stage's dimensions, type values for width and height in the appropriate fields of the Dimensions section (**Figure 1.38**). Flash automatically assigns the units of measure currently selected in Ruler Units.

   ▲ To create a Stage big enough to cover all the elements in your movie, select the Contents radio button in the Match section (**Figure 1.39**).

continues on next page

About the Pasteboard

Flash CS4's Pasteboard grows to accommodate your need for extra space. As you drag items from the Stage to the Pasteboard area, Flash enlarges the Pasteboard to hold them. If you move a large graphic element onto the Pasteboard, and some of it lies outside the area of the open document window, you can see the scroll bar move back toward the center of its range. There is now more Pasteboard area that's hidden from view. Use the scroll bars to view your graphic element and the enlarged Pasteboard. (You'll learn about creating graphic elements in Chapter 2 and repositioning them in Chapter 4.)

▲ To set the Stage size to the maximum print area currently available, select the Printer radio button in the Match section (**Figure 1.40**).

2. Click OK.

✔ Tips

■ If you've entered new dimensions, either manually or by selecting Printer or Contents for matching, you can return to the default Stage dimensions by selecting the Default radio button.

■ To set the units of measure for your document, in the Document Properties dialog, from the Ruler Units menu, choose the units of measure you prefer (**Figure 1.41**). Flash uses these units to calculate all measured items on the Stage: rulers, grid spacing, and dimensions.

■ If you want a banner that's 1 inch tall and 5 inches wide, but you don't know what that size is in pixels, first set Ruler Units to inches. Type 1 in the height field and 5 in the width field. Then, return to Ruler Units and choose pixels. Flash does the math and sets the Stage dimensions.

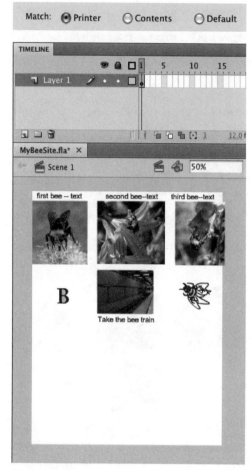

Figure 1.40 When you select the Printer radio button in the Match section of the Document Properties dialog, Flash creates a Stage that fits within the margins currently set for Page Setup.

Figure 1.41 To set the units of measure for your Flash document, choose from the Ruler Units menu in the Document Properties dialog.

Figure 1.42 To assign your Stage a new color, choose one from the Background Color control in the Document Properties dialog.

Figure 1.43 Typing a frame rate for your movie in the Frame Rate field of the Document Properties dialog sets Flash to display that number of frames in 1 second.

To set the background color:

1. Open the Document Properties dialog.

2. Click the Background Color control.

   The pointer changes to an eyedropper, and a set of swatches appears (**Figure 1.42**).

3. To select a background color, do either of the following:

   ▲ Click a swatch with the eyedropper.

   ▲ Click the hexadecimal-color field, type a value, and press Enter.

   The selected color appears in the Background Color control.

4. Click OK.

   The Stage appears in the color you selected.

✔ Tip

■ The Properties section of the Document Property inspector contains a Stage color control for selecting the movie's background color.

To set the frame rate:

1. Open the Document Properties dialog.

2. In the Frame Rate field, type the number of frames you want Flash to display in 1 second (**Figure 1.43**).

3. Click OK.

   The frame-rate setting appears in the Status bar of the current document.

✔ Tip

■ You can also set the frame rate in the Properties section of the Document Property inspector or by using the fps hot text in the Status bar.

To save your settings as the default:

◆ In the Document Properties dialog, click the Make Default button (**Figure 1.44**).

The current settings in the Document Properties dialog become the defaults.

Figure 1.44 To save the current document-property settings as the defaults for all new documents, click the Make Default button in the lower-left corner of the Document Properties dialog.

Touring the Edit Bar

The Edit bar, which appears at the top of each Flash document, is the key to identifying what mode you're working in (editing your document or editing a graphic element). Pop-up menus in the Edit bar give you the power to switch scenes, to choose a symbol to edit and immediately switch to symbol-editing mode, and to change the magnification for viewing the Stage. When you edit a drawing-object, group, or symbol, the Edit bar identifies the element you're editing (**Figure 1.45**). To learn about editing drawing-objects and groups, see Chapter 5; for symbols, see Chapter 7.

By default, the Edit bar is visible; to hide it, choose Window > Toolbars > Edit Bar. If you hide the Edit bar, however, you may find it more difficult to know when you're editing drawing-objects, groups, or symbols within your document and when you're working on the Stage in the main document.

Figure 1.45 The Edit bar is located at the top of the document window. You can use the Edit bar to access symbols and scenes and to change magnification for viewing the Stage. When you're editing a drawing-object, group, or symbol, the Edit bar identifies the item you're editing. Clicking the Back button takes you up the hierarchy of items you are editing, eventually returning you to document-editing mode.

Figure 1.46 Flash offers three visual drawing aids: rulers, grids, and guides. To show or hide these features during authoring, use the View menu. Here, for example, is the command for showing grids.

Figure 1.47 Choosing View > Rulers (left) makes rulers visible on the Stage (right).

Figure 1.48 Visible grid lines help you position elements on the Stage during authoring.

Using Rulers, Grids, and Guides

Flash offers rulers, grids, and guides to help you place graphic elements on the Stage. You turn on these visual aids from the View menu (**Figure 1.46**). Choose the feature you want to use; a check mark indicates that the feature is on. None of the visual aids appear in your final movie.

To show/hide grids, guides, and rulers:

From the View menu, choose any of the following (or use a keyboard shortcut):

◆ Choose Rulers, or press Option-Shift-⌘-R (Mac) or Ctrl-Alt-Shift-R (Windows).

Ruler bars appear on the left side and top of the Stage (**Figure 1.47**). You can set ruler units in the Document Properties dialog.

◆ Choose Grid > Show Grid, or press ⌘-apostrophe (') (Mac) or Ctrl-apostrophe (') (Windows).

When Show Grid is active, Flash superimposes crisscrossing vertical and horizontal lines on the Stage (**Figure 1.48**). The grid acts as a guide for drawing and positioning elements, the way graph paper functions in the nondigital world. Flash also uses the grid to position elements when you activate the Snap to Grid feature.

◆ Choose Guides > Show Guides, or press ⌘-semicolon (;) (Mac) or Ctrl-semicolon (;) (Windows).

When Show Guides is active, any guides you've placed become visible. To place guides, see "To work with guides," later in this section.

◆ To access all of the snapping, guide, ruler, and document options quickly, Ctrl-click (Mac) or right-click (Windows) in an empty part of the stage or in the Pasteboard and choose the appropriate submenu.

To set grid parameters:

1. Choose View > Grid > Edit Grid, or press Option-⌘-G (Mac) or Ctrl-Alt-G (Windows).

   The Grid dialog appears (**Figure 1.49**).

2. To set grid spacing, do the following:

   ▲ Type a value in the width field.

   ▲ Type a value in the height field (**Figure 1.50**).

3. To select a grid color, do the following:

   ▲ Click the Color control.

   ▲ The pointer changes to an eyedropper, and a set of swatches appears.

   ▲ Click a color in the swatch set (**Figure 1.51**).

   ▲ The new color appears in the Color control in the Grid dialog.

4. To control how close an item must get to the grid before Flash snaps the item to the grid, from the Snap Accuracy menu, choose a tolerance setting.

5. Click OK.

✔ Tips

■ Grids need not consist of perfect squares.

■ You can create new default settings for the grids in all new documents. After entering the desired settings in the Grid dialog, click the Save Default button, and then click OK.

Figure 1.49 Choosing View > Grid > Edit Grid opens the Grid dialog, where you can change grid parameters.

Figure 1.50 Type values in the width and height fields to set grid spacing.

Figure 1.51 To select a new grid color, with the eyedropper pointer, click anywhere in the pop-up set of swatches. The swatch set displays the currently selected color set.

USING RULERS, GRIDS, AND GUIDES

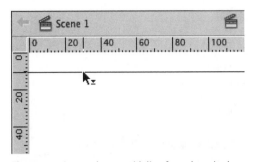

Figure 1.52 As you drag a guideline from the ruler bar, a direction indicator appears next to the selection tool.

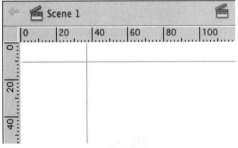

Figure 1.53 You can position individual vertical and horizontal guides anywhere you want on the Stage. The original guide location remains visible as you drag (top). Release the mouse button to confirm the new position (bottom).

- To set parameters for guides, open the Guide dialog by choosing View > Guides > Edit Guides or pressing Option-Shift-⌘-G (Mac) or Ctrl-Alt-Shift-G (Windows).

To work with guides:

1. With rulers visible, position the pointer over the vertical or horizontal ruler bar.

   If you're using a tool other than the selection tool, the pointer changes to the selection arrow on the Mac. In Windows, the pointer of the currently selected tool remains visible until you click the ruler bar.

2. Click and drag the pointer onto the Stage.

   As you click, a small directional arrow appears next to the pointer, indicating which direction to drag (**Figure 1.52**).

3. Release the mouse button.

   Flash places a vertical or horizontal line on the Stage.

✔ Tips

- To move a guide, position the selection tool over the guide. A direction arrow appears next to the pointer, indicating that the guide can be dragged (**Figure 1.53**). Drag the guide to a new location, and release the mouse button. To remove a guide, drag it completely out of the open document window.

- To avoid repositioning guides accidentally, choose View > Guides > Lock Guides, or press Option-⌘-semicolon (;) (Mac) or Ctrl-Alt-semicolon (;) (Windows). The directional arrow no longer appears next to the selection tool when you place it over a guideline. To unlock the guides, choose View > Guides > Lock Guides or press the keyboard shortcut again.

- If you've placed numerous guides in your document, dragging them from the Stage may get tedious. To remove them all at once, choose View > Guides > Clear Guides, or access the Guides dialog and click the Clear All button.

USING RULERS, GRIDS, AND GUIDES

Working with Snapping

Flash's five snapping features help you align elements on the Stage. Snap to Grid helps you position the edge or center of an element to sit directly on top of a user-defined grid. Snap to Guide does the same thing with elements and guidelines. Snap to Objects helps you position one element in relation to another. Snap to Pixels helps you move elements in whole-pixel steps; at magnifications of 400 percent or greater it displays a 1-pixel-by-1-pixel grid. Snap Align helps you align elements once you've dragged them within a user-definable distance from one another or from the edge of the Stage.

To turn snapping options on and off:

1. Choose View > Snapping.

   The menu items with check marks are currently active (**Figure 1.54**). Select an unchecked item to activate it; select a checked item to deactivate it.

2. To activate/deactivate a snapping option, from the Snapping submenu, choose any of the following:

   ▲ *To snap elements to a grid,* choose Snap to Grid, or press Shift-⌘-apostrophe (') (Mac) or Ctrl-Shift-apostrophe (') (Windows).

   With Snap to Grid active, as you drag an element, a circle called the *snap ring* appears near the tip of the selection tool. As the element comes close to a grid line, Flash highlights potential snap points by enlarging the snap ring (**Figure 1.55**).

   ▲ *To snap elements to guides,* choose Snap to Guides, or press Shift-⌘-semicolon (;) (Mac) or Ctrl-Shift-semicolon (;) (Windows).

   ▲ *To snap elements to elements,* choose Snap to Objects, or press Shift-⌘-U (Mac) or Ctrl-Shift-U (Windows).

Figure 1.54 Choose View > Snapping to open a submenu with Flash's snapping options. Select an unchecked item to activate it; select a checked item to deactivate it.

Figure 1.55 As you drag elements, the snap ring, a small circle, appears near the tip of the pointer (top). The snap ring grows larger when it moves over an item that you've chosen to snap to, such as a grid, a guide, or the edge or center of another element.

Figure 1.56 With Flash's Snap to Pixels feature enabled, a 1-pixel grid becomes visible at magnifications of 400 percent or greater. You can use this mode for precise positioning of graphic elements.

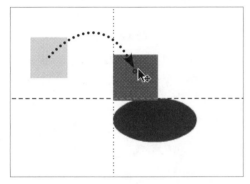

Figure 1.57 Flash's Snap Align feature displays a dotted alignment guide whenever the element you're dragging meets certain conditions. For example, you can set Snap Align to display a dotted line when the edge of the object you're dragging aligns with the edge of another object, or when the dragged object's edge gets to a certain distance from the edge of the Stage.

Figure 1.58 Choose a Snap Accuracy setting to determine how close an element must be to the grid before Flash snaps the element to the grid line. Choosing Always Snap forces the edge or center of an element to lie directly on a grid line.

▲ *To snap elements to pixels,* choose Snap to Pixels.

Flash creates a grid whose squares measure 1 pixel by 1 pixel. To see the grid, you must set the Stage's magnification to at least 400 percent (**Figure 1.56**). You'll learn more about magnified views in "Viewing at Various Magnifications," later in this chapter.

▲ *To view alignment guides while positioning elements,* choose Snap Align.

With Snap Align active, as you drag elements on the Stage, Flash displays an alignment guide (a dotted line) whenever the element's edge or center gets close to aligning with the edge or center of another element, or when the element gets within a user-specified distance of another element's edge, its center, or the edge of the Stage (**Figure 1.57**).

✔ Tip

■ Although the Snap to Pixels feature uses a 1-pixel grid, the graphic elements you move don't snap to the grid's coordinates unless you set the element's x and y position to a whole number in the Info panel or Property inspector. (You'll learn to set coordinates for graphic elements in Chapter 4.)

To set parameters for snapping to the grid:

1. Choose View > Grid > Edit Grid or press Option-⌘-G (Mac) or Ctrl-Alt-G (Windows).

2. In the Grid dialog, choose a parameter from the Snap Accuracy pop-up menu (**Figure 1.58**).

3. Click OK.

To set parameters for snapping to guides:

1. Choose View > Guides > Edit Guides or press Option-Shift-⌘-G (Mac) or Ctrl-Alt-Shift-G (Windows).

2. In the Guides dialog, choose a setting from the Snap Accuracy pop-up menu (**Figure 1.59**).

3. Click OK.

To set snap-align options:

1. Choose View > Snapping > Edit Snapping. The Edit Snapping dialog opens. If the Snap Align settings aren't visible in the dialog, click the Advanced/Basic button (**Figure 1.60**).

2. To adjust the way Snap Align interacts with elements and the Stage, do any of the following.

   ▲ To have alignment guides appear when a dragged object reaches a specified distance from the edge of the Stage, enter a value in the Stage Border field.

   ▲ To have alignment guides appear when the top or bottom edge of a dragged object reaches a specified distance from the top or bottom edge of another object, in the Object Spacing section, enter a value in the Vertical field.

   ▲ To have alignment guides appear when the side of a dragged object reaches a specified distance from either side of another object, in the Object Spacing section, enter a value in the Horizontal field.

   ▲ To have guides appear when the center of a dragged object aligns horizontally and/or vertically with the center of another object, in the Center Alignment section, select the Horizontal and/or Vertical check boxes.

Figure 1.59 In the Guides dialog, you can set how close items must be before they snap to the guides. You can also set a guide color, the visibility of guides, and their status as locked or unlocked.

Figure 1.60 You set the tolerance for Snap Align in the Advanced section of the Edit Snapping dialog. Flash's default settings are shown here.

Figure 1.61 Choose 100% magnification to display graphics at the size they will be in the final movie.

Figure 1.62 Enter a percentage greater than 100 in the Zoom Control field to magnify elements on the Stage. The pop-up menu to the right of the field offers several common magnification levels.

Viewing at Various Magnifications

Flash offers several ways to adjust the magnification of elements on the Stage.

To view elements at actual size:

◆ Choose View > Magnification > 100% (**Figure 1.61**), or press ⌘-1 (Mac) or Ctrl-1 (Windows).

or

◆ In the Zoom Control field, at the right side of the Stage's Edit bar, type 100%. Press Enter.

At 100%, Flash displays elements as close as possible to the size they will be in the final movie. (Some monitors and video cards may display elements at a slightly different size than the system on which you created the element.)

To zoom in or out on the Stage:

1. In the Zoom Control field, type the desired percentage of magnification (**Figure 1.62**).

2. Press Enter.

✔ Tip

■ Click the scroll button next to the Zoom Control field to open a menu that duplicates the choices in the View > Magnification submenu. Choose a percentage from this menu to change magnification immediately. This menu also lets you choose Fit in Window (to display the full Stage area in the current window, without scroll bars), Show Frame (to display the full Stage area in the current window, with scroll bars), and Show All (to scale the Stage so that all elements on the Stage and in the Pasteboard appear in the current window).

To reduce or enlarge specific areas:

1. In the Tools panel, select the zoom tool (or press M on the keyboard).

   The pointer changes to a magnifying glass.

2. To enlarge an area or element, click and drag to create a selection rectangle that encompasses the area or element.

   Flash fills the window with your selection (**Figure 1.63**). This technique works whether the zoom tool is set to Enlarge or Reduce mode.

To zoom in or out:

1. With the zoom tool active, in the lower portion of the Tools panel, select one of the tool's modifiers:

   ▲ Enlarge (the magnifying-glass icon with the plus sign)

   ▲ Reduce (the magnifying-glass icon with the minus sign)

2. On the Stage, click the area or element you want to enlarge or reduce.

   Flash places the spot you clicked at the center of the viewing window and changes the percentage of magnification specified in the Zoom Control field. With the zoom tool set to Enlarge, Flash doubles the percentage; with the zoom tool set to Reduce, Flash halves the percentage.

✔ Tip

■ With the zoom tool selected, to switch temporarily from Enlarge to Reduce, and vice versa, hold down the Option key (Mac) or Alt key (Windows).

Zoom tool

Reduce modifier

Enlarge modifier

Figure 1.63 Use the zoom tool (top) to draw a selection rectangle around an element (middle). Flash enlarges your selection to fill the open window (bottom).

VIEWING AT VARIOUS MAGNIFICATIONS

CREATING SIMPLE GRAPHICS

About Strokes and Fills

What do *stroke* and *fill* mean? A stroke is an outline, and a fill is a solid area of color. Think of a coloring book, with black lines creating the pictures: those lines are strokes. When you fill in the areas outlined by strokes that colorful area is the fill. In a coloring book, you start with an outline and create the fill inside it. In Flash, you can also work the other way around— start with a solid shape and then create the outline as a separate element.

Flash's rectangle, oval, rectangle-primitive, oval-primitive, and polystar tools can create an element that's just a stroke or just a fill; they can also create the stroke and fill elements simultaneously. The line and pen tools, as you might guess, create only strokes.

The concept of fills and strokes is a bit trickier to grasp in relation to the brush tool. This tool creates fills. These fills may look like lines or brushstrokes, but they are shapes you can outline with a stroke. Flash has special tools for adding, editing, and removing strokes and fills: the ink bottle, the paint bucket, and the faucet eraser. See Chapter 4 for more details.

This chapter teaches you to use Adobe Flash CS4 Professional's drawing tools to create basic shapes from lines and areas of color— in Flash terminology, *strokes* and *fills.* Flash offers natural drawing tools that imitate the feel of working on paper with a pencil or brush; geometric-shape tools that create pre-defined shapes; and a pen tool that lets you draw with precision, using Bézier curves.

These tools let you create three types of shapes. Tools set to Merge Drawing mode create raw shapes—shapes that interact with other raw shapes on the same layer (you'll learn about shape interactions in Chapter 5). Tools set to Object Drawing mode create editable shapes that don't interact with other shapes. Flash's rectangle- and oval-primitive tools create *primitive-shapes*—non-interactive shapes with a set of defining parameters. You can edit a primitive's parameters (changing the roundness of a rectangle's corners, for example), but you can't freely edit a primitive's outline (turning an oval into a free-form blob, for example). Once you create a shape, you can edit it (see Chapter 4).

Flash CS4 introduces two new tools—spray brush and deco—that create patterns using multiple shapes (see Chapter 5). You can also import graphics from other programs for use in Flash (see Chapter 16).

Touring the Tools

The Tools panel holds all the tools you need to create and modify graphic elements (**Figure 2.1**). Flash CS4 gives you tools for creating graphic elements, for scrolling the Stage and zooming in and out, and for setting colors for the elements you create.

You click a tool to select it for use. Additional options and settings for a selected tool may appear at the bottom of the Tools panel and/or in the Property inspector.

To access tools and options:

1. With the Tools panel open, click a tool—for example, the brush tool.

   The relevant modifiers for the selected tool appear at the bottom of the Tools panel.

2. Click a button or select an option to modify the way the selected tool works (**Figure 2.2**).

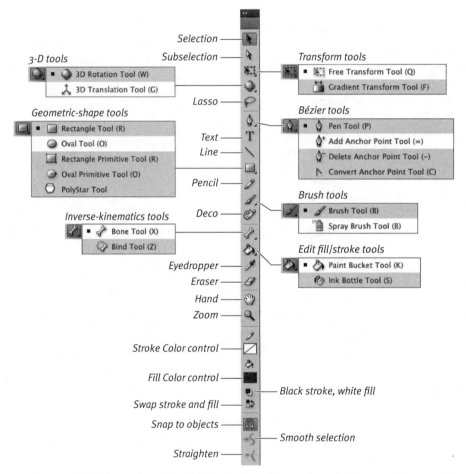

Figure 2.1 The Tools panel contains tools for drawing, editing, and manipulating graphic elements in Flash. To save space, some tools are grouped. Click the current tool icon to view a submenu from which to choose a different tool in that group.

Merge/Drawing
Object mode

Brush mode
(how fills interact)

Brush shape

Use tilt

Lock fill

Brush size

Use pressure

Figure 2.2 When selected, some tools display modifiers at the bottom of the Tools panel. Here the settings for using the brush appear. Click a button to toggle settings such as Merge mode. Access a menu (indicated by a small black triangle) to select settings such as Brush mode.

✔ Tips

- Flash's default setting makes tool tips active (when the pointer hovers over a tool, an identifying label appears). You can change the tool tip setting in the Preferences dialog: Select the General category, select (or deselect) the Show Tooltips check box, and click OK to close the dialog. (For details on opening the Preferences dialog, see Chapter 1.)

- In addition to displaying tool names, tool tips show keyboard shortcuts. As you get more familiar with the tools, activating them from the keyboard will speed your operations.

Customize Your Tool Set

Flash CS4 lets you customize the Tools panel to make the best use of space. You can resize the panel vertically and horizontally, as you would any other panel (see Chapter 1). You can also combine tools in pop-up submenus, or completely remove tools from the panel.

To change which tools appear where in the panel, from the Flash application menu (Mac) or Edit menu (Windows), choose Customize Tools Panel; a dialog with the same name appears. The default layout of tool icons appears on the left; a scrolling list of all Flash's tools appears next to it. To make modifications, select a tool icon in the layout; Flash outlines the slot containing that icon in red and the places the name of the tool (or tools) assigned to that slot in the Current Selection list, on the right side of the dialog. You can now assign tools to the selected slot.

To add a tool to the highlighted slot, select the tool name in the Available Tools list, then click the Add button. To remove a tool from the highlighted slot, select the name in the Current Selection list and click the Remove button. To return the Tools panel to its original state, click the Restore Default button. Click OK to confirm the new set of tools. The tools panel now contains the tool set you created. When you assign multiple tools to one slot, Flash makes them available through submenus.

Touring the Tools

Creating Solid Colors and Gradients

Although you can define fill and stroke colors from most color controls (see the sidebar "The Mystery of Color Controls," later in this chapter), the Color panel gives you the widest variety of options for defining fill and stroke colors. You can choose colors visually, by clicking a graphic representation of a *color space*—all the available colors in a given color-definition system; or you can choose colors numerically, by entering specific values for color components. You can also set a color's transparency in the Color panel. To define new gradients, you must use the Color panel.

Before you define a color or gradient, you must choose whether the color or gradient applies to fills or strokes by activating the Fill Color control or the Stroke Color control. As you define new colors, Flash updates all the related color controls. If you define a new fill color, for example, that color becomes the current setting for all the tools that use fills.

To assign solid-color attributes in the Color panel:

1. Access the Color panel (if it's not open, choose Window > Color or press Shift-F9).

2. From the Type menu, choose Solid.

3. To choose a color space, from the panel menu, choose one of the following:

   ▲ To define colors as mixtures of red, green, and blue, choose RGB.

   ▲ To define colors by percentage of hue, saturation, and brightness, choose HSB (**Figure 2.3**).

Fill Color control
Stroke Color control   *Panel menu*

Figure 2.3 The Color panel lets you choose a color from the color-space window or enter values directly to define a color in the RGB or HSB color space. Choose the desired color space from the panel menu.

What Are Hex Colors?

The term *hex color* is short for *hexadecimal color,* which is a fancy way of saying "a color defined by a number written in base 16." Hexadecimal coding is the language of bits and bytes that computers speak.

Hex coding is the way to specify color in HTML. In Flash, entering a single hex code for your color may be easier than entering three different values for red, green, and blue (RGB).

If you remember studying bases in high-school math, you'll recall that the decimal system is base 10, represented by the numbers 0 through 9. In hex color, to get the extra six digits, you continue coding with letters A through F.

Figure 2.4 The Color panel displays a color-space window (A), a luminosity/lightness slider (B), a text field for entering the precise hex value of a color (C), and a preview window for the new color (D). Click in the color-space window to choose a new color visually.

Figure 2.5 Enter RGB values to specify the amount of red, green, and blue that make up the color. Enter HSB values to specify the color by hue, saturation, and brightness. The new color appears in the selected color control.

✔ Tip

■ To change values in the Color panel interactively, click and drag the small triangle to the right of the R, G, B, or Alpha fields. A slider pops up; drag up to increase values, down to decrease values. When the color you want appears in the preview window, release the mouse button. Flash enters the current slider value in the field.

4. To determine where Flash applies the new color, do one of the following:

   ▲ To set a new stroke color, choose the Stroke Color control by clicking the pencil icon.

   ▲ To set a new fill color, choose the Fill Color control by clicking the paint-bucket icon.

To define a new color visually in the Color panel:

1. With the Color panel open, choose a color space.

2. Position the pointer over the desired hue in the color-space window, and click.

   Flash places a crosshair cursor in the window where you clicked and selects the color within the crosshairs (**Figure 2.4**).

✔ Tip

■ If you have trouble clicking exactly the right color, click and drag around within the color-space window. A preview of the new color appears above the old color in the preview window. When the color you want appears, release the mouse button. Flash enters the values for that color in the appropriate fields.

To define a new color numerically in the Color panel:

1. With the Color panel open, choose a color space.

2. To define a new color, do one of the following:

   ▲ For RGB colors, enter values from 0 to 255 for red, green, and blue in the R, G, and B fields (**Figure 2.5**).

   ▲ For HSB, enter values for hue, saturation, and brightness in the H, S, and B fields.

To define a color's transparency:

1. With the Color panel open, define a color.

2. Enter a value in the Alpha field (**Figure 2.6**).

   A value of 100 (100 percent) results in a completely solid color; a value of 0 results in a completely transparent color.

To create a linear gradient:

1. Open the Color panel.

2. From the Color panel's Type menu, choose Linear (**Figure 2.7**).

   The tools and options for defining gradients appear (**Figure 2.8**). The default gradient starts with two pointers, black on the left and white on the right.

3. For Overflow, leave the default setting, Extend (on the Mac the Overflow menu setting is labeled Extend; in Windows, the menu is iconic and the Extend setting appears as a black-to-white gradient).

   Overflow determines how gradient colors fill a shape when you resize the gradient to be narrower than the shape it fills. (To learn about resizing gradients, see Chapter 4.)

4. To add a new color to the gradient, do the following:

   ▲ Position the pointer on or below the gradient-definition bar.

   ▲ Flash adds a plus sign to the pointer, indicating that you can add a new gradient pointer in this area.

   ▲ Click anywhere along the gradient-definition bar.

   ▲ Flash adds a new gradient pointer.

Figure 2.6 Enter an Alpha value of less than 100 percent to define a transparent color.

Figure 2.7 Choose Linear from the Type menu to access the tools for defining linear gradients.

Color-space window

Brightness control

Gradient-definition bar

Gradient-preview window

Gradient pointer selected

Figure 2.8 When you choose Linear or Radial as the Type, the Color panel displays the gradient-preview window, gradient-definition bar, and a color-space window.

Gradient starts with white, and blends first to gray and then to black

Move pointers in to increase width of outside bands

Click to add pointers

Figure 2.9 Choose a color for each gradient pointer. The colors and positions of the pointers on the bar define a gradient's color transitions. Place pointers closer together to make the transition between colors more abrupt; place them farther apart to spread the transition out over more space.

5. To change the color of a gradient pointer, click it to select it, and define a new color using any of the methods described in the preceding section.

   or

   Double-click the gradient pointer to open a pop-up swatch set, and do one of the following:

   ▲ Click a swatch to copy the swatch color.

   ▲ Click an item on the desktop to copy its color.

   ▲ Enter a new value in the Hex field.

   ▲ Click the Color Picker button in the upper-right corner of the pop-up swatch set to access the System Color Picker for assigning new colors.

6. To remove a color from the gradient, drag its pointer downward, away from the gradient-definition bar. The pointer disappears as you drag. The gradient preview changes to blend the colors in the remaining gradient pointers.

7. Repeat steps 4 through 6 to create the colors you want in your gradient.

   You can add up to 13 pointers (for a total of 15 colors) to a gradient.

8. Drag the pointers to position them on the gradient-definition bar (**Figure 2.9**).

   As you modify the gradient, your changes appear in all the Color controls for strokes or fills, depending on whether you assigned the gradient to strokes or fills.

CREATING SOLID COLORS AND GRADIENTS

To create a radial gradient:

1. Open the Color panel.

2. From the Type menu, choose Radial.

   The tools for defining circular gradients appear. The gradient-definition bar looks the same as it does for linear gradients, but the preview shows your gradient as a set of concentric circles (**Figure 2.10**). The leftmost pointer defines the inner ring; the rightmost pointer defines the outer ring.

3. Follow steps 3 through 8 of the previous task, "To create a linear gradient," to define the color transitions in the radial gradient.

✔ Tips

■ To modify an existing gradient, choose it in the Swatches panel. Flash switches the Color panel to gradient mode and displays the selected gradient. Now you can make any changes you need.

■ Gradients can have transparency. You simply use a transparent color in one or more gradient pointers (see "To define a color's transparency," earlier in this chapter). If a gradient has transparency, a grid shows up in the gradient pointer, in the Fill Color or Stroke Color control, and in the transparent part of the gradient in the preview window (**Figure 2.11**).

■ Each pointer in a gradient can have a different alpha setting. To create fade effects, try creating a gradient that blends from a fully opaque color to a transparent one.

■ The panel menu for the Swatches panel also offers some handy shortcuts for dealing with color sets, including Sort by Color to arrange colors by hue. Note that you can't undo the color sorting. Be sure to save your current set of colors if there's any chance you'll want to restore the unsorted order.

Figure 2.10 Choose Radial from the Type menu to create a circular gradient. The preview window translates the horizontal gradient-definition bar into the appropriate circular color transitions.

Figure 2.11 When transparent colors make up part of a gradient, grid lines appear in the gradient pointer, the Fill Color or Stroke Color control, and the gradient-preview window.

Figure 2.12 The panel menu in the Color panel has an Add Swatch command for adding the current color to the Swatches panel.

Figure 2.13 Positioning the pointer over a blank spot in the Swatches panel changes the pointer to a paint bucket. Click to add whatever color is currently specified in the Color panel. Solid color swatches are added to the upper half of the Swatches panel; gradient swatches, to the lower half.

Working with Swatches

You can save a new color or gradient for the duration of your work session by adding the color currently displayed in the Color panel to the Swatches panel. The Fill Color and Stroke Color controls found in the Tools panel, in the Property inspector, and in the Color panel also give you quick access to the current set of swatches.

To add a color or gradient to the Swatches panel:

1. Create a new color or gradient using any of the techniques outlined in the preceding sections.

2. In the Color panel, do either of the following:

   ▲ From the panel menu, choose Add Swatch (**Figure 2.12**).

   ▲ Position the pointer over the blank area of the Swatches panel; when the paint-bucket pointer appears, click.

   Flash adds the new solid color or gradient to the appropriate section of the Swatches panel (**Figure 2.13**).

✔ Tips

■ You can add new colors to the Swatches panel even if it's closed. But if you want to get feedback when you add a swatch, open the Swatches panel. Resize the panel window so that a bit of space appears below the existing swatches.

■ To remove a swatch from the Swatches panel, select a swatch, and from the panel menu, choose Delete Swatch.

■ If the swatches in the Swatches panel are too small for you, resize the panel. The swatches grow bigger as the window widens.

Color Sets and Kuler Themes

Flash stores a default set of colors and gradients in the system color file and stores just the specific colors and gradients used in each document with that document. You can define the default set and create additional sets for loading into the Swatches panel. Color sets, which help maintain a consistent color palette across several documents, are particularly useful for projects with multiple contributors.

Flash's Kuler panel offers another way to maintain consistency with color. The panel integrates with Adobe Kuler, an Internet application for creating and sharing simple five-color palettes called *themes*.

Saving Color Sets

Once you've defined a set of swatches, from the panel menu in the Swatches panel choose Save Colors (**Figure 2.14**). When the Export Color Swatch dialog appears, choose a format: Flash Color Set saves colors and gradients in Flash's proprietary Flash Color Set (CLR) format; Color Table saves colors (but no gradients) in Color Table (ACT) format. Choose where to save the file and click Save.

Loading Color Sets

To display a color set, from the panel menu in the Swatches panel choose one of the following: Add Colors adds new colors to the current swatch set; Replace Colors removes

Figure 2.14 The panel menu in the Swatches panel offers commands for working with color sets.

the current swatch set and displays the new colors. When the Import Color Swatch dialog appears, choose which file format to view in the dialog, navigate to your color set, select it, and click Open.

Using the Kuler Panel

Adobe's Kuler extension helps people use color creatively. Kuler users can post themes (sets of five colors) on the Web where other Kuler users can rank them. Much like the Kuler application available on the Internet, Flash's Kuler panel lets you create a theme according to the rules of color theory. You select a base color, choose a rule, and Kuler picks four colors that should work well with the base. You can also choose five colors independently. The Kuler panel provides a direct link to the Web for browsing and sharing themes. You can load the Kuler panel's current theme into the Swatches panel. To access the Kuler panel, choose Window > Extensions > Kuler. To connect to the Kuler Web site, click the Browse button at the top of the panel. To create a theme, click the Create button. Kuler's color tools appear; use them to define the theme's colors. To add the theme colors to the Swatches panel, click the Add Theme to Swatches button. Flash adds the colors below the current swatch set in the Swatches panel.

Fill Color control

Expand/collapse section — Fill Color control

Figure 2.15 Selecting a tool or graphic element that uses fills activates the Property inspector's Fill and Stroke section, which contains a Fill Color control. If the control isn't visible, click the expand/collapse triangle to display the contents of the section. The Fill Color control in the Tools panel is always visible.

Current fill color — Hex hot text
Choose new color
Alpha hot text

Figure 2.16 Click the Fill Color control—the color chip identified by a paint-bucket icon—to open a set of swatches. Click a swatch to choose the new color or use the hot text to enter new hex or alpha values. The Fill Color control works the same way in the Tools panel and the Fill and Stroke portion of the Property inspector.

Setting Fill Attributes

You can use any Fill Color control to assign colors or gradients to selected tools or graphic elements. A Fill Color control is always available in the Color panel and Tools panel. A Fill Color control also appears in the Fill and Stroke section of the Property inspector when you select a tool or graphic element that uses fills (for example, when you select the rectangle tool in the Tools panel, or when you select a rectangle shape on the Stage). When you change the fill color in one panel, the Fill Color controls in the other panels change to match.

To assign fill colors from the Property inspector or Tools panel:

1. With the Property inspector open, in the Tools panel, select a tool that creates fills. (The rectangle, oval, rectangle-primitive, oval-primitive, polystar, brush, and paint-bucket tools all create fills.)

   When one of these tools is selected, the Property inspector's Fill and Stroke section appears. This section is where you'll find a Fill Color control—a color chip identified by a paint-bucket icon (**Figure 2.15**).

   or

   Access a Fill Color control in the Tools panel.

2. Click on the Fill Color control.

   A set of swatches pops up; as you move the pointer over the swatches, it changes to an eyedropper (**Figure 2.16**).

   continues on next page

SETTING FILL ATTRIBUTES

3. To assign a new fill color or gradient, do one of the following:

▲ To assign a gradient, select one of the linear or radial gradient swatches.

▲ To select a solid color, click a solid swatch or an item on the Stage; the color directly below the tip of the eyedropper becomes the assigned fill color.

▲ To define a new fill color, use the Hex hot text (to the right of the current-color chip) to enter a new hex value. Click the hot text to enter a precise value; drag the hot text's invisible slider to choose a value interactively.

▲ To define transparency for the current fill color, use the Alpha hot text to enter a percentage less than 100. Note there is no Alpha hot text when a gradient is the current fill color; transparency is a part of the gradient definition.

The new color appears in all Fill Color controls (in the Tools panel, the Fill and Stroke section of the Property inspector, and the Color panel). Flash changes the fills of any shapes or drawing-objects selected on the Stage; any tools that create fills are set to use the new color.

✔ Tips

■ To assign new fill colors, you can also use the Color panel. Its Fill Color control works just like the ones in the Tools panel and Property inspector.

■ To access a System Color Picker for assigning fill colors, click the color chip in one of the Fill Color controls and then click the Color Picker button from the pop-up swatch window (**Figure 2.17**).

Color Picker

Figure 2.17 Click the Color Picker button to access the system's color picker(s) for defining a color that's not in the current swatch set.

The Mystery of Color Controls

You'll find color controls—a color chip with an open-menu triangle in the lower right corner—throughout Flash. To operate a color control, click the color chip; a panel of color swatches pops up, and the pointer changes to an eyedropper. To assign a new color, position the pointer over a swatch and click the color you want; enter a new value in the Hex Color field; enter a transparency value in the Alpha field; choose No Color; or click the Color Picker button to access the System Color Picker(s). With many color controls you can also position the eyedropper pointer over an element on the Stage or desktop and click to select that color. The pointer may lose its eyedropper shape as it moves over certain areas of the interface, but it's still picking up the color beneath its tip.

You can use any Stroke Color or Fill Color control to assign color attributes. The specs for the color you select appear in the Color panel, and all the other color controls update to match.

Figure 2.18 Clicking the Stroke Color control (the color chip identified by a pencil icon) in the Fill and Stroke section of the Property inspector opens a set of color swatches and provides an eyedropper pointer for selecting a new color.

Figure 2.19 Entering a new value in the Stroke field sets the weight, or thickness, for strokes created by tools that draw strokes.

Setting Stroke Attributes

A line has three main attributes: color, thickness (also known as *weight* or, in Flash, *stroke height*), and style. You set all three in the Fill and Stroke section of the Property inspector for any tool that creates strokes. That section also lets you control the way the ends of lines (*caps*) look and the way lines connect (*joins*).

To set stroke properties:

1. With the Property inspector open, in the Tools panel, choose a tool that creates strokes. (The pen, line, rectangle, oval, rectangle-primitive, oval-primitive, polystar, pencil, and ink-bottle tools all create strokes.)

   The Fill and Stroke section appears in the Property inspector, displaying current stroke settings for the selected tool.

2. To select a stroke color, do the following:

   ▲ In the Fill and Stroke section of the Property inspector (or in the Tools panel), click the Stroke Color control—the color chip identified by a pencil icon.

   ▲ A set of swatches pops up; as you move the pointer over the swatches, it changes to an eyedropper (**Figure 2.18**).

   ▲ Click the swatch with the desired color (or use any of the techniques described in step 3 of the preceding task).

3. To set the stroke's weight, in the Stroke field, enter a number between 0.25 and 200, or drag the slider next to the field (**Figure 2.19**).

continues on next page

4. To set the stroke's style, choose from the Style pop-up menu (**Figure 2.20**).

There are seven styles to choose from: Hairline, Solid, Dashed, Dotted, Ragged, Stippled, and Hatched.

5. To set the way a solid or hairline stroke ends, from the Cap pop-up menu, choose a cap style.

▲ *None* ends the stroke exactly where you stop drawing it.

▲ *Round* extends the stroke by half the current stroke height, creating a rounded end.

▲ *Square* extends the stroke by half the current stroke height, creating a square end (**Figure 2.21**).

6. To set the way solid or hairline strokes meet, click the Join pop-up menu.

▲ *Miter* creates a sharp corner.

▲ *Round* creates a slightly curved corner.

▲ *Bevel* creates a slightly flattened corner (**Figure 2.22**).

✔ Tips

■ The Tools panel displays two buttons for setting basic stroke and fill colors quickly. Clicking the overlapping black and white squares sets the Stroke Color control to black and the Fill Color control to white. Clicking the small squares with an arrow next to them makes the current stroke and fill colors change places.

■ In Flash, the hairline setting is considered a stroke style, not thickness, or stroke height. (Use the stroke-style pop-up menu to get the Hairline setting.) Hairlines in a symbol don't change thickness when you resize the symbol. Other lines in a symbol grow thicker or thinner as you scale the symbol up or down. (To learn about symbols, see Chapter 7.)

Preview of current stroke settings

Selected stroke style

Figure 2.20 Choose a stroke style from the pop-up menu in the Fill and Stroke section of the Property inspector.

Figure 2.21 Set a Cap style in the Fill and Stroke section of the Property inspector to control the look of the ends of lines. The None option keeps the line's original length and makes the end flat; Round extends and rounds the line's end; and Square extends and squares off the end.

Miter (set to 1)   Miter (set to 2)

Round

Bevel

Join: ☒ ▼   Mit
✓ **Miter**
  Round
  Bevel

Figure 2.22 Set a join style in the Fill and Stroke section of the Property inspector to control the way lines connect. Miter makes a pointed corner, Round makes a rounded corner, and Bevel slices a flat piece off the corner. Choosing Miter activates the Miter hot text, which accepts values between 1 and 60. With Miter set to 1, Flash flattens the join slightly by slicing off the very tip of the point; the flat area is smaller than in a bevel join. Settings of 2 and above create a very sharp point.

■ To constrain the way strokes scale in your published movie, with a stroke (or stroke-creating tool) selected, choose a setting from the Scale menu in the Fill and Stroke section of the Property inspector. In the default (Normal) mode, a 1-pixel stroke becomes a 2-pixel stroke if your final movie gets enlarged to 200 percent. To prevent a selected stroke from scaling at all, choose None. To allow the stroke to scale in one direction only, choose Horizontal or Vertical.

■ Click the Hinting check box in the Fill and Stroke section of the Property inspector to ensure crisp lines in your final output. Without hinting, lines sometimes appear slightly blurry on some monitors.

■ You can modify Flash's stroke styles. You might, for example, want larger dots in the dotted line or bigger spaces in the dashed line. Select a stroke-creating tool; in the Fill and Stroke section of the Property inspector, select the stroke style you want to modify, and then click the Edit Stroke Style button (the pencil icon). The Stroke Style dialog appears, in which you can assign new settings. Click OK to close the dialog and confirm the settings. Those settings continue in force for that style until you change them or end the work session.

■ You can also set stroke color from any Stroke Color control (in the Property inspector, the Tools panel, or the Color panel). Click the Stroke Color control, and select a color as described in "Setting Fill Attributes," earlier in this chapter.

■ You can set the Join property for rectangles created with the rectangle-primitive tool, but you'll only see the joins on sharp corners (those with a corner radius setting of 0).

SETTING STROKE ATTRIBUTES

Making Geometric Shapes

Flash provides separate tools for drawing ovals, rectangles, and polygons (or stars). The tools work similarly; all can draw a shape as an outline (just a stroke) or as a solid object (a fill). You can also create a geometric shape with a fill and a stroke simultaneously. There are special properties for defining rectangles and ovals that you can set as precise values in the Property inspector.

Merge Drawing vs. Object Drawing vs. Primitive-Shapes

Flash CS4 creates three types of graphic objects: *merge-shapes* (also called *raw shapes),* *drawing objects,* and *primitive-shapes.* You can use most of the drawing tools to create merge-shapes or drawing objects simply by selecting the appropriate drawing mode. To create primitives, you must select either the rectangle-primitive or the oval-primitive tool.

In **Merge Drawing** mode, the strokes and fills you create are raw shapes and are ready for editing directly on the Stage; raw shapes on a single layer interact with one another (you'll learn more about shape interactions in Chapter 5).

In **Object Drawing** mode, the strokes and fills you create are directly editable on the Stage but don't interact with other shapes on the same layer. Shapes created in Object Drawing mode act somewhat as if they were isolated on a separate layer or protected using the Group command (you'll learn about working with grouped shapes in Chapter 5 and about shapes on separate layers in Chapter 6). But shapes created in Object Drawing mode can be modified directly on the Stage (see Chapter 4), whereas grouped objects generally can't.

Primitive-shapes do not interact with other shapes on the same layer. Behind the scenes, Flash creates these shapes in Object Drawing mode but locks and constrains them so that they always exhibit certain defining characteristics. Those characteristics are editable and appear as properties in the Property inspector when you select a primitive tool in the Tools panel or a primitive-shape on the Stage. You can edit these properties of a primitive anytime, but you can't freely edit a primitive the way you can edit a shape created in Merge/Object Drawing mode. For example, you can change the inner radius setting for an oval-primitive to transform a solid oval to a donut shape, but you can't edit an oval-primitive's outline to give it pointy ends and transform it into a football shape.

continues on next page

Figure 2.23 The Tools panel combines all the geometric-shape tools under a pop-up submenu. To view them all, click the geometric-shape tool that's visible, then click a tool to select it and close the submenu.

To create geometric outlines:

1. To select a geometric-shape tool, do the following:
   - ▲ In the Tools panel, click the active geometric-shape tool.
   - ▲ From the submenu that appears, choose a tool—for example, the oval tool (**Figure 2.23**).

2. In the Fill and Stroke section of the Property inspector, enter values and choose settings for the stroke properties you wish to control.

continues on next page

Merge Drawing vs. Object Drawing vs. Primitive-Shapes *continued*

Flash's default mode for drawing tools is Merge Drawing. To turn on Object Drawing mode, select a tool that creates strokes and/or fills, then click the Object Drawing button in the Tools panel (**Figure 2.24**). Once you activate Object Drawing mode, it remains active until you click the Object Drawing button again to return to Merge Drawing mode (or press J on the keyboard to toggle between Merge Drawing and Object Drawing). Whichever Merge/Object Drawing setting is active when you end a work session will be active the next time you open Flash. The Merge/Object Drawing mode button is absent from the Tools panel when you choose one of the primitive tools (**Figure 2.25**).

For many tasks, you'll see no difference between working with the three types of shapes; in some tasks, however, the difference is crucial. For the exercises in this book, unless otherwise noted, you can create shapes using either drawing mode or the primitive-shape tools.

Object Drawing mode

Figure 2.24 You can set the drawing tools to create shapes that don't interact with other shapes on the same layer. Select Object Drawing mode in the Tools panel.

Oval-primitive tool selected

Drawing mode unavailable

Figure 2.25 The drawing-mode button does not appear in the Tools panel when you select the oval-primitive (or rectangle-primitive) tool.

When creating an outline shape, you choose the stroke's color, height, and style (see "Setting Stroke Attributes," earlier in this chapter). Specific oval and rectangle properties also appear in the Property inspector when you select the rectangle, rectangle-primitive, oval, and oval-primitive tools.

3. To set the tool to create an outline with no fill, do the following:

▲ Access the Color Panel and click the paint-bucket icon of its Fill Color control; Flash highlights Fill Color as the active control.

▲ Click the No Color button (**Figure 2.26**).

4. Move the pointer over the Stage.
The pointer turns into a crosshair.

5. Click and drag to create the geometric shape (**Figure 2.27**).
Flash previews the shape as you drag.

6. Release the mouse button.
Flash draws an outline.

✔ Tips

■ To draw a perfect circle (or square), hold down the Shift key while you draw with the rectangle, oval, rectangle-primitive, or oval-primitive tool.

■ To make ovals (or rectangles) grow outward from the center point as you draw, position the pointer where you want the center of the shape to be; hold down the Option key (Mac) or Alt key (Windows) as you drag. Shapes drawn with the polystar tool always grow from the center.

■ In step 3 of the preceding task, you can click any Fill Color control and choose No Color from the pop-up swatch set.

Active control

No Color button

Figure 2.26 To set the geometric shape tools to create outline shapes (ones without fills), you need to set the fill to No Color. A quick way to do that is via the Color panel. Click the Fill Color control's paint-bucket icon; Flash highlights the control in gray, meaning it's the control to which the current panel settings apply. Then click the No Color button (top). Flash sets the fill type to None (bottom).

Figure 2.27 With a geometric-shape tool selected, click the Stage and drag to create an outline preview of a shape (top). Release the mouse button, and Flash creates a shape using the current settings for fills and strokes. In this case, the oval tool is set to black stroke color, no fill, dashed stroke style, and a stroke height of 1 point (bottom).

No Color

Figure 2.28 To create a geometric shape that's just a fill (no outlining stroke), you must set the stroke to No Color. One way to do that is to click any Stroke Color control (here it's the one in the Tools panel); when the swatch set pops up, click the No Color button.

Figure 2.29 As you drag the rectangle tool, Flash creates an outline preview of a rectangle (left). To complete the fill shape, release the mouse button (right).

To create geometric fills:

1. To select a geometric-shape tool, follow steps 1 and 2 in the preceding exercise.

   For this task, for example, select the rectangle tool.

2. To set the tool to create just a fill with no outline, do the following:

   ▲ Click any Stroke Color control (in the Tools panel, the Fill and Stroke section of the Property inspector, or the Color panel).

   ▲ Choose No Color from the pop-up swatch set (**Figure 2.28**).

3. Follow steps 4 through 6 in the preceding exercise.

   Flash draws a geometric fill, using the currently selected fill color (**Figure 2.29**).

✔ Tips

■ You can create polygons and star shapes with the polystar tool. To set the number of sides in the polygon and to switch from polygons to stars, select the polystar tool (choose it from the geometric-shape tool's submenu in the Tools panel). A Tool Settings section appears in the Property inspector. Click the Options button in that section. Enter values for the number of sides and how sharp the star points are, then click OK.

■ In step 2 of the preceding task, you could use the Color panel to set the stroke to No Color. Click the pencil icon to apply settings to the Stroke Color control, then click the No Color button.

MAKING GEOMETRIC SHAPES

To set rectangle properties:

1. In the Tools panel, select the rectangle (or rectangle-primitive) tool.

   The Property inspector displays settings for the selected tool (**Figure 2.30**). The properties are the same for both tools.

2. To create a rectangle with four identical corners, set the Lock Corner Radius button to the constrained state (**Figure 2.31**).

   Clicking the chain-link icon toggles between the unconstrained (open link) and constrained (closed link) states.

3. To create a rectangle with rounded corners, in the Rectangle Corner Radius field enter a positive number.

   or

   To create a rectangle with indented corners, in the Rectangle Corner Radius field enter a negative number.

To set oval properties:

1. In the Tools panel, select the oval (or oval-primitive) tool.

   The Property inspector displays settings for the selected tool (**Figure 2.32**). The properties are the same for both tools.

2. To create variations on the oval shape, in the Oval Options section of the Property inspector, do any of the following:

   ▲ To create a pie-wedge shape, in the Start Angle and/or End Angle field, enter a number from 0 to 360 (**Figure 2.33**).

Figure 2.30 When you select the rectangle or rectangle-primitive tool, the Property inspector's Rectangle Options section displays special properties for defining a rectangle's corners. The properties are the same for both tools.

Constrain corner radius

Figure 2.31 By default, the rectangle and rectangle-primitive tools create shapes whose corners all have the same radius. When the closed-link icon appears (Constrained mode), only the first field is active for entering values because the settings are linked.

Figure 2.32 When you select the oval or oval-primitive tool, the Property inspector's Oval Options section displays special properties for defining an oval. The properties are the same for both tools.

Drag slider to reposition control point

Figure 2.33 Entering values in the Start Angle and End Angle fields creates partial ovals like those often used in pie charts. You can also use the sliders to enter start- and end-angle values.

MAKING GEOMETRIC SHAPES

Shape with closed path

Shape with open path

Figure 2.34 Deselecting the Close Path check box lets you create arcs out of pie-wedge oval shapes. If the shape has an inner-radius setting greater than 0, in its open-path form it appears as two arcs.

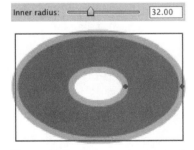

Figure 2.35 Entering a number greater than 0 in the Inner Radius field creates an oval with a hollow center.

▲ To create an open arc, deselect the Close Path check box. When you create a pie-wedge shape, this setting creates an open path. Flash removes the shape's fill (if one is present) and deletes the straight line segments from the wedge shape (**Figure 2.34**).

▲ To create an oval with a hollow center, in the Inner Radius field, enter a number from 0 to 99.

Flash draws a hollow oval inside the first oval (**Figure 2.35**). The inner-radius setting corresponds to the percentage of the outer oval's "fill" that gets removed by the inside oval. (The outer oval may have a fill of No Color, in which case the inner oval just appears as an outline.)

✔ Tips

■ You can change an oval-primitive's start- or end-angle settings interactively. Select the shape on the Stage. In the Oval Options section of the Property inspector, drag the Start Angle or End Angle slider to change the setting; the shape on the Stage changes.

■ You can also change start and end angles interactively from the keyboard. Click the pointer of the slider for the value you want to change. The pointer highlights in blue, indicating that it has focus. Press the up (or right) arrow to increase the value by 1; press the down (or left) arrow to decrease the value by 1. Hold down the Shift key as you press the arrows to increase or decrease the value by 72 degrees at a time.

Setting Oval Options

How do the settings in the Oval Options section of the Property inspector work? Imagine drawing a circle on the face of an analog clock. The start angle is the point where you put your pencil down to begin drawing; the end angle is the point where you lift the pencil and stop drawing. For oval-primitives, those points become control points for modifying the shape.

The values in the Start Angle and End Angle fields in the Property inspector correlate to degrees of a circle. The value 0 corresponds to 3 o'clock, 90 to 6 o'clock, 180 to 9 o'clock, and so on; When the start and end angles have the same value, both control points sit on the same spot, and the circle is complete. When the values differ, there's a gap.

When you click the Close Path check box, Flash finishes the shape by drawing straight-line segments to the center of the oval, creating a pie-wedge (**Figure 2.36**). If the inner-radius value is greater than 0, the segments connect with an inner oval, creating a C shape or a partial C shape.

Figure 2.36 The Start Angle and End Angle values in the Oval Options section of the Property inspector let you define an oval or oval-primitive shape as a full circle or a pie wedge.

About Drawing Assistance

Flash's pencil tool offers two assisted line-drawing modes: Straighten and Smooth. For total freedom in drawing, the pencil's Ink mode leaves shapes exactly as you create them.

Straighten mode refines any blips and tremors in a rough hand-drawn line into straight-line segments and regular arcs. This mode also carries out what Flash calls *shape recognition*. Flash evaluates each rough shape you draw, and if the shape comes close enough to Flash's definition of an oval or a rectangle, Flash turns your rough approximation into a shape neat enough to please your high-school geometry teacher.

Smooth mode transforms your rough drawing into one composed of smooth, curved line segments. Note that Smooth mode doesn't recognize shapes; it simply smoothes out the curves you draw. Smoothing reduces the number of points in a shape, resulting in smaller files and thus improving the performance of your final, published work.

Tolerance settings are all-important, especially for Straighten mode. You can set Flash to change almost anything ovoid into a circle and anything slightly more oblong into a rectangle. You set the degree of drawing assistance in the Preferences dialog. Choose Flash > Preferences (Mac) or Edit > Preferences (Windows); in the Preferences dialog that opens, choose Drawing from the Category list, then choose tolerance levels from the Connect Lines, Smooth Curves, Recognize Lines, and Recognize Shapes menus. Click OK to close the dialog.

Creating Free-form Shapes

Flash offers three tools for creating free-form shapes: the pencil, pen, and brush. The pencil and pen tools create stroke outlines, and the brush tool creates fills without strokes. The pencil and pen tools create only outlines, even if you draw a closed shape. Once you've created a shape, you can always modify it—say, to fill an empty outline or add an outline to a plain fill shape.

The pencil tool lets you draw lines (strokes) naturally, as you would with a real-world pencil, but using the mouse or a graphics tablet and pen. Flash hides information about the anchor points and curves of a stroke drawn with the pencil. With the pen tool, you place anchor points and adjust Bézier curves to create strokes. You can use the pen tool not only to create Bézier curves initially, but also to modify them once they are on the Stage. In addition there are three anchor-point tools for modifying Bézier curves on the Stage—the add-anchor-point tool, the delete-anchor-point tool, and the convert-anchor-point tool. In this chapter, you'll use the pen tool to create free-form shapes; in Chapter 4, you'll learn to use the pen tool and the anchor-point tools to modify shapes.

For the tasks below, make sure the grid is visible (see Chapter 1) and set drawing preferences as follows: choose Flash > Preferences (Mac) or Edit > Preferences (Windows) to open the Preferences dialog; choose Drawing from the Category list, and select the Show Pen Preview and Show Solid Points check boxes; leave the other items at their default settings. Click OK to close the dialog.

To draw free-form strokes with the pencil tool:

1. In the Tools panel, select the pencil tool, or press Y.

2. From the Pencil Mode menu (**Figure 2.37**), choose one of the following assistance modes:

   Straighten resolves minor variations into straight-line segments.

   Smooth resolves minor variations into smooth curves.

   Ink provides very little assistance, leaving minor variations.

3. Move the pointer over the Stage.

   The pointer changes to a pencil icon.

4. Click, and draw a squiggle.

   Flash previews your rough line.

5. Release the mouse button.

   Flash recasts the line you've drawn according to the assistance mode you chose in step 2, creating a set of straight-line segments and regular curves (**Figure 2.38**).

✔ Tips

- You can apply smoothing and straightening (even shape recognition) after you've drawn an outline or shape, by selecting it on the Stage and then clicking the Straighten or Smooth modifier of the Selection tool (you'll learn more about making and modifying selections in Chapter 4).

- To apply smoothing and straightening with more control, select an outline or shape, then choose Modify > Shape > Advanced Smooth (or Advanced Straighten). In the dialog that appears, enter new values to refine your shape, then click OK. To preview various settings, click the Preview check box; Flash applies the dialog's current settings to the selected shape.

Figure 2.37 When the pencil tool is selected, the Tools panel displays a pop-up menu of pencil modes.

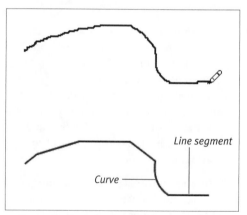

Figure 2.38 With the pencil tool in Straighten mode, when you draw a squiggle, Flash previews it for you. When you release the mouse button, Flash applies straightening, turning your rough squiggle (top) into a set of straight-line segments and smooth curves (bottom).

Figure 2.39 Select the pen tool to create paths.

Figure 2.40 The x next to the pen tool indicates that you're about to start a new path. Click to place the first anchor point.

First point previewed   *Preview line segment*

Click to place second point   *Completed line segment*

Figure 2.41 Flash previews points as you place them (top), and it adds a stroke to the path as soon as you complete a segment (bottom).

Figure 2.42 Continue clicking to add segments to your free-form shape. A quick click (top) adds a straight line segment (bottom).

To draw free-form strokes with the pen tool:

1. In the Tools panel, select the pen tool, or press P (**Figure 2.39**).

2. In the Fill and Stroke section of the Property inspector, set the stroke attributes for your path.

3. Move the pointer over the Stage.

   The pen tool appears with a small *x* next to it (**Figure 2.40**). The *x* indicates that you're ready to place the first point of a path.

4. Click where you want your line segment to begin.

   The pointer changes to a solid arrowhead; a small hollow circle indicates the location of the anchor point on the Stage.

5. Reposition the pen tool where you want your line segment to end.

   With Drawing Preferences set to Show Pen Preview, Flash extends a preview of the line segment from the first point to the tip of the pen as you move around the Stage.

6. Click.

   Flash completes the line segment using the selected stroke attributes. With Drawing Preferences set to Show Solid Points, the anchor points appear as solid squares (**Figure 2.41**).

7. To add a straight segment to your line, click the Stage where you want the segment to end, and release the mouse button (**Figure 2.42**).

continues on next page

CREATING FREE-FORM SHAPES

8. To add a curve segment, click the Stage where you want the curve segment to end, then drag the pointer.

Flash places a preview point on the Stage, the pointer changes to a solid arrowhead, and Bézier handles (sometimes referred to as tangent handles) appear (**Figure 2.43**).

Figure 2.43 Click and drag to create a curve point; as you drag, the point's Bézier handles activate. The bulge of the curve grows away from the direction of your drag. For example, to make the curve bulge upward, drag downward.

9. Drag the pointer in the opposite direction from which you want your curve to bulge.

The Bézier handles extend from the anchor point, growing in opposite directions as you drag. Flash previews the curve you're drawing (**Figure 2.44**).

Figure 2.44 To make the curve bulge downward, drag upward. Dragging the handles out farther deepens the curve.

10. Still keeping the mouse button down, drag the pointer to reposition the Bézier handle.

Dragging the handle clockwise or counterclockwise around its anchor point controls the direction of the bulge; dragging the handle farther from the anchor point deepens the curve (**Figure 2.45**).

11. When the curve preview looks the way you want, release the mouse button.

Flash completes your curve segment with a stroke (**Figure 2.46**).

12. To create an open path, #-click (Mac) or Ctrl-click (Windows) the Stage.

or

To create a closed shape, do the following:

▲ Position the pointer over your first anchor point.

▲ Flash previews the closing segment of your shape. A small hollow circle appears next to the pen tool (**Figure 2.47**).

▲ Click the first anchor point.

▲ Flash closes the shape, adding a stroke to the path.

Figure 2.45 Move the handles clockwise or counterclockwise around the anchor point to modify the curve shape (top). Drag the handles in or out to make the curve deeper or shallower (bottom).

Figure 2.46 When you finish positioning handles for a segment and release the mouse button, Flash adds a stroke to the segment.

Figure 2.47 To create a closed shape, position the pointer over the first anchor point you placed. When you see the hollow-circle icon, click that first point (left). Flash adds the finishing segment, creating a closed path (right).

Extend Line

Join Line

Modifier icon for drawing-object ⎯

Modifier icon for merge-shape ⎯

Figure 2.48 You can use the pen tool to add to existing line segments. Position the pointer over the end point of the existing line and click (top), then continue clicking to place more points. Or, place new points first, then position the pointer over the end point of the line you want to join (bottom). When the modifier icon appears, click to join the lines.

Once the path is complete, the pen tool pointer displays a small *x*, indicating that the tool is ready to place the first anchor point of a new path.

✔ Tips

- There are other ways to end open paths. Choose Edit > Deselect All, or press ⌘-Shift-A (Mac) or Ctrl-Shift-A (Windows). In the Tools panel, click a different tool. You can also double-click the last point you placed. To use this technique you must be drawing a path that ends with a straight-line segment that doesn't involve Bézier handles.

- The pen tool can add to a line created earlier (**Figure 2.48**). To extend outward from the original line, position the pointer over the end of the line (the terminal anchor point). A modifier—a small slash—appears next to the pen icon. Click the terminal anchor point and the pen links to that point as if you'd just placed it; continue adding segments as you learned to do in the previous exercises. You can also join to an existing line during the process of creating a new line. To join, the pen tool must be in the same mode (merge or drawing-object) as the existing line. Click to place the anchor points of the new line, but don't double-click to end the line. Instead, position the pointer over one of the terminal anchor points of the line you want to join. A modifier appears next to the pen icon; if the pen is in merge mode, the modifier is a small hollow circle; if the pen is in drawing-object mode, the modifier is a chain-link icon. Click the existing terminal anchor point, and Flash joins the two lines.

- The pen tool creates only strokes. To add a fill to a closed shape drawn with the pen, use the paint-bucket tool.

To create free-form solid fills with the brush tool:

1. In the Tools panel, click the current brush tool; and from the submenu that opens, select the brush tool, or press B (**Figure 2.49**).

Figure 2.49 The brush tool and its modifiers.

About Path Math in Flash

A *path*—a series of points and connecting lines—is the skeleton of your graphic-object. With most Flash tools, the math that goes into creating a path takes place behind the scenes. You draw a complete line or a shape; Flash places points (without showing them), connects them, and adds a stroke. With the pen tool, you place the defining points—called *anchor points*—and adjust the curve segments that connect them, using controllers called *Bézier handles* (also known as *tangent handles*). When you've finished placing points with the pen tool, Flash fleshes out the path by applying a stroke to it.

Figure 2.50 The Brush Mode options give you control over how fills created with the brush tool interact with other shapes on the same layer. Choosing Paint Normal lets you paint merge-shape fills that act like any other fills when they overlap other shapes.

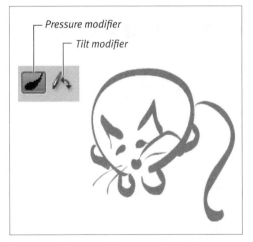

Figure 2.51 Selecting the brush tool's Use Pressure modifier activates the pressure-sensitive capabilities of a connected pressure-sensitive pen and graphics tablet. To vary line thickness, apply more or less pressure as you draw. Flash created all the lines in this cat with a single brush size and shape.

2. To optimize the brush for a particular painting task, in the lower portion of the Tools panel, select any of the following:

   ▲ From the Brush Mode pop-up menu, choose a painting mode; for this exercise, choose Paint Normal (**Figure 2.50**). The painting modes let you control how brushstroke fills act when you use the brush tool to paint over other shapes.

   Overlapping shapes interact in different ways depending on whether they are merge-shapes, drawing-objects, or primitives. (You'll learn about how overlapping shapes interact in Chapter 5.)

   ▲ From the Brush Size pop-up menu, choose a size for the brush tip.

   ▲ From the Brush Shape pop-up menu, choose a shape for the brush tip.

   ▲ To paint brushstroke fills that vary in thickness, choose Use Pressure. This option appears only when a graphics tablet is connected to your computer.

3. Select or define a solid fill color using any of the techniques outlined earlier in this chapter.

4. Move the pointer over the Stage.

   The pointer changes to reflect the current brush size and shape. When Use Pressure is active, the pointer changes to a crosshair within a circle; as you draw, the pointer changes to reflect brush-tip size and shape (**Figure 2.51**).

continues on next page

5. Click and draw on the Stage.

Flash previews your brushwork in the currently selected fill (**Figure 2.52**).

6. When you complete your shape, release the mouse button.

Flash creates the final shape, smoothing it according to settings in the Property inspector (see the sidebar "The Mystery of Brush Smoothing," later in this chapter).

✔ Tip

■ You can change the size of your brush-stroke by changing the magnification at which you view the Stage. To create a fat stroke without changing your brush-tip settings, set the Stage view to a small percentage. To switch to a thin stroke, zoom out to a higher percentage (**Figure 2.53**). Be sure to check your work in 100% view.

To paint with gradients:

1. Follow steps 1 and 2 in the preceding task.

2. Using one of the methods described earlier in this chapter, select (or define) a linear or radial gradient fill.

Figure 2.52 Drawing with the brush creates a preview of your shape (left); Flash recasts the shape as a vector graphic with the currently selected fill color and smoothing settings (right).

Created with 200% magnification

Created with 100% magnification

Created with 50% magnification

Figure 2.53 Flash created these three brushstrokes with exactly the same brush size—only the magnification level of the Stage was changed for each stroke.

The Mystery of Brush Smoothing

Flash's Smoothing setting controls how brushstrokes translate into vector shapes. When the brush tool is active, the Property inspector contains a Smoothing section, with hot text for Smoothing. This control sets the brush tool's stroke-smoothness value (from 0 to 100, with a default of 50). Stroke smoothness determines how closely Flash re-creates each movement of the brush as a separate vector segment. The lower the setting, the more faithfully Flash reproduces the shapes you draw (by using more vectors, which has an impact on the size and animation performance of your final file). A higher setting re-creates your flourishes more roughly, using fewer vectors.

To see the difference clearly, select the brush tool, assign a Smoothing value of 1, and draw a curved line on the Stage. Change the Smoothing setting to 30 and draw a second curved line. Using the subselection tool (you'll learn about using this tool in Chapter 4), select each shape. The line drawn with Smoothing set to 1 displays many more points—that is, it contains many more vector segments.

Figure 2.54 Deselect the Lock Fill modifier to paint with an unlocked gradient.

Unlocked

Unlocked

Figure 2.55 A brushstroke shape painted with an unlocked linear-gradient fill (top) and one painted with an unlocked radial-gradient fill (bottom).

3. To lock or unlock the gradient, in the Tools panel, do either of the following:

▲ To paint shapes that contain the full gradient-spectrum, deselect Lock Fill (**Figure 2.54**).

▲ To paint shapes that reveal just a portion of the gradient (as if the shape were a window onto a gradient that filled the whole Stage area), select Lock Fill.

4. Paint with the brush as described in steps 4 through 6 in the preceding task.

Flash can't preview the shape you paint with a gradient fill. The preview shape has a black-and-white pattern.

Flash redraws the painted shape, using the current lock-fill and fill-color settings (see the sidebar "The Mystery of Gradients and Flash's Drawing Models," later in this chapter).

For unlocked fills, the full gradient is visible in the shape (**Figure 2.55**).

For locked fills, just a portion of the gradient is visible in the shape (**Figure 2.56**).

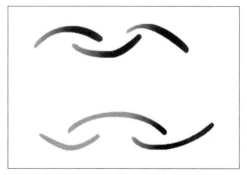

Figure 2.56 With the brush tool's Lock Fill modifier deselected, each brushstroke fill you paint contains the full range of the current gradient (top). With Lock Fill selected, each brushstroke fill appears to reveal a section of a gradient that runs the width of the Stage and the Pasteboard (bottom).

✔ Tips

■ Try painting a variety of brushstrokes in both drawing modes; use locked and unlocked gradients; use different areas of the Stage; and make the shapes different lengths. Notice the way each shape displays the gradient.

■ If the first gradient you paint in a work session has a locked fill, Flash puts the center of the underlying locked gradient along the left edge of the Stage. That means half the gradient lies on the Pasteboard, not on the Stage. To choose a different location for the center of a locked gradient, first use the brush tool to paint an unlocked gradient that's centered the way you want. When you switch to painting with Lock Fill active, the underlying locked gradient aligns with the last unlocked gradient you painted. You can then delete the unneeded unlocked gradient.

■ After you've created a shape with a gradient fill, you can adjust the location of the center of the gradient by using the gradient-transform tool (see Chapter 4).

The Mystery of Gradients and Flash's Drawing Models

When you use the brush tool to paint a shape with a gradient fill and the Lock Fill modifier is deselected, it makes no difference if you're painting in Merge Drawing mode or Object Drawing mode. Flash centers the gradient in the shape's bounding box (an invisible rectangle that's just the right size to enclose the shape); the full gradient is visible in the shape.

When you paint the same kind of shape and Lock Fill is selected, however, shapes created in the two drawing modes behave differently.

For locked fills, Flash creates a virtual gradient that underlies the Stage and Pasteboard. (By default, Flash aligns the center of the locked gradient with the left edge of the Stage.) Each shape you create with a locked fill reveals just the portion of the gradient that corresponds to that area of the Stage. If you paint multiple merge-shapes with a locked gradient, the same virtual gradient underlies each shape; you can use the gradient-transform tool to shift the gradient within all the shapes. Multiple drawing-objects each have their own personal virtual gradient. These virtual gradients are all centered in the same way, so initially it looks as though there's one underlying gradient, as with merge-shapes. But the gradient-transform tool shifts the gradient in each drawing-object separately.

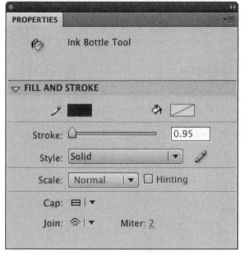

Figure 2.57 The ink-bottle tool applies all the stroke attributes currently set in the Fill and Stroke section of the Ink Bottle Tool Property inspector.

Adding Strokes and Fills

As you've learned earlier in this chapter, you can use the line, pencil, pen, and geometric-shape tools to create outline shapes—strokes without fills. To create fill shapes that have no stroke outline, you use the brush, pen, and geometric-shape tools. At any point you can add the missing element to such shapes. The ink-bottle tool adds strokes that outline plain fill shapes; the paint-bucket tool adds fills inside plain outline shapes. (You can also use these tools to modify existing strokes and fills; see Chapter 4.)

To add strokes to fills:

1. On the Stage, draw a fill that has no stroke, or work with an existing unstroked shape.

   For a merge-shape, make sure the fill is deselected; for a drawing-object, the fill can be selected or deselected.

2. In the Tools panel, click the current fill/stroke tool; and from the submenu that opens, select the ink-bottle tool, or press S (**Figure 2.57**).

3. In the Fill and Stroke section of the Ink Bottle Tool Property inspector, set the desired stroke attributes (see "Setting Stroke Attributes," earlier in this chapter).

4. Position the pointer over a fill shape that has no stroke.

   The pointer appears as a little ink bottle spilling ink.

   continues on next page

5. With the ink bottle's hot spot, click a fill shape in one of the following ways:

▲ To add a stroke around the outside of the shape, click near the outside edge of the shape (**Figure 2.58**).

▲ To add a stroke around the inside of a shape that has a hole cut out of it, click near the inside edge of the shape.

▲ To outline both the outside of a shape and the hole inside the shape, click in the middle of the shape (**Figure 2.59**).

Flash adds strokes to the outside edge, inside edge, or both, using the color, thickness, and style currently specified in the Fill and Stroke section of the Property inspector.

✔ Tips

■ Flash lets you use gradients for strokes. In step 3 of the preceding task, in the Fill and Stroke section of the Property inspector, choose a linear or radial gradient from the Stroke Color control's pop-up swatch set. Why might you want a gradient stroke? For an oval shape, adding a thick stroke with a radial gradient can help create the illusion of 3D depth or make the shape appear to glow.

■ Another way to "add" missing strokes to drawing-objects and primitive-shapes is to modify them using the Property inspector. First select the drawing-object or primitive on the Stage. Then change the stroke properties, including color, in the Property inspector. You can use this technique to add strokes to multiple drawing-objects and/or primitives (the technique doesn't work for merge-shapes, however). You'll learn more about modifying graphic objects in Chapter 4.

ADDING STROKES AND FILLS

Before

After

Figure 2.58 As you move the ink bottle over a filled shape, the hot spot appears as a white dot at the end of the ink drip that's spilling out of the bottle. To add a stroke around the outside edge of your fill shape, position the hot spot along that edge (top) and then click. Flash adds a stroke with the current attributes set in the Fill and Stroke section of the Ink Bottle Tool Property inspector (bottom).

Hot spot

Outside edge of fill shape

Stroke

Before

After

Inside stroke

Outside stroke

Figure 2.59 Position the ink bottle's hot spot in the middle of your fill shape (top), then click. Flash uses the current stroke attributes to add a stroke around the outside and inside of your shape (bottom).

Paint-bucket tool

Fill color

Lock fill

Gap size

Figure 2.60 The paint-bucket tool and its modifiers.

○ Don't Close Gaps
■ ○ Close Small Gaps
○ Close Medium Gaps
○ Close Large Gaps

Figure 2.61 The Gap Size menu controls Flash's capability to fill shapes that aren't fully closed.

Figure 2.62 Clicking inside an outline shape with the paint bucket (left) fills the shape with the currently selected fill color (right).

Figure 2.63 The paint bucket can't fill this apple shape with the setting of Close Large Gaps and a magnification of 100 percent (left). But in a 50 percent view, the paint bucket with the same large-gap closure setting recognizes this shape as complete and fills it.

To fill an outline shape with solid color:

1. On the Stage, draw an outline stroke that has no fill, or work with an existing outline shape.

   The outline can be selected or deselected.

2. In the Tools panel, click the current fill/stroke tool; and from the submenu that opens, select the paint-bucket tool, or press K (**Figure 2.60**).

3. From the Gap Size menu in the Tools panel, choose the amount of assistance you want (**Figure 2.61**).

   If you draw your shapes precisely, a medium or small gap closure serves you best; you don't want Flash to fill areas that aren't meant to be shapes. If your drawings are rougher, choose Close Large Gaps. This setting enables Flash to recognize less-complete shapes.

4. From any Fill Color control, select a solid fill color.

5. Place the paint bucket's hot spot (the tip of the drip of paint) inside the outline shape, and click.

   The shape fills with the currently selected fill color (**Figure 2.62**).

✔ Tips

- You may be unaware that your shape has any gaps. If nothing happens when you click inside a shape with the paint bucket, try changing the Gap Size setting in step 3.

- Gap-closure settings are relative to the amount of magnification you're using to view the Stage. If the paint bucket's largest gap-closure setting fails at your current magnification, try again after reducing magnification (**Figure 2.63**).

ADDING STROKES AND FILLS

73

To fill outline shapes with unlocked gradients:

1. In the Tools panel, click the current fill/ stroke tool, and from the submenu that opens, select the paint-bucket tool, or press K.

2. In the Color panel, define a new gradient (see "Creating Solid Colors and Gradients," earlier in this chapter).

   or

   From any Fill Color control, select an existing linear or radial gradient (see "Setting Fill Attributes," earlier in this chapter).

3. In the Tools panel, make sure that Lock Fill is deselected (**Figure 2.64**).

4. Follow steps 5 and 6 in the preceding task.

   Each outline shape you click fills with the gradient currently displayed in the Fill Color control. If you chose a linear gradient in step 2, Flash centers the unlocked gradient within the outline shape (**Figure 2.65**). If you chose a radial gradient, the location you click with the paint bucket's hot spot determines where the center of the unlocked gradient appears (**Figure 2.66**).

Deselect Lock Fill

Figure 2.64 Deselect the Lock Fill button to fill a shape with an unlocked gradient.

Figure 2.65 You can use the paint-bucket tool to apply a linear-gradient fill. An unlocked gradient is centered within the outline shape's bounding box.

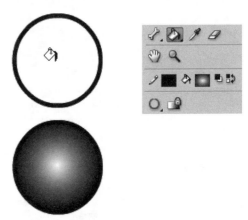

Figure 2.66 The paint-bucket tool can also apply a radial-gradient fill. Click where you want to locate the center of the gradient.

To fill outline shapes with locked gradients:

1. Follow steps 1 and 2 in the preceding task.

2. In the Tools panel, select the Lock Fill button.

3. Follow steps 5 and 6 in "To fill an outline shape with solid color," earlier in this section.

   Each outline shape you click fills with a portion of the gradient currently set in the Fill Color control (see the sidebar "The Mystery of Gradients and Flash's Drawing Models," earlier in this chapter).

✔ Tip

■ Gradients increase file sizes and thereby slow the loading of published movies. Each area of gradient fill requires an extra 50 bytes of data that a solid fill doesn't need. In addition, gradients take processor power. If you use too many, you may see slower frame rates, which translate to slower animations in your finished movie.

ADDING STROKES AND FILLS

Creating Simple Patterns

Flash CS4 introduces two tools that create patterns: the spray-brush tool and the deco tool (**Figure 2.67**). By default, the spray-brush tool creates a random dot pattern. You determine where the pattern goes by painting with the tool on the Stage. The deco tool uses predefined patterns that fill space automatically. To make the finished spray-brush and deco patterns easier to work with, Flash unites all the elements of the pattern in a special object called a *group*. You'll learn about groups and about using the pattern tools in Chapter 5.

Dots from one "brushstroke"

Vine pattern fills a shape

Deco tool   *Spray-brush tool*

Figure 2.67 Flash CS4 offers two tools for creating patterns: the spray-brush tool and the deco tool. The spray brush works something like a real-world airbrush to create a pattern of dots or symbols as you move the mouse. The deco tool fills a shape (or the Stage) with a predefined pattern.

Working with Text

Adobe Flash CS4 Professional's text tool doesn't just create graphic-objects in the shape of letters, it also creates text fields filled with live text; in the authoring environment, the contents of a text field are fully editable. As you create text elements, you must decide how they will be used in the published movie and assign them a type property. If you want the end user to interact with a text field (for example, to enter personal information), set the text field's type property to *input*. If you want to update the text at runtime (for example, using ActionScript to download and display new basketball scores to a sports site), set the type property to *dynamic*. If the text will just sit there looking pretty, set the type property to *static*.

Flash Type, Flash's text-rendering engine, makes fonts more legible, especially at small sizes. This legibility shows up in the authoring environment, as you create your movies, but it also comes into play for your end users if you publish your files for Adobe Flash Player 8 or later (see Chapter 18).

In this chapter you'll learn about using static text. The manipulation of input and dynamic text fields requires a more advanced level of ActionScripting than this book can cover; if you need to know more, check out Adobe Flash CS4 Professional; Visual QuickPro Guide (Peachpit Press).

Using the Text Tool

The text tool creates blocks of editable text. You can set the text to read horizontally or vertically. You can also apply a variety of text attributes to text—including text and paragraph styles.

To create a single line of text for use as a graphic element:

1. In the Tools panel select the text tool (**Figure 3.1**), or press T.

   The Text Tool Property inspector appears with options for setting text attributes.

2. To set the attributes for text you are about to create, do the following,

   ▲ From the Text Type menu at the top of the Property inspector, choose Static Text. Static text acts as a purely graphic element in Flash. Unless otherwise instructed, use static text for all the tasks in this book.

   ▲ In the Character and Paragraph sections of the Property inspector, use the current settings. You learn to change these settings in upcoming tasks.

3. Move the pointer over the Stage.

   The pointer turns into a crosshair with a letter *T* in the bottom-right corner (**Figure 3.2**).

4. Click the Stage at the spot where you want your text to start.

   Flash creates a resizable bounding box with a blinking insertion point, ready for you to enter text (**Figure 3.3**).

   Each corner of the box has a draggable resize handle; the round handle in the upper-right corner indicates that word wrap hasn't been set on this text field.

5. Start typing your text.

   The bounding box grows to accommodate whatever you type (**Figure 3.4**).

Text tool

Figure 3.1 Select the text tool in the Tools panel to start creating text fields on the Stage.

Figure 3.2 The text-tool pointer.

Figure 3.3 Click the Stage with the text tool to create a text field. The round resize handle indicates that the text field does not have word wrap turned on.

Squares|

Squares at a square|

Squares at a square dance generally|

Figure 3.4 As you type, the text field grows horizontally to accommodate your text. The text doesn't wrap.

Resize pointer

Resize pointer

Resize handle for text
field with word wrap

Squares at a square

Squares at a square
dance

Squares at a square
dance generally dance
with squares|

Figure 3.5 Click and drag any resize handle of a text field's bounding box to create a text field with a specific width. The top-right handle changes to a square, indicating that the text you enter will wrap to fit the column width of the text field. The text field continues to grow in length—but not width—as you enter more text.

■ To restore a text field to its original state (in which text doesn't wrap), double-click the square handle in the upper-right corner of the field's bounding box. It changes back to a circle, which indicates the text field will grow horizontally.

6. When you finish typing, click elsewhere on the Stage (or change tools) to deselect the text.

Flash hides the bounding box, leaving just the text visible. When you click this text with the selection tool, Flash selects the text field so that you can reposition it, resize it, or change the text's attributes directly.

To create a text field with set width and word wrap:

1. With the text tool selected in the Tools panel, click the Stage to place the text field.

2. Move the pointer over any of the resize handles at the corners of the field's bounding box.

The pointer changes to a double-headed arrow.

3. Click and drag one of the handles until the text field's bounding box is as wide as you want it (**Figure 3.5**).

The resize handle in the upper-right corner changes to a square, indicating that word wrap is set for this text field.

4. Release the mouse button.

The blinking insertion point appears in the text field.

5. Enter your text.

Flash wraps the text horizontally to fit inside the column that the text field's bounding box defines. The box automatically grows longer (not wider) to accommodate your text.

✔ Tips

■ To reposition a text field with the text tool active, position the pointer along the edge of the bounding box. The pointer changes to the selection arrow. Now you can drag the text field to a new location.

USING THE TEXT TOOL

Setting Text Attributes

You can set the attributes of your text in the context-sensitive Property inspector. When you choose the text tool in the Tools panel, a large T (for text) and the name Text Tool appear at the top of the Property inspector; sections named Character and Paragraph appear in the body of the inspector. Character governs text attributes, such as font, style, size, and color. Paragraph governs attributes, such as paragraph alignment and line spacing. When you select a chunk of text (or a text field) on the Stage, the name Text Tool disappears from the inspector, but the T icon and the Character and Paragraph sections remain. Three new sections—Position and Size, Options, and Filters—appear. Position and Size deals with the attributes of the text field itself: its width, height, and location on the Stage. The Options section lets you turn text into a live link to a URL. The Filters section lets you apply special effects to text.

When you need to distinguish one Property inspector from the other, this book will refer to them as the Text Tool Property inspector and the Text Property inspector; when referring to either or both, this book will use the name Text (Tool) Property inspector.

You can set attributes in advance so that as you type, the text tool applies them automatically, or you can apply attributes to existing text. The text tool always uses whatever settings currently appear in the Text (Tool) Property inspector (**Figure 3.6**).

For the following tasks, keep the Property inspector open (choose Window > Properties if it's not already open) and expand the Character section (click the triangle to the left of the section name to toggle between the expanded and collapsed views).

✔ Tip

■ In addition to setting text attributes in the Text (Tool) Property inspector, you can set the font, size, style, paragraph alignment, and letterspacing from the Text menu. You can use the Text menu to change the properties of selected text or to load text properties into the text tool.

Figure 3.6 When you have selected the text tool in the Tools panel (or you have selected a text block on the Stage), the Text (Tool) Property inspector displays the type attributes to be created by the text tool (or applied to the current text selection).

To select text to apply character attributes:

◆ Do either of the following:

▲ With the text tool active, drag over existing text to highlight just a portion of text.

▲ With the selection tool active, click a text field to select all the text within it.

✔ Tips

■ You can select multiple text fields with the selection tool and modify them at the same time. (You'll learn more about selections in Chapter 4.)

■ The contact-sensitivity settings in the General category of the Preferences dialog also apply to selecting text fields with a selection outline. (You'll learn more about making such selections in Chapter 4.)

To choose a font family:

1. On the Stage, select the text you want to modify and access the Property inspector.

2. In the Character section, from the Family pop-up menu, choose a font name.

   The menu opens as a scrolling list displaying the font families installed on your system. A font sample (showing the word *Sample*, set in that font) appears to the right of the font name in the list (**Figure 3.7**).

3. Scroll to view the available font families.

4. Move the pointer over a font-family name. Flash highlights the name.

5. Click to select the currently highlighted font family and close the scrolling list.

   The selected font name appears in the Family field. Flash changes the selected text to the new font.

Figure 3.7 Use the Family pop-up menu in the Character section of the Text (Tool) Property inspector to choose a font family. The scrolling list contains all the installed font families. The word Sample shows what text looks like in that font.

✔ Tips

■ Another way to select a font family is to choose it from the Text > Font menu.

■ You can allow end users to copy text from static text fields. During authoring, select the text that you want users to be able to copy. In the Character section of the Text (Tool) Property inspector, click the Selectable Text button (the button labeled with the letters *Ab*, just below the Anti-Alias menu).

■ You can also enter a font-family name by typing it in the Family field in the Character section of the Text (Tool) Property inspector. As you type, Flash autocompletes the name from the list of installed fonts. In earlier versions of Flash you had to be careful about making typos. No longer. Flash CS4 goes for the closest match from the installed list; if Flash can't find something similar, it leaves the current font in place.

Figure 3.8 The Style menu in the Character section of the Text (Tool) Property inspector lists the bold and italic variants of the font currently active in the Family field. If that font has no bold or italic variants, the Style menu is disabled.

The Mystery of Anti-aliasing

Anti-aliasing is a method of *rendering*—drawing lines and curves—that softens edges. For text, this means making the letterforms appear slightly blurry. Anti-aliasing text at large point sizes makes it easier to read, but at smaller sizes, text may appear fuzzy and indistinct. In early versions of Flash, applying anti-aliasing to text in small sizes made that text difficult to read. Flash Type (the font-rendering engine found in Flash versions 8 and later) lets you apply anti-aliasing to small font sizes and still have readable text, provided the text isn't animated.

To choose a style:

1. Select the text you want to modify and access the Text Property inspector.

2. In the Character section, from the Style pop-up menu, choose one of the available font styles (**Figure 3.8**).

   The Style menu displays the available variants of the font selected in the Family field. If the current font has no variants, the Style menu is disabled.

✔ Tip

■ If selected text is currently set in a font that has a boldface variant, you can toggle between the regular and bold variant by pressing Shift-⌘-B (Mac) or Ctrl-Shift-B (Windows). (Take note of that Shift key if you're accustomed to using another application for creating text: it's not part of the usual command.) To toggle an italic variant, press Shift-⌘-I (Mac) or Ctrl-Shift-I (Windows). If the font of the selected text lacks bold or italic variants, these commands won't change the selected text. You can apply faux bold or faux italic by using the commands in the Text menu (see the sidebar "The Mystery of Faux Styles").

To set the font size:

1. Select the text you want to modify and access the Text Property inspector.

2. To enter a new size, in the Character Section, use the Size hot text to enter a value between 0 and 2500 points.

   To use a precise value, click the hot text, enter a number in the field that activates, then press Enter. To choose a value interactively, position the pointer over the hot text; when the pointing finger with a double arrow appears, drag left (or down) to lower the value, or drag right (or up) to increase the value (**Figure 3.9**). Flash previews the changes on the Stage as you drag the hot text's invisible slider.

Figure 3.9 Drag the Size hot text to change the point size of selected text interactively on the Stage.

✔ Tip

■ You can also choose Text > Size to select from 13 common sizes ranging from 8 points to 120 points.

The Mystery of Faux Styles

There are two ways to achieve bold and italic font styles. To get the best looking text, use a font family that includes variants designed from the ground up as bold or italic versions of the font. The Arial family, for example, includes Arial Bold, Arial Italic, and Arial Bold Italic. A less sophisticated way to create styles is to tweak the letterforms graphically, making them thicker to imitate bold or slanting them to imitate italic.

Flash CS4 makes it easy to get the best-looking font styles from the font families you use. When the currently selected font family has variants (say a bold or italic version), the styles for those variants appear in the Text > Style menu and in the Style menu in the Character section of the Text (Tool) Property inspector. When the currently selected font family lacks style variants, Flash disables the Style menu in the Character section of the Property inspector. When you create text using a font that lacks variants, you can have Flash tweak it to approximate bold and italic styles. Select your text (or select the text tool and set its Family to the font without variants), then choose Text > Style; the submenu offers Faux Bold and Faux Italic options (**Figure 3.10**).

Figure 3.10 For text set in a font whose family contains no italic, bold, or bold italic variants, you can approximate bold and italic with faux styles. Select the text, choose Text > Style, and from the submenu choose Faux Bold or Faux Italic.

The Mystery of Device Fonts

When you assign an installed font to a static text field, usually you want the text to look exactly the same during playback as it does during authoring. Yet you have no way of knowing if the font that you assigned is installed on the end user's system. In order to re-create your static text field font accurately during playback, Flash saves information about the outlines of the letterforms with the published (SWF) file (you'll learn more about publishing files in Chapter 18). During playback, Flash Player uses those outlines to draw the letters correctly. Saving outline information increases the size of your SWF file. Device fonts allow you to eliminate that information. You can apply device fonts two ways: Select one from a font-family menu, or choose Use Device Fonts from the Anti-Aliasing menu in the Character section of the Text (Tool) Property inspector.

By choosing a device font from one of the menus, you retain some control over the look of the text the end user sees, but you give up the use of a specific font. Three device fonts appear in the Family menu in the Text (Tool) Properties tab and the Text > Font menu: _sans, _serif, and _typewriter. During movie playback of static text for which you chose a specific device font, the end user's system supplies a font that has the same type style. For static text set as _serif, the end user's system supplies a font with *serifs*, those little hooks and tails you see at the ends of some letters' strokes in fonts such as Times Roman. For _sans (short for *sans serif*, or "without serifs"), the end user's system supplies a plainer font, one without hooks and tails; Helvetica and Arial are good examples. For _typewriter, the end user's system supplies a *monospaced* font (one in which each letterform takes up the same amount of space, like the letters on a typewriter); Courier is one example.

Choosing a specific font for your static text and then choosing Use Device Fonts from the Anti-Alias menu in the Character section of the Text (Tool) Property inspector gives the end user's system the greatest liberty in choosing a substitute font. The system looks for the closest match from its installed fonts, but there's no guarantee that it will substitute a font with the same style as the font you originally specified.

Although the use of Device Fonts helps keep your SWF files slim, the results are often unattractive. If you want to try this option, be sure to test your published movie on a variety of systems to get an idea of what your users might actually wind up seeing. The savings in file size may not be worth the loss of quality.

To adjust space between letters and/or words:

1. Within a text field in a Flash document, select the text whose spacing you want to change, and access the Text Property inspector.

   To adjust only the space between letters, select the letters or select a single word. To adjust the space between letters and words, select a larger chunk of text: an entire line, paragraph, or text field.

2. In the Character section, use the Letter Spacing hot text to enter a value between –60 and 60 points.

   Click the hot text to enter a precise value; drag the hot text to choose a value interactively. A negative value reduces the space between letters in the selection; a positive value increases it (**Figure 3.11**). If the selection contains multiple words, the setting also adjusts the space between words.

✔ Tips

■ Another way to increase spacing for selected text is to choose Text > Letter Spacing > Increase or press Option-⌘–right arrow (Mac) or Ctrl-Alt–right arrow (Windows). To decrease spacing, choose Text > Letter Spacing > Decrease, or use the keyboard commands with the left arrow. Adding the Shift key to the keyboard shortcuts doubles the amount of increase or decrease.

■ You can also adjust letterspacing interactively by using the keyboard shortcuts. The space between letters continues to expand or contract as long as you hold down the key combination.

■ To reset the font's original letterspacing, choose Text > Letter Spacing > Reset or press Option-⌘–up arrow (Mac) or Ctrl-Alt–up arrow (Windows).

Letter spacing: 0.0

Spaced Out

Letter spacing: –1.0

Spaced Out

Letter spacing: 2.0

Spaced Out

Figure 3.11 Enter a negative value for Letter Spacing to bring characters (or words) closer together. Enter a positive value to space them out. Enter 0 to use a font's built-in letterspacing value.

SETTING TEXT ATTRIBUTES

Figure 3.12 You can choose a color for text created with the text tool from the Color control in the Text (Tool) Properties tab of the Property inspector.

To choose a text color:

1. Select the text you want to modify and access the Text Property inspector.

2. In the Character section, click the Color control.

   The standard color-control swatch set appears (**Figure 3.12**).

3. Select a color.

   Flash applies the color to the selected text.

✔ Tips

■ Flash changes all the settings in the Text (Tool) Property inspector to match the attributes of selected text, which means that by selecting text, you load the text tool with that text's attributes. Keep blocks of text with formatting you use often on the Pasteboard, and click one to re-create its settings for the text tool quickly.

■ Flash considers text to be a fill. When the text tool is active, or text is selected on the Stage, you can change the text color by using any of the methods described for setting fill attributes in Chapter 2.

What Is Kerning?

Whereas letterspacing affects the space between characters and words in an entire chunk of selected text, *kerning* affects the space between a pair of letters. Because of the way fonts are constructed, with each letter being a separate element, some pairs of letters look oddly spaced when you type them. The space between a capital *T* and a lowercase *o*, for example, may seem too large because of the white space below the crossbar of the *T*. To make the characters look better, you can reduce the space between them, or *kern in* the pair. Some letters may seem to be too close together—say, a *t* and an *i*. You can *kern out* the pair so that it looks better.

Font designers often build into their fonts special information about how to space troublesome pairs of letters. Flash takes advantage of that embedded kerning information when you select the Auto Kern check box in the Character section of the Text (Tool) Property inspector. It's a good idea to turn on kerning to make your type look its best.

You can kern manually in Flash instead of or in addition to using the embedded kerning. Select the character pair that you want to kern, then use Flash's Letter Spacing feature to bring the letters closer together or move them farther apart.

To set the font-rendering method:

1. Select the text field you want to modify and access the Text Property inspector.

    Font rendering applies to the whole text field. You can't apply different methods to individual words or selections within one field.

2. In the Character section, from the Anti-Alias menu (**Figure 3.13**), choose one of the following:

    Use device fonts. Choose this setting when smaller file sizes are more important than re-creating the precise font outlines on the end user's system (see the sidebar "The Mystery of Device Fonts").

    Bitmap text (no anti-alias). Choose this setting when you want your text to have hard edges instead of softened (anti-aliased) edges. Fonts are embedded in your published movie, without anti-aliasing. (Bitmap text can greatly increase your SWF file size.)

    Anti-alias for animation. Choose this setting for animated text fields or when you plan to publish your movie to Flash Player 7 or earlier. Flash embeds font outlines for these text fields but ignores some information about aligning and kerning to help speed playback. Flash Type doesn't do the rendering.

    Anti-alias for readability. (This is the default setting for publishing to Flash Player 8 and later; see Chapter 18.) Choose this setting for text fields that you don't plan to animate. The Flash Type font-rendering engine draws text with this setting on the Stage as you create your FLA file. When you publish, Flash embeds the fonts in the SWF file. The Flash Type engine renders this text for playback.

Figure 3.13 To control the degree of anti-aliasing, in the Character section of the Text (Tool) Property inspector, choose an option from the Anti-Alias menu (top). The Custom Anti-Aliasing option gives you access to a dialog for setting more precise anti-aliasing controls (bottom).

Custom anti-alias. Choosing this setting gives you access to the Custom Anti-Aliasing dialog, where you can determine how soft and blurry the anti-aliased letterforms are. The dialog's Thickness and Sharpness settings control the transitional blurred area between each letter and the background against which it appears. Flash Type renders the text with custom settings.

✔ Tip

- Even when you choose an option that evokes Flash Type anti-aliasing, certain situations cause Flash to turn off anti-aliasing. When you skew, flip, or distort a text field, Flash Type doesn't anti-alias that text. Flash Type doesn't work on fonts larger than 255 points.

Vertical Text

Using Flash's static text fields, you can create a single vertical text column, or create a paragraph containing text that flows vertically in columns; columns can read left to right (as in English text) or vice versa (as in Japanese text). To set the text-flow direction, access the Paragraph section of the Text (Tool) Property inspector and choose one of the vertical modes from the Orientation menu (**Figure 3.14**). Vertical text fields work similarly to horizontal ones: resizing sets the word wrap. In vertical text, the wrap forces words to the next column, not the next line. As you enter text, Flash places one character below another until the text reaches the bottom edge of the text field's bounding box, then text jumps to the next column. To force text to flow to the next column, add a paragraph return.

Figure 3.14 The Paragraph section of the Text (Tool) Property inspector contains an Orientation menu, which lets you set the direction of your text flow.

Setting Paragraph Attributes

Flash allows you to work with paragraph formatting much as you would in a word processor. For static text, the Paragraph section of the Text (Tool) Property inspector contains settings for paragraph alignment (flush left, flush right, centered, or justified), a first-line indent, line spacing, left and right margins, and text orientation (**Figure 3.15**). You can set paragraph attributes in advance so that as you type, the text tool applies them automatically. And you can apply paragraph attributes to existing text. The text tool uses whatever settings currently appear in the Property inspector.

The following tasks show you how to modify existing text. Keep the Property inspector open (choose Window > Properties if it's not already open) and expand the Paragraph section (click the triangle to the left of the section name to toggle between the expanded and collapsed views).

Figure 3.15 The Paragraph section of the Text (Tool) Property inspector contains settings for text attributes that apply to paragraphs, such as alignment, indents, space between lines of text, and margins.

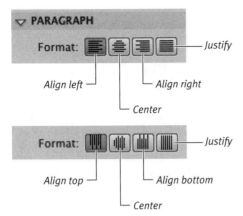

Figure 3.16 Flash's paragraph-format buttons let you align the text of a paragraph in four ways. Each Format button depicts its paragraph-alignment style graphically. The images on the buttons reflect whether the text field is set for horizontal (left) or vertical (right) text flow.

To select paragraphs to modify:

◆ Do one of the following:

▲ With the text tool, click within the paragraph you want to modify.

▲ With the text tool, click and drag to select multiple paragraphs within one text field.

▲ With the selection tool, click a text field to select all the paragraphs within the field.

To set paragraph alignment:

1. Select the paragraphs you want to modify and access the Text Property inspector.

2. In the Format area of the Paragraph section, do one of the following (**Figure 3.16**).

▲ To align horizontal text on the left (vertical text on the top), click the first (far left) alignment button.

▲ To center horizontal or vertical text, click the second alignment button.

▲ To align horizontal text on the right (vertical text on the bottom), click the third alignment button.

▲ To justify text (force all lines except the last line of a paragraph to fill the full column width), click the fourth alignment button.

✔ Tip

■ To select all the paragraphs within a text field, click with the text tool anywhere inside the text field, then choose Edit > Select All. Flash highlights the entire text field.

SETTING PARAGRAPH ATTRIBUTES

To set a first-line indent:

1. In the Text (Tool) Property inspector, access the Paragraph section.

2. In the Spacing area use the Indentation hot text (on the left) to enter an amount between –720 and 720 pixels (**Figure 3.17**). Click the hot text to enter a precise value; drag the hot text to choose a value interactively. Flash calculates the indent from the left margin; when the left margin is set to 0, Flash measures the indent from the left edge of the text field's bounding box.

✔ Tip

■ You can use Flash's Indentation hot text to create paragraphs with hanging indents (ones where the first line starts farther to the left than the other lines), but there's a bit of a trick to it. You can't simply enter a negative Indentation value; the left margin must be wide enough to hold that "negative" first-line text. To create a paragraph where the first line starts 5 pixels to the left of the other lines, for example, set Indentation to –5 and set Left Margin to 5 or greater.

Figure 3.17 The first hot text in the Spacing area lets you set an indent for the first line of a paragraph of text.

Spacing: 11.0 pt   0.0 px

Squares at a square dance generally dance with squares.

Squares at a square dance gꞮenerally dance with squares.

Figure 3.18 The line spacing for the text block on the left is set to 0 points. The space you see between lines is specified as part of the font. Because the text is all one size, the spacing above and below the middle line of text is the same. In the text block on the right—with the same o-point line spacing—one letter is a larger point size. Flash increases the space between lines to make room for the larger text.

Measuring Indents and Margins

By default, Flash uses pixels as the unit of measure for indentation and margins; that's because pixels are the default ruler units for a document. If you choose different units in the Document Properties dialog (see Chapter 1), Flash uses those units in the Indentation and Margins settings, and the range of available values adjusts to match the current units of measure. The unit abbreviations next to the hot text in the Paragraph section of the Text (Tool) Property inspector also change to reflect the units in use by the document.

To set line spacing:

1. In the Text (Tool) Property inspector, access the Paragraph section.

2. In the Spacing area use the Line Spacing hot text (on the right) to enter a value between –360 and 720 points.

   Line spacing governs the amount of space between lines of text. Negative values place lines closer together; positive values place lines farther apart. If your text contains various point sizes, Flash bases the spacing between two lines on the larger font (**Figure 3.18**).

✔ Tips

■ *Points* are the most common units of measure for working with text. Regardless of the units you've set in the Document Properties dialog, Flash always enters the line-spacing value with the abbreviation *pt* (for *points).

■ If you set different values for different paragraphs within a single text field— different line spacing, for example—you need to be a little careful whenever the entire field is selected. Let's say you move a field by dragging it with the selection tool. Then, while the field is still selected, you accidentally click the Line Spacing hot text. Even if you enter no value, Flash applies the spacing of the last paragraph in the text field to all the selected paragraphs.

To set margins:

1. In the Text (Tool) Property inspector, access the Paragraph section.

2. In the Margins area, use the Left Margin and/or Right Margin hot text to enter a value between 0 and 720 pixels (**Figure 3.19.**).

   Click the hot text to enter a precise value; drag the hot text to choose a value interactively.

✔ Tip

- Flash incorporates the current margin settings into text fields as you create them. With margins set to the default (0 pixels), clicking the text tool on the Stage creates a small bounding box, just large enough for the blinking insertion point. If you get a longer box than you expect when you click the Stage with the text tool, check Margins settings in the Paragraph section of the Text (Tool) Property inspector and adjust them as needed.

Figure 3.19 The Margins hot text in the Paragraph section of the Text (Tool) Property inspector lets you enter values for left and right margins (horizontal text) or top and bottom margins (vertical text). Flash uses the values that you enter to create margins from the left and right sides of the text field's bounding box. Your audience won't see the margins unless you're creating text that they can edit, in which case you can make the border of the text field visible.

MODIFYING SIMPLE GRAPHICS

One way to modify graphics in Adobe Flash CS4 Professional is to select one or more shapes and edit them by changing their attributes (such as color, size, and location) in the Property inspector or in other appropriate panels.

You can also modify the path that creates the shape of an element. Some operations—such as straightening lines, adjusting Bézier curves, and assigning new attributes—require that the element be selected. Others, such as reshaping a line segment or curve with the selection tool, require the element to be deselected. A few operations let you edit the element whether it's selected or not—using the paint-bucket tool to change a fill color, for example.

This chapter covers using the selection, lasso, and subselection tools to select and modify the elements you learned to make in Chapter 2. You also learn about using the Property inspector and other panels to modify elements' attributes.

Setting Selection Preferences

There are two basic ways to make a selection in Flash: one is to click an element directly, and the other is to enclose all or part of an element with a selection outline. You can set preferences to gain more control over these two methods. For the click method, you choose whether you must Shift-click to select multiple items or whether you can merely click additional items to add to a selection. For the selection-outline method, you decide if the outline must fully enclose a graphic-object to select it or if enclosing any part of a graphic-object selects the whole thing.

To set selection methods for the selection tools:

1. From the Flash menu (Mac) or the Edit menu (Windows), choose Preferences.

   The Preferences dialog appears.

2. From the Category list, choose General (**Figure 4.1**).

3. In the Selection section, choose either of the following check boxes:

   Shift Select. In Shift Select mode (Flash's default setting), you must Shift-click to add items to the current selection. With Shift Select turned off, each new item you click with the selection tool is added to the current selection.

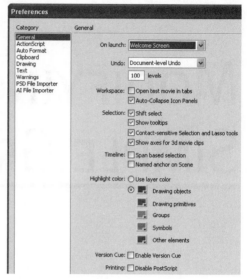

Figure 4.1 Choose General in the Category list of the Preferences dialog to choose a selection method.

Contact-Sensitive Selection and Lasso Tools. With Contact-Sensitive Selection on (the default), when a selection outline touches a graphic-object or text field (see Chapter 3), a grouped shape (see Chapter 5), or a symbol instance (see Chapter 7), Flash selects the whole thing. When Contact-Sensitive Selection is off, the selection outline must fully enclose the item to select it. This setting has no effect on merge-shapes; a selection outline always defines the precise area of the merge-shape that is selected (see the next section, "Making Selections").

4. Click OK.

Choose Your Own Highlights

Whenever you select a graphic element on the Stage, Flash highlights it. By default, Flash CS4 uses a different color to highlight each type of graphic-object (drawing-objects, primitives, groups, symbols, and all other elements). In certain situations the selection highlight may be difficult to see. If you're using a background color that's similar to a highlight color, for example, the selection highlight may blend in. You can change these highlight colors in the Preferences dialog. From the Flash menu (Mac) or Edit menu (Windows), choose Preferences; in the Category list, choose General. To use the layer-outlines color as the selection-highlight color for all graphic-objects on a layer, click the Use Layer Color radio button (you'll learn about layers and their outline view in Chapter 6).

To use separate colors for each type of graphic-object, click the radio button next to the list of objects (Drawing Objects, Drawing Primitives, Groups, Symbols, and Other Elements). To choose a new color, click the color control for the type of graphic-object whose highlight you want to change. Then choose a color from the set of swatches that pops up (**Figure 4.2**).

Figure 4.2 In the General category of the Preferences dialog, you can choose new colors for highlighting selection elements. Click the color control next to the type of graphic-object to choose its new selection-highlight color.

Making Selections

Merge-shapes, drawing-objects, and primitives all behave slightly differently when being selected. What you think of as a single shape may contain several segments. The rectangle tool creates a square whose stroke is actually four separate line segments. Clicking one side of a merge-shape square's stroke selects just that segment. To fully select the square's stroke, you must select each segment (you could use Shift-click to add the remaining sides to the initial selection). If you create the square as a drawing-object or a rectangle-primitive, Flash treats the four stroke segments as a unit. Clicking the stroke on any side of a drawing-object square or rectangle-primitive selects the entire stroke.

Flash highlights selected areas of merge-shapes with a pattern of tiny dots. Make sure all the parts of the merge-shape stroke or fill you intend to select display this pattern.

To make selections by clicking:

1. In the Tools panel, choose the selection tool, or press V on the keyboard.

2. To select elements created as merge-shapes, do one of the following:

   ▲ To select a merge-shape fill, position the pointer over the fill and click.

   The selection icon appears next to the selection pointer when it is over the fill. Flash highlights the selected fill with a dot pattern (**Figure 4.3**).

   ▲ To select a merge-shape stroke, position the pointer over a line segment and click.

   Flash appends a little arc or a little right-angle icon to the selection tool (**Figure 4.4**).

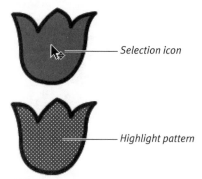

Selection icon

Highlight pattern

Figure 4.3 When the pointer sits above a filled area, it changes into the selection arrow (the cross icon appears next to the pointer, indicating that the tool is ready to move or select an item). Click a fill to select it. A dot pattern in a contrasting color highlights the selected fill.

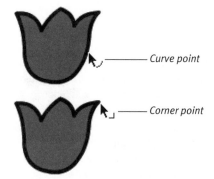

Curve point

Corner point

Figure 4.4 As you prepare to select a line, additions to the pointer icon indicate what kind of point lies beneath the pointer.

Double-Click Tricks

Double-clicking any segment in a series of connected merge-shape strokes selects all the segments. Double-clicking the fill of a merge-shape that has a fill and a stroke selects the fill and the stroke together.

Selected curve segment

Selection cursor in selection mode

Figure 4.5 When you click a merge-shape line, Flash selects and highlights just one segment.

Figure 4.6 When you position the selection tool over an unselected drawing-object (left), the pointer displays the same icons as for merge-shapes (move/select cross for fills, curve-point arc or corner-point angle for strokes). Click anywhere on the drawing-object, and Flash selects the entire drawing-object, highlighting its bounding box (right).

Figure 4.7 Whether you position the selection pointer over the stroke (top) or fill (middle) of a primitive-shape, the selection icon appears by the pointer. Clicking anywhere on the shape selects the whole thing (bottom).

These icons indicate that the tool is over a point in a line segment and show what type of point it is: a curve point or a corner point. (For more information about points, see the sidebar "About Curve and Corner Points," later in this chapter). Flash highlights just the segment you clicked, using a dot pattern (**Figure 4.5**).

3. To select elements created as drawing-objects, position the pointer over any portion of the shape and click.

    The arc or angle icon appears next to the selection pointer as described above for merge-shape fills and strokes. Flash selects the entire shape and highlights it by displaying the bounding box—a rectangle that encloses the shape (**Figure 4.6**).

4. To select elements created as primitives, position the pointer over any portion of the shape and click.

    The selection icon appears next to the selection pointer whether it's over a fill or a stroke. Flash selects the entire shape and highlights its bounding box (**Figure 4.7**).

continues on next page

MAKING SELECTIONS

5. To add elements to a selection, do one of the following:

- ▲ With Shift Select (Flash's default selection style) active, hold down the Shift key as you click each item you want to add (**Figure 4.8**).

- ▲ If you turned off the Shift Select option in the General category of the Preferences dialog, click each item you want to include.

Flash highlights each new item and adds it to the selection.

✔ Tips

■ To switch to the selection tool temporarily while using another tool, press ⌘ (Mac) or Ctrl (Windows). The selection tool remains in effect as long as you hold down the modifier key.

■ To select everything that's currently on the Stage, choose Edit > Select All, or press ⌘-A (Mac) or Ctrl-A (Windows).

■ The bounding box for a round or irregular drawing-object or primitive-shape is easy to see because the box sits outside the shape like a frame, and the bounding box for a rectangle-primitive has control points that make it more visible; but the bounding box for a drawing-object rectangle sits right on the edge of the rectangle. Therefore, depending on the color of your drawing-object rectangle, the highlighted bounding box can be difficult to see. If you have trouble seeing the highlight on selected drawing-object rectangles, choose a contrasting highlight color in the General category of the Preferences dialog (see the sidebar "Choose Your Own Highlights," earlier in this chapter).

1st selection

1st addition

2nd addition

Figure 4.8 With Flash's default Preferences setting for selections, Shift-click unhighlighted line segments or fill areas to add them to a selection.

Figure 4.9 Clicking and dragging with the selection tool creates a selection rectangle (top). Be sure to start from a point that allows you to enclose all the elements you want to select within the rectangle (bottom). Release the mouse button, and Flash selects those elements.

Drag selection rectangle

Selection outline partly encloses shapes

Selected shapes

Merge-shape partly selected

Drawing-object fully selected   *Primitive-shape fully selected*

Figure 4.10 When Flash's default contact-sensitive selection mode is active, any drawing-objects or primitives that are touched or partially enclosed by the selection rectangle are fully selected. But when it comes to merge-shapes, only the parts that fall within the selection rectangle are selected. (Here the star shapes are drawing-objects, the indented rectangles are primitives, and the circles are merge-shapes.)

To use a contact-sensitive selection rectangle:

1. Make sure the selection preferences are set for contact sensitivity (see "Setting Selection Preferences," earlier in this chapter).

2. In the Tools panel, select the selection tool.

3. Click and drag to pull out a selection rectangle (**Figure 4.9**).

   This rectangle isn't a graphic element; it just defines the boundaries of your selection.

4. Continue dragging until the rectangle encloses all the merge-shapes you want to select and at least some part of each drawing-object.

5. Release the mouse button.

   Merge-shapes. Flash highlights any portions of fill or stroke that fall inside the selection rectangle; portions of merge-shape fills or strokes that lie outside the rectangle remain unselected (**Figure 4.10**).

   Drawing-objects and primitive-shapes. If the selection rectangle touches any part of a drawing-object or primitive, Flash selects the entire thing, highlighting its bounding box.

To use a non–contact-sensitive selection rectangle:

1. Make sure contact sensitivity is turned off (see "Setting Selection Preferences," earlier in this chapter).

2. Follow steps 2 through 4 in the preceding exercise, but this time, fully enclose the drawing-objects you want to select.

    Merge-shapes. Flash highlights any portions of fill or stroke that fall inside the selection rectangle; portions of merge-shape fills or strokes that lie outside the rectangle remain unselected (**Figure 4.11**).

    Drawing-objects and primitive-shapes. Flash selects only those drawing-objects or primitives that are completely enclosed within the selection rectangle. If the selection rectangle touches or includes just a part of a drawing-object or primitive, Flash leaves the entire object deselected.

✔ Tips

- If the lines or shapes you want to select are located close to other lines, you may have difficulty selecting just what you want with a rectangle. The lasso tool can create an irregular selection outline. In the Tools panel, select the lasso tool, or press L. Click and draw a free-form line around the elements you want to select (**Figure 4.12**). Close the selection outline by bringing the lasso pointer back over the spot where you began the selection outline. Release the mouse button. Flash highlights whatever falls inside the shape you drew with the lasso.

- The lasso's Polygon mode lets you define a selection area with a series of connected straight-line segments. With the lasso tool selected, click the Polygon mode button in the Tools panel. Now you can click your way around the elements you want to select (**Figure 4.13**). Double-click to end the selection outline.

Drag selection rectangle

Selection outline partly encloses shapes

Selected shapes

Merge-shape partly selected

Drawing-object not selected   *Primitive-shape not selected*

Figure 4.11 When contact-sensitivity is inactive, a selection includes just the parts of merge-shapes that fall within the selection rectangle. For drawing-objects or primitives to be selected, they must be fully enclosed by the selection rectangle. (Here again the star shapes are drawing-objects, the indented rectangles are primitives, and the circles are merge-shapes.)

Figure 4.12 The lasso tool lets you select elements that are oddly shaped or too near other elements to allow use of the selection rectangle. Any merge-shapes inside the selection outline become highlighted and selected when you release the mouse button. Whether or not you must fully enclose drawing-objects and primitives in a lasso selection outline to select them depends on the contact-sensitivity setting in the Preferences dialog.

2nd click —
1st click —
6th click

Positioning polygon —
lasso for 18th click
— 17th click

Figure 4.13 In Polygon mode, the lasso tool creates a series of connected line segments to outline whatever element you want to select. Double-clicking finishes the shape by drawing a line from the point where you double-clicked to the starting point.

To deselect individual items:

1. In the Tools panel, select the selection tool.

2. Hold down the Shift key.

3. Click any highlighted drawing-objects, primitives, or merge-shape strokes or fills you want to remove from the current selection.

   Flash deselects the items you clicked (**Figure 4.14**). No matter which method you used to select items, you must Shift-click with the selection tool to remove items from a selection.

✔ Tips

■ To deselect everything, choose Edit > Deselect All, or press Shift-⌘-A (Mac) or Ctrl-Shift-A (Windows).

■ To deselect all elements quickly, click the selection tool in an empty area of the Stage or Pasteboard.

Figure 4.14 With the selection tool selected, position the pointer over the element you want to remove from the selection (left). Shift-click the item to deselect it (middle). Repeat the process to deselect another item (right). (In this image, the stars are drawing-objects, and the circles are merge-shapes.)

MAKING SELECTIONS

Using the Clipboard

Flash supports the standard cut, copy, and paste operations familiar to most computer users. Flash also provides special pasting operations for graphic elements; you can paste items in the center of the Stage or in their original location.

To perform basic editing operations:

1. Select the elements you want to delete, cut, or copy.

2. From the Edit menu (**Figure 4.15**), choose one of the following:

   ▲ To delete the selection, choose Clear, or press the Delete key.

   ▲ To cut the selection, choose Cut, or press ⌘-X (Mac) or Ctrl-X (Windows).

   ▲ To copy the selection, choose Copy, or press ⌘-C (Mac) or Ctrl-C (Windows).

Figure 4.15 The Edit menu offers all the basic cut, copy, and paste commands for working with graphic elements.

Figure 4.16 When you copy a selected graphic element (top) and choose Edit > Paste in Center, Flash pastes a copy of the element from the Clipboard to the center of the current view (bottom).

To paste the Clipboard's contents in the center of the window:

◆ Choose Edit > Paste in Center, or press ⌘-V (Mac) or Ctrl-V (Windows).

Flash pastes the Clipboard's contents in the center of the current view (**Figure 4.16**).

To paste the Clipboard contents in their original location:

◆ Choose Edit > Paste in Place, or press Shift-⌘-V (Mac) or Ctrl-Shift-V (Windows).

Flash pastes the Clipboard contents to their original location on the Stage. When creating animation, it can be crucial to maintain the position of elements you cut and paste between layers and frames.

✔ Tips

■ Another way to make copies of selected elements: Choose Edit > Duplicate, or press ⌘-D (Mac) or Ctrl-D (Windows). The duplicate appears on the Stage, offset from the original item. The duplicate is selected, to prevent a merge-shape duplicate from interacting with the original.

■ Using the selection tool, Option-click (Mac) or Alt- or Ctrl-click (Windows) and drag any single element to create a copy. Be sure to keep the modifier key down until the copy appears.

Resizing Graphic Elements

Flash gives you several ways to resize, or *scale*, graphic elements. You can scale selected elements interactively on the Stage. You can also set specific scale percentages or dimensions for your element in the Transform panel, the Position and Size section of the Property inspector, and the Info panel.

To resize a graphic element interactively:

1. In the Tools panel, from the transform-tools submenu, select the free-transform tool (**Figure 4.17**).

2. On the Stage, click the element you want to resize.

   Flash selects and highlights the element and places transformation handles on all four sides and at the corners of the ele-ment's bounding box.

3. In the Tools panel, select the Scale modifier.

4. Position the pointer over a handle.

   The pointer changes to a double-headed arrow, indicating the direction in which the element will grow or shrink as you drag the handles inward or outward.

5. To resize the graphic element, do one of the following:

   ▲ To change the graphic element's width, click and drag one of the side handles.

   ▲ To change the element's height, click and drag the top or bottom handle.

   ▲ To change the size of the element proportionally, click and drag one of the corner handles.

   Dragging toward the center of the element reduces it; dragging away enlarges it (**Figure 4.18**).

Free-transform

Rotate and skew

Scale

Distort

Envelope

Figure 4.17 The free-transform tool lets you select and scale elements interactively.

Original

Drag top or bottom handle to change height

Drag left or right handle to change width

Drag corner to scale proportionally

Figure 4.18 Activating the free-transform tool's Scale modifier places a set of handles around a selected element. Click and drag the handles to change the size of the element.

Constrain mode (preserve aspect ratio)

Unconstrain mode

TRANSFORM

Reset
dimensions

Select to rotate
the element

Select to skew
the element

Remove
transform

Duplicate selection and transform

Figure 4.19 To resize a selected element, use the Transform panel's Width and Height hot text to enter new percentages. In Constrain mode (the closed-link icon), as you change the percentage of one dimension, Flash automatically updates the other. The Transform panel also lets you enter values for rotating and skewing selected elements.

✔ Tip

■ In the default scaling mode, the selection scales graphic elements from the control point opposite the one you're dragging. To scale relative to the center of a selection, hold down the Option key (Mac) or Alt key (Windows) as you drag. For symbols (see Chapter 7), it's the reverse: the default mode scales the symbol from its transformation point (which is the center by default), and pressing the Option key (Mac) or Alt key (Windows) lets you scale from the opposite control point.

To resize an element via the Transform panel:

1. With the Transform panel open, on the Stage select the element you want to resize.

   Percentages appear in the Width and Height hot text in the top section of the Transform panel. When you select an element that's never been resized, width and height are set to 100%.

2. To resize the element and maintain its aspect ratio (the ratio of width to height), do the following:

   ▲ In the top section of the Transform panel, set the chain-link icon to Constrain mode (the closed-link icon). Clicking the icon toggles between modes.

   ▲ Use the Width (or Height) hot text to enter a new percentage (**Figure 4.19**).

   To use a precise value, click the hot text, enter a number in the field that activates, then press Enter. To choose a value interactively, position the pointer over the hot text; when the pointing finger with a double arrow appears, drag left (or down) to lower the value or drag right (or up) to increase the value. Flash previews the changes on the Stage as you drag the hot text's invisible slider.

continues on next page

RESIZING GRAPHIC ELEMENTS

In Constrain mode, changing the Width percentage also changes the Height percentage (and vice versa).

or

To resize the element and allow the aspect ratio to change, do the following:

▲ Set the chain-link icon to Unconstrain mode (the broken-link icon).

▲ Use the Width and Height hot text to enter new percentages.

In Unconstrain mode, entering new values for Width and Height changes those dimensions of the selected element independently.

✔ Tips

■ Once you've gotten pleasing proportions for an element by adjusting its width and height independently, choose the Constrain mode to lock in the aspect ratio. Now using the Width or Height hot text scales the element while preserving the new aspect ratio.

■ Flash resizes merge-shapes on an absolute scale as long as the shape remains selected. Deselect the shape, and the current width and height become the shape's new 100%. To transform merge-shapes on a relative scale, select the shape and enter new values for Width and/or Height using the Transform panel, then deselect the shape. Select the shape again (Width and Height now show a value of 100%). Enter new percentages for the second transformation.

■ Flash always resizes drawing-objects, primitives, text fields, groups, and symbols on an absolute scale (applying the percentage you enter into the panel to the element's original size).

■ To undo changes you made to an element's width and height (whether made using the free-transform tool or a panel setting), click the Reset button in the top section of the Transform panel or press Shift-⌘-Z (Mac) or Ctrl-Shift-Z (Windows). For merge-shapes, you must not have deselected the transformed element; for drawing-objects, primitives, text fields (see Chapter 3), groups (see Chapter 5), and symbols (see Chapter 7), you can select the object and click the Reset button anytime to restore the item to its original 100% width and height.

■ A Remove Transform button appears at the bottom-right corner of the Transform panel; that button undoes all the transformations you applied to the selected item, not just the width and height changes.

■ To scale several elements at the same time, select all the elements and then use any of the scaling methods described earlier in this section. When you use the Transform panel, the bounding box that contains the elements scales relative to its center point, and the entire selection grows or shrinks to fit the new box. When you use the free-transform tool, the bounding box scales from the corner opposite to the one you're dragging.

Constrain

Unconstrain

Figure 4.20 The Width and Height hot text in the Position and Size section of the Property inspector displays the dimensions of the bounding box of a selected element. Enter new values to resize the element. In Constrain mode (the closed-link icon), Flash preserves the ratio of width to height. In Unconstrain mode (the broken-link icon), you can enter independent width and height values.

Figure 4.21 You can enter precise dimensions for an element's width and height in the Info panel. The Registration/Transformation Point icon shows whether changes will be relative to the top-left corner of the element's bounding box or to the transformation point. To apply the values you entered in the panel to the selected graphic element, press Enter or click the Stage.

To resize an element via the Property inspector:

1. With the Property inspector open, in the workspace, select the element you want to resize.

   The Position and Size section of the Property inspector contains Width and Height hot text displaying the dimensions of the selected shape's bounding box.

2. To resize the element, do either of the following:

   ▲ To preserve the aspect ratio, set the chain-link icon to Constrain mode (the closed-link icon). Use the Width or Height hot text to enter a new percentage (**Figure 4.20**). Click the hot text to enter a precise value; drag the hot text's invisible slider to choose a value interactively. Changing the value for one dimension automatically changes the other.

   ▲ To allow the aspect ratio to change, set the chain-link icon to Unconstrain mode (the broken-link icon); use the Width and/or Height hot text to enter new percentages.

✔ Tip

■ The Info panel lets you resize a selected element relative to its *registration point* (the top-left corner of its bounding box) or *transformation point*. Click the Registration/Transformation Point icon to toggle between modes (**Figure 4.21**). A crosshair in the upper-left corner of the icon means the values are relative to the registration point; a circle in the icon's lower-right corner means the values are relative to the transformation point. Values in the Property inspector are always relative to the registration point. (For more details, see the sidebar "How Flash Tracks Elements," later in this chapter.)

Positioning Graphic Elements

If you aren't happy with the position of an element, you can always move it. You can position elements visually by dragging them around on the Stage with the selection tool. You can also position a selection numerically by specifying a precise Stage location in *x*- and *y*-coordinates. You can enter the *x*- and *y*-coordinates in either the Property inspector or the Info panel.

To reposition an element via the Property inspector:

1. With the Property inspector open, select an element on the Stage.

   A label—for example, Drawing Object—appears at the top of the Property inspector, identifying the type of element selected. The Position and Size section of the Property inspector displays the –*x*- and *y*-coordinates of the element's registration point (**Figure 4.22**).

2. To move the element, do one or both of the following:

   ▲ To position the element along the horizontal axis, use the X hot text to enter a new *x*-coordinate.

   ▲ To position the element along the vertical axis, use the Y hot text to enter a new *y*-coordinate.

   Click the hot text to enter a precise value; drag the hot text's invisible slider to choose a value interactively (**Figure 4.23**). The element moves to its new position.

✔ Tip

■ By default, the transformation point corresponds to a point at the center of a shape's bounding box. You can change that. With the free-transform tool, drag the hollow circle that represents the transformation point to a new location.

Figure 4.22 The Property inspector shows attributes of a selected element, including the x- and y-coordinates of the registration point. This drawing-object's registration point is ½ inch to the right along the horizontal axis and ¼ inch down the vertical axis.

Figure 4.23 Changing the x- and y-coordinates in the Position and Size section of the Property inspector changes the location of a selected element. This arrow is now located 1 inch to the right along the horizontal axis and 1 inch down the vertical axis.

POSITIONING GRAPHIC ELEMENTS

How Flash Tracks Elements

To keep track of an element's size and position on the Stage, Flash encloses each element in a *bounding box*—an invisible rectangle just big enough to hold the element. Flash then treats the Stage as a giant graph, with the top-left corner of the Stage as the center of the *x*- and *y*-axis (**Figure 4.24**). The units of measure for the graph are those currently selected in the Document Properties dialog (to learn more about document properties, see Chapter 1). The Property inspector and the Info panel display information about the size of the element (the width and height of the bounding box) and the position of the element (the *x*- and *y*-coordinates for one important point in the element).

Representation of x-y axis   Origin   Pasteboard

Figure 4.24 The dotted line here represents the x-y axis of the Stage. The origin—the 0 point both horizontally and vertically—is the top-left corner of the Stage.

By entering new values for Height and Width in the Position and Size section of the Property inspector or in the Info panel, you can change an element's size. By entering new *x*- and *y*-coordinates in those panels, you can change an element's position on the Stage. (For more information about resizing elements, see "Resizing Graphic Elements," earlier in this chapter.)

Depending on which panel you use to enter values for an element, you can use either of two points to position an element: the *registration point* or the *transformation point*. For merge-shapes, drawing-objects, and primitives, the registration point is always located at the top-left corner of an element's bounding box. For symbols, you determine the location of registration point, which stays the same for all instances of the symbol. For all types of objects, Flash initially places the transformation point at the center of the bounding box; you can reposition it using the free-transform tool. You can position the transformation point differently for individual symbol instances (see Chapter 7).

The Property inspector always tracks elements by the registration point. The Info panel lets you track elements by either point. You choose the point by clicking the Registration/ Transformation icon to toggle between the two tracking styles. When a crosshair appears in the top-left corner of the icon, the Info panel settings position and size elements by the registration point. When a circle appears in the bottom-right corner of the icon, the Info panel settings position and size elements by the transformation point.

When you use ActionScript to dynamically move symbols at runtime, Flash always uses the registration point to position them.

Flipping, Rotating, and Skewing

Flash lets you flip, rotate, and skew selected elements. You can either manipulate elements freely with the free-transform tool's Rotate and Skew modifier or use a variety of commands to do the job with more precision.

To flip a graphic element:

1. Select the element you want to flip.

2. Choose Modify > Transform.

3. From the submenu (**Figure 4.25**), choose either of the following:

   ▲ To reorient the element so that it spins 180 degrees around its horizontal central axis like a Rolodex file, choose Flip Vertical.

   ▲ To reorient the element so that it spins 180 degrees around its vertical central axis like a weathervane, choose Flip Horizontal.

   Figure 4.26 shows the results of the two types of flipping.

✔ Tip

■ You can flip and scale selected elements simultaneously by using the free-transform tool in Scale mode. Drag one handle all the way across the transform box and past the handle on the other side. To flip a selected element vertically and horizontally, for example, drag the handle in the bottom-right corner diagonally upward, past the handle in the top-left corner (**Figure 4.27**). The flipped element starts small and grows as you continue to drag away from the element's top-left corner. Flash previews the flipped element; release the mouse button when the element is the size you want.

Rotate 90 degrees clockwise

Rotate 90 degrees counterclockwise

Flip 180 degrees like a Rolodex card file

Flip 180 degrees like a weathervane

Figure 4.25 The Modify > Transform submenu offers commands for flipping graphic elements vertically and horizontally. It also provides commands for rotating an element in 90-degree increments, both clockwise and counterclockwise.

Original

Flipped horizontally

Flipped vertically

Figure 4.26 The results of flipping an element by using the Flip commands in the Modify > Transform submenu.

End drag

Flipped vertically and horizontally

Start drag

Figure 4.27 The free-transform tool can flip and scale an element simultaneously. Here, the tool with its Scale modifier active is flipping the element both vertically and horizontally.

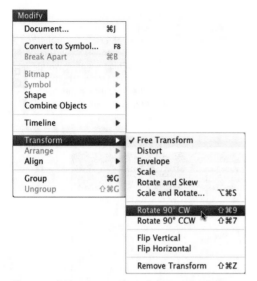

Figure 4.28 To rotate a selected element in 90-degree increments, use the Modify > Transform menu. Repeat the command to rotate the element 180, 270, or 360 degrees.

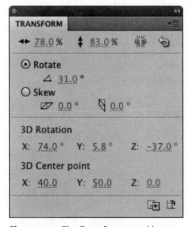

Figure 4.29 The Transform panel lets you rotate graphic elements in precise increments. Select the Rotate radio button and use the hot text to enter a value for the degrees of rotation. Positive values rotate the element clockwise; negative values rotate it counterclockwise.

To rotate an element in 90-degree increments:

1. Select the element you want to rotate.

2. Choose Modify > Transform (**Figure 4.28**).

3. From the submenu, choose either of the following:

   ▲ To rotate the element clockwise 90 degrees, choose Rotate 90° CW.

   ▲ To rotate the element counterclockwise 90 degrees, choose Rotate 90° CCW.

To rotate an element by a user-specified amount:

1. Select the element and access the Transform panel (**Figure 4.29**).

   If the panel isn't open, choose Window > Transform.

2. Click the Rotate radio button.

3. To specify the direction and amount of rotation, do either of the following:

   ▲ To rotate the element counterclockwise, use the Rotate hot text to enter a negative value (–1 to –360).

   ▲ To rotate the element clockwise, use the Rotate hot text to enter a positive value (1 to 360).

   Click the hot text to enter a precise value; drag the hot text's invisible slider to choose a value interactively.

✔ Tips

■ When you work with drawing-objects and primitive-shapes, you can undo changes in width, height, rotation, and skewing at any time, even after you've deselected the item and made changes to other items. To restore the original Width, Height, Rotate, and Skew settings, select the item and click the Transform panel's Remove Transform button (**Figure 4.30**).

■ For merge-shapes, the Reset and Remove Transform buttons work only as long as the shape remains selected.

To skew an element by a user-specified amount:

1. With the Transform panel open, select the element you want to skew.

2. In the Transform panel, select the Skew radio button.

3. Using the Skew Horizontal and Skew Vertical hot text, enter the desired skew values (**Figure 4.31**).

   Click the hot text to enter a precise value; drag the hot text's invisible slider to choose a value interactively.

✔ Tip

■ You can quickly create step-and-repeat versions of a transformed object. Say you need three squares with the same dimensions, but with Horizontal Skew values of 10, 20, and 30 degrees. Create the original square, select it, and set the Horizontal Skew to 10 degrees in the Transform panel. With the square still selected, click the Duplicate Selection and Transform button. Flash duplicates the square with the 10-degree horizontal skew, then applies the current Horizontal Skew value to the already skewed square. The effect is to increase the Horizontal Skew value by 10 degrees with each duplication.

Figure 4.30 To undo all the changes you've made to a selected object, in the Transform panel, click the Remove Transform button. This technique works whether you made the changes via the Transform panel or interactively with the free-transform tool.

Duplicate Selection and Transform button

Figure 4.31 Use the Transform panel to skew selected elements. You can set separate values for horizontal and vertical skewing.

Free-transform tool

Rotate and Skew modifier

Figure 4.32 Select the free-transform tool's Rotate and Skew modifier to access handles for rotating or skewing a selected element interactively.

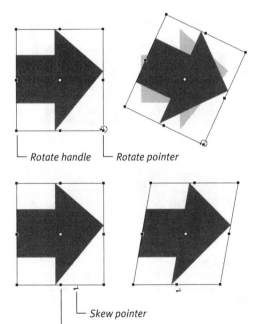

— *Rotate handle* └ *Rotate pointer*

— *Skew pointer*

└ *Skew handle*

Figure 4.33 With the free-transform tool's Rotate and Skew modifier selected, you can drag one of the corner handles of a selected element's transform box to rotate that element (top). Drag one of the side handles to skew the element (bottom).

To rotate or skew an element interactively:

1. Select an element to rotate or skew.

2. In the Tools panel, select the free-transform tool; then click the Rotate and Skew modifier (**Figure 4.32**).

   A transform box (similar to the element's bounding box, but with square handles at the corners and on all four sides) encloses the element.

3. To modify the selected element, do either of the following:

   ▲ To rotate the element, position the pointer over one of the corner handles.

   The pointer changes to a circular arrow. Click and drag to rotate the element. Flash spins the element around its transformation point (**Figure 4.33**).

   ▲ To skew the element, position the pointer over one of the side handles of the transform box.

   The pointer changes to a two-way arrowhead. Click and drag the side handle to skew the element.

4. Release the mouse button.

   Flash redraws the modified element.

✔ Tips

■ To rotate an element around one of its corners instead of its transformation point, press Option (Mac) or Alt (Windows) while dragging.

■ To constrain rotation by 45-degree increments, hold down the Shift key while rotating.

FLIPPING, ROTATING, AND SKEWING

115

Distorting Graphic Elements

The free-transform tool's Distort modifier lets you distort some graphic elements by changing the shape of the transform box. You can move the box's corners individually; move paired corner handles simultaneously to turn the rectangular box into a trapezoid; and move the side handles to stretch, shrink, or skew the box. The selected element(s) redraw to fit the altered box. The Distort modifier works only on merge-shapes and single, selected drawing-objects; Distort doesn't work on primitive-shapes, text fields (see Chapter 3), groups (see Chapter 5), symbols (see Chapter 7), or selections with multiple drawing-objects.

To distort an element freely:

1. Using the free-transform tool, select the element you want to distort.

   A transform box with handles appears.

2. In the Tools panel, select the Distort modifier (**Figure 4.34**).

   The center point of the selection disappears, indicating that you are in Distort mode.

3. Position the pointer over one of the transform handles.

   The pointer changes to a hollow arrowhead.

4. To change the shape of the transform box, do one of the following:

   ▲ To relocate one corner of the box, position the pointer over one of the corner handles; then click and drag the handle to the desired location. You can position each corner handle independently (**Figure 4.35**).

   ▲ To skew the element, position the pointer over one of the side handles; then drag the handle to the desired position. The element skews toward the direction you drag.

Free-transform tool

Distort modifier

Figure 4.34 Choose the free-transform tool's Distort modifier to reposition the corner points of a selected item's transform box independently.

Drag a corner handle...   ...to distort a shape

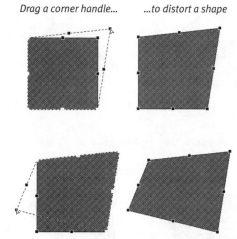

Figure 4.35 Use the free-transform tool's Distort modifier to redefine the shape of an element's transform box. You can drag each corner handle separately.

Drag a side handle...   *...to skew and stretch a shape*

Skew

← Stretch →

Figure 4.36 When the Distort modifier is selected, dragging the side handles of a selected element's transform box skews the element. To enlarge (or shrink) the element at the same time, move the side handle away from (or in toward) the center of the original shape.

▲ To stretch the element as you skew it, move the selected side handle away from the element's center (**Figure 4.36**).

▲ To shrink the element as you skew it, move the selected side handle toward the element's center.

5. Release the mouse button.

Flash redraws the selection to fill the new transform-box shape.

✔ Tips

■ When you select multiple drawing-objects, the free-transform tool's Distort modifier is inactive. To distort multiple drawing-objects simultaneously, you must combine them into a single drawing-object (see "Converting Shape Types," later in this chapter).

Adding Perspective

As beginning art students discover, it's not difficult to add depth to two-dimensional objects made up of rectangular shapes. You adjust the appropriate edges to align with imaginary parallel lines that converge at a distant point on the horizon—the *vanishing point*. Doing so creates the illusion that the objects recede into the distance. Adding perspective to nonrectangular shapes takes a bit more experience and the ability to imagine the way those shapes should look. The Distort modifier of Flash's free-transform tool helps you because it encloses your selected shape—circle, oval, or squiggle—within a rectangular transform box. All you need to do is adjust that box as you would a rectangular shape.

Flash CS4 also provides more-sophisticated tools for making two-dimensional objects appear to inhabit three-dimensional space. The 3D-rotation and 3D-translation tools work only on movie-clip symbols (you learn to create symbols in Chapter 7 and animated movie-clip symbols in Chapter 12). Flash's 3D tools let you rotate and position movie clips not only along the *x* and *y* axis (for horizontal and vertical positions) but also along the *z* axis (for depth), redrawing the object to make it appear to recede into space. The use of the 3D tools to create artwork that simulates three-dimensional environments is complex and is beyond the scope of this *Visual Quickstart Guide*. After you learn to create symbols, however, try using the 3D tools on a movie-clip symbol containing a simple shape, such as a square. Experimenting on this basic level gives you a feel for how the tools distort the "plane" that the movie clip resides in and create the 3D illusion.

DISTORTING GRAPHIC ELEMENTS

To distort a graphic element symmetrically:

1. Follow steps 1 and 2 of the preceding task to prepare an element for distorting.

2. To taper the element, do either of the following:

   ▲ To make the top of the transform box narrower than the bottom, Shift-click and drag the top-right corner handle toward the top-left corner handle (**Figure 4.37**), or vice versa.

   ▲ To make the top of the transform box wider than the bottom, Shift-click and drag the top-right corner handle away from the top-left corner handle, or vice versa.

   As you drag, the two corner handles move in tandem, coming together if you drag in or moving apart if you drag out.

3. Release the mouse button.

   Flash redraws the transform box and its contents. If you dragged in, the box appears to taper toward the top. If you dragged out, the box appears to taper toward the bottom. You can follow these procedures for the sides or bottom of the bounding box to taper the box in any direction.

✔ Tips

- When you've already selected an element with the free-transform tool, you can access the hollow-arrow pointer temporarily without selecting the Distort modifier, press ⌘ (Mac) or Ctrl (Windows). Then you can drag or Shift-drag to distort selected elements.

- If you make a mistake while distorting a graphic, and you choose Edit > Undo so you can fix it, your graphic will be selected with the free-transform tool but the Distort modifier won't be active. You must reselect the Distort modifier in the Tools panel to continue your distortion.

Shift-drag a corner handle...

...to taper a shape

Figure 4.37 Using the Distort modifier of the free-transform tool, Shift-click and drag a corner handle to taper selected elements.

- Although you can use the free-transform tool on text fields, groups, and symbols, the Distort modifier doesn't work on these items. If your selection includes merge-shapes and one or more text fields, groups, or symbols, the free-transform tool's Distort modifier is available, but the distortion affects only the merge-shapes.

- You can use the free-transform tool to distort multiple merge-shapes simultaneously. Select the merge-shapes you want to modify. Then, using the Distort modifier of the free-transform tool, redefine the shape of the transform box that surrounds the shapes. The shapes change as a unit.

Figure 4.38 Clicking a fill with the paint-bucket tool applies whatever color is selected in the Fill Color control. Use this technique to change existing fills.

Modifying Fills and Strokes

Flash provides two methods for modifying existing fills and strokes: you can apply new attributes with a tool (the paint-bucket tool for fills, the ink-bottle tool for strokes), or you can select the fill or stroke on the Stage and choose new attributes in an appropriate panel. For fills or strokes that contain a gradient, you can also modify the way the gradient fits in the shape by using the gradient-transform tool.

To change fill color with the paint-bucket tool:

1. In the Tools panel, click the active edit-fill/stroke tool and select the paint-bucket tool from the submenu, or press K.

2. Select new fill attributes (see Chapter 2).

3. Click the paint bucket's hot spot (the tip of the drip of paint) somewhere inside the fill you want to change.

   The fill can be selected or deselected. The fill changes to the new color (**Figure 4.38**).

✔ Tip

- To pick up the color of a stroke or fill and use it for both strokes and fills, Shift-click with the eyedropper tool. Flash loads the selected color into the Fill Color and Stroke Color controls in the Tools panel, the Color panel, and the Property inspector.

- When you select multiple merge-shapes, clicking one shape with the paint bucket changes all selected merge-shape fills. The ink-bottle tool works the same way on merge-shape strokes (see "To change stroke color with the ink-bottle tool," in the next section). When you select multiple drawing-objects or primitive-shapes, however, these tools can't modify all the fills or strokes in the selection; you must click each fill and stroke individually, or use a panel to make the changes (see the sidebar "Use Panels to Change Selected Fills and Strokes," below).

MODIFYING FILLS AND STROKES

Use Panels to Change Selected Fills and Strokes

You can modify the fill and stroke attributes of a selected graphic element by changing the settings in any appropriate panel. For example, draw an oval with a red fill and a solid, 1-point, blue stroke; then select the whole shape (note that if you create the oval as a drawing-object or primitive-shape, Flash automatically selects it). Now access the Fill and Stroke section of the Property inspector; it displays the attributes of the selected shape (or drawing-object or primitive). Select green from the Fill Color control; the oval fill changes to green. Increase the stroke height or choose a new stroke style; the oval stroke changes to match.

You can choose new colors for selected fills and strokes from any appropriate panel—Color, Swatches, Tools, or Property inspector. When you choose a new color from the Swatches panel, Flash uses the Color panel to determine whether that color is for fills or strokes. When the Fill Color control is selected in the Color panel, Flash applies the swatch color to selected fills; if the Stroke Color control is selected, Flash applies the color to strokes.

When a selected merge-shape has a stroke or fill set to No Color, however, the only way to change that setting is to add a fill or stroke by using the paint-bucket or ink-bottle tool (see Chapter 2).

When your selected shape is a drawing-object or primitive-shape, changing the fill or stroke attributes in a panel adds the missing element (**Figure 4.39**).

Selected merge-shapes *Selected drawing-objects* *Selected primitives*

Fill set to No Color

Stroke set to No Color

Select new attributes

Drawing-objects and primitives add stroke and fill

Figure 4.39 Changing the attributes of a drawing-object or primitive-shape whose fill or stroke was originally set to No Color causes Flash to add the missing element, whereas doing the same thing for a selected merge-shape has no effect.

For merge-shapes, drawing-objects, primitives

With nothing selected, click stroke or fill

With fill and stroke selected, click stroke or fill

For merge-shapes only

With just fill selected, click stroke

With part of stroke selected, click selection

Warning: Clicking a selected fill with unselected stroke does nothing

Figure 4.40 You don't have to select a stroke to change its attributes; just click the stroke or the unselected fill with the ink bottle. Warning: If the fill is selected, you must click the stroke itself; you can't click the selected fill to change an unselected stroke.

To change stroke color with the ink-bottle tool:

1. In the Tools panel, click the active edit-fill/stroke tool and select the ink-bottle tool, or press S.

2. Select new stroke attributes (see Chapter 2).

3. Click the ink bottle's hot spot (the tip of the drip of paint) in one of the following ways:

   ▲ Click directly on the stroke.

   ▲ If a shape has both stroke and fill, and both are deselected, click the fill.

   ▲ If a shape has both stroke and fill, and both are selected, click the fill.

   ▲ If a shape has both stroke and fill, and only the fill is selected, click the stroke.

   The stroke takes on its new attributes (**Figure 4.40**).

✔ Tip

■ To save time, you can copy the fill and stroke attributes of one element and apply them to another. In the Tools panel, select the eyedropper tool, or press I. The pointer changes to an eyedropper. To copy a fill color or gradient, position the eyedropper over a fill and click. To copy all of a stroke's attributes, position the eyedropper over the stroke and click. Flash switches tools; the paint bucket appears for fills, the ink bottle for strokes. The attributes of the clicked item appear in all related panels; when you click a fill, for example, the fill type and fill color appear in the Tools panel, the Color panel, and the Property inspector. You can then use the loaded paint-bucket or ink-bottle tool to apply the attributes to a different graphic element.

To change a gradient fill's center point:

1. In the Tools panel, from the transform-tools submenu, select the gradient-transform tool, or press F (**Figure 4.41**).

2. Position the pointer over the graphic element whose gradient you want to modify; the gradient can be located in a fill or in a stroke.

   The pointer changes to the gradient-transform pointer.

3. Click.

   Handles for manipulating the gradient appear (**Figure 4.42**). You can rotate the gradient or change its size and/or center point.

4. Position the pointer over the gradient's center-point handle, the circle icon.

   The move icon appears.

5. Drag the center-point handle to reposition the center point of the gradient (**Figure 4.43**).

✔ Tip

- When you create a graphic element containing a locked gradient, by default Flash positions the gradient so that its center aligns with the left-hand side of the Stage. With the Stage set to larger viewing magnifications, when you select such an element with the gradient-transform tool, all of the gradient-transform handles may be outside the viewing area of your computer screen. It can seem as if the gradient-transform tool doesn't work. If you click a gradient with the gradient-transform tool and nothing seems to happen, try choosing a new magnification level. Depending on your workspace setup, you may need to view the Stage at 50%—or even 25%—to see all the gradient-transform handles for a selected gradient.

Figure 4.41 Flash pairs the free-transform tool and gradient-transform tool in a submenu of the Tools panel; select the gradient-transform tool to manipulate the way gradients appear within fills and strokes.

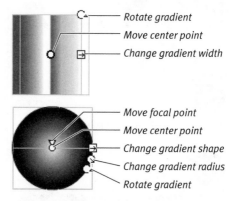

Figure 4.42 Handles for transforming gradients appear when you click a gradient with the gradient-transform pointer.

Figure 4.43 Drag the center-point handle to reposition the center of the gradient within your shape.

Preview of new focal-point position *Repositioned focal point*

Figure 4.44 This gradient blends from white (in the leftmost gradient pointer) to black (in the rightmost). This arrangement puts white at the center of a radial gradient, giving the illusion of highlighting on a three-dimensional object. By moving the focal point, you can mimic changes in the way light hits the object.

Preview width

Transform gradient width

Color bands on outer edges of blend get wider

Figure 4.45 With a linear gradient selected, use the gradient-transform tool to drag the square handle inward and create a narrower rectangle for a gradient.

To change a radial gradient's focal point:

1. Follow steps 1 through 3 in the preceding task.

2. Position the gradient-transform pointer over the focal-point handle, the triangle. The pointer changes to a triangle.

3. Click and drag the focal-point handle to a new location (**Figure 4.44**).

   The focal point, where you have the most concentrated amount of the gradient's central color, shifts to the new location.

To resize a gradient in a fill or stroke:

1. With the gradient-transform tool selected in the Tools panel, click the graphic element that contains the gradient you want to modify.

2. To change the way the gradient fits inside the fill or stroke, do one of the following:

   ▲ To change the width of a linear gradient, drag the square handle (**Figure 4.45**).

   The pointer changes to a double-headed arrow. Dragging toward the center of your shape squeezes the transition into a narrower space; dragging away from the center of your shape spreads the transition over a wider space.

continues on next page

MODIFYING FILLS AND STROKES

▲ To change the shape of a radial gradient, drag the square handle (**Figure 4.46**).

The pointer changes to a double-headed arrow. Dragging toward the center of your shape creates a narrower oval space for the transition; dragging away from the center of your shape creates a wider oval space.

▲ To change the radius of a radial gradient, drag the circular handle next to the square handle (**Figure 4.47**).

The pointer changes to an arrow within a circle. Dragging toward the center of your shape squeezes the transition into a smaller circular space; dragging away from the center of your shape spreads the transition over a larger circular space.

Preview shape

Transform gradient width

Outer rings of blend get wider

Circular blends become oval

Figure 4.46 With a radial gradient selected, use the gradient-transform tool to drag the square handle inward to create a narrower oval for a gradient.

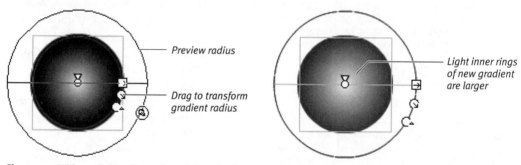

Preview radius

Drag to transform gradient radius

Light inner rings of new gradient are larger

Figure 4.47 With a radial gradient selected, drag the first round handle outward to create a larger radius.

Figure 4.48 When you're set to publish your movie to Flash Player 8 or later (see Chapter 18), the Color panel's Overflow menu is active. You can choose how Flash fills out a gradient that you have made narrower than the shape it sits in.

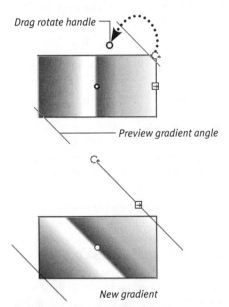

Figure 4.49 As you drag the gradient's rotate handle with the gradient-transform tool, you spin the gradient around its center point.

To control overflow:

1. Follow the steps in the preceding task to create a gradient that is narrower than the shape it sits in.

2. In the Color panel, from the Overflow menu (**Figure 4.48**), choose one of the following:

   ▲ To extend the colors in the leftmost and rightmost gradient pointers, choose Extend (the first menu item).

   ▲ To repeat the gradient, but with the colors in reverse order, choose Reflect (the second menu item).

   ▲ To repeat the gradient with colors in the original order, choose Repeat.

   Note that to view the Overflow menu, your Publish Settings must be set to publish for Flash Player 8 or later (see Chapter 18).

To rotate a gradient fill:

1. With the gradient-transform tool selected in the Tools panel, click the fill or stroke containing the gradient you want to modify.

2. To rotate the gradient, do either of the following:

   ▲ To rotate a linear gradient, drag the round handle (**Figure 4.49**).

   ▲ To rotate a radial gradient, drag the round handle farthest from the square handle.

   The pointer changes to a circular arrow. You can rotate the gradient clockwise or counterclockwise.

✔ Tip

■ Click and drag with the paint-bucket tool to rotate the gradient as you apply it. To constrain the gradient angle to vertical, horizontal, or 45-degree angles, hold down the Shift key as you drag.

Modifying Shapes: Natural Drawing Tools

All the strokes and fills you create in Flash can be edited after you've drawn them. You can edit merge-shapes and drawing-objects in Flash's natural-drawing style, using the selection tool to change the path that defines the shape, or you can work directly with the path's anchor points and Bézier curves by using the subselection, pen, and anchor-point tools (see "Modifying Shapes: Bézier Tools," later in this chapter). You can modify primitive-shapes by manipulating their control points with the selection or subselection tools, or you can change their properties in the Property inspector.

When you use the selection tool, the merge-shape or drawing-object you want to modify must be deselected. If the element is selected, the selection tool moves the element as a unit. Always note what kind of icon the selection pointer is displaying as it hovers over the path you want to modify.

For the following tasks, make sure the item you want to modify is deselected. These tasks all deal with modifying strokes, but the same techniques work for modifying fills by reshaping their paths (see the sidebar "The Mystery of Fill Paths," later in this chapter).

About Curve and Corner Points

Flash's selection and subselection tools let you modify an element's curves and lines. The subselection tool lets you do so by moving the curve and corner points that define the element's path and by rearranging the curves' Bézier handles. When you drag a selection rectangle to enclose a path with the subselection tool, Flash reveals any curve points' Bézier handles. (Corner points have no handles.)

When you use the selection tool, Flash hides all that technical stuff. You simply pull on a line to reshape it. Still, the selection tool has its own hidden version of curve and corner points, which are evident only in the changing icons that accompany the tool as it interacts with an unselected line or curve (**Figure 4.50**).

Over an empty spot

Over a selected line on the Stage

Over an unselected curve point

Over an unselected corner point

Figure 4.50 The small icons appearing with the selection pointer indicate what lies beneath the pointer.

For the selection tool, corner points appear at the end of an unselected segment or at the point where two segments join to form a sharp angle. All those other in-between points—even those in the middle of a completely flat line segment—are curve points. When you tug on a curve point with the selection tool, you pull out a range of points in a tiny arc. When you tug on a corner point with the selection tool, you pull out a single point.

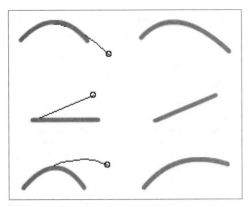

Figure 4.51 Drag away from the existing curve or line segment to lengthen it (top). Reposition the end point to change the direction of the line or curve segment (middle, bottom).

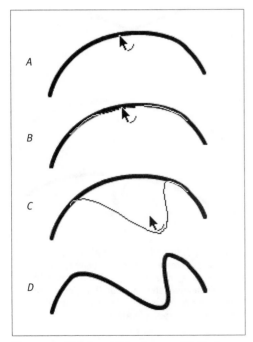

Figure 4.52 Click the middle of a curve (A). Flash activates the curve segment (B). Drag the curve to a new position (C). When you release the mouse button, Flash redraws the curve (D).

To activate the end of a segment with the selection tool:

1. Position the pointer over the end point of a deselected line segment.

   The corner-point modifier appears.

2. Click the end point.

   The end of the segment becomes active.

3. Reposition the end point in any of the following ways:

   ▲ Drag away from the existing line or curve to lengthen the segment.

   ▲ Drag toward the existing line or curve to shorten the segment.

   ▲ Drag at an angle to the original line to pivot a straight-line segment to a new position or reshape the end of a curve segment.

   As you drag, the end of the line changes to a small circle, showing that the line is active for modifications; Flash previews the modified segment as you drag (**Figure 4.51**).

4. Release the mouse button.

   Flash redraws the line segment.

To reshape a curve with the selection tool:

1. Position the selection tool's pointer over the middle of an unselected curve segment.

   The curve-point modifier appears.

2. Click and drag the curve to reshape it (**Figure 4.52**).

   Flash previews the curve you're drawing.

3. Release the mouse button.

   Flash redraws the curve.

MODIFYING SHAPES: NATURAL DRAWING TOOLS

To turn a straight-line segment into a curve segment with the selection tool:

1. Position the selection tool's pointer over the middle of an unselected line segment.

   The curve-point modifier appears.

2. Click and drag the line to reshape it (**Figure 4.53**).

   Flash previews the curve that you're drawing.

3. Release the mouse button.

   Flash redraws the line, giving it the curve you defined.

To create a new corner point with the selection tool:

1. Position the selection tool's pointer over the middle of an unselected line or curve segment.

   The curve-point modifier appears.

2. Option-click (Mac) or Alt- or Ctrl-click (Windows).

   After a brief pause, the selection tool's modifier changes to the corner-point modifier, and a circle appears where the pointer intersects the line. You're now activating a corner point.

3. Drag to modify the line or curve segment and add a new corner point (**Figure 4.54**).

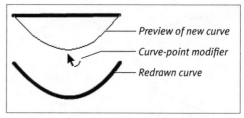

Figure 4.53 Although this line doesn't look curved (top), Flash considers all its middle points to be curve points. Drag one of those points to create a line that looks like a curve (bottom).

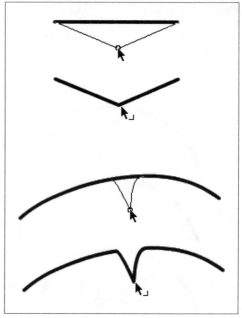

Figure 4.54 Option-click (Mac) or Alt- or Ctrl-click (Windows) to create a new corner point for editing your line. Dragging a corner point from a straight-line segment creates a sharp V (top). Dragging a corner point from a curve creates a V with curving sides that comes to a sharp point (bottom).

Figure 4.55 Use the subselection tool to modify the path of a line segment.

The Mystery of Fill Paths

Although a fill shape without a stroke has no outline, it does have a path that defines its shape. The selection, pen, and subselection tools all work to reshape fill paths just as they do to reshape strokes, as outlined in the tasks in this chapter (**Figure 4.56**).

Figure 4.56 When you position the pointer over the edge of a fill shape, the selection tool displays either the curve-point or corner-point modifier. Clicking the edge of the fill activates a portion of the path outlining the shape (top). Selecting the edge of a fill shape with the subselection tool highlights the full path and its anchor points. You can reposition anchor points and Bézier handles to modify the fill shapes (bottom).

Modifying Shapes: Bézier Tools

The subselection tool lets you see and manipulate the anchor points of a path. You can reposition anchor points to change the path and you can manipulate a point's Bézier handles to modify the slope and depth of the curve. You can add and delete points and convert existing curve points to corner points, or vice versa, with the three anchor-point tools or the pen tool. Flash has two styles for displaying anchor points: hollow (the default) and solid. To pick a style, from the Flash menu (Mac) or the Edit menu (Windows), choose Preferences. In the dialog that appears, from the Category list, choose Drawing. In the Pen Tool section, select/deselect the Show Solid Points check box; click OK.

The tasks in this book assume that Show Solid Points is active.

To view a path and anchor points:

1. In the Tools panel, choose the subselection tool (**Figure 4.55**), or press A.

   The pointer changes to a hollow arrow.

2. On the Stage, click the line or curve you want to modify.

   Flash selects and highlights the path and anchor points. To manipulate a particular point, you must select it directly.

✔ Tip

■ When the subselection tool is selected in the Tools panel, the Select All command—⌘-A (Mac) or Ctrl-A (Windows)—highlights the path and anchor points for all the graphic elements on the Stage and Pasteboard.

To select an anchor point:

1. In the Tools panel, select the subselection tool.

2. Move the subselection pointer over the path you want to modify.

   A small solid square appears next to the hollow arrow when the pointer is above a curve or line segment; a small hollow square appears next to the hollow arrow when the pointer is directly above an anchor point (**Figure 4.57**).

3. Click an anchor point.

   Flash highlights the selected point and displays its Bézier handles.

✔ Tip

■ You can select multiple points on a merge-shape path directly with the sub-selection tool. Draw a selection rectangle that includes the points you want to select. Flash highlights the entire path and selects any points that fall within the rectangle. This technique won't work on paths created as drawing-objects.

To move a corner point:

1. Use the subselection tool to highlight the path and anchor points of the element you want to modify.

2. Position the pointer over a corner point.

3. Click and drag the desired corner point to a new location.

   Flash redraws the path (**Figure 4.58**).

✔ Tip

■ Corner points are often easy to identify without highlighting the path. You can click and drag such points directly without first highlighting the path. If you don't click right on the point, however, you'll move the whole path, not just the intended point.

Figure 4.57 A solid square appears next to the subselection tool when it's ready to select the entire path (top). When a hollow square appears (bottom), the tool is ready to select and manipulate a single anchor point.

Figure 4.58 Using the subselection tool, drag a corner point to reposition it.

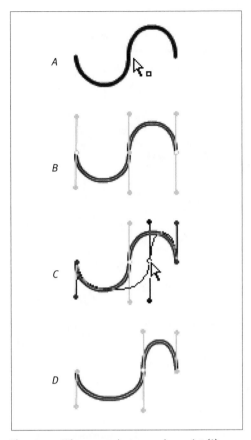

Figure 4.59 When you select an anchor point (A), Flash highlights the entire path (B). You can drag the anchor point to modify the path (C). The path and anchor points remain highlighted when you're done (D).

To move a curve point:

1. Use the subselection tool to highlight the path and anchor points of the element.

2. Position the pointer over a curve point.
   The anchor-point modifier appears.

3. Click and drag the point to a new location (**Figure 4.59**).
   Flash previews the new curve as you drag.
   After you move a curve point, the path remains selected, and the Bézier control handles become active so that you can further manipulate the curve.

To reshape a curve with the Bézier handles:

1. With the subselection tool, click the curve you want to modify.

2. Click one of the anchor points that define the curve you want to modify.
   Bézier handles appear.

3. Click and drag one of the Bézier handles.
   The pointer changes to a solid arrowhead as you drag.

continues on next page

MODIFYING SHAPES: BÉZIER TOOLS

4. To modify the curve, do one or more of the following:

- ▲ To make the curve bulge in the opposite direction, move the Bézier handle past the existing curve, in the opposite direction from the current bulge.

- ▲ To make the curve deeper, position the Bézier handle farther from the anchor point.

- ▲ To make the curve shallower, position the Bézier handle closer to the anchor point.

Flash previews the new curve as you manipulate the Bézier handle (**Figure 4.60**).

✔ Tips

- ■ A curve point that connects two curve segments has two Bézier handles. By default, the handles act in concert as you move them, modifying the curves on either side of the anchor point. You can adjust just one handle (one curve) at a time. Using the subselection tool, press Option (Mac) or Alt (Windows) while dragging the handle. Or, with the anchor point selected and the Bézier handles active, in the Tools panel select the convert–anchor-point tool. Use the caret pointer to drag a handle independently.

- ■ For paths created in Merge Drawing mode, you can select an anchor point and activate its Bézier handles quickly. Use the subselection tool to draw a selection rectangle around the curve you want to modify. Flash highlights the path, selects the curves and the anchor points that fall within the selection, and activates their handles.

- ■ You can move selected anchor points with the arrow keys. To move in larger increments, press the Shift–arrow key.

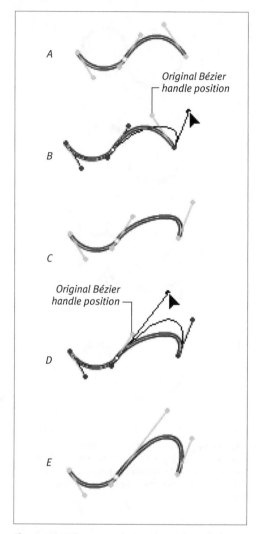

Figure 4.60 When you select anchor points, their Bézier handles appear (A). Leaning a Bézier handle away from a curve (B) makes that curve segment more pronounced (C). Leaning the handle toward the curve flattens that part of the curve. Dragging the Bézier handle away from its anchor point (D) makes the curve deeper (E); dragging the handle toward the anchor point makes the curve shallower.

The Mysterious Modes of the Pen Tool

Flash CS4 has three Bézier tools: add anchor point, delete anchor point, and convert anchor point. The pen tool can perform many of those functions. As you position the pen pointer over the Stage and existing paths, various modifiers appear next to the pen icon, indicating the tool's current function (**Figure 4.61**).

Create initial anchor point. A small x indicates the pen is ready to place the first point in a path. Click any empty spot on the Stage to start your path.

Create sequential points. The pen tool has no modifier when you are in the middle of placing a series of anchor points. Clicking the Stage adds points and segments to the path you are creating.

Add anchor point. A plus sign appears when you position the pointer over a selected path, between anchor points. In this mode, double-clicking the path between two corner points adds a new corner point; double-clicking between two curve points (or between a curve and a corner point) adds a curve point. Single-clicking the path starts a new branching path; click away from the existing path to complete the first segment of the branch.

Convert curve point to corner point. A caret appears when you position the pen pointer over a curve point in a selected path. Click the curve point and it changes to a corner point.

Delete corner point. A minus sign appears when you position the pen pointer over a corner point in a selected path. Click the corner point and Flash removes it.

Extend path. A slash appears when you position the pen pointer over a terminal anchor point (the first or last point in an open path). Clicking the point links the pen tool to that path; now clicking on the Stage creates a new point that extends the existing path.

Close path. A circle appears when you position the pen pointer over the initial anchor point of the path you are currently creating. (The circle modifier also appears if you are using the pen tool to create a merge-shape path and you position the pointer over a terminal anchor point in a different merge-shape path.)

Join drawing-object path. A chain-link icon appears when you are creating a new path, and you position the pen pointer over one of the terminal anchor points in an existing drawing-object path.

Create initial anchor point Create sequential anchor points Add anchor point Convert curve point to corner point Delete corner point Extend path

Close path Join path, merge-shape Join path, drawing-object

Figure 4.61 The pen tool icon changes to reflect what function the tool can perform at any given moment.

To convert a corner point to a curve point:

1. Use the subselection tool to highlight the path and anchor points of the path you want to modify.

2. In the Tools panel, click the current Bézier tool and from the submenu that opens, choose Convert Anchor Point Tool (**Figure 4.62**).

   The pointer changes to an upward-pointing caret.

3. Position the caret pointer over a corner point.

4. To activate Bézier handles, click the point, then drag away.

   Flash converts the corner point to a curve point that has Bézier handles (**Figure 4.63**). As you drag, the handles extend and move, modifying the curve.

✔ Tips

■ You can also use the subselection tool directly to convert a corner point to a curve point. Position the hollow-arrow pointer over a selected corner point, then Option-drag (Mac) or Alt-drag (Windows) away from the point to pull out the Bézier handles.

■ To switch between the Bézier and sub-selection tools quickly, use the keyboard shortcuts: press A for the subselection tool, P for the pen tool, = (equals sign) for the add–anchor-point tool, – (minus sign) for the delete–anchor-point tool, and C for the convert–anchor-point tool.

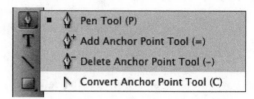

Figure 4.62 Flash has four tools for modifying the anchor points and Bézier curves of a path. Click the current Bézier tool in the Tools panel to access a submenu showing all four.

Figure 4.63 To change a corner point into a curve point (one with Bézier handles) using the convert–anchor-point tool, click (top) and drag a corner point. You pull Bézier handles out of the point instead of relocating the point (middle). When you release the mouse button, Flash redraws the curve (bottom).

Figure 4.64 Clicking a curve point with the convert–anchor-point tool (left) reduces the point to a corner point (right). Flash redraws the path accordingly.

Figure 4.65 Click an anchor point with the delete–anchor-point tool to remove the point. Flash redraws the path accordingly.

✔ Tips

■ To access the delete–anchor-point tool temporarily while using the add–anchor-point tool, hold down the Option key (Mac) or Alt key (Windows).

■ While you can also delete anchor points by selecting them with the subselection tool and pressing Backspace or Delete, the results may surprise you. If the selected anchor point connects two segments, pressing Delete removes the anchor point and reshapes the path. If the anchor point lies at the intersection of three or more segments, however, Flash removes not only the anchor point, but also all the line and curve segments that directly attach to the point. You may wind up removing more than you bargained for.

To convert a curve point to a corner point:

1. Using the subselection tool, select the path you want to modify.

2. In the Tools panel, from the Bézier-tools submenu, select the convert–anchor-point tool.

3. Position the caret pointer over a curve point.

4. Click the curve point.

   Flash converts the curve point to a corner point, removing the Bézier handles and flattening the curved path (**Figure 4.64**).

✔ Tip

■ When using the pen tool, you can access the convert–anchor-point tool temporarily by holding down the Option (Mac) or Alt (Windows) key.

To delete an anchor point:

1. Using the subselection tool, select the path you want to modify.

2. In the Tools panel, click the current Bézier tool, and from the submenu that opens, choose the delete–anchor-point tool.

   The pointer changes to a pen icon with a remove-point modifier (a minus sign).

3. Position the pointer over an anchor point and click.

   Flash removes the anchor point and reshapes the path to connect the remaining points (**Figure 4.65**).

To add a point within a path:

1. Use the subselection tool to select the path you want to modify.

2. In the Tools panel, from the Bézier-tool menu, select the add–anchor-point tool.

   The pointer changes to a pen with a plus-sign modifier.

3. Position the pointer over the path and do any of the following:
   ▲ Click between two corner points to create a new corner point.
   ▲ Click between two curve points to create a new curve point.
   ▲ Click between a corner point and a curve point to create a new curve point.

   Flash adds a new point (**Figure 4.66**).

To extend an existing path:

1. In the Tools panel, from the Bézier-tool submenu, select the pen tool.

2. Position the pointer over the anchor point at either end of the path (a terminal anchor point).

   The continue-path modifier—a small slash—appears next to the pen icon.

3. Click the terminal anchor point.

   The pen links to that point as if you'd just placed it.

4. Click to add points as you learned to do in Chapter 2.

   Note that to create a single unified path, the pen tool and the existing path must be in the same drawing mode. If the existing path is a drawing-object and the pen is set to Merge Drawing mode (or vice versa), Flash places the points, but the segments remain separate.

Figure 4.66 When you position the pen tool between existing anchor points, a small plus sign appears next to the pointer (left). With the plus-sign modifier active, click the path to add a new point (right).

✔ Tips

■ To access the add–anchor-point tool temporarily while using the delete–anchor-point tool, hold down the Option key (Mac) or Alt key (Windows).

■ When the path and the pen tool are in the same drawing mode, you can link the path you are creating to an existing path. Use the pen tool to place the anchor points of your path. When you're ready to link, position the pointer over a terminal anchor point in the path you want to join. One of two modifiers appears next to the pen icon: when the pen is in Merge Drawing mode and you link to a merge-shape path, the close-path modifier (a hollow circle) appears; when the pen is in Drawing Object mode and you link to a drawing-object path, the join-paths modifier (a chain-link icon) appears. Click the existing terminal anchor point, and Flash joins the two merge-shape, or drawing-object, paths.

Figure 4.67 The rectangle-primitive has two control points for the corner radius of each corner. When the corner radius is set to 0, the corner is a sharp 90-degree angle, and the control points sit directly on top of one another.

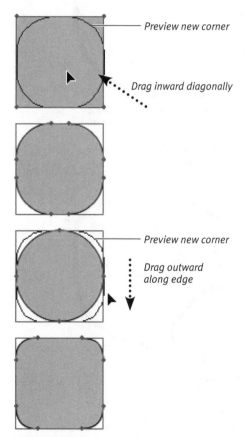

Figure 4.68 As the corner radius increases, two control points appear at the end of the arc defining the corner. Drag inward to round the corner more, outward to round it less.

Modifying Primitive-Shape Paths

Flash's rectangle- and oval-primitive tools create shapes whose paths are defined by a set of properties specific to that shape. You can't change the outline of a primitive-shape freely the way you can reshape the outline of a merge-shape or drawing-object. You can change the primitive's defining properties by dragging control points in the shape or by setting new values for those properties in the Property inspector.

To change a rectangle-primitive's properties interactively:

1. Using the selection or subselection tool, on the Stage select the rectangle-primitive you want to modify.

   The shape's bounding box highlights, and control points appear (**Figure 4.67**). Each corner has two control points. For sharp corners with a corner-radius setting of 0, the points sit directly on top of one another; for rounded corners, a control point appears at either end of the arc that defines the corner. The two points work in concert; dragging one moves the other.

2. Position the pointer over one of the control points.

   The pointer changes to a small solid arrow.

3. To modify the shape, do one of the following:

   ▲ To increase the radius (make the corner more rounded), drag the point inward.

   ▲ To decrease the radius (make the corner less rounded), drag the point outward.

   You can drag diagonally toward (or away from) the center of a shape, or you can drag vertically or horizontally toward (or away from) the center of the edge containing the control point (**Figure 4.68**).

✔ Tip

■ By default, Flash constrains the corner-radius settings so that all four corners of a rectangle-primitive have the same degree of roundness. To create corners with various degrees of roundness, select the rectangle-primitive, access the Rectangle Options section of the Rectangle Primitive Tool Property inspector, and click the Constrain Corner Radius button to change to the unlinked state (the open-link icon). You can then drag the control points for each corner independently, creating a variety of shapes (**Figure 4.69**).

To change a rectangle-primitive's properties precisely:

1. With the rectangle-primitive selected on the Stage, access the Rectangle Options section of the Rectangle Primitive Property inspector.

2. To modify the shape, in the Rectangle Corner Radius fields, do one of the following:

   ▲ To create rounded corners, enter positive values.

   ▲ To create indented corners, enter negative values.

   For more details about setting the values of the various properties for rectangle-primitives, see Chapter 2.

✔ Tip

■ You can't change a square or rounded corner to an indented corner by dragging the control points; you must set a negative value in the Property inspector. Once the rectangle-primitive has an indented corner, however, you can drag its control points to adjust the size of the indent (**Figure 4.70**).

Figure 4.69 With the Constrain Corner Radius button set to the unlinked state (open-link icon), you can enter values for each corner separately to create a variety of shapes.

Figure 4.70 Dragging the control points of an indented corner (one with a corner radius value less than 0) changes the size of the indent. If you drag all the way back to a sharp corner, however, the control points revert to creating rounded corners as you drag. To get another indented corner, you must enter a negative value in the Property inspector.

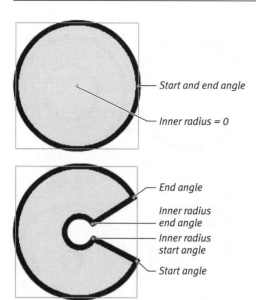

Figure 4.71 An oval-primitive has control points that control the start angle and end angle for the outer and inner oval shapes.

Figure 4.72 Drag the control points on the outer edge of an oval-primitive clockwise or counterclockwise to change the start and end angle of the shape.

To change an oval-primitive's properties interactively:

1. Using the selection or subselection tool, on the Stage select the oval-primitive you want to modify.

   The shape's bounding box highlights, and control points appear. Oval-primitives have four control points: one pair for the start and end angle of the outer oval and another pair for the start and end angle of the inner oval (**Figure 4.71**). When the start angle and end angle of an oval have the same value, the control points lie directly on top of one another.

2. Position the pointer over a control point.

   The pointer changes to a solid arrow.

3. To modify the shape, do any of the following:

   ▲ To change the start angle, drag the control point clockwise or counter-clockwise around the perimeter of the oval (**Figure 4.72**).

   ▲ To change the end angle, drag the control point clockwise or counter-clockwise around the perimeter of the oval.

continues on next page

▲ To increase the inner radius (to create a larger space inside the oval), drag outward (**Figure 4.73**).

▲ To decrease the inner radius (to create a smaller space inside the oval), drag inward.

To change an oval-primitive's properties precisely:

1. With the oval-primitive selected on the Stage, access the Oval Options section of the Oval Primitive Property inspector.

2. In the Start Angle, End Angle, or Inner Radius fields, enter new values.

   For more details about setting the values of the various properties for oval-primitives, see Chapter 2.

✔ Tip

■ Although you can't alter the paths of primitives to create fanciful free-form shapes, you can use a primitive as the starting point from which to create a shape whose paths can be modified freely. After you set the primitive's properties, convert the shape to a merge-shape or drawing-object (see "Converting Shape Types," later in this chapter). Then modify the merge-shape or drawing-object using any of the techniques discussed earlier in this chapter.

Preview larger inner radius

Preview smaller inner radius

Figure 4.73 Drag the control points on the inner edge of an oval-primitive to resize the radius of the inner oval: Drag toward the center of the shape to close down the opening in the middle of the shape; drag away from the center to open up a bigger space.

Modifying Shapes with the Eraser Tool

Flash's eraser tool lets you modify merge-shapes and drawing-objects by deleting parts of fills and strokes. (The eraser tool doesn't work on primitive-shapes, except in its Faucet mode.) To use the eraser tool, click and scrub on the Stage, as you'd rub an eraser over a piece of paper.

The eraser tool has five modes; you select one from the Eraser Mode menu in the Tools panel. The eraser modes govern how the tool interacts with fills and strokes. For simple shapes on a single layer, Erase Normal is a good setting; it enables the eraser tool to remove any line or fill you drag over. The other eraser modes limit what the tool affects. In Erase Fills, the tool affects only fills; in Erase Lines, the tool affects only strokes; in Erase Selected Fills, the tool erases only from fills that have been selected; and in Erase Inside, the tool affects only the fill in which you begin an erasure. These modes become important when you work with complex graphics that have multiple elements (see Chapter 5).

Another eraser option is the Faucet modifier. The faucet speeds removal of strokes and fills for any type of shape. Clicking a deselected stroke with the eraser in Faucet mode deletes all the segments that make up that stroke. In a selection containing multiple merge-shape strokes and/or fills, clicking any of the selected items with the faucet deletes the entire selection. In a selection containing multiple drawing-objects or primitive-shapes, however, the faucet deletes the individual fills or strokes you click, one at a time. (Undoing changes for primitives is a bit unreliable.)

In addition, the Faucet mode overrides the complex eraser-mode settings. For example, with the eraser set to Erase Lines, you can't scrub to erase a fill; but without changing the Erase Lines setting, you can choose the Faucet mode and then click a fill to erase it.

The eraser tool's quickest trick is to clear the decks completely. Double-click the eraser tool in the Tools panel to delete the entire contents of the Stage.

Converting Shape Types

Flash offers a variety of shape types: fills, strokes, merge-shapes, drawing-objects, primitives, and text. It's possible to convert some types of shapes into others. For example, you can convert strokes to fills; you can convert merge-shapes to drawing-objects and vice versa; you can convert primitive-shapes to merge-shapes and drawing-objects; and you can convert text, a special type of fill, to a regular merge-shape fill. You cannot, however, convert merge-shapes or drawing-objects to primitive-shapes.

To convert a stroke to a fill:

1. Select a stroke on the Stage.

2. Choose Modify > Shape > Convert Lines to Fills (**Figure 4.74**).

   Flash converts the stroke to a fill shape that looks exactly like the stroke. You can now edit the path of the "stroke's" outline as though you were working with a fill created with the brush tool (**Figure 4.75**).

Figure 4.74 To transform strokes into fills, choose Modify > Shape > Convert Lines to Fills.

Figure 4.75 You can convert a stroke, such as this line drawn with the pencil tool (top), to a fill. The fill's outline then has its own editable path (middle and bottom).

The Mystery of Text Fills

Flash considers text to be a type of fill, but the letterforms don't act like fill shapes you sketch with the drawing tools. The letter shapes are unified as text within a container that acts as a single graphic-object. Flash lets you *break apart* text—that is, divide one text block containing multiple editable characters into multiple text blocks, each containing one editable character. This feature lets you scale, reposition, or distort individual letters. The ability to place letters in separate text fields also comes in handy for animating text. (You learn more about animation techniques in Chapters 8–13.) These single-letter text fields are still graphic-objects, however. To convert text fills to true merge-shape fills, you must break them apart twice: once to get them into separate text fields, then a second time to convert each letter to a merge-shape. This technique is useful when you have a small amount of text that you can't (or don't want to) supply to every end user, but you need to ensure the text looks exactly the same in the finished product as it did during the authoring phase.

Selected merge-shape
(fill and stroke)

Converted to
drawing-object

Figure 4.76 Choose Modify > Combine Objects > Union to convert the shape selected on the Stage into a drawing-object.

Figure 4.77 Choose Modify > Break Apart to convert a drawing-object or primitive-shape to a merge-shape.

To convert a merge-shape or a primitive to a drawing-object:

1. Select a merge-shape or primitive-shape on the Stage.

2. Choose Modify > Combine Objects > Union.

   Flash converts the selected shape to a drawing-object; it remains selected (**Figure 4.76**).

✔ Tip

- The Modify > Combine Shapes commands (Union, Intersect, Punch, and Chop) work on multiple, selected drawing-objects and primitives; the last three commands work on overlapping drawing-objects or primitives. In effect, these commands convert the drawing-objects or primitives to merge-shapes (so that they interact) and then convert the resulting shape(s) back into a drawing-object. Note that primitives lose their status as primitives once you combine them. You'll learn more about combining shapes in Chapter 5.

To convert a drawing-object or a primitive to a merge-shape:

1. Select a drawing-object or primitive-shape on the Stage.

2. Choose Modify > Break Apart, or press ⌘-B (Mac) or Ctrl-B (Windows) (**Figure 4.77**).

   Flash converts the selected drawing-object or primitive-shape to a merge-shape; it remains selected.

CONVERTING SHAPE TYPES

To divide a text block into single-letter text fields:

1. Select a text block on the Stage.

2. Choose Modify > Break Apart (**Figure 4.78**).

   Flash places each letter in its own text field and selects all the text fields. Each text field is just wide enough to hold one letter. Each letter is fully editable on its own, although the group is no longer linked.

To transform letters into merge-shapes:

1. Follow the steps in the preceding task to place letters in individual text fields.

2. Choose Modify > Break Apart.

   This second Break Apart command transforms the editable letters into raw shapes on the Stage (**Figure 4.79**). You can edit them as you would any other fill, but you can no longer change their text attributes with the text tool.

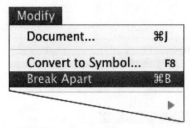

Figure 4.78 Choose Modify > Break Apart to place each letter of a text block in its own text field.

Figure 4.79 Applying the Break Apart command once transforms selected text (top) into single-letter text fields (middle); applying the command again creates merge-shapes out of the individual letters (bottom).

COMPLEX GRAPHICS ON A SINGLE LAYER

In Chapters 2 and 4, you learned to make and modify simple individual shapes from strokes (lines) and fills by using Adobe Flash CS4 Professional's drawing tools. In your movies, you'll want to use many shapes together, and you'll need to combine strokes and fills in complex ways. You might combine several shapes, such as ovals and rectangles, to create a robot character, for example. To work effectively with complex graphics, you must understand how multiple graphic elements—merge-shapes, drawing objects, and primitive-shapes—interact when they're on the same layer or on different layers. In this chapter, you learn how to work with multiple graphic elements on one layer in a Flash document. (To learn more about the concept of layers, see Chapter 6.)

Two of Flash's drawing tools—the brush tool and the eraser—offer special modes for use with multiple fills and strokes on a single layer. In this chapter, unless you're specifically requested to do otherwise, leave both tools at their default settings of Paint Normal (for the brush tool) and Erase Normal (for the eraser).

When Merge-Shapes Interact

You can think of each frame in a Flash movie as being a stack of transparent acetate sheets. In Flash terms, each sheet is a layer. Graphics on different layers have a depth relationship: items on higher layers block your view of items on lower layers, just as a drawing on the top sheet of acetate would obscure drawings on lower sheets.

Imagine you have two layers in your movie. If you draw a little yellow square on the bottom layer, then switch to the top layer and draw a big red square directly over the yellow one, the little square remains intact, but you can't see it. The square on the top layer is in the way.

On a single layer in Flash, however, merge-shapes interact with one another, almost as though you were painting with wet finger paint. Here's a quick rundown of how lines (strokes) and shapes (fills) created in Merge Drawing mode interact within a single layer.

When Merge-Shape Lines Intersect

Intersecting merge-shape lines drawn on the same layer affect one another. Draw one line in Merge Drawing mode, and then draw a second line that intersects the first. The second line cuts—or, in Flash terminology, *segments*—the first. Segmentation happens whether the lines are the same color or different colors, but it's easiest to see with contrasting colors (**Figure 5.1**).

You might expect that the second line you drew would wind up on top of the first, but sometimes that's not the case. Start with a red line, and then draw a blue line across it; the blue line jumps *behind* the red one when you release the mouse button. Flash creates a stacking order for merge-shape lines based on the hex-color value of the line's stroke-color setting. The higher the hex value of the stroke color, the higher the line sits in a stack of merge-shape lines drawn in one layer. A merge-shape line whose stroke color is set to a hex value of 663399 always winds up on top of one whose stroke color is set to 333399.

continues on next page

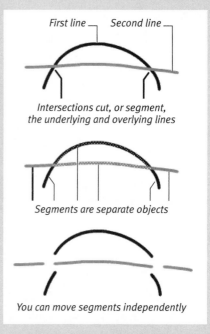

First line ⎯ *Second line* ⎯

Intersections cut, or segment, the underlying and overlying lines

Segments are separate objects

You can move segments independently

Figure 5.1 When you draw one line across another in Merge Drawing mode, every intersection creates a separate segment.

When Merge-Shapes Interact *continued*

When Merge-Shape Lines and Fills Intersect

A fill that has no stroke still has a path (the invisible outline that describes the fill shape). When you work in Merge Drawing mode, fill paths can cut the strokes of other shapes. When you place merge-shape lines over merge-shape fills, you can wind up with lots of little segments. Try drawing lines (strokes) with the pencil tool and arcs (fills) with the brush tool; set the tools to Merge Drawing mode. If you paint a fill that intersects a stroke, the fill remains one solid object, but the stroke gets segmented (**Figure 5.2**). If you draw a stroke that intersects a fill, the stroke cuts the fill, and the path of the fill cuts the stroke (**Figure 5.3**).

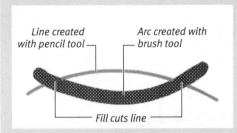

Figure 5.2 When a merge-shape fill overlays a merge-shape stroke, the fill segments the stroke. As the selection highlighting shows, the fill remains one solid object.

Figure 5.3 When a merge-shape line overlays a merge-shape fill, the line's path cuts the fill, and the fill's path cuts the line.

When Merge-Shape Fills Intersect

When intersecting fills created in Merge Drawing mode are the same color, the newer fill adds to the merge-shape (**Figure 5.4**).

When fills of different colors interact, the newer fill replaces the older one where the two overlap (**Figure 5.5**).

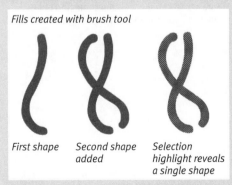

Figure 5.4 When you draw overlapping fills in the same color in Merge Drawing mode, Flash puts the two shapes together to create a single merge-shape.

Figure 5.5 When one merge-shape fill overlaps another of a different color, the fills don't meld but remain separate. The second oval here replaces the first where they overlap.

Working with Groups

A *group* is a type of virtual container that holds graphic elements. Groups serve several functions. They prevent selected merge-shapes from interacting. They also lock down the attributes of shapes and preserve spatial relationships among graphic elements. Although you can also group drawing-objects and primitive-shapes, for the tasks in this section you want to see the interaction with merge-shapes; make sure the Object Drawing button in the Tools panel is deselected.

To create a group:

1. Select one or more items on the Stage using any of the methods discussed in Chapter 4 (**Figure 5.6**).

2. Choose Modify > Group, or press ⌘-G (Mac) or Ctrl-G (Windows).

   Flash groups the items, placing them within a bounding box (**Figure 5.7**). The visible bounding box lets you know that the group is selected. When the group isn't selected, the bounding box is hidden.

✔ Tip

■ If you choose Modify > Group when nothing is selected, you immediately enter group-editing mode: anything you draw on the Stage is part of a new group.

To return objects to ungrouped status:

1. Select the group that you want to return to ungrouped status.

2. Choose Modify > Ungroup, or press Shift-⌘-G (Mac) or Ctrl-Shift-G (Windows).

   Flash removes the bounding box and selects all the items.

Figure 5.6 The first step in grouping is selecting the shapes you want to use in the group.

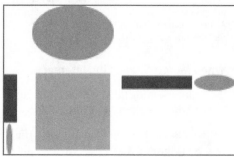

Figure 5.7 The Modify > Group command unites multiple selected shapes within a single bounding box.

WORKING WITH GROUPS

✔ Tips

- The command for breaking apart symbols (Modify > Break Apart or ⌘-B [Mac] or Ctrl-B [Windows]) also works to ungroup groups.

- Interactions between strokes and fills occur not only when you draw a shape but also when you place a copy of a shape or move a shape. Be careful when placing copies of merge-shape fills and strokes on a single layer; you can inadvertently add to or delete part of an underlying merge-shape. If you ungroup a grouped shape that overlaps merge-shapes on a single layer, the shapes will segment one another.

Preventing Interactions

Shapes created in Merge Drawing mode act as if their paint is still wet. Here are some ways to "dry" the paint and prevent interactions.

Drawing-objects. In Drawing Object mode, the drawing tools create merge-shapes, but Flash isolates them inside a container. Fills and strokes inside the drawing-object container don't interact with fills and strokes outside the container, but you can modify the path and the fill and stroke attributes of a drawing-object directly on the Stage (see Chapter 4). You can also open a drawing-object container to work with its merge-shape contents directly.

Primitive-shapes. The rectangle- and oval-primitive tools create drawing-objects with specific properties that define the shape. Flash places those drawing-objects inside a more restrictive, primitive container. Primitive fills and strokes don't interact with fills and strokes outside the container. You can modify the fill and stroke attributes of a primitive directly, using the paint-bucket and ink-bottle tools. You can modify the defining properties of the shape (such as the corner radius for rectangle-primitives) using the selection tool and the primitive's control points, but you can't freely modify the shape's outline. You can open a primitive's container, to modify the drawing-object inside, but doing so converts the shape to a drawing-object permanently.

Groups. When you group selected fills and strokes, they stop interacting with other fills and strokes. Grouped items also stop being directly editable. To modify any attributes of the shapes in a group, you must enter a special editing mode.

Symbols. Fills and strokes inside symbols don't interact with fills and strokes of other graphic elements. Symbols also require editing in a special mode (see Chapter 7).

Layers. Placing merge-shapes on separate layers prevents them from interacting (see Chapter 6).

To prevent interaction between merge-shapes on one layer:

1. In the Tools panel, choose the oval tool in Merge Drawing mode.

2. Set the stroke color to No Color and the fill color to red.

3. On the Stage, draw a fairly large oval (**Figure 5.8**).

4. In the Tools panel, switch to the selection tool, and select the oval you just drew.

5. To make the oval a grouped element, Choose Modify > Group (**Figure 5.9**).

6. Deselect the grouped oval.

7. In the Tools panel, choose the oval tool and a different fill color.

8. On the Stage, draw a smaller oval in the middle of your first oval (**Figure 5.10**).

    When you finish drawing the new oval, it immediately disappears behind the grouped oval (**Figure 5.11**). Grouped objects always stack on top of ungrouped objects (see the sidebar "Understanding Stacking Order," later in this chapter).

9. Switch to the selection tool, and reposition the large oval so that you can see the small one (**Figure 5.12**).

10. Deselect the large oval, and select the small oval (**Figure 5.13**).

11. To make the small oval a grouped element, Choose Modify > Group.

    Flash puts the small oval in a bounding box and brings it to the top of the stack (**Figure 5.14**). The most recently created group is always on the top of the stack. Now the two ovals won't interact.

Figure 5.8
The oval before grouping.

Figure 5.9
The oval after grouping.

Figure 5.10
Draw a second oval on top of the grouped oval.

Figure 5.11
The ungrouped oval stacks beneath the grouped oval.

Figure 5.12
Drag the grouped oval to make the ungrouped oval visible.

Figure 5.13
Select the small oval.

Figure 5.14
After grouping, the small oval—the most recently created group—pops to the top of the stack.

Document-editing mode

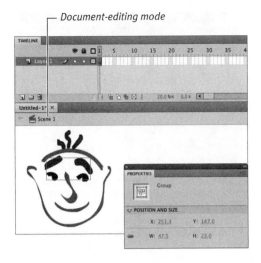

Click the Back button to return
to document-editing mode

Click the scene name to return
to document-editing mode

Group-editing mode

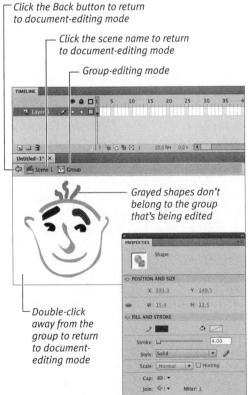

Grayed shapes don't
belong to the group
that's being edited

Double-click
away from the
group to return
to document-
editing mode

Figure 5.15 The eyes and eyebrows are a selected group (top). In group-editing mode (bottom), the selected shapes are ready to edit; the other items on the Stage are grayed out to indicate that you can't edit them.

Editing Groups

Although you can transform a group as a whole (scale, rotate, and skew it), you can't directly edit the individual shapes within the group the way you can edit an ungrouped shape. To edit the shapes within a group, use the Edit Selected command.

To edit the contents of a group:

1. In the Tools panel, choose the selection tool.

2. On the Stage, select the group you want to edit.

3. Choose Edit > Edit Selected.

   Flash enters group-editing mode (**Figure 5.15**). The Edit bar just above the Stage changes to indicate that you're in group-editing mode. The bounding box for the selected group disappears, and Flash dims all the items on the Stage that aren't part of the selected group. These dimmed items aren't editable; they merely provide context for editing the selected group.

4. Make changes to the contents of the group.

5. To return to document-editing mode, do one of the following:

   ▲ Choose Edit > Edit All.

   ▲ Double-click an empty area of the Stage or the Pasteboard.

   ▲ Click the current scene name in the Edit bar.

   ▲ Click the Back button in the Edit bar.

✔ Tips

- To enter group-editing mode quickly, double-click a grouped item on the Stage with the selection tool.

- When the Property inspector is open, you can use it to modify the *x*- and *y*-coordinates and the height and width of a selected group's bounding box (**Figure 5.16**).

- When you're editing a group nested within another group, clicking the Back button moves you up one level in the nesting hierarchy.

- You can also enter group-editing mode for a selected item by choosing Edit > Edit in Place. When you edit groups, there is no difference between this command and Edit > Edit Selected. There is a difference when you use these commands to edit symbols. (You'll learn about symbols in Chapter 7.)

Figure 5.16 The Position and Size section of the Group Property inspector contains hot text for adjusting the x- and y-coordinates and the height and width of the bounding box of a group you've selected on the Stage. Enter new values to change any of those parameters.

Editing Inside the Drawing-Object Container

As you learned in Chapter 4, you can modify drawing-objects directly as they sit on the Stage (in essence reaching through the drawing-object container). But you can also work directly with the merge-shapes inside the container. To do so, you must open the container and work in drawing-object–editing mode. There is no menu command for entering this edit mode, but double-clicking a drawing-object on the Stage opens that object's container so you can edit the contents. (Note that double-clicking a primitive-shape brings up a dialog that lets you convert the primitive to a drawing-object and open its container for editing the contents.)

In drawing-object–editing mode—as in group-editing mode—selected shapes appear in full color, and other shapes appear dimmed. In drawing-object–editing mode, you can modify or delete the original merge-shapes or add new shapes. Note that the contents of a drawing-object must be merge-shapes. You can create new drawing-objects or primitives while you work in drawing-object–editing mode, but when you return to document-editing mode, Flash converts your original drawing-object to its constituent merge shapes, adds the new drawing-object(s) or primitive(s), selects all these items, and turns them into a group.

To return to document-editing mode, you use the same techniques as when editing a group (for example, click the Back button in the Edit bar).

Controlling Stacking Order

Within a single layer, text fields, grouped objects, drawing-objects, and primitives stack as if they were sitting on sublayers above any ungrouped merge-shapes. Stacking order exists even if objects don't literally lie on top of one another. If you have a group on one side of the Stage and a drawing-object on the other, you can't see which one stacks higher than the other; but if you drag the objects so they overlap, the order becomes apparent. (Symbols, which you'll learn about in Chapter 7, are another type of graphic-object that stacks on top of ungrouped merge-shapes.)

Understanding Stacking Order

Merge-shapes on a single layer always stay on the same layer, segmenting one another whenever they inhabit the same space on the Stage. All graphic-objects (drawing-objects, primitives, text fields, groups, and symbols) stack on top of one another. By default, Flash stacks each new graphic-object that you create on top of the preceding one; the last graphic-object created winds up on top of all the others (**Figure 5.17**). A higher-level graphic-object obscures any graphic-object that lies directly beneath it.

Primitive-shape created 7th

Drawing-object created 6th

Text field created 5th

Group created 4th

Primitive-shape created 2nd

Merge-shape created 1st

Merge-shape created 3rd

Figure 5.17 This schematic shows Flash's default stacking order for graphic-objects. The most recently created graphic-object is on top. Merge-shapes are always on the bottom.

You can change the stacking order of graphic-objects via the Modify > Arrange menu. You can move objects up or down in the stacking order one level at a time, or you can send an object to the top or bottom of the stack of sublayers.

To change position in a stack by one level:

1. On the Stage, create at least three graphic-objects.

   Use any combination of grouped shapes, drawing-objects, primitives, or text fields.

2. Select one of the graphic-objects.

3. From the Modify > Arrange menu, choose either of the following:

   ▲ To move the selected item up one level, choose Bring Forward, or press ⌘–up arrow (Mac) or Ctrl–up arrow (Windows).

   ▲ To move the selected item down one level, choose Send Backward, or press ⌘–down arrow (Mac) or Ctrl–down arrow (Windows).

   Flash moves the selected item up (or down) one sublayer in the stacking order (**Figure 5.18**).

To move an element to the top or bottom of the stack:

1. On the Stage, select one of the graphic-objects you created in the previous task.

2. From the Modify > Arrange menu, choose either of the following:

   ▲ To bring the item to the top of the stack, choose Bring to Front, or press Option-Shift–up arrow (Mac) or Ctrl-Shift–up arrow (Windows).

   ▲ To move the item to the bottom of the stack, choose Send to Back, or press Option-Shift–down arrow (Mac) or Ctrl-Shift–down arrow (Windows).

   Flash places the selected item at the top (or bottom) of the heap.

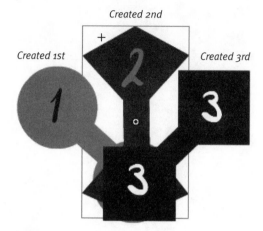

Created 1st · Created 2nd · Created 3rd

Figure 5.18 Each dumbbell-like shape here is a separate group (top). Choose Modify > Arrange > Bring Forward (middle) to move a selected group up one level in the stacking order (bottom).

Figure 5.19 Applying the Modify > Combine Objects > Union command to drawing-object or primitive-shape fills of the same color (left) melds the fills and creates a single drawing-object (right).

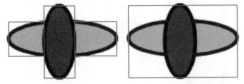

Figure 5.20 Applying the Modify > Combine Objects > Union command to drawing-objects (or primitive-shapes) of different colors (left) causes the selected fills and strokes to replace and segment one another as merge-shapes would. The resulting shapes unite in a single drawing-object (right).

Figure 5.21 Try double-clicking the new drawing-object after you've applied Union to drawing-objects (or primitives) of different colors. In drawing-object–editing mode, you can see how the shapes segment one another. Each chunk of stroke and fill is a separate shape.

Combining Drawing-Objects and Primitives

Drawing-objects and primitive-shapes don't interact with one another or with merge-shapes, even when they overlap. You can force them to interact by using the Modify > Combine Objects commands. Flash converts combined primitives to drawing-objects.

To unite multiple drawing-objects or primitives:

1. Use the drawing tools in Object Drawing mode, or the rectangle- or oval-primitive tools, to create overlapping shapes:

   ▲ Make two or more overlapping fills with the same colors.

   ▲ Make two or more overlapping shapes with fills and strokes; use different colors for the fills and strokes in each shape.

2. Select the overlapping fills that are the same color.

3. Choose Modify > Combine Objects > Union.

   The two fills become a single drawing-object shape (**Figure 5.19**).

4. Select the overlapping shapes of different colors.

5. Repeat step 3.

   The fills and strokes of the shapes segment one another, but you wind up with a single drawing-object containing all those segmented shapes (**Figure 5.20**).

✔ Tips

■ You can also use the Modify > Combine Objects > Union command to combine a mix of merge-shapes, drawing-objects, and primitives into a single drawing-object.

■ To access and edit merge-shapes inside a drawing-object, double-click it (**Figure 5.21**).

To use one drawing-object to remove part of another:

1. Use the drawing tools in Object Drawing mode, or the rectangle- or oval-primitive tools, to create two or more overlapping shapes with a variety of fills and strokes.

2. From the Modify > Combine Objects menu, choose one of the following:

   Intersect retains fills and strokes only where all the selected shapes overlap, and deletes all other fills and strokes. The resulting shape(s) take stroke and fill attributes from the topmost shape.

   Punch uses the topmost shape like a cookie cutter to remove any shapes directly below it. (Imagine the shape left in the cookie dough after you've cut out a cookie; that's what Punch creates.) The resulting shape(s) retain their original attributes.

   Crop uses the topmost shape like a cookie cutter to select a new shape from any shapes that lie below it. (Imagine the cookie cutter again, but this time you wind up with the cookie itself.) The resulting shape(s) retain their original attributes (**Figure 5.22**).

✔ Tips

- When you select merge-shapes, the Modify > Combine Objects menu only offers the Union command. You can use this command instead of grouping merge-shapes. The Union command preserves the spatial relationships between shapes but gives you the ability to change fills and strokes directly on the Stage as described in Chapter 4.

- If you choose Modify > Combine Objects > Intersect and all your shapes disappear, it means there was no place where they all intersected. That result may seem self-evident, but if you've selected many shapes or your shapes are complex, it may be difficult to see.

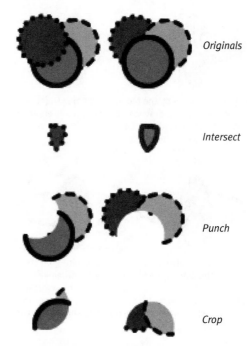

Originals

Intersect

Punch

Crop

Figure 5.22 The last three commands in the Modify > Combine Objects menu have different results depending on which object lies on top of the stack. The Intersect command creates a new shape from the intersection of all selected shapes, using the top shape's attributes. With Punch, the top shape takes a bite out of the others and removes it; the remaining shapes keep their original attributes. With Crop, the top shape takes the same bite but this time removes everything else; the resulting shapes keep their original attributes.

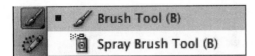

Figure 5.23 The spray-brush tool is located in the same submenu as the brush tool.

Creating Patterns

Flash CS4 introduces two tools for creating patterns: the spray-brush and deco tools. The spray brush creates a random dot pattern as you move the tool over the Stage. The deco tool fills an area with a pattern. Once you finish filling an area, Flash selects the elements that make up the pattern and groups them. In the following tasks, you use the tools to create simple patterns in default merge-shapes. The tools can also create more-complex patterns, and can use custom elements (see the sidebar "Customizing Patterns").

To paint a random dot pattern:

1. In the tools panel, click the active brush tool.

2. From the submenu that appears, select the spray bush tool (**Figure 5.23**).

3. To set parameters for the pattern element, access the Symbol section of the Spray Brush Tool Property inspector and do the following:

   ▲ Select the Default Shape check box. The default shape is a small, black dot.

   ▲ To change the dot color, click the color control to access the pop-up swatch set and select a new color.

   ▲ To change the dot size, use the Scale hot text to enter a percentage between 0 and 40,000. Click the hot text to enter a precise value; drag the hot text's invisible slider to choose a value interactively. Flash previews the changes on the Stage as you drag the hot text's invisible slider.

   ▲ To use dots of random sizes, select the Random Scaling check box.

   continues on next page

Customizing Patterns

The tasks in this section use the pattern-creation tools at a basic level, creating random dots with the spray brush, and a grid of squares with the deco tool. The deco tool can also create more intricate patterns, such as a sinuous vine with leaves and flowers. You adjust the parameters of all the patterns in the Property inspector. Although you can't create new underlying patterns, you can create new pattern elements. You might, for example, set the spray-brush tool to spew forth stars instead of dots, or set the deco tool to make a grid out of flapping birds. To use different pattern elements, deselect the Default Shape check box (or click the Edit button) in the appropriate section of the Property inspector. A dialog appears displaying the symbols currently in your document; choose a symbol to be the new element (you'll learn about creating symbols in Chapter 7).

CREATING PATTERNS

4. To modify the brush's shape (to change the shape of the "nozzle" through which the pattern elements get "sprayed"), access the Brush section of the Property inspector (**Figure 5.24**) and use the hot-text controls to specify new values for any of the following:

▲ *Width* specifies how wide the nozzle is.

▲ *Height* specifies how tall the nozzle is.

The range of possible values for width and height is based on the dimensions of the Flash document. In one that is 550 by 400 pixels, for example, spray-brush width ranges from 0 to 550 pixels, height from 0 to 400 pixels (**Figure 5.25**).

▲ *Brush Angle* determines how the nozzle orients itself in space. Acceptable values are 0 to 360 (**Figure 5.26**).

5. Move the pointer over the Stage.

The pointer turns into a spray can.

6. Click and drag.

As you move the pointer, Flash adds more dots radiating away from the pointer location according to the settings you chose in step 4. Dragging slowly places dots close together; dragging quickly spreads dots out more.

7. Release the mouse button.

Flash combines all the shapes it just created into a single group.

✔ Tip

■ If the dot pattern seems too light, or too light in some areas, after you finish spraying, you can spray over the area again, starting in a different place. To avoid creating lots of separate spray-brush groups, double-click the initial group of sprayed dots to enter group-editing mode, then do your additional spray brushing inside the group.

Figure 5.24 The Spray Brush Tool Property inspector lets you set how the tool creates its spray pattern. You can also set the tool to use your own symbols.

Figure 5.25 When setting the Width and Height values for the spray brush, think of using a spray bottle. Smaller values close down the "nozzle" to create a narrower spay; larger ones open it up. With a width of 1 and a height of 20, Flash lays down the dots in a single line as you draw vertically, but lays down a swatch roughly 20 pixels across when you draw horizontally.

Figure 5.26 Choosing unequal values for width and height creates an elliptical spray-brush "nozzle." The Brush Angle setting lets you rotate that ellipse (as you might tilt a real calligraphy pen with a wide nib), so that the brush creates thick and thin areas as you paint.

Figure 5.27 To create patterns that fill the Stage or a shape, select the deco tool.

Figure 5.28 The deco tool offers three patterns to choose from: Vine Fill, Grid Fill, and Symmetry Brush. Select one from the pop-up menu in the Drawing Effect section of the Property inspector. Choosing Grid Fill and selecting the Default Shape check box creates a grid pattern using squares.

To fill space with a repeating grid:

1. In the tools panel, select the deco tool, or press U (**Figure 5.27**).

2. Access the Drawing Effect section of the Property inspector, and from the pop-up menu, choose Grid Fill (**Figure 5.28**).

   Flash CS4 comes with three Drawing Effects: Vine Fill, Grid Fill, and Symmetry Brush. In Grid Fill mode, the deco tool lays down a regular pattern of squares to create a grid that fills the Stage or a shape.

3. Click the Default Shape check box (**Figure 5.29**).

   The default shape is a small, black square.

4. To change the square's color, click the Color control to access the pop-up swatch set and select a new color.

5. To set the grid's parameters, access the Advanced Options section of the Property inspector (**Figure 5.30**) and use the hot text to enter values for any of the following:

   continues on next page

Figure 5.29 Use the Deco Tool Property inspector to set parameters for the pattern elements.

Figure 5.30 To change the attributes of the grid's default square, access the Advanced Options section of the Deco Tool Property inspector.

▲ *Horizontal Spacing* sets the amount of horizontal space between squares in the grid.

▲ *Vertical Spacing* sets the amount of vertical space between squares in the grid.

▲ *Pattern Scale* sets the size of the grid pattern as a whole. Larger percentages increase the size of the squares as well as the amount of space between them; smaller percentages decrease the size and space.

6. Position the pointer over the Stage.

The pointer turns into a paint bucket spilling squares.

7. To fill the Stage with the grid pattern, click a blank area of the Stage.

Flash creates a grid of squares that fills the Stage. If graphic objects already exist on the Stage, Flash places the squares only in the empty space around the existing objects (**Figure 5.31**).

or

To fill a shape with the grid pattern, click within the shape (**Figure 5.32**).

Flash places the squares to fill as much of the shape as possible. Flash combines the squares of the grid into a single group.

✔ Tips

■ The grid is a group; double-click it to enter group-editing mode. In group-editing mode, you can modify the grid elements individually.

■ You can fill a shape that already has a fill; simply click within the filled shape. The deco-pattern group winds up above the shape's fill and stroke in the stacking order.

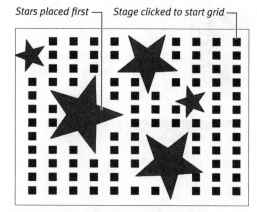

Stars placed first —⏐ *Stage clicked to start grid* —⏐

Figure 5.31 When you click a blank area of the Stage, the deco tool fills all blank areas with the grid. The pattern flows around any graphic elements already on the Stage.

Figure 5.32 Click the deco tool within a shape to fill the shape with the current deco pattern.

■ The deco tool places only whole grid elements. When filling a circle shape with a grid of squares, for example, the deco tool leaves out any squares that would intersect the edge of the circle, leaving a gap in the grid. If you wind up with too many gaps, select the grid group, delete it, and try clicking a different spot to start the grid. Alternatively, try changing the pattern parameters until you get a grid that fills the shape in a pleasing way. You can also edit the grid group; in group-editing mode, copy and paste grid elements to fill gaps, then trim the elements manually to fit the shape.

GRAPHICS ON MULTIPLE LAYERS

In Adobe Flash CS4 Professional, you can create an illusion of three-dimensional depth by overlapping graphic elements. As you learned in Chapter 5, you can create this overlapping effect on one layer by stacking drawing-objects, primitive-shapes, groups, and symbols. The more elements the layer contains, however, the more difficult it becomes to manipulate and keep track of their stacking order. Layers help you to bring that task under control.

You can think of a Flash document as a stack of filmstrips: a sheaf of long, clear acetate strips divided into frames. Each filmstrip is analogous to a Flash layer. Shapes painted on the top filmstrip obscure shapes on lower strips; where the top filmstrip is blank, elements from the lower strips show through.

When you place items on separate layers, it's easy to control and rearrange the way the items stack up. You can make shapes appear to be closer to the viewer by putting them on a higher layer. Additionally, raw shapes on different layers don't interact, so you don't need to worry about grouping merge-shapes or having one merge-shape inadvertently delete another. You can hide and show layers and label them to make it easier to work with multiple layers and elements in a Flash document.

Touring the Timeline's Layer Features

Flash graphically represents each layer as one horizontal section of the Timeline and provides controls for viewing and manipulating these graphic representations. Several handy features help you work with graphics on layers, such as viewing the items on layers as outlines and assigning different colors to those outlines so you can easily see which items are on which layers. You can lock layers so you don't edit their contents accidentally, and you can hide layers to make it easier to work with individual graphics in a welter of other graphics. You can create guide layers for help in positioning elements, masks for hiding and revealing layer contents selectively, and motion-guide layers for animating classic-tween elements along a curving path. (You learn more about classic-tween motion-guide layers in Chapter 9.)

Complex movies contain dozens of layers. Viewing and navigating such hefty Timelines can get tedious and confusing. Flash lets you create *layer folders* to organize the layers in a movie. You can keep all the layers related to one character or element together in one folder, for example. Flash considers a folder to be another type of layer, and the methods for adding and deleting layer folders are similar to those for adding and deleting layers. Layer folders don't by themselves hold graphic content, however, and folders have neither frames nor keyframes in the Timeline. (Keyframes are special frames in which you place your graphic elements; you'll learn about them in Chapter 8.)

Figure 6.1 offers a road map to the important layer features in the Timeline.

Touring the Timeline's Layer Features

Figure 6.1 The Timeline graphically represents all the layers in a Flash movie. Layer folders let you organize layers in a complex movie. You can do much of the work of creating and manipulating layers and folders by clicking buttons in the Timeline.

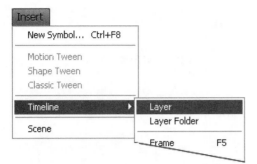

Figure 6.2 Choose Insert > Timeline > Layer to add a new layer to the Timeline.

Figure 6.3 Select the layer that you want to wind up beneath the new layer (top); Flash inserts a new layer directly above the selected layer and gives the new layer a default name (bottom).

Creating and Deleting Layers and Folders

While creating the ingredients of a particular scene in your movie, you can add new layers and layer folders as you need them.

To add a layer or a layer folder:

1. In the Timeline, select a layer or a folder.

 Flash always adds the new layer or folder directly above the one you selected, so be sure to select the layer or folder that should wind up directly beneath the new one. To add a layer or folder beneath the current bottom layer, create the layer first, then click and drag it to reposition it at the bottom of the stack.

2. To add a layer, do either of the following:

 ▲ Choose Insert > Timeline > Layer (**Figure 6.2**).

 ▲ In the Timeline's Status bar, click the New Layer button (the folded-page icon).

 Flash adds a new layer and gives it a default name—for example, *Layer 4* (**Figure 6.3**).

 continues on next page

3. To add a folder, do either of the following:

▲ Choose Insert > Timeline >
Layer Folder.

▲ In the Timeline's Status bar, click the
New Folder button (the folder icon).

Flash adds a new layer folder and gives it
a default name—for example, *Folder 1* or
Folder 2 (**Figure 6.4**). The folder is open
by default, making it easy to place layers
within (see "Organizing with Layers and
Folders," later in this chapter).

Flash bases the number in default names
on the number of layers or folders already
created in the active scene of the movie,
not on the number of layers and folders
that currently exist or their current position.
Flash tracks layer and folder numbers separately; the first folder you insert among
numerous layers gets the name *Folder 1*.

Figure 6.4 Select the layer that should be below
the new folder (top). Flash creates a new folder
above the layer you selected (bottom). Flash
names new folders based on the number of
folders that have been created in the current
scene of the movie.

To delete a layer or a folder:

1. In the Timeline, select the layer or folder
you want to delete.

2. Click the Delete button (the Trash icon)
(**Figure 6.5**).

Flash removes that layer (and all its
frames) or that folder from the Timeline.
If your selection includes folders containing layers, a dialog appears, warning that
deleting the layer folder will also delete all
the layers it contains.

3. To delete the folder and its layers, click Yes.

or

To cancel the delete operation, click No.

✔ Tip

■ The contextual menu for layers offers some
choices that otherwise are available only
via buttons in the Timeline—for example,
the Delete Layer and Delete Folder commands (**Figure 6.6**). To access this menu,
Control-click a layer on the Mac or right-
click it in Windows.

— Delete layer or folder

Figure 6.5 Click the Delete button to delete a
selected layer or folder.

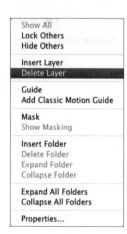

Figure 6.6
The contextual menu
for layers gives you
easy access to layer
commands, including
some that you can
otherwise access only via
buttons—for example,
Delete. To access the
contextual menu for
layers, Control-click (Mac)
or right-click (Windows)
the icon of the layer you
want to work with.

Layers selected for deletion

Click to delete selected layers

After deletion

Figure 6.7 To delete noncontiguous layers, ⌘-click (Mac) or Ctrl-click (Windows) the layers you want to add to your selection; then click the Delete button.

To delete multiple layers and/or folders:

1. In the Timeline, select the first layer or folder you want to remove.

2. ⌘-click (Mac) or Ctrl-click (Windows) every layer or folder you want to remove.

   This method of selection allows you to choose multiple layers that aren't contiguous (**Figure 6.7**).

3. Click the Delete button (the Trash icon).

   Flash removes the selected layers (and their frames) from the Timeline. If your selection includes folders containing layers, follow step 3 of the preceding task to deal with the warning dialog.

✔ Tips

- To select a range of layers, click the lowest layer you want to delete, then Shift-click the highest layer you want to delete. Flash selects the clicked layers and all the layers in between.

- You can't delete all the layers in the Timeline. If you select all the layers and folders and click the Delete button, Flash keeps the bottom layer and deletes the rest. Even if the bottom layer is nested in a folder, Flash keeps it and promotes it to regular layer status.

- You can also Control-click (Mac) or right-click (Windows) selected layers or folders to bring up the contextual menu, which contains commands for deleting layers and folders.

Controlling Layers and Folders

Layer properties are the settings that define the look and function of a layer. Layer folders are a type of layer in Flash. You can name layers and folders. You can hide or show the contents of layers and folders, lock them to prevent editing their contents, and view them in outline form. Flash generally gives you three ways to control the properties of a selected layer or folder: set the property in the Layer Properties dialog, set the property via button controls in the Timeline, or set the property via the contextual menu.

To work with the Layer Properties dialog:

1. In the Timeline, select the layer whose properties you want to define or change.

2. Choose Modify > Timeline > Layer Properties.

   The Layer Properties dialog appears (**Figure 6.8**).

3. To name the layer, enter text in the Name field.

4. To define the layer type, click one of the following radio buttons.
   - ▲ Normal (the default layer type)
   - ▲ Mask (hides and reveals elements on linked layers)
   - ▲ Masked (contains elements to be masked)
   - ▲ Folder (used to organize layers)
   - ▲ Guide (aids in positioning elements; not part of the published movie)

5. To hide the contents of a layer (or layer folder), deselect the Show check box.

   To show the contents, select the box.

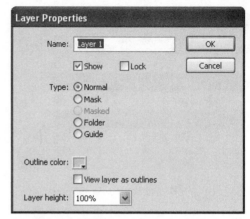

Figure 6.8 You can define a layer's type and other features in the Layer Properties dialog. You can also set these properties directly in the Timeline via buttons or via the contextual menu for layers. The Layer Properties dialog is the only place to change the height or outline color for a layer.

Where Should You Set Layer Properties?

If you just want to set layer visibility, lock layer contents, or view layer elements as outlines, it makes no difference whether you call up the Layer Properties dialog to do so, click the various layer-property controls in the Timeline, or choose a command from the contextual menu for layers. Selecting a property in the dialog offers no more permanence than setting that property in the Timeline or from the contextual menu.

The Layer Properties dialog does offer functions that lack button equivalents: creating plain guide layers, changing the height of a layer in Timeline view, choosing an outline color, and changing an existing layer from one type to another.

The contextual menu is your only choice for creating classic motion-guide layers.

Figure 6.9 Flash offers two enlarged layer views. The larger layers in the Timeline are especially useful for working with sounds. To increase the height of a selected layer, choose a larger percentage from the Layer Height menu in the Layer Properties dialog.

6. To prevent changes in the contents of a layer or folder, select the Lock check box.

   To permit changes, deselect the box.

7. To view the contents of a layer as outlines, select the "View layer as outlines" check box.

   To view the contents as solid graphic elements, deselect the box.

8. To choose a color for the outlines on this layer, use the Outline Color control (see Chapter 2, "Creating Solid Colors and Gradients").

   You can change this property only via the Layer Properties dialog.

9. To change the height at which layers or folders display in the Timeline, choose a percentage from the Layer Height pop-up menu (**Figure 6.9**).

   You can change this property only via the Layer Properties dialog.

10. Click OK.

    Flash applies all the selected settings to the current layer.

✔ Tips

■ Double-clicking a layer's folded-page icon or folder icon in the Timeline opens the Layer Properties dialog for that layer or folder.

■ When the "View layer as outlines" check box is selected for a layer folder, Flash displays the contents of all the layers contained in the folder as outlines. Although you can specify an outline color for a layer folder, the color has no effect on what you see on the Stage. When you turn on outline view for the folder, each layer within the folder displays its contents in the outline color for that layer.

■ To change the size of the graphic representation of all the layers in the Timeline, choose a size from the Frame View pop-up menu located in the top-right corner of the Timeline. The Preview and Preview in Context options display thumbnails of the contents of each key-frame in the layers.

■ You can have Flash use each layer's outline color as the selection highlight color for all types of graphic elements on that layer. Open the Preferences dialog—from the Flash menu (Mac) or Edit menu (Windows), choose Preferences—then in the General category, in the Highlight Color section, click the Use Layer Color radio button.

Setting Layer Properties via the Timeline

The Timeline represents each layer or layer folder as a horizontal field containing a name and three buttons for controlling the way the layer's or folder's contents look on the Stage. You can hide a layer or folder (making all the elements on that layer or within that folder temporarily invisible), lock a layer or folder (making the contents visible but uneditable), and view as outlines the items on the layer or within the folder. These controls are helpful when you're editing numerous items on several layers.

To rename a layer or folder:

1. In the Timeline, double-click the layer or folder name.

   Flash activates the name's text-entry field.

2. Type a new name.

3. Press Enter, or click anywhere outside the name field.

To hide/show the contents of a layer or folder:

◆ In the Timeline for the layer or folder that you want to hide or show, click the icon in the Eye column (**Figure 6.10**).

   The layer or folder toggles between the hidden and visible state. A red *X* in the column indicates that the layer or folder is hidden; its contents no longer appear on the Stage. A bullet indicates that the layer is visible. The hidden setting has no effect on the final movie. When you publish a movie (see Chapter 18), Flash includes all the contents of hidden layers and folders.

Toggles visibility of the layer's contents

Layer contents hidden

Folder contents hidden

Contents of Star layer hidden

Contents of all layers in Corner folder hidden

Figure 6.10 The column below the eye icon controls the visibility of layers. Each of the six graphic elements (top) is on a separate layer. The four triangles at the corners are located in the Corners folder. Hiding the Star layer makes the star disappear from the Stage; hiding the Corners folder makes the four triangles disappear as well (bottom).

Figure 6.11 The padlock icon indicates that a layer is locked. The contents of a locked layer appear on the Stage, but you can't edit them.

Figure 6.12 A hollow square in the Outline column indicates that graphic elements on that layer appear as outlines. Setting a folder to outline mode automatically changes all the layers within it to outline mode.

To lock/unlock a layer or folder:

◆ In the Timeline for the layer or folder that you want to lock or unlock, click the icon in the Lock column (**Figure 6.11**).

The layer or folder toggles between the locked and unlocked state. A padlock icon in the column indicates that the layer or folder is locked; its contents appear on the Stage, but you can't edit them. A bullet indicates that the layer or folder is unlocked; its contents are editable. Locking a layer or folder has no effect on the final movie.

To view the contents of a layer or folder as outlines or solids:

◆ In the Timeline for the layer or folder that you want to view as outlines or solids, click the icon in the Outline column—the one topped by a square icon (**Figure 6.12**).

The layer or folder toggles between outline mode and solid mode. When the square in the column has a thick color outline, the contents of the layer or folder appear on the Stage as outlines. When the square in the column is a solid color, the layer or folder contents appear in their complete form. For regular layers, the color of the outline square indicates what color Flash uses to create the outlines for the contents of that layer. (For layer folders, the color of the square has no meaning; the square just shows which mode the folder is in.) Placing a layer or folder in outline mode doesn't affect the final movie.

✔ Tip

■ Setting a folder to outline mode makes all the layers within the folder display their contents as outlines. Click the outline square of individual layers within the folder to see that layer's content as solid shapes.

Organizing with Layers and Folders

You can organize layers by rearranging their position in the Timeline and by placing them within folders. Layers and folders make it easy to change the stacking order of numerous elements at the same time. You can, for example, bring all the elements on one layer to the top of the stack by dragging that layer to the top of the list in the Timeline. Doing so brings those elements to the front of the Stage (overlapping any items on other layers) in every frame of the movie. Repositioning a folder in the Timeline changes the stacking order of all the layers within that folder. When you place layers in a folder, you have the ability to hide or show those layers within the Timeline by collapsing or expanding the folder.

To reorder layers (or folders):

1. In a document with several layers and folders, in the Timeline, position the pointer over the layer icon (or folder icon) of the layer (or folder) you want to move.

2. Click and drag the layer (or folder).

   A black bar with a small circle on its left end previews the new location of the layer (or folder).

3. Position the preview bar in the layer order you want (**Figure 6.13**).

4. Release the mouse button.

   Flash moves the layer (or folder) to the new location and selects it in the Timeline. The contents of single layers are selected on the Stage; the contents of the layers inside a repositioned folder are not selected.

Figure 6.13 The black bar with a small circle at its left end (top) represents the new location for the layer you're dragging (here it's the Rectangle layer). Release the mouse button to drop the layer into its new position. Flash selects the layer and its contents (bottom). The rectangle shape moves from the bottom of the heap, below the square, to just under the star.

Layer goes inside folder

Layer goes outside folder

Figure 6.14 When you position a layer below the last layer in an open folder, you need to let Flash know whether you want the dragged layer to wind up inside or outside the folder. As you drag into the open folder, the preview bar's circle automatically aligns with the right side of the target-folder icon (top), indicating that the dragged layer will go inside the target folder. To place the layer outside the folder, drag to the left until the preview bar's circle aligns with the left side of the folder icon (bottom). The option to drag to the left is available only when you place a layer at the bottom of the folder.

✔ Tips

- Positioning layers (or folders) beneath the layers in an open folder is a bit tricky; you must choose to put the dragged layer (or folder) inside the folder or outside. See the next task for further details.

- A folder to be moved can be open or closed (see "To hide/show layers inside folders in the Timeline," later in this section).

To move existing layers (or folders) into open folders:

1. Follow steps 1 and 2 of the preceding task.

2. Do either of the following:

   ▲ Position the preview bar directly beneath the target folder layer (or beneath a layer within the target folder other than the last layer).

   The preview bar's circle automatically aligns with the right side of the target folder's icon.

   ▲ Position the preview bar beneath the last layer within the target folder.

   Drag to the right until the circle aligns with the right side of the target folder's icon.

3. Release the mouse button.

   The dragged layer winds up inside the target folder.

✔ Tip

- To position a layer or folder directly below the last layer of an open folder without placing it inside the folder, drag to the left until the preview bar's circle aligns with the left side of the folder icon (**Figure 6.14**). Then release the mouse button.

To move existing layers into closed folders:

1. In a document with several layers and folders, in the Timeline, position the pointer over the layer you want to place in a folder.

2. Click and drag the layer until the preview bar appears directly above or below the folder where you want to place it (**Figure 6.15**).

3. Position the pointer directly over the target folder.

   Unfortunately, there is no feedback to let you know that you are on the folder; the preview bars make it look like you're placing the layer above or below the folder. To be sure you're on the target folder, position the pointer precisely over the folder name.

4. Release the mouse button.

   Flash moves the layer into the folder (making the moved layer the first layer in the folder), selects the folder in the Timeline, and selects the contents of all the layers in the folder on the Stage.

Figure 6.15 When you drag a layer over a folder, there is no feedback to let you know you are on the folder; the preview bar remains visible above or below the target folder layer (top). You just have to be sure to position the pointer directly over the target-folder name. Release the mouse button to drop the layer into that folder. Flash selects the folder and its contents (bottom).

Figure 6.16 Clicking the triangle to the left of the folder icon toggles between open (top) and closed (bottom) folder views.

Figure 6.17 To open or close all folders at the same time, Control-click (Mac) or right-click (Windows) any layer to access the contextual menu for layers. Then choose Expand All Folders or Collapse All Folders.

To hide/show layers inside folders in the Timeline:

◆ In the Timeline, click the triangle to the left of the folder icon (**Figure 6.16**).

The folder toggles between the open and closed state. When the triangle points to the right, the closed-folder icon appears, and the Timeline hides all the layers contained in that folder. When the triangle points downward, the open-folder icon appears, and the Timeline displays all the layers contained in the folder.

✔ Tip

■ You can open or close all the folders in a movie at the same time via the contextual menu. Access the menu by Control-clicking (Mac) or right-clicking (Windows) any Timeline layer. Then, choose Expand All Folders or Collapse All Folders (**Figure 6.17**).

ORGANIZING WITH LAYERS AND FOLDERS

Working with Graphics on Different Layers

Unless you lock shapes, or lock or hide layers, the merge-shapes and drawing-objects on all layers are available for editing using the selection, paint-bucket, and ink-bottle tools; primitive-shapes are available for editing using the paint-bucket and ink-bottle tools. You can add shapes only on the active (currently selected) layer.

To activate a layer:

◆ To select the layer where you want to add a graphic-object, do either of the following:

   ▲ In the Timeline, click the layer name.

   The area containing the layer name highlights in blue, and a pencil icon appears to the right of the layer name. Flash selects all the graphic-objects on that layer.

   ▲ On the Stage, click a graphic-object.

   Flash selects that graphic-object, highlights the layer name in gray, and puts the pencil icon to the right of the layer name.

To edit merge-shape and drawing-object outlines on inactive layers:

1. In a document with merge-shapes or drawing-objects on two or more layers, using the selection tool, position the pointer over a shape on an inactive layer (one without the pencil icon).

   The curve or corner-point icon appears.

2. Drag the outline of the shape on the inactive layer.

3. Release the mouse button.

   Flash redraws the shape (**Figure 6.18**). The layer that was active originally remains active.

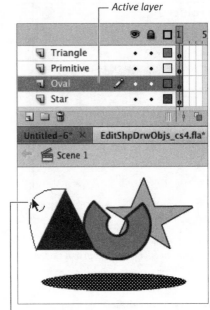

Active layer

Use selection tool to modify shape on inactive layer

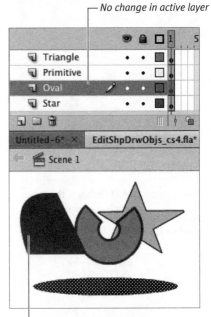

No change in active layer

Flash redraws shape

Figure 6.18 Oval is the active layer, but you can still edit merge-shapes or drawing-objects on inactive layers. Modifying a shape's outline with the selection tool doesn't activate the shape's layer.

Use paint bucket to modify fill on inactive layer

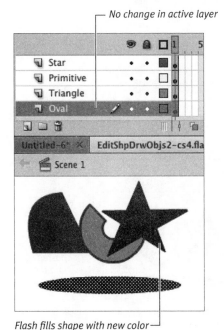

Flash fills shape with new color

Figure 6.19 Using the paint-bucket tool to change a fill color on an inactive layer doesn't activate that layer.

✔ **Tips**

■ Unlike with merge-shapes and drawing objects, using the selection tool to modify the outline of a primitive on an inactive layer makes that layer active. You can start the modification—for example, using the selection tool to reposition the control points for a rectangle-primitive's corner radius—while the primitive is deselected; once you finish the modification, however, Flash selects the primitive on the Stage, and that layer becomes the active layer in the Timeline.

■ The Bézier tools work to modify shapes only on active layers.

To edit fills across layers:

1. In a document with shapes on two or more layers, select the paint-bucket tool from the Tools panel.

2. From the Color panel, choose a new fill color.

3. Position the paint bucket over a shape on an inactive layer and click.

   Flash fills the shape with the new color, but the layer remains inactive (**Figure 6.19**).

✔ **Tips**

■ When you're working with merge-shapes, get into the habit of creating each one on a separate layer. That way, if you need to tweak the stacking order, you can. It won't hurt to have drawing-objects or primitives on separate layers too; more layers don't increase the file size of your final movie.

■ Remember that any fill shapes that are selected when you choose a new fill color will change to that color. When you select a layer, all its elements get selected; be sure to deselect any shapes whose color you want to preserve before choosing a new fill color.

Cutting and Pasting Between Layers

Flash lets you create and place graphics only on the active layer of a document. But you can copy, cut, or delete elements from any visible, unlocked layer. You can select items on several layers, cut them, and then paste them all into a single layer. Or you can cut items individually from one layer, and redistribute them to separate layers.

To paste across layers:

1. Create or open a document that contains several layers.

2. Place at least one element on all but one layer.

   To make the elements easier to work with, create them as drawing-objects or primitives, or group each merge-shape. Leave one layer empty.

3. On the Stage, select a shape.

   Flash highlights the layer in the Timeline in gray.

4. Choose Edit > Copy.

5. In the Timeline, select the empty layer.

6. Choose Edit > Paste in Center.

   Flash pastes the copy of the shape in the empty layer, in the middle of the window (**Figure 6.20**). Now you can move the shape to a new position, if you wish.

Active layer

Selected and copied shape

Select new active layer

Shape pasted into the new layer

Figure 6.20 Copying a shape from one layer to another involves selecting the shape (top), copying it, selecting the target layer, and then pasting the copy there. The Paste in Center command (middle) positions the pasted shape in the center of the window (bottom).

Active layer is the layer of the item last selected

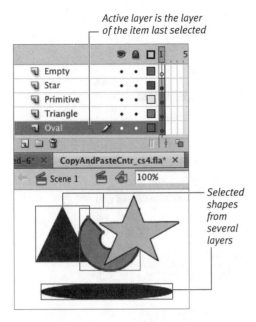

Selected shapes from several layers

After cutting the shapes

Figure 6.21 The first step in consolidating items from several layers on a single new layer involves selecting all the items and cutting them. Later, you'll paste them into the new active layer.

To use the Paste in Place command across layers:

1. In a document that has several layers containing shapes and one layer that has no shapes, select one shape.

   In the Timeline, the layer containing the selected shape becomes the active layer.

2. Using the techniques you learned in Chapter 4, add other shapes to your selection.

   In the Timeline, the layer containing the most recent addition to the selection becomes the active layer.

3. Choose Edit > Cut.

   Flash removes the selected shapes (**Figure 6.21**).

4. In the Timeline, select the empty layer.

5. Choose Edit > Paste in Place (**Figure 6.22**).

   Flash pastes all the shapes back into their original locations on the Stage but on a different layer (**Figure 6.23**). Try hiding the empty layer temporarily; you should no longer see those shapes.

Two Ways to Paste

Flash offers two pasting modes: Paste in Center and Paste in Place. Paste in Center puts elements in the center of the open Flash window. (Note that the center of the window may not necessarily be the center of the Stage; if you want to paste to the center of the Stage, you must center the Stage in the open window.) Paste in Place puts an element at the same *x*- and *y*-coordinates it had when you cut or copied it. Paste in Place is useful for preserving the precise relationships of all elements in a scene as you move items from one layer to another.

✔ Tips

- Selecting an element on the Stage causes Flash to select that element's layer in the Timeline. As you move elements between layers, it helps to know that selections work the other way around, too. When you select a layer in the Timeline, Flash selects all the elements for that layer on the Stage.

- The process of cutting elements and using the Paste in Place command is time-consuming, because you have to keep selecting new layers as you place the elements. To automate the process, use the Distribute to Layers command (see "Distributing Graphic Elements to Layers," the next section in this chapter).

- The highlight color of the active layer in the Timeline changes depending on whether the Timeline or the Stage has focus. Blue highlighting means the Timeline has focus (for example, you just clicked the layer in the Timeline). Gray highlighting means the Stage has focus (for example, you just selected an item on the Stage, or you used the Paste command to paste an element onto the Stage). It's a subtle distinction, but it can help you keep track of what operation you've just completed.

Where Do Pasted Graphic Elements Go?

A Flash document can have only one layer active at a time. Any new shapes you create wind up on the currently selected, or active, layer. The same is true of placing copies of shapes or instances of symbols; if you copy and paste an element, Flash pastes the copy on the active layer. When you drag a symbol instance from the Library window, it winds up on the active layer.

Figure 6.22 Choose Edit > Paste in Place to paste items back into their original positions.

Shapes after pasting in place

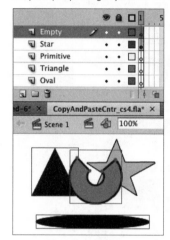

Click to hide the layer

Layer containing the shapes is now hidden

Figure 6.23 The Paste in Place command positions the pasted items in the new layer. Each shape occupies the same coordinates it had on its former layer, but now all the shapes are together on the new layer. Hide the new layer to make sure you moved the elements from their old layers.

CUTTING AND PASTING BETWEEN LAYERS

Figure 6.24 Selecting elements on the Stage (top) and choosing Modify > Timeline > Distribute to Layers (middle) automatically cuts each element and pastes it in place in a new layer. The new layers follow the order in which you placed the elements on the Stage originally. In this series of numbers, the numeral 1 was drawn first, so it winds up at the top of the section of new layers (bottom).

Distributing Graphic Elements to Layers

As you draw elements for your movie, you may not always remember to create a new layer for each one. Using the Cut and Paste in Place commands can be tedious. Flash's Distribute to Layers feature automates the process, putting each element of a selection on a separate layer. This feature comes in handy when you start creating two types of animation—*motion tweening* and *classic tweening*—in which each element being animated must be on its own layer. (You'll learn about classic tweening in Chapter 9 and motion tweening in Chapter 11.)

To place selected elements on individual layers:

1. Open a new document, and, on the Stage, create several separate shapes on a single layer.

2. Choose Edit > Select All.
   Flash highlights all the shapes.

3. Choose Modify > Timeline > Distribute to Layers, or press Shift-#-D (Mac) or Ctrl-Shift-D (Windows) (**Figure 6.24**).
   Flash creates a layer for each shape and adds the new layers to the bottom of the Timeline. Each shape winds up in the same location on the Stage, but on a separate layer.

✔ Tip

■ Distribute to Layers works with selected graphic-objects (text fields, drawing-objects, primitives, groups, and symbols) as well as with selected raw shapes. (You learn about symbols in Chapter 7.) Flash distributes each selected graphic-object to its own layer; the various elements of the graphic-object remain joined.

Working with Guide Layers

Flash offers two types of guide layers: guides and motion guides. Plain old guides can contain any kind of content—lines, shapes, or symbols. The contents of a regular guide layer merely serve as a point of reference to help you position items on the Stage. Flash doesn't include the graphic content of guide layers in the final exported movie.

Motion-guide layers contain a single line that directs the movement of an animated element in a classic tween. (To learn more about using motion guides with classic tweens, see Chapter 9.) Another distinction to remember is that Flash creates motion guides by adding a new layer directly to the Timeline. To create plain guides, you must redefine an existing layer as a guide layer.

To create a plain guide layer:

1. Do either of the following:
   - ▲ Create a new layer in the Timeline (for example, by clicking the Insert Layer button). Flash selects the new layer.
   - ▲ Select a layer that already exists.

2. Control-click (Mac) or right-click (Windows) the layer you want to define as a guide, and choose Guide from the contextual menu (**Figure 6.25**).

   Flash turns the selected layer into a guide layer and places a little T-square icon before the layer name (**Figure 6.26**).

   You can rename the layer to identify it as a guide, if you wish.

Figure 6.25 Choose Guide as the layer type in the contextual menu for layers to change a normal layer to a guide layer.

Figure 6.26 Select a layer (top) and define it as a guide layer. In the Timeline, Flash identifies the guide layer with a T-square icon; compare that with the icon for the motion-guide layer (bottom).

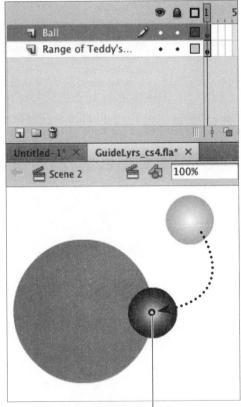

Center point snaps to other elements as you drag

Figure 6.27 Choose View > Snapping > Snap to Objects (top) to force items that you drag to snap to other lines or shapes, such as those on a guide layer (bottom).

3. To make guide elements easier to use, choose View > Snapping, and from the submenu, choose any of the following settings:

▲ Choose Snap to Objects (**Figure 6.27**). Flash forces items that you draw or drag to snap to lines or shapes.

▲ Choose Snap Align.

Flash displays alignment guides as you drag shapes or graphic-objects near to other shapes or graphic-objects. Now you can more easily align items to the elements on your guide layers.

✔ Tips

■ When you've placed guide elements where you need them for a certain scene, lock the guide layer so you don't move the guides accidentally as you draw on other layers.

■ The Snap to Guide feature doesn't help you snap to items on a guide layer; the guides in that feature are the guide lines you drag out from rulers (see Chapter 1).

■ Because the graphic content of guide layers doesn't become part of your published movie, you can use guide layers as a space for making notes.

■ When positioning layers beneath a guide layer, it's easy to transform the guide layer into a motion-guide layer by accident. (Motion guides are used in classic tweening.) As you drag a layer beneath a guide layer, watch the preview bar and the icon in the guide layer. To maintain the guide layer as a guide layer, drag to the left until the preview bar's gray circle aligns with the left side of the guide layer's T-square icon. To create a motion-guide layer, drag to the right to align the circle with the right side of the T-square icon; the guide icon changes to a dotted arc icon indicating a motion guide (to learn about motion guides, see Chapter 9).

Working with Mask Layers

Mask layers are special layers that let you hide and show elements on underlying layers. In the final movie, shapes on the Mask layer become holes that let items on linked layers show through.

To create a mask layer:

1. Do either of the following:

   ▲ Create a new layer in the Timeline (for example, by clicking the Insert Layer button). Flash selects the new layer.

   ▲ Select a layer that already exists.

   In general, it's easier to create (or select) a layer directly above the layer containing content you want to mask, although you can always create the mask separately and link the masked layers to it later.

2. Control-click (Mac) or right-click (Windows) the layer to access the contextual menu for layers, and choose Mask (**Figure 6.28**).

   Flash automatically defines the layer as a mask, links the layer beneath the selected layer to the mask, and locks both layers so that masking is in effect (**Figure 6.29**). You can also rename the layer to identify it as a mask, if you wish.

✔ Tips

■ To link existing layers to a mask layer quickly, drag them in the Timeline so they sit directly below the mask or one of its linked layers.

■ Once you have linked a layer to the mask, you can create additional new linked layers for that mask quickly. Select the linked (masked) layer, then follow the steps for creating a new layer. Flash adds the new layers as masked layers directly above the selected layer.

Figure 6.28 To define a layer as a mask, choose Mask from the contextual menu for layers.

Figure 6.29 The mask-layer icon imitates the masking effect with a dark mask shape over a checkerboard pattern. Masked layers are indented and have a checkerboard pattern on the layer icon in the Timeline, indicating that the layer is masked.

When you define this layer as a mask...

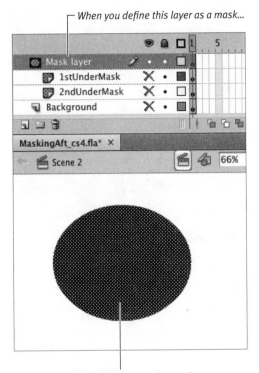

...this merge-shape fill becomes the mask

Figure 6.30 The content for the layers that the mask will reveal is just like any other content. You must use fill shapes to create "holes" in the mask; all those shapes must be on the same sublevel of the mask layer. In other words, you must either use only merge-shapes or combine all your shapes into a single drawing-object.

To create the mask:

1. Create one or more layers containing graphic elements you want to reveal only through a mask.

2. Create a mask layer above your masked-content layers, and make sure that it's selected, visible, and unlocked.

   The layer should be highlighted in the Timeline, and the Eye and Lock columns should contain bullets (not X or padlock icons).

3. Use the drawing tools to create a fill shape on the mask layer (**Figure 6.30**).

   Flash uses only fills to create the mask and ignores any strokes on the mask layer.

✔ Tips

■ It's best to limit your mask to a single merge-shape or a single graphic-object (drawing-object, primitive-shape, group, symbol, or text field with static text). If the mask layer contains multiple merge-shapes, the mask may work initially. Move one of the parts, however, and Flash may stop treating that shape as part of the mask. If the mask layer contains a merge-shape and a graphic-object, Flash uses just the merge-shape to create the mask. If the mask layer contains multiple graphic-objects, Flash uses just the bottom-most one. (For more details on stacking order for graphic-objects, see Chapter 5.)

■ If you want to use multiple shapes in a mask, select them and turn them into a single drawing-object: choose Modify > Combine Objects > Union. You could also convert the selected shapes into a symbol: press F8 to access the Convert to Symbol dialog.

■ You can set up mask and masked layers in the Layer Properties dialog (see "Controlling Layers and Folders," earlier in this chapter).

To see the mask's effect:

1. Lock the mask layer and all linked layers.

or

Control-click (Mac) or right-click (Windows) a mask (or masked) layer.

2. From the contextual menu, choose Show Masking (**Figure 6.31**).

Flash automatically locks the mask layer and all the layers linked to it.

In document-editing mode, you must lock the mask layer and any masked layers beneath it to see the mask effect (**Figure 6.32**). You can see the effect without locking the layers in one of Flash's test modes (see Chapter 8).

Figure 6.31 The Show Masking command in the contextual menu for layers locks the selected mask layer and all its linked layers.

Transparent fill helps you see what the mask will reveal

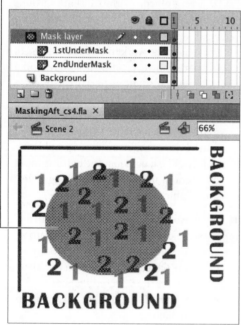

Masking not on

Masking turned on

Figure 6.32 After defining the mask and masked layers, you must lock them to see the mask in effect in document-editing mode.

Working with Symbols

In previous chapters, you learned to create and edit static graphics. Ultimately, you'll want to animate those graphics, and you'll probably want to use the same graphic over and over again. You may want an element to appear several times in one movie, or you may want to use the same element in several movies. You can save graphic elements for reuse by storing them in a library; to do that, you first turn the graphics into *symbols*.

Every Flash document has its own library; the library contains the symbols you create and other *assets*—reusable elements that you import for use in your movie (see the sidebar "Library Terminology").

In this chapter, you learn to work with libraries and to create symbols that are static graphics. In later chapters, you learn about creating animated symbols and buttons (see Chapters 12 and 14), using bitmapped graphics (see Chapter 16), and adding sound and video (see Chapter 17).

Library Terminology

The general term for an item stored in a Flash library is an *asset*. More specifically, graphics created with Flash's drawing tools and stored in a library are called *symbols;* fonts stored in a library are called *font symbols;* and imported sounds, video clips, and bitmaps (which are always stored in a library) are just called *sounds, video clips,* and *bitmaps.* Flash refers to each copy of a library asset that you use in a movie as an *instance* of that asset.

Using the Library Panel

The Library panel offers several ways to view a library's contents and allows you to organize your symbols, sounds, video clips, and bitmaps in folders. The Library panel provides information about when an item was last modified, what type of item it is, and how many times the movie uses it. The Library panel also contains a search feature for locating specific assets.

To open the library of the current movie:

◆ Choose Window > Library, or press ⌘-L (Mac) or Ctrl-L (Windows) **Figure 7.1**).

The Library panel appears on the desktop (**Figure 7.2**.). The Library panel contains the libraries of all the Flash documents currently open on your desktop.

Figure 7.1 Choose Window > Library to open the Library panel of the currently active Flash document.

Figure 7.2 The Library panel lists the assets assigned to the current document. Items are sorted by the selected column; click the triangle in the column heading to reverse the sort order.

USING THE LIBRARY PANEL

Figure 7.3 The Library panel contains the libraries of all the currently open documents. To view a different library without switching documents, choose one from the menu of open documents.

To view the library of another open document:

1. Open two or more Flash documents.

2. With the Library panel open, do either of the following:

   ▲ In the Library panel, from the menu of open documents, choose the desired inactive document (**Figure 7.3**).

   or

   ▲ Select the open document whose library you want to view.

   For documents in a tabbed window, click the document's tab; for documents in separate windows, click the desired window to make it active.

   The contents of the Library panel change to display the assets of the selected document.

✔ Tips

■ The Library panel displays the assets of just one document at a time. To view libraries for multiple documents simultaneously, open multiple Library panels. In the open Library panel, click the New Library Panel button (the double-document-arrow icon just below the panel menu). Flash opens the current library in a new panel window; you have two panels showing the assets of the same document. Choose a different library in one of the panels.

■ The variety of menus from which you can open a library of some sort can be daunting at first. Here's a short rundown. To open the Library panel for an open, active document, choose Window > Library; to view the library of an open, inactive document, choose it from the menu of open documents in the Library panel; to open the library of a closed document, choose File > Import > Open External Library; to open one of the common libraries, choose Window > Common Libraries (see the sidebar "What Are Common Libraries?").

USING THE LIBRARY PANEL

To open the library of a closed Flash document:

1. Choose File > Import > Open External Library, or press Shift-⌘-O (Mac) or Ctrl-Shift-O (Windows) (**Figure 7.4**).

   The Open As Library dialog appears.

2. Navigate to the file whose library you want to open, select it, and click Open.

   The Library panel appears on the desktop, making those symbols available for use in other movies.

Figure 7.4 Choose File > Import > Open External Library to access symbols from the library of a closed Flash document.

What Are Common Libraries?

Flash makes a set of *common libraries* available from the Menu bar—a sort of library of libraries. Flash ships with three common libraries, but you can add your own. The libraries in the Common Libraries menu are Flash files that live in the Libraries folders of the language-specific Configuration folders at the application level (see the sidebar "The Mystery of the Configuration Folder," in Chapter 1). If you have administrative privileges, you can add FLA files to that folder. If you don't have privileges, you must add a folder named Libraries to the User-Level Configuration folder for your language installation. Any files you add to that Libraries folder also appear in the Common Libraries menu when you restart the application (**Figure 7.5**). Choosing an item from the Common Libraries menu opens only the library, not the file itself.

You might create a common library to keep all the symbols, sounds, video clips, and bitmaps for a work project accessible from the Menu bar. As you create or import assets, add a copy of each item to a special file with a meaningful name—for example, MyShapes. Make the file one of your common libraries. When you choose MyShapes from the Window > Common Libraries menu, Flash opens the library containing all your project's items.

Figure 7.5 The Common Libraries menu gives you quick access to the libraries of Flash Documents located inside a Libraries folder that's available to all users.

Drag to resize

Figure 7.6 Drag the divider between column headers to resize a column in the Library panel.

To resize library columns:

1. In the Library panel, position the pointer over a column-head divider.

   The pointer changes to a double-arrow icon.

2. Click and drag the divider (**Figure 7.6**).

✔ Tips

■ You can also resize the Library panel's preview window. Position the pointer over the gray area at the bottom of the preview window. When the divider-moving pointer appears, drag up to make the window shorter, down to make it taller. The preview image for the asset resizes to fit the new window.

■ When in doubt about whether or not to make a graphic element a symbol, opt for making it a symbol. You can always break it apart into its original shapes. When you publish a movie to make it available to end users, unused symbols don't export (unless you specifically set them up to export). So unused symbols add nothing to the SWF file's size. Check it out for yourself by generating a size report when you publish your movie (see Chapter 18).

USING THE LIBRARY PANEL

To find an asset by name:

◆ In the Library panel's search field (identified by a magnifying-glass icon), enter the name of the desired asset.

As you type, Flash narrows the asset list, showing only assets whose names contain the letter (or letters) you enter. For example, type the letter *o* into the search field, and the list shows only assets whose names contain *o*. When you add another letter—*w*, for example —the list narrows to just assets that contain both *o* and *w* (**Figure 7.7**). Flash pulls assets out of the folder hierarchy to create the reduced list.

To restore full asset list:

◆ Click the *X* at the right side of the search field.

Flash ends the search session and restores the original asset list to the scrolling list in the Library panel.

Full list

After typing ow

After typing owl

Figure 7.7 To find a specific asset, enter its name in the search field of the Library panel. Flash narrows the field of assets to choose from, displaying just those whose names contain the letters you enter. The letters can be in any order. To reduce the list to a single asset, you must type enough of the asset name to distinguish it from all other assets (and it must have a unique name).

Figure 7.8 From the panel menu in the Library panel, choose New Folder to create a library folder.

Select root-level item...   *...to add root-level folder*

— New Folder button   — Enter folder name

Select item within a folder...   *...to add a subfolder*

Figure 7.9 To create new folders and subfolders, click the New Folder button.

Understanding Library Hierarchy

Flash lets you create folders and subfolders to organize assets hierarchically within the library.

To create a library folder:

1. Open the Library panel.

2. To select a location, do either of the following:
   ▲ To add a root-level folder, select an item at the root level.
   ▲ To add a subfolder, select an item within the folder where you want to add the new subfolder. (Do not select the folder itself.)

3. To create the new folder, do either of the following:
   ▲ From the panel menu, choose New Folder (**Figure 7.8**).
   ▲ At the bottom of the window, click the New Folder button (**Figure 7.9**).

   Flash creates a new folder, selects it, and activates the text field.

4. Type a name for your folder.

5. Press Enter.

✔ Tips

■ To sort items in the Library panel, click the heading of the column you want to sort by. To sort by name, for example, click the Name column header.

■ To toggle between alphanumeric and reverse-alphanumeric sort order, click the triangle on the far-right side of the column heading (see Figure 7.2).

To work with library folders:

1. To open a closed folder, do either of the following:
   - ▲ Click the triangle to the left of the folder icon.
   - ▲ Double-click the folder icon.

   The folder's contents appear in the Library panel (**Figure 7.10**).

2. To close an open folder, do either of the following:
   - ▲ Click the triangle to the left of the folder icon.
   - ▲ Double-click the folder icon.

✔ Tip

■ The panel menu contains commands for working with folders in the Library panel. Choose Expand Folder to open the currently selected folder; choose Collapse Folder to close it. Choose Expand All Folders to open all library folders at the same time; choose Collapse All Folders to close them.

To move items between library folders:

1. In the open Library panel, select the item you want to move.

2. Drag the selected item over the icon or name of the destination folder.

   Flash highlights the target folder in green (**Figure 7.11**).

3. Release the mouse button.

   Flash moves the item into the new folder.

✔ Tip

■ To move a selected asset to a new folder quickly, from the panel menu, choose Move To. The Move To dialog appears. Select the New Folder radio button, enter a name in the active text field, and click Select. Flash creates a folder on the same level as the selected item and places that item inside.

Figure 7.10 Open folders in the Library panel to display their contents.

Figure 7.11 In the Library panel, you can drag assets (or folders) between folders. The target folder highlights when it's ready to receive the dragged item.

UNDERSTANDING LIBRARY HIERARCHY

Figure 7.12 To turn a selection into a symbol, choose Modify > Convert to Symbol. In the Convert to Symbol dialog, name your symbol, choose a type, and set the registration-point location. (Click the Advanced button to expand the box to set linkages for sharing and import/export. Click the Folder hot text to place the symbol into a folder in the library.)

Converting Graphics to Symbols

Not all graphics in a Flash movie are symbols; you need to take special steps to define the items you create as symbols. You can convert elements you've already created into symbols or create symbols from scratch in the symbol editor. Symbols reside in the library of the document in which you create them. You can copy a symbol from one document to another or from one library to another document; the symbol then resides separately in each document's library.

The standard library of a Flash document contains all the symbols used in that document; it can also contain unused symbols.

The following task covers creating static graphic symbols. But you can also turn graphics into symbols that are animations (see Chapter 12) or buttons (see Chapter 14).

To turn an existing graphic into a symbol:

1. On the Stage, select the graphic element(s) you want to convert to a symbol.

   Flash highlights the selected element(s).

2. Choose Modify > Convert to Symbol, or press F8 on the keyboard.

   The Convert to Symbol dialog appears (**Figure 7.12**). Flash gives the symbol a default name—for example, Symbol 16—based on the number of symbols previously created for the library.

3. If you don't want to use the default name, type a new name for your symbol.

4. From the Type menu, choose Graphic.

continues on next page

5. To set the symbol's registration point (see the sidebar "Registration Point vs. Transformation Point for Symbols"), click one of the squares in the registration model.

By default, Flash registers a symbol by the upper-left corner of its bounding box. Click a different square on the registration model—another corner, the center, or the middle of a side—to make Flash register the symbol by the corresponding point on the symbol's bounding box.

6. Click OK.

Flash adds the symbol to the library hierarchy at the level currently set in the Folder area. The selected graphic element(s) on the Stage become an instance of the symbol. A crosshair appears, indicating the location of the registration point; a circle, known as the transformation point, appears at the center of the symbol (**Figure 7.13**). You can no longer edit the item directly on the Stage; you must open it in one of Flash's symbol-editing modes.

Selected merge-shape

Converted to a symbol

Registration point

Transformation point

Bounding box for symbol

Figure 7.13 A selected merge-shape on the Stage is highlighted with dots. When you convert that shape to a symbol, the bounding box is the only item that gets highlighted. A crosshair indicates where the symbol's registration point is. A circle indicates the symbol's transformation point.

About Symbol Types

In Flash, you must specify a symbol type for each symbol. (In early versions of Flash, this was called the symbol's behavior.) You have three choices: graphic, button, and movie clip.

Graphics are, as you might expect, graphic elements, but they can also be animated graphic elements. The feature that distinguishes one symbol type from another is the way the symbol interacts with the Timeline of the movie in which it appears. Graphic symbols operate in lock step with the Timeline of the movie. A static graphic symbol takes up one frame of the movie in which you place it (just as any graphic element would). A three-frame animated graphic symbol takes up three frames of the movie (see Chapter 12).

Buttons have their own four-frame Timeline; a button instance sits in a single frame of the main movie Timeline but displays different frames as a user's mouse interacts with the button (see Chapter 14).

Movie clips have their own multiframe Timeline that plays independently of the main movie Timeline (see Chapter 12).

✔ Tips

■ The Folder hot text in the Convert to Symbol dialog lets you control where the new symbol winds up in the library hierarchy. By default, Flash puts new symbols at the root level of the library (the hot text says Library root). Clicking the hot text opens the Move To dialog, which lets you select an existing folder or create (and select) a new folder. Flash places the new symbol into the selected folder.

■ A graphic symbol can consist of one or more merge-shapes, drawing-objects, primitive-shapes, grouped shapes—you name it. You can even include symbols within symbols. Whatever is selected on the Stage when you choose Convert to Symbol becomes part of the symbol.

■ To convert a graphic element to a symbol quickly, select the elements on the Stage and drag the selection to the lower half of the document's Library panel. The Convert to Symbol dialog appears. Name and define your symbol as described in the preceding task.

■ The registration model is elusive. It appears only in the Convert to Symbol dialog. That means you get one chance to use the model to position the registration point at preset locations on the symbol's bounding box or at its center. However, you can always go into symbol-editing mode and reposition the graphic elements in relation to the registration point (see "Editing Master Symbols," later in this chapter).

CONVERTING GRAPHICS TO SYMBOLS

Registration Point vs. Transformation Point for Symbols

The *registration point* (represented by a small crosshair) is the point that Flash uses to *register* a graphic-object—that is, to locate the object via coordinates on the Stage during authoring and playback. For drawing-objects, primitives, groups, and text fields, the registration point is always the upper-left corner of the object's bounding box. For symbols, the location of the registration point is flexible (**Figure 7.14**). When you select elements on the Stage and convert the selection to a symbol, you can put the point at any of nine preset locations (see "Converting Graphics to Symbols," earlier in this chapter). When you create a symbol from scratch in symbol-editing mode, you determine where the registration point goes by positioning elements around a crosshair icon on the Stage (see the next section, "Creating Symbols from Scratch"). The location of the registration point stays the same for all instances of the same symbol.

The *transformation point* (represented by a small circle) is the reference point Flash uses for transforming the symbol. When you rotate a symbol with the free-transform tool in Rotate and Skew mode, for example, the transformation point is the pivot around which the symbol spins. You can also use the transformation point for snapping operations. By default, Flash places the transformation point in the center of a symbol instance, but you can change the transformation point's location for individual symbol instances by using the free-transform tool.

Registration/Transformation Point button

Converted symbol

Registration point — Transformation point

Symbol from scratch

Transformation point — Registration point

Figure 7.14 When you convert a selection to a symbol, the registration model lets you position the registration point in the center, in any corner, or in the middle of any side of the symbol's bounding box; the location highlighted in the model becomes the registration point in the symbol. When you create a symbol from scratch, you can position the registration point freely.

The Info panel and the Position and Size section of the Property inspector display coordinates that locate a selected symbol instance in space during authoring. The Position and Size section of the Property inspector always displays the coordinates of a symbol's registration point. The Info panel gives you the option to view coordinates for the registration point or the transformation point. You choose which method via the Registration/Transformation Point button (for more details about using the Info panel and the Position and Size section of the Property inspector, see Chapter 4).

Figure 7.15 From the library's panel menu, choose New Symbol to create a symbol from scratch.

New symbol button ———

Figure 7.16 Click the New Symbol button in the bottom-left corner of the Library panel to create a symbol from scratch.

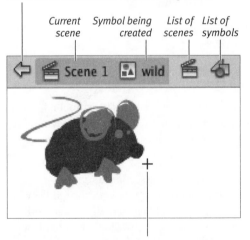

Back button (return to document-editing mode)

Current scene | Symbol being created | List of scenes | List of symbols

Registration crosshair for symbol being created

Figure 7.17 In symbol-editing mode, the name of the symbol being worked on appears in the Edit bar just above the Stage.

Creating Symbols from Scratch

You can avoid the conversion process described in the preceding section by creating graphics directly in symbol-editing mode. This practice makes all the tools, frames, and layers of the Flash editor available, but Flash defines the element you're creating as a symbol from the start.

To create a new symbol:

1. To enter symbol-editing mode, do one of the following:
   ▲ Choose Insert > New Symbol, or press ⌘-F8 (Mac) or Ctrl-F8 (Windows).
   ▲ From the library's panel menu, choose New Symbol (**Figure 7.15**).
   ▲ In the bottom-left corner of the Library panel, click the New Symbol button (**Figure 7.16**).

   The Create New Symbol dialog appears.

2. Type a name for your symbol.

3. From the Type menu, choose Graphic.

4. Click OK.

   Flash enters symbol-editing mode. Flash displays the name of the symbol you're creating in the Edit bar, places a crosshair in the center of the Stage, and hides the Pasteboard (**Figure 7.17**). The crosshair indicates the symbol's registration point.

5. Create your graphic on the Stage of the symbol editor as you would in the regular editing environment.

continues on next page

6. To return to document-editing mode, do one of the following:

▲ Choose Edit > Edit Document. Flash returns you to the current scene.

▲ In the Edit bar, click the Back button or the Current Scene link (**Figure 7.18**). Flash returns you to the current scene.

▲ From the Edit Scene pop-up menu in the Edit bar, choose a scene (**Figure 7.19**). Flash takes you to that scene.

✔ Tips

■ When you're creating new symbols, be sure to consider how the registration point should work with your finished symbol so you can place your graphic elements appropriately in relation to the registration crosshair. Will you want to align this symbol by its center? Then position your elements evenly around the crosshair. Will you want to align this symbol by a specific area? (You might want to register a bird figure, for example, by a point at the tip of the beak.) Then position your elements accordingly.

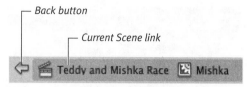

Back button

Current Scene link

Figure 7.18 Click the Back button or the Current Scene link to return to document-editing mode.

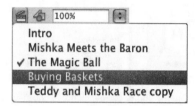

Figure 7.19 Choose a scene from the Edit bar's Edit Scene menu to return to document-editing mode.

■ When you start editing a symbol, the registration crosshair may be outside the current viewing area. To bring the registration crosshair to the center of your window, choose View > Magnification > Show Frame.

Where Am I?

When you edit symbols in a Flash document, the current window switches to symbol-editing mode. It's easy to get confused about whether you're editing the main document or a symbol. Learn to recognize the following subtle visual cues; they're the only indication that you're in symbol-editing mode.

In symbol-editing mode, a Flash document displays the name of the scene and symbol you're editing in the Edit bar and activates the Back button. If you entered symbol-editing mode by choosing Insert > New Symbol *or* Edit > Edit Symbols *or* Edit > Edit Selected, the Pasteboard disappears. If you double-click an existing symbol on the Stage, or choose Edit > Edit in Place, the pasteboard remains visible. Also, a small crosshair, which acts as a registration point for the symbol, appears on the Stage. If you entered symbol-editing mode via the Edit in Place command, any elements on the Stage that aren't being edited appear in a ghostly form. Apart from these changes, the Timeline, the Stage, and the tools all appear and work just as they do in document-editing mode.

CREATING SYMBOLS FROM SCRATCH

Preview location of symbol on the Stage

Use count updated

Figure 7.20 When you drag a symbol from the Library panel to the Stage (top), Flash places the symbol on the Stage, selects it, and updates that symbol's use count.

Using Symbol Instances

A *symbol instance* is a pointer to the full description of the symbol. Symbols help keep file sizes small. If you converted a graphic on the Stage to a symbol, you have one symbol instance on the Stage. To use the symbol again, or if you created your symbol in symbol-editing mode, you'll need to get a copy out of the library and onto the Stage.

To place a symbol instance in your movie:

1. In the Timeline, select the layer and key-frame where you want the graphic symbol to appear.

   Flash can place symbols only in key-frames. If you select an in-between frame, Flash places the symbol in the preceding keyframe. (To learn more about key-frames, see Chapter 8.)

2. Access the library containing the symbol.

3. In the Library panel, navigate to the symbol you want; click it to select it.

   Flash highlights the chosen symbol and displays it in the preview window.

4. Position the pointer over the preview window.

5. Click and drag a copy of the symbol onto the Stage.

   Flash previews the symbol's location on the Stage with a rectangular outline as you drag (**Figure 7.20**).

6. Release the mouse button.

   Flash places the symbol on the Stage and selects it.

✔ Tip

■ To place a symbol instance quickly, drag the symbol name directly from the Library panel to the Stage without using the previewed image.

199

Modifying Symbol Instances

You can change the appearance of individual symbol instances without changing the master symbol itself. As with any other element, you can resize and reposition an instance (for example, scale and rotate it) by using the tools in the Tools panel, Info and Transform panels, and the Position and Size section of the Property inspector (see Chapter 4).

You can also change a symbol instance's color and transparency, but the method differs from the methods you've learned for assigning colors to merge-shapes, drawing-objects, and primitive-shapes. You modify the color, intensity, and transparency of a symbol instance in the Color Effect section of the Property inspector.

To change an instance's color property:

1. On the Stage, select the symbol instance you want to modify.

2. Access the Property inspector.
   Settings for the symbol instance appear.

3. In the Color Effect section, from the Style menu, choose one color property to modify.
   The properties available for you to modify are Brightness (amount of black or white in the color), Tint, Alpha (transparency), and Advanced (simultaneous changes to alpha and RGB values).

4. Enter settings for your selected color change as outlined in the tasks that follow.

5. Press Enter to confirm the new settings.
   Flash applies the new settings to the symbol on the Stage.

Tips for Transforming Symbols

You can change the dimensions and orientation of symbol instances using the same techniques you use to modify graphic-objects (see Chapter 4). You can enter precise values in the Position and Size section of the Property inspector or in the Transform or Info panels; you can also modify symbol instances interactively with the free-transform tool. Here are some tips for using that tool.

When you use the free-transform tool to scale a symbol instance, it scales in relation to the instance's transformation point (by default, the center of the symbol instance). Hold down the Option key (Mac) or Alt key (Windows) to scale the symbol instance relative to the bounding-box corner diagonally, opposite the corner you're dragging.

You can change the transformation point of individual symbol instances. Using the free-transform tool, click the small white circle in the middle of the symbol instance. Drag the circle to a new location.

To position a symbol instance's transformation point at the same location as the symbol's registration point, select the instance with the free-transform tool. Then double-click the transformation point.

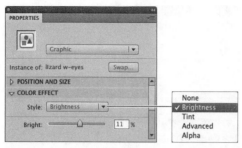

Figure 7.21 Use the Brightness settings in the Color Effect section of the Property inspector to change the intensity of a symbol instance. Enter a high value to make the symbol instance lighter or a low value to make it darker.

−100 percent brightness setting

100 percent brightness setting

Figure 7.22 At its extremes, the Brightness setting lets you turn a symbol instance completely black or completely white.

Figure 7.23 Use the Tint settings in the Color Effect section of the Property inspector to change the color of a symbol instance.

To change an instance's brightness:

1. In step 3 of the preceding task, from the Style menu, choose Brightness.

   A Bright slider and a field for entering a brightness percentage appears (**Figure 7.21**).

2. To change the symbol's brightness, use the Bright slider or type a percentage in the brightness-amount field.

   A value of −100 makes the symbol black; a value of 0 leaves the symbol at its original brightness; a value of 100 makes the symbol white (**Figure 7.22**).

To change the instance's color:

1. In step 3 of the first task in this section, from the Style menu, choose Tint.

   Tint settings appear (**Figure 7.23**).

2. To choose a new color, do either of the following:

   ▲ Use the Red, Green, and Blue sliders or type new values in the Red Color, Green Color, and Blue Color fields.

   ▲ Click the Tint Color control, and choose a color from the pop-up swatch set.

3. Use the Tint slider or type a percentage in the tint-amount field.

   The tint percentage indicates how much of the new color to blend with the existing colors. Applying a tint of 100 percent changes all the lines and fills in the symbol to the new color. Applying a lesser percentage mixes some of the new color with the existing colors in the symbol; it's almost like placing a transparent film of the new color over the symbol.

MODIFYING SYMBOL INSTANCES

To change the instance's transparency:

1. In step 3 of the first task in this section, from the Style menu, choose Alpha.

   The Alpha settings appear (**Figure 7.24**).

2. To change the amount of transparency, use the Alpha slider or type a new value in the alpha-amount field.

   A value of 0 makes the symbol completely transparent; a value of 100 makes the symbol completely opaque.

Figure 7.24 To change the transparency of a selected symbol instance, access the Color Effect section of the Property inspector. From the Style menu choose Alpha, then use the Alpha slider or the text field to enter a new alpha amount. A lower percentage makes the symbol instance more transparent.

The Mystery of Advanced Effect Settings

The Advanced color-effect settings let you change the RGB values and alpha values for a symbol instance simultaneously. The percentage hot-text controls (in the left-hand column) determine what percentage of the master symbol's original RGB and alpha values to apply to the symbol instance. The offset hot-text controls (in the right-hand column) add to or subtract from the alpha, red, green, and blue values of the original colors.

Imagine a symbol with three ovals. One is pure red, one is pure green, and one is pure blue. The alpha setting is 50 percent. Decreasing the red-percentage value affects only the red oval, making it less red. (A red-percentage of 0 would make the red oval totally black). The green and blue ovals contain 0 percent red to start with; decreasing the red-percentage value makes no visible change to these ovals. Increasing the red-offset value adds red to everything; the green and blue ovals change color. (If you decrease the red-offset value, you'll see no difference in the green and blue ovals because they contained no red to begin with, but you will see a lower percentage of red in the red oval.)

Figure 7.25 To change the color and transparency of a selected symbol instance, choose Advanced from the Style menu in the Color Effect section of the Property inspector. Use the hot-text controls in the left-hand column to enter new percentages for Alpha, Red, Green, and Blue; use the hot-text controls in the right-hand column to enter new values for the offset of Alpha, Red, Green, and Blue.

To change the instance's tint and alpha simultaneously:

1. In step 3 of the first task in this section, from the Style menu, choose Advanced.

   Settings for percentage and offset for Alpha, Red, Green, and Blue appear in the Color Effect section of the Property Inspector (**Figure 7.25**).

2. Adjust the values to fine-tune the color and transparency of the symbol instance (see the sidebar "The Mystery of Advanced Effect Settings").

   Click the hot text to enter a precise value; drag the hot text's invisible slider to choose a value interactively.

Duplicating Master Symbols

If you need to use one variation of a symbol repeatedly, you can duplicate the original master symbol and then modify the duplicate to create a new master symbol with those variations. In the Library panel, select a symbol. From the panel menu, choose Duplicate. Flash opens the Duplicate Symbol dialog, giving the duplicate symbol a default name. If you want, type a new name for your symbol. Choose the symbol type—for example, Graphic. Click OK. Use the Folder hot text to place the duplicate in a specific location. (Note that when you select a symbol that's nested in a folder, the Duplicate Symbol dialog's Folder hot text says Library Root, but the duplicate symbol winds up in the same folder as the nested symbol unless you specify a different location. To place a nested symbol's duplicate at the library's root level, click the Folder hot text; in the Move To dialog that appears, click the Existing Folder radio button, but don't choose any of the listed folders, just click the Select button; then click OK in the Duplicate Symbol dialog.). A duplicate symbol doesn't link to the original symbol in any way. You can change the duplicate without changing the original, and vice versa.

Swapping One Symbol Instance for Another

Flash lets you replace one symbol instance with another while retaining all the modifications you've made in the symbol instance. If, for example, you want to change the look of a logo in certain places in your site but not everywhere, you can create the new logo as a separate symbol and swap it in as needed. (To change the look for every instance, edit the master logo symbol directly, as you learn to do in "Editing Master Symbols," later in the chapter.) You can perform symbol swapping via menu command or in the Property inspector (**Figure 7.26**).

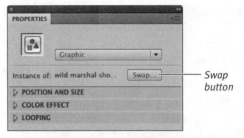

Figure 7.26 The Swap button in the Property inspector lets you replace a selected symbol instance with an instance of a different symbol from the same document.

To switch symbols:

1. On the Stage, select the symbol instance you want to change.

2. Do either of the following:
   ▲ Choose Modify > Symbol > Swap Symbol
   ▲ In the Property inspector, click the Swap button.

   The Swap Symbol dialog appears, listing all the symbols in the current document's library (**Figure 7.27**). Flash highlights the name of the symbol you're modifying. In Windows, Flash places a bullet next to the name in the Symbol list.

Figure 7.27 Select a replacement symbol from the list in the Swap Symbol dialog, and click OK to exchange one symbol for another.

Before swapping: mouse scaled and rotated

After swapping: scaling and rotation applied to cat

Figure 7.28 When you swap symbols, any modifications you have made for the selected instance you're swapping apply to the replacement instance.

3. From the Symbol list, select the replacement symbol.

   In Windows, the original symbol remains bulleted; Flash highlights the new symbol and places it in the preview window.

4. Click OK.

   Flash places the new symbol on the Stage, locating the new symbol where the old one was located and applying any modifications you previously made for that instance (**Figure 7.28**).

✔ Tips

- To swap symbols quickly, double-click the new symbol in the Swap Symbol dialog. Flash replaces it and closes the dialog.

- The Duplicate Symbol button in the Swap Symbol dialog lets you make a copy of whatever symbol is selected in the list (Figure 7.27). If you know you need to tweak the master version of the replacement symbol for this instance, but you also want to keep the current version, click the Duplicate Symbol button, enter a name in the dialog that appears, and click OK. Make sure you select the duplicate as the replacement in the Swap Symbol dialog, and click OK. You can edit the duplicate's master symbol later.

Editing Master Symbols

After you create a symbol, you can refine and modify it in symbol-editing mode. Unlike modifications of a symbol instance, which affect just that instance on the Stage and leave the master symbol in the library unchanged, modifications made in symbol-editing mode affect the master symbol and all instances of that symbol in your movie.

You can enter symbol-editing mode in several ways.

To enter symbol-editing mode from the Stage:

1. On the Stage, select the symbol you want to edit.

2. To open the symbol editor, do one of the following:

   ▲ Choose Edit > Edit Symbols, or press ⌘-E (Mac) or Ctrl-E (Windows) (**Figure 7.29**).

   ▲ Choose Edit > Edit Selected.

   ▲ From the pop-up list of symbols in the Edit bar, choose the symbol you want to edit (**Figure 7.30**).

Flash opens the symbol editor in the current window. You can edit the symbol using any of the techniques you've learned for modifying graphics and creating and deleting content.

✔ Tip

■ The Edit in Place command lets you edit your master symbol in context on the Stage with all other items grayed out (**Figure 7.31**). To evoke the Edit in Place command, select a symbol instance and choose Edit > Edit in Place or double-click a symbol instance on the Stage. Any changes you make affect all instances of that symbol.

Figure 7.29 Choosing Edit > Edit Symbols takes you from document-editing mode to symbol-editing mode. If you have selected a symbol on the Stage, choosing Edit > Edit Selected also takes you to symbol-editing mode.

Figure 7.30 Choosing a symbol from the Edit Symbol pop-up menu in the Edit bar takes you into symbol-editing mode.

Figure 7.31 The Edit in Place command lets you see your symbol instance in context with other items on the Stage. The symbol instance appears in full color (here it's the large ant); the other elements on the Stage are grayed out. In this mode, changes made to the instance affect the master symbol and all the instances in the movie.

— *Delete selected item*

Figure 7.32 Click the trash-can icon to delete a selected library item.

Figure 7.33 You can also choose Delete from the library's panel menu to remove selected symbols from the active document.

Deleting Master Symbols

Deleting symbols can be a little trickier than deleting shapes or groups on the Stage. Deleting one instance of a symbol from its place on the Stage is easy; use the methods for cutting or deleting graphics discussed in Chapter 4. Deleting symbols from the library isn't difficult but does require some thought, because instances of the symbol may still be in use in your movie.

To delete one symbol from the library:

1. In the Library panel, select the symbol you want to remove.

2. To delete the symbol, do any of the following:
   ▲ At the bottom of the panel, click the Delete button (the trash-can icon) (**Figure 7.32**).
   ▲ From the panel menu in the top-right corner of the window, choose Delete (**Figure 7.33**).
   ▲ Press the Delete key.

To delete a folder of symbols from the library:

1. Select the folder you want to remove.

2. Follow step 2 of the preceding task.
   Flash removes the folder and all the symbols it contains from the library.

✔ Tip

- Always check the numbers in the Use Count column before you delete library items (**Figure 7.34**). You don't want to delete a symbol that you're currently using in a movie, which is especially easy to do if you've nested symbols within symbols. Some earlier versions of Flash warned you when you tried to delete an item that was in use in a movie. Flash CS4 doesn't.

Figure 7.34 Before deleting a symbol from the library, be sure to check the use count. It's safest to delete only items with a use count of zero. If the use count is not zero, track down where instances of the symbol appear in the movie and delete them there first; then you can safely delete the master symbol in the library.

The Mystery of Object-Level Undo

Every computer user gets familiar with the Undo command. ⌘-Z (Mac) or Ctrl-Z (Windows) becomes an automatic "oops" response to fix mistakes. Flash CS4 provides two types of undo: *document-level* undo and *object-level* undo.

In document-level undo, Flash tracks every undoable step you take. Open the History panel (choose Window > Other Panels > History); you'll see the steps you've done listed in order. In object-level undo, Flash also tracks every undoable step but makes a distinction between steps that pertain to working in the main document and steps that pertain to working on master symbols.

Object-level undo tracks the steps for each master symbol separately; each time you create a master symbol, object-level undo starts a separate History-panel list for that symbol. Within one work session (provided you haven't made changes in the History panel yourself), whenever you edit that master symbol, the History panel loads the steps for that symbol; any edits you make are added to the list. If you edit a different symbol, the panel loads the steps for that symbol. When you leave symbol-editing mode and return to document-editing mode, the History panel displays only the steps you've used in the main document.

Note that modifications you make to an instance of a symbol on the Stage are part of the history of the document, not of the master symbol.

To change from one type of undo to the other, choose Flash > Preferences (Mac) or Edit > Preferences (Windows). In the General category, from the Undo menu, choose the style you want. To track the history of master symbols separately, choose Object-Level Undo; to track all your steps in one integrated list, choose Document-Level Undo. It's best to choose your undo style at the beginning of a work session. If you switch in the middle, Flash wipes the current History panel clean.

Figure 7.35 The Property inspector reveals that the selected graphic is an instance of a symbol named anteater (top). To break the link with its master symbol, choose Modify > Break Apart. The Property inspector reveals that the selection now consists of shapes; it's no longer a symbol instance (bottom).

Converting Symbol Instances to Graphics

At times, you'll want to break the link between a placed instance of a symbol and the master symbol. You may want to redraw the shape in a specific instance but not in every instance, for example. To convert a symbol back to an independent shape or set of shapes, break it apart.

To break the symbol link:

1. On the Stage, select the symbol instance whose link you want to break.

2. Choose Modify > Break Apart, or press ⌘-B (Mac) or Ctrl-B (Windows) (**Figure 7.35**).

    Flash breaks the link to the symbol in the library and selects the symbol's elements. The Property inspector no longer displays information about the instance of the symbol; it displays information about the selected shapes.

    If the original symbol contained any grouped elements, they remain grouped after you break the link; ungrouped elements stay ungrouped. Any symbols that existed within the original symbol remain as instances of their respective master symbols. Now you can edit these elements as you learned to do in previous chapters.

A Note About Blend Modes

Blend modes give designers control over the way graphics in different layers and sublayers interact, letting you create new colors and interesting effects. They can be used for compositing—overlapping multiple images so that parts of each appear in one combined image—or to enhance or correct flaws in digital photos (for example, to lighten the areas of a photo where there is too much shadow). You can use blending with two types of symbols: buttons and movie clips. Select a button or movie-clip instance on the Stage. In the Display section of the Property inspector, from the Blending menu, choose a blend mode (**Figure 7.36**). Blending changes the selected symbol's colors on a pixel-by-pixel basis. Whether a particular pixel in the selected symbol instance actually changes color depends on the type of blend, the color of the pixel in the symbol instance, and the color of the pixel that lies on the layer below the movie clip. The pixels on lower layers may be other buttons, movie clips, graphic elements, or the background color of the Stage.

Figure 7.36 On the Stage, select a button or movie-clip instance to which you would like to apply a blend; then choose a mode from the Blending menu in the Display section of the Property inspector.

FRAME-BY-
FRAME ANIMATIONS

8

When to Use Frame-by-Frame Animation

Frame-by-frame animation displays multiple images, each slightly different from the next to create the illusion of motion; each image requires its own keyframe. Each keyframe adds a bit to your final movie's file size, which in turn affects the download time for people viewing your movie over the Web.

Reserve frame-by-frame techniques for animations where shapes must constantly change in subtle ways that you can best control by redrawing. Otherwise, use Flash's classic-tweening, shape-tweening, and motion-tweening features (see Chapters 9 through 12).

In this chapter you place a shape in multiple keyframes, making a circle seem to bounce like a ball. You could minimize file size by converting the ball shape to a symbol and reusing it in the keyframes (adding keyframes with the same symbol adds little to the size of the file). In the real world, however, if you can use a symbol, it would be more efficient to use one of Flash's tweening methods.

Frame-by-frame animation was the conventional form of animation used before the days of computers. Live-action movies and video are really a form of frame-by-frame animation. The camera captures motion by snapping a picture every so often. Animation simulates motion by showing drawings of elements at various stages of a movement.

Traditional animators, such as those who worked for the early Walt Disney or Warner Bros. studios from the 1930s through the 1960s, had to create hundreds of images, each one slightly different from the next, to achieve every movement of each character or element in the cartoon. To turn those drawings into animations, they captured the images on film, putting a different image in each frame of the movie.

Traditional animators painted individual characters (or parts of characters) and graphics on transparent sheets called *cels*. They stacked the cels to create the entire image for the frame. The cel technique allowed animators to save time by reusing parts of an image that stayed the same in more than one frame.

In Adobe Flash CS4 Professional, you, too, can make frame-by-frame animations by placing different content in different frames. Flash calls the frames that hold new content *keyframes*.

Touring the Timeline

When you create a new Flash document, the Timeline displays a single layer with hundreds of little boxes. The first box has a solid black outline and displays a hollow bullet; the bullet indicates that the frame has been defined as a *keyframe* (a container for content, such as graphics, sound, and video). A hollow bullet indicates a *blank keyframe* (one with no content on the Stage). When you place graphics on the Stage for a keyframe, the Timeline displays a solid bullet. The rest of the boxes have gray outlines; these are undefined placeholder frames, or *protoframes*. Every fifth protoframe is tinted gray.

As you work with the Timeline to create animation, you will convert protoframes into *frames* (or *in-between frames*) and *keyframes*, creating *spans* in the process. A span consists of a keyframe plus any in-between frames that follow it. Flash CS4 creates three types of spans: *keyframe spans,* which are used in frame-by-frame animation, classic tweening (Chapter 9), and shape tweening (Chapter 10); *tween spans,* which are used in motion tweening (Chapter 11); and *pose spans,* which are used in inverse kinematics (Chapter 13). In this chapter, you'll work solely with keyframe spans.

Flash outlines keyframe spans with black in the Timeline and puts a hollow rectangle in the last frame of the span. When the keyframe at the beginning of a span has content, the in-between frames in the span continue to display that content on the Stage. If you've set Frame View to Tinted Frames (the default), the in-between frames of a keyframe span with content also have a gray tint in the Timeline. **Figure 8.1** shows a Timeline with a variety of defined frames and spans.

Figure 8.1 Similar to an interactive outline, the Timeline represents each frame of your movie. Click any frame, and Flash displays its contents on the Stage.

Controls frame size

Controls layer height

Applies gray shade to frames with content

Thumbnail of content at relative Stage position, sized proportionally in Timeline frame

Thumbnail of content centered, fills Timeline frame

Figure 8.2 The Timeline's panel menu gives options for viewing the frames in the Timeline.

Optimizing the Timeline

The Timeline is the framework that holds all the little slices of motion that make up an animation. The Timeline displays the layers and frames of the currently active document. New documents automatically start with a Timeline containing one layer and a blank keyframe as the first frame. You add more frames to hold content and tweens.

To view frames at different sizes:

◆ In the Timeline, from the panel menu (also known as the Frame View menu), choose a display option (**Figure 8.2**).

Flash resizes the frame representations in the Timeline to reflect your choice (see the sidebar "Frames of Many Sizes").

Timeline History

In versions of Flash before CS4, each document had its own Timeline that appeared within the document itself (on the Mac, if you had multiple open documents, you saw multiple Timelines). In CS4, each document has its own Timeline information, but the Timeline appears in a separate panel. You can see just one Timeline at a time.

The Timeline offers five size options for viewing frames and two options for previewing thumbnails of frame contents. A Flash movie may contain hundreds of frames; the Timeline's scroll bars let you access frames not currently visible in the Timeline panel. The Timeline works just like any other Flash panel. You can open and close the Timeline, resize it, dock it, collapse it to an icon, and so on (see Chapter 1).

Frames of Many Sizes

The Timeline's panel menu (also known as the Frame View menu) gives you options for setting frame size for viewing the Timeline. For documents with many layers and frames, choosing Tiny from the menu lets you squeeze the greatest number of frames into the panel, but it can be hard to distinguish what you're seeing. Normal and Medium are better choices when you need to distinguish keyframes with content from blank keyframes or in-between frames. The Preview mode and Preview in Context mode let you see thumbnails of a keyframe's content within the Timeline. **Figure 8.3** shows some of the frame views available.

Figure 8.3 Flash can display the frames in the Timeline in a variety of sizes, from Tiny to Large. You can also preview the contents of each frame in the Timeline.

Figure 8.4 Select a frame in the Timeline (top) and then choose Insert > Timeline > Blank Keyframe (middle) to add a new blank keyframe (bottom).

Context Menu for Frames

The tasks in this section access frame-related commands from the Menu bar, but all the relevant commands for working with frames are available from the contextual frame menu as well. Control-click (Mac) or right-click (Windows) a frame in the Timeline to bring up the contextual frame menu.

Creating Keyframes

Flash offers two commands for creating keyframes. Insert > Timeline > Blank Keyframe defines a keyframe that's empty; use this command when you want to change the contents of the Stage completely. Insert > Timeline > Keyframe defines a keyframe that duplicates the content of the preceding keyframe in that layer; use this command when you want to modify the content of the preceding keyframe.

To add a blank keyframe to the end of your movie:

1. Create a new Flash document.

   The new document by default has one layer and one blank keyframe at frame 1. If you like, add content to frame 1.

2. In the Timeline, click the protoframe for frame 10 to select it.

3. Choose Insert > Timeline > Blank Keyframe (**Figure 8.4**).

   Flash revises the Timeline to give you information about the frames you've defined. A hollow rectangle appears in frame 9, and a black line separates frame 9 from frame 10. This line indicates where the content for one keyframe span ends and the content for the next keyframe begins. Flash replaces the gray bars separating protoframes 2–9 with tiny gray tick marks and removes the gray highlight that appeared in every fifth frame of the undefined frames.

To create a blank keyframe within a keyframe span:

1. Follow the steps in the preceding task to create a single-layer, ten-frame movie.

2. In the Timeline, select frame 1.

3. Draw a shape on the Stage.

   Flash updates the Timeline, adding a solid bullet to frame 1 (**Figure 8.5**).

   With Tinted Frames chosen in the panel menu (Flash's default setting), Flash shades frames 1–9 with gray. The shading indicates that keyframe 1 has content that remains visible through frame 9 in this layer. A hollow rectangle appears in frame 9, indicating the end of the span of in-between frames that displays the content of keyframe 1.

   Frame 10 still contains a hollow bullet, meaning that it has no content.

4. In the Timeline, in the area above the layers, click the number 5 or drag the playhead to position it in frame 5.

   Flash displays frame 5 on the Stage. Notice that this in-between frame continues to display the content of the preceding keyframe, frame 1.

5. Choose Insert > Timeline > Blank Keyframe.

   Flash converts the selected in-between frame to a keyframe and removes all content from the Stage (**Figure 8.6**).

Figure 8.5 When you place content in a keyframe, Flash displays that frame in the Timeline with a solid bullet. The gray tint on the in-between frames indicates that content from the preceding keyframe appears during these frames. The hollow square indicates the end of the span of in-between frames displaying the same content. The hollow circle indicates a blank keyframe.

Figure 8.6 When you convert an in-between frame that displays content to a blank keyframe, Flash removes that frame's content from the Stage. Frames 6–9 are tinted when they display the content of frame 1 (left). When you insert a blank keyframe at frame 5 (right), the tint disappears, because these frames now display the content of the most recent keyframe, frame 5, which is empty.

Current frame

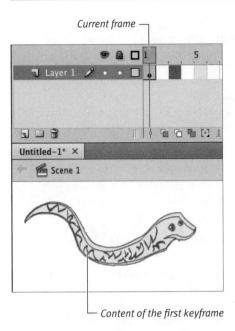

Content of the first keyframe

Duplicate of the first keyframe

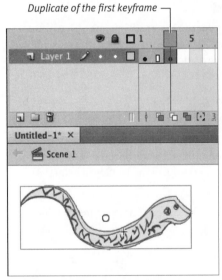

Figure 8.7 The Insert > Timeline > Keyframe command creates a keyframe that duplicates the contents of the preceding keyframe in that layer.

To duplicate the contents of the preceding keyframe:

1. Open a new Flash document and place content in keyframe 1.

2. In the Timeline, select frame 3.

   The playhead doesn't move into the protoframe area, but frame 3 is highlighted as the current selected frame.

3. Choose Insert > Timeline > Keyframe.

   Flash creates a new keyframe, duplicates the contents of frame 1 in frame 3, and places a solid bullet in the Timeline at frame 3 and a hollow rectangle in frame 2 (**Figure 8.7**). The content of frames 1 and 3 is totally separate.

✔ Tips

- The word insert used in connection with keyframes is a bit misleading. Choosing Insert > Timeline > Keyframe adds frames only if you've selected a protoframe. If you select an existing in-between frame, Insert > Timeline > Keyframe converts that frame to a keyframe and leaves the length of the movie as it was. The Insert > Timeline > Frame command always adds frames to your movie.

- You can't add a blank keyframe between back-to-back keyframes. With keyframes in frames 5 and 6, select frame 5 and choose Insert > Timeline > Blank Keyframe. The playhead moves to frame 6, but Flash doesn't add a new blank keyframe. With frame 5 selected, you must choose Insert > Timeline > Frame. Flash creates an in-between frame at frame 6. Now select frame 5 or frame 6 and choose Insert > Timeline > Blank Keyframe; Flash converts frame 6 to a keyframe.

Keyframe Mysteries: Insert vs. Convert

In addition to the Insert > Timeline > Keyframe and Insert > Timeline > Blank Keyframe commands, Flash offers commands for converting frames to keyframes. Choose Modify > Timeline > Convert to Keyframes (or press F6) or choose Modify > Timeline > Convert to Blank Keyframes (or press F7). These conversion commands are also found in the contextual menu for frames—Control-click (Mac) or right-click (Windows) a frame in the Timeline to access the menu.

Whether you should insert or convert keyframes depends on how many frames you have selected when you issue the command and how many frames you want to create. The Insert commands create a single keyframe regardless of how many frames you have selected; the Modify commands create multiple keyframes, one for each selected frame.

With a single frame selected, the Insert > Timeline > Keyframe command and the Modify > Timeline > Convert to Keyframe command work identically. If you select one protoframe or in-between frame, both commands transform that frame to a keyframe and duplicate the content of the preceding keyframe (if any). If you select a keyframe that is followed by an in-between frame or a protoframe, both commands transform that following frame to a keyframe with the same content as the selected frame. Neither command has any effect on a selected keyframe that is followed by another keyframe.

With multiple protoframes or in-between frames selected, the Insert > Timeline > Keyframe command creates a single keyframe, usually in the same frame as the playhead (if you select frames at the end of your movie, Flash places the new keyframe in the last selected frame). The remaining selected frames become in-between frames.

With multiple protoframes or in-between frames selected, the Modify > Timeline > Convert to Keyframes command creates a keyframe in every selected frame.

The commands for blank keyframes work similarly. Insert > Timeline > Blank Keyframe creates one keyframe in the same frame as the playhead; the remaining frames become in-between frames. Modify > Timeline > Convert to Blank Keyframe creates a blank keyframe in all the selected frames.

These commands work a bit differently when used within the tween span of a motion tween (see Chapter 11).

Figure 8.8 Choose Insert > Timeline > Frame to add in-between frames to the Timeline.

Timeline before evoking Insert > Timeline > Frame

Timeline after evoking Insert > Timeline > Frame

Figure 8.9 The Insert > Timeline > Frame command adds an in-between frame after the frame where the playhead is located.

Creating In-Between Frames

The frames that appear between keyframes are in a sense tied to the keyframe that precedes them. They display its content and allow you a space in which to create classic tweens and shape tweens (see Chapters 9 and 10). Flash makes the connections between these frames clear by tinting them and placing a hollow rectangle at the end of the keyframe span. Motion tweens also rely on a span containing in-between frames to display content, but the span works differently (see Chapter 11).

To add in-between frames:

1. Open or create a Flash document with keyframes and content in frames 1 and 2.

2. In the Timeline, position the playhead in keyframe 1.

3. Choose Insert > Timeline > Frame, or press F5 (**Figure 8.8**).

   Flash adds an in-between frame (**Figure 8.9**). Your movie now contains a keyframe at frame 1, an in-between frame at frame 2, and another keyframe at frame 3.

What Are Keyframes and In-Between Frames?

In the early days of animation, it took veritable armies of artists to create the enormous number of drawings that frame-by-frame animation requires. To keep costs down, the studios broke the work into categories based on the artistic skill required and the pay provided. The work might start with creating spec sheets for each character. Then came storyboards that outlined the action over the course of the animation. Eventually, individual artists drew and painted hundreds of cels, each slightly different, to bring the animation to life.

To make the process manageable, animators broke each movement into a series of the most crucial frames that defined a movement, called *keyframes*, and frames that incorporated the incremental changes necessary to simulate the movement, called *in-between frames*.

Keyframes define a significant change to a character or graphic. Imagine a 25-frame sequence in which Bugs Bunny starts out facing the audience and then turns to his right to look at Daffy Duck. This scene requires two keyframes—Bugs in a face-on view and Bugs in profile—and 23 in-between frames.

In the early days, some artists specialized in creating keyframes. Other artists—usually lower-paid—had the job of creating the frames that fell in between the keyframes. These *in-betweeners* (or *tweeners*, for short) copied the drawings in the keyframes, making just the slight adjustments necessary to create the intended movement in the desired number of frames while retaining the continuity of the character. In Chapters 9 through 13, you learn how to turn Flash into your own personal wage slave. The program takes on the drudgery of in-betweening for certain types of animation.

Flash's classic- and shape-tween features require that you use keyframes to define any change in the content or image, even if the change affects just one property of an object. Flash's motion-tween feature works a bit differently. A motion tween relies on one keyframe that holds the tweened object; the tween then uses *property keyframes* to define changes to individual properties (see Chapter 11). Flash's inverse kinematics (IK) feature also relies on just one keyframe per span; *pose frames* indicate changes to the IK object (see Chapter 13).

Flash doesn't use the term *in-between frames;* it uses the term *frame* for any frames that aren't defined as keyframes, property keyframes, or pose frames. For clarity, the tasks in this book use the term *in-between frames* when referring to such frames.

Figure 8.10 Both frame-selection styles treat protoframes identically for selection. Position the pointer over a protoframe (top) and click to select it (bottom).

Selecting Frames in Keyframe Spans

Flash offers two styles for selecting frames in the Timeline; you set the style in Preferences. Frame-based selection, the default style, treats every frame individually. Span-based selection treats frames as members of a *keyframe span*—the keyframe plus any in-between frames that follow it and display its content. In the span-based selection style, clicking one frame in the middle of a span selects the entire span.

Flash CS4 introduces a new twist on the concept of spans with motion-tween spans and pose spans. No matter which selection style you set in Preferences, there is only one way to make selections within these spans; it's similar to the span-based selection but with a few variations. (You'll learn about working with these new types of spans in Chapters 11 and 13.)

Except where noted, the examples in this book use Flash's default selection style, frame-based selection.

To select undefined frames:

To work with protoframes in either selection style, do any of the following:

◆ To select one protoframe, click it (**Figure 8.10**).

◆ To select two protoframes and all the frames between them, Shift-click the first and last protoframes.

◆ To select noncontiguous protoframes, ⌘-click (Mac) or Ctrl-click (Windows) the protoframes.

The process of selecting frames that have not been defined works identically in Flash's two frame-selection styles.

To choose a selection style:

1. Choose Flash > Preferences (Mac) *or* Edit > Preferences (Windows).

   The Preferences dialog appears.

2. From the Category list, select General.

   The General settings appear in the right-hand pane of the dialog (**Figure 8.11**).

3. In the Timeline section, choose either of the following frame-selection styles:

   ▲ To manipulate keyframe spans in the Timeline, select the Span-Based Selection check box (**Figure 8.12**).

   ▲ To manipulate individual frames in the Timeline, deselect the Span-Based Selection check box (**Figure 8.13**).

To select frames inside keyframe spans—frame-based mode:

In the Timeline—with preferences set to frame-based selection style—do one of the following:

◆ To select a keyframe, click it.

◆ To select the last frame in a keyframe span, click it.

◆ To select just a middle frame in a keyframe span, click that frame (**Figure 8.14**).

◆ To select an entire keyframe span, double-click any frame in the span.

◆ To add frames to your selection, Shift-click the additional frames. Flash selects all the frames between the last selected frame and the frame you Shift-click.

◆ To select a range of frames, Shift-click the first and last frame in the range; or with no frames selected, click and drag through the range of frames.

Figure 8.11 Choose the way frame selection works in the Timeline from the General category of the Preferences dialog.

Timeline: ☑ Span based selection

Figure 8.12 In the General section of the Preferences dialog, select the Span-Based Selection check box to work with keyframe spans as a unit in the Timeline.

Timeline: ☐ Span based selection

Figure 8.13 In the General section of the Preferences dialog, deselect the Span-Based Selection check box to work with individual keyframes in the Timeline.

Figure 8.14 In Flash's frame-based selection style, clicking a frame in the middle of a keyframe span (top) selects just that frame (bottom).

Figure 8.15 In Flash's span-based selection style, clicking a frame in the middle of a keyframe span (top) selects the whole span (bottom).

Figure 8.16 With Flash's span-based frame-selection style, you can Shift-click to select keyframe spans that aren't contiguous.

To select frames inside keyframe spans—span-based mode:

In the Timeline—with preferences set to span-based selection style—do one of the following:

◆ To select a keyframe, click it.

◆ To select the last frame in keyframe span, click it.

◆ To select one in-between frame, ⌘-click (Mac) or Ctrl-click (Windows) that frame.

◆ To select an entire keyframe span, click a middle frame in the keyframe span (**Figure 8.15**); or Shift-click the first or last frame in the span.

◆ To add other spans to your selection, Shift-click any frame in each additional span. The selection can include noncontiguous spans (**Figure 8.16**).

◆ To select a range of frames, ⌘-drag (Mac) or Ctrl-drag (Windows) through the frames.

✔ Tips

■ In both selection styles, you can select all the frames in a layer by clicking the layer name. In the span-based selection style, you can also select all the frames in a layer by double-clicking any frame.

■ In both selection styles, you can select noncontiguous frames by ⌘-clicking (Mac) or Ctrl-clicking (Windows) each frame that you want to include. Note that this technique does not work within the tween span of a motion tween (Chapter 11) or within an IK pose span (Chapter 13).

Manipulating Frames in One Layer

You can't copy or paste frames with the standard Copy and Paste commands that you use for graphic elements. Flash's Edit menu provides special commands for copying and pasting frames. Flash also lets you drag selected frames to new locations in the Timeline.

For the following tasks, open a new Flash document. Create a ten-frame movie with keyframes at frames 1, 3, 5, and 9. Using the text tool, place a text field in each keyframe, and enter the number of the frame in the text field; this technique makes it easy to tell what frame winds up where as you practice.

To copy and paste a single frame:

1. In the Timeline, select keyframe 3.

2. Choose Edit > Timeline > Copy Frames, or press Option-⌘-C (Mac) or Ctrl-Alt-C (Windows) (**Figure 8.17**).

   Flash copies the selected frame to the Clipboard.

3. In the Timeline, click frame 4 to select it as the location for pasting the copied frame.

4. Choose Edit > Timeline > Paste Frames, or press Option-⌘-V (Mac) or Ctrl-Alt-V (Windows).

   Flash pastes the copied frame into frame 4 (**Figure 8.18**).

Figure 8.17 Flash's Edit menu provides special commands for copying and pasting frames in the Timeline.

Copy Keyframe 3

Selected location for pasting

Flash pastes copied Keyframe 3 content into Frame 4

Figure 8.18 When you paste a frame with new content into an in-between frame, Flash converts the frame to a keyframe.

Keyframe 5 selected

Pasted content from keyframe 3

Figure 8.19 When you paste a frame with new content into a keyframe, Flash replaces the keyframe's content.

5. Paste another copy into frame 5 (**Figure 8.19**).

Flash replaces the contents of keyframe 5 with the content of keyframe 3.

6. Paste another copy into protoframe 12.

Flash extends the movie to accommodate the pasted frame. Note that the playhead won't move to protoframe 12 until after you've pasted the copy to create a defined frame.

✔ Tips

■ You can copy and paste multiple frames; in step 1 of the preceding task, select a range of frames.

■ To copy and paste the content of a keyframe, you can also copy an in-between frame that displays that content. When you paste, Flash creates a new keyframe.

■ Warning: Flash always replaces the content of the selected frame with the pasted frame (or, for multiple-frame pastes, with the first pasted frame). If you're not careful, you may eat up the content of keyframes you intended to keep. To be safe, always paste frames into in-between frames or blank keyframes. You can always delete an unwanted keyframe separately.

To move frames using drag and drop:

1. In the Timeline of your practice document, select the keyframe span that starts with keyframe 5 and ends with frame 8. Flash highlights the selection in blue.

2. Position the pointer over the selected frames.

3. Click and drag the selected frames.

   A darker blue outline appears around the selection highlight as you drag. Use the blue rectangle to preview the new location for the selected frames in the Timeline.

4. To move the selected frames to the end of your movie, drag the rectangle past the last defined frame and into the area of protoframes, and release the mouse button.

   Flash adds frames to the end of the movie; these frames display the content from frames 5–8. In frame-based selection style, Flash completely removes the content from frames 5–8 and adds those frames to the preceding span. In span-based selection style, Flash removes the content but keeps a blank keyframe at frame 5 (**Figure 8.20**).

5. To move the selected frames to the very beginning of your movie, drag the selected frames to frame 1 and release the mouse button.

   The dragged frames replace the content of frames 1–4; there is no longer a keyframe at frame 5.

Select and drag: either selection style

Preview of new frame location

After drop: frame-based selection style

After drop: span-based selection style

Figure 8.20 The process of dragging and dropping frames in the Timeline to relocate them is the same in Flash's two frame-selection styles (top). The results, however, are quite different (bottom). The frame-based selection style removes selected keyframes from their original location, leaving only in-between frames. The span-based style retains the original keyframes but removes their content.

✔ Tips

- To drag a copy of selected frames in the Timeline, hold down Option (Mac) or Alt (Windows) as you drag.

- No matter which frame-selection style you use, pressing the ⌘ key (Mac) or Ctrl key (Windows) lets you access some of the functionality of the other style temporarily. In frame-based selection, the modifier lets you access the double-headed arrow pointer for extending keyframe spans. In span-based mode, the modifier gives you the arrow pointer for selecting individual frames.

- If you make a mistake in modifying the frames in the Timeline, you can undo your steps by choosing Edit > Undo. Flash tracks the selection and deselection of frames as part of the undo history. Operations such as dragging frames to move them or to extend spans may require repeated Undo commands, because some of the steps involved are things Flash does behind the scenes.

The Trick to Extending Keyframe Spans

In span-based selection style, the pointer becomes a double-headed arrow when it hovers over the first or last frame of a keyframe span. You can use this pointer to drag a keyframe or end-of-span frame to the right or the left to increase or decrease the length of the span.

Resizing a span in the middle of other spans gets a bit tricky. Flash won't let your expanding span eat up the content of other keyframes. Your expansion can reduce the length of a neighboring span, however. In your practice document, for example, using span-based selection, position the pointer over frame 4 (the end of keyframe 3's span); the frame must not be selected. With the double-headed arrow pointer, drag frame 4 to the right. When you get to frame 7, you can drag no farther. Release the mouse button. The span that starts at frame 3 now extends through frame 7. The content that was originally in keyframe 5 still exists, but Flash has pushed it into frame 8.

To increase the length of a span without affecting the length of neighboring spans, select the span or any frame within it; then choose Insert > Timeline > Frame, or press F5. Flash adds an in-between frame to the selected span and pushes all subsequent spans to the right in the Timeline.

When you reduce the size of a span by dragging, Flash creates blank keyframe spans to cover any gaps between the end of the span you're resizing and the beginning of the neighboring span. To simply reduce the number of in-between frames, you can use the Remove Frames command (see "Removing Frames," the next section in this chapter). Note that you must use different techniques for resizing tween spans for motion tweens (Chapter 11) and pose spans for inverse kinematics (Chapter 13).

MANIPULATING FRAMES IN ONE LAYER

Removing Frames

Flash has two commands for removing frames: Clear Keyframe and Remove Frames. Clear Keyframe removes keyframe status from a selected frame or range of frames (converting the keyframes to in-between frames) and deletes the keyframes' content from the movie. Clear Keyframe has no effect on the number of frames in the movie. Remove Frames removes frames (and their content, if they're keyframes) from the movie. Remove Frames reduces the number of frames in the movie. For the following tasks, use the same practice document you created for working with the tasks in "Manipulating Frames in One Layer," earlier in this chapter.

To remove keyframe status from a frame:

1. In the Timeline, select keyframe 5.

2. Choose Modify > Timeline > Clear Keyframe, or press Shift-F6.

   Flash removes the bullet from frame 5 in the Timeline (indicating that the frame is no longer a keyframe) and removes the graphic element it contained. Frame 5 becomes an in-between frame, displaying the contents of the keyframe at frame 3 (**Figure 8.21**). The total number of frames in the movie remains the same.

Before clearing the keyframe

Selected keyframe is frame 5

Content of selected keyframe

After clearing the keyframe

Frame 5 becomes an in-between frame

Frame 5 displays the content of the previous keyframe

Figure 8.21 The Modify > Timeline > Clear Keyframe command removes the contents of the selected keyframe from the Stage and converts the keyframe to an in-between frame. The Clear Keyframe command doesn't change the overall length of the movie.

Selected in-between frame

After deleting

Content originally in keyframe 5 is now in keyframe 4

Figure 8.22 The Edit > Timeline > Remove Frames command removes frames from the movie and thus reduces its length.

To delete a frame from a keyframe span:

1. With your practice file in its original state (keyframes at 1, 3, 5, and 9), select frame 4 in the Timeline.

   Frame 4 is an in-between frame associated with keyframe 3.

2. Choose Edit > Timeline > Remove Frames, or press Shift-F5.

   Flash deletes what was frame 4, reducing the overall length of the movie by one frame (**Figure 8.22**). The keyframe content that was in frame 5 moves back one frame to become keyframe 4.

3. Select keyframe 3 and choose Edit > Timeline > Remove Frames again.

   Flash deletes the selected keyframe and its content, and reduces the length of the movie by one frame. The keyframe content that was just in frame 4 moves back one frame to become keyframe 3.

✔ Tip

■ Flash doesn't let you use Clear Keyframe to remove keyframe status from the first frame of a movie, but you can delete it. If you select all the frames in one layer and choose Edit > Timeline > Remove Frames, Flash removes all the defined frames in the Timeline, leaving only protoframes. You must add back a keyframe at frame 1 to place content on that layer.

REMOVING FRAMES

To delete a range of frames:

1. Using your practice file in its original state (keyframes at 1, 3, 5, and 9), in the Timeline, select frames 3–6.

2. Choose Edit > Timeline > Remove Frames. Flash removes all the selected frames (**Figure 8.23**).

✔ Tip

■ With the frame-based selection style active, you can quickly replace the contents of one keyframe with those of another. Select an in-between frame that displays the contents you want to copy. Drag that source frame over the keyframe whose contents you want to replace. Flash replaces the contents of the target keyframe with the contents of the source keyframe.

Figure 8.23 The Edit > Timeline > Remove Frames command can delete a selected range of frames. Because an entire keyframe span (frames 3 and 4) is included in the selection (top), Flash not only reduces the number of frames but also removes the content of that keyframe span (middle). Where only part of a span was selected (originally frames 5 and 6), the span gets shorter, but the content remains the same (bottom).

Figure 8.24 In keyframe 1, using the oval tool, draw a circular fill near the top of the Stage. This shape will become a bouncing ball.

Making a Simple Frame-by-Frame Animation

In traditional cel animation or flip-book animation, you create the illusion of movement by showing a series of images, each slightly different from the rest. When you create each of these drawings and place them in a series of keyframes, that process is called *frame-by-frame animation*. When you create only the most crucial images and allow Flash to interpolate the minor changes that take place between them, you're creating *tweened animation*. You learn more about tweening in Chapters 9 through 12.

A time-honored example of frame-by-frame animation is a bouncing ball. A crude animation of a bouncing ball takes just three frames. Each frame shows the ball in a different position.

To set up the initial keyframe:

1. Create a new Flash document, and name it something like FrmByFrmBounce.

   By default, Flash creates a document with one layer and a keyframe at frame 1. Choose View > Grid > Show Grid to help with positioning graphics in this task.

2. In the Timeline, select keyframe 1.

   From the Panel menu, choose Preview in Context mode. This setting makes it easy to keep track of what you do in the example.

3. Near the top of the Stage, using the oval tool, draw a circle (**Figure 8.24**).

   The circle will be your ball. Make it fairly large.

To create the second keyframe:

1. In the Timeline, click the protoframe for frame 2 to select it.

2. Choose Insert > Timeline > Keyframe.

   Flash creates a keyframe in frame 2 that duplicates your ball from keyframe 1.

3. In keyframe 2, select the ball and reposition it at the bottom of the Stage (**Figure 8.25**).

To create the third keyframe:

1. In the Timeline, select frame 3.

2. Choose Insert > Timeline > Keyframe.

   Flash creates a keyframe in frame 3 that duplicates your ball from keyframe 2.

3. In keyframe 3, select the ball and reposition it, placing the ball roughly two-thirds of the way back up the Stage, almost back to the original position (**Figure 8.26**).

   That's it. Believe it or not, you have just created all the content you need to animate a bouncing ball. To see how it works, in the Timeline, click keyframes 1, 2, and 3 in turn. As Flash changes the content of the Stage at each click, you see a very crude animation.

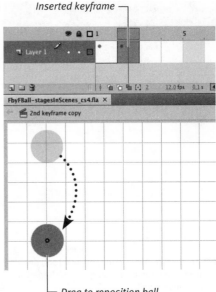

Inserted keyframe

Drag to reposition ball

Figure 8.25 Use the Insert > Timeline > Keyframe command to duplicate the ball from keyframe 1 in keyframe 2. Then drag the ball to reposition it.

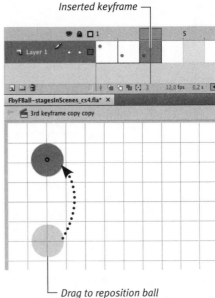

Inserted keyframe

Drag to reposition ball

Figure 8.26 Use the Insert > Timeline > Keyframe command to duplicate the ball from keyframe 2 in keyframe 3. Drag the ball to reposition it again.

Smoother Frame-by-Frame Animation

The three-frame bouncing ball you created in the preceding task is crude; it's herky-jerky; and at Flash CS4's default 24 frames per second, it's much too fast. You can spread out the action of a frame-by-frame animation (and slow it down) by separating the back-to-back keyframes with in-between frames (see the tasks in "Varying Frame-by-Frame Speed," later in this section). To smooth the movement of a frame-by-frame animation, you need to create more snapshots that define the ball's position in the air as it moves up and down in smaller increments. This means adding more keyframes (see "Creating Keyframes," earlier in this chapter) and repositioning the ball slightly in each one (**Figure 8.27**). The smoothest frame-by-frame animations make tiny changes to graphic elements over numerous keyframes. Adding keyframes does add to file size, though not as much as adding multimedia elements such as sound and video.

Figure 8.27 With frames set to Preview in Context, the Timeline shows the location of the ball in this frame-by-frame animation; the ball moves from the top of the Stage to the bottom in a single step (left). Adding more keyframes and moving the ball in smaller steps creates a smoother animation (right).

Previewing the Action

Flash's Controller window offers VCR-style playback buttons for playing animations during authoring. You can also have Flash export the file and open it for you in Flash Player.

To use the Controller:

1. Choose Window > Toolbars > Controller (**Figure 8.28**).

   Flash opens a window containing standard VCR-style buttons.

2. In the Controller window, click the button for the command you want to use (**Figure 8.29**).

✔ Tips

- The Control menu in the Menu bar duplicates the Controller's functions and offers options for stepping through a movie one frame at a time.

- You can use keyboard commands to move one frame at a time: to go forward, press the period (.) key; to go backward, press the comma (,) key.

- To scrub (scroll quickly) through the movie, drag the playhead backward or forward through the frames in the Timeline. Flash displays the content of each frame as the playhead moves through it.

Figure 8.28 To access the Controller, choose Window > Toolbars > Controller.

Figure 8.29 The Controller window contains VCR-style buttons for controlling playback of Flash movies.

PREVIEWING THE ACTION

Figure 8.30 Choose Control > Test Movie to see your movie in action in Flash Player.

To play through all frames in the Flash editor:

Do one of the following:

◆ To play through the frames once, choose Control > Play, or press Enter.

Flash displays each frame in turn, starting with the current frame and running through the end of the movie. The Play command in the Control menu changes to a Stop command, which you can use to stop playback at any time.

◆ To play through the frames repeatedly, choose Control > Loop Playback.

When you issue a Play command, Flash plays the movie repeatedly until you issue a Stop command.

To play through frames in Flash Player:

◆ Choose Control > Test Movie or press ⌘-Enter (Mac) or Ctrl-Enter (**Figure 8.30**).

Flash exports your movie to a Flash Player (SWF) file and opens it in a separate window. Flash stores the SWF file at the same hierarchical level of your system as the original Flash file. The SWF file has the same name as the original, except that Flash appends the .swf extension.

PREVIEWING THE ACTION

Setting the Frame Rate

In Flash, you can set only one frame rate for the entire movie. You set the frame rate in the Document Properties dialog.

To set the frame rate via Status bar:

1. Open a Flash document and access the Timeline.

2. To enter a playback speed for this movie, in the Status bar, use the Frame Rate hot text to enter a value between 0 and 120 (**Figure 8.31**).

   To use a precise value, click the hot text, enter a number in the field that activates, then press Enter. To choose a value interactively, position the pointer over the hot text; when the pointing finger with a double arrow appears, drag left (or down) to lower the value or drag right (or up) to increase the value.

   Frame rate is measured in frames per second and indicates how quickly Flash displays the frames to your viewers (see the sidebar "Understanding Frame Rate").

✔ Tips

- You can also set the frame rate in the Document Property inspector.To access it, select a frame in the Timeline, or using the selection tool, click an empty area of the Stage or Pasteboard. In the Properties section of the inspector, use the FPS hot text to enter a playback speed for your movie. Flash updates the frame rate in the Status bar.

- Another way to set a document's frame rate is via the Document Properties dialog. Choose Modify > Document, or press ⌘-J (Mac) or Ctrl-J (Windows). The Document Properties dialog appears. Enter a value in the Frame Rate field, then click OK.

Elapsed time ⎯

Frame rate ⎯

Current frame ⎯

Figure 8.31 The Status bar contains Frame Rate hot text for quick entry of the speed for your movie.

Varying Frame-by-Frame Speed

Although the frame rate for a movie is constant, you can make any particular bit of animation go faster or slower by changing the number of frames it takes to complete the action. You can lengthen a portion of an animation by adding more keyframes or by adding in-between frames. In the bouncing-ball example, the ball may drop down slowly (say, over five frames) but rebound more quickly (over three frames). The smoothest frame-by-frame animation has many keyframes, each showing the ball in a slightly different position. Adding keyframes, however, increases file size. Sometimes you can get away with adding in-between frames to slow the action. In-between frames add little to the exported movie's file size.

To add in-between frames:

1. Open (or create) a five-frame bouncing-ball movie.

   Keyframe 1 shows the ball at the top of the Stage, keyframes 2 and 3 show the ball at two places in its descent, keyframe 4 shows the ball at the bottom of the Stage, and keyframe 5 shows the ball bouncing most of the way back up.

2. Choose File > Save As, and make a copy of the file.

   Give the file a distinguishing name, such as BounceSlower.

3. In the copy's Timeline, select frame 1.

4. Control-click (Mac) or right-click (Windows) to access the contextual menu for frames.

   continues on next page

Understanding Frame Rate

The illusion of animation relies on the human brain's ability to fill in gaps in continuity. When you see a series of images in very quick succession, your brain perceives a continuous moving image. In animation, you must display the sequence of images fast enough to convince the brain that it's looking at a single image.

Frame rate controls how fast Flash delivers the images. If the images come too fast, the movie turns into a blur. Slow delivery too much, and your viewers start perceiving each frame as a separate image; then the movement seems jerky. In addition, when you're working in Flash, you're most likely planning to deliver the movie over the Internet, and you don't always know what types of systems your viewers will be using. That means you won't necessarily be able to deliver a fast frame rate.

Flash CS4's default rate matches the standard rate for film—24 frames per second (fps). For graphic animation that's going out over the Internet to a target audience using low-bandwidth connections, consider lowering the frame rate to 15 or 12 fps. Today's high-bandwidth connections and Flash Player 10's capabilities, however, make still higher frame rates a possibility. If you're confident that your target audience has the capability to handle it, and you want to deliver even smoother animations or lots of video, you may want to use a frame rate as high as 31 fps.

5. Choose Insert Frame.

Flash inserts an in-between frame at frame 2 and pushes the keyframe that was there to frame 3 (**Figure 8.32**).

6. Repeat steps 3–5 for the second and third keyframes in the movie.

You wind up with keyframes in frames 1, 3, 5, 7, and 8 (**Figure 8.33**).

7. Choose Control > Test Movie.

Flash exports the movie to a SWF file and opens it in Flash Player. Play through the regular five-frame bouncing ball, and then play through the one you just created (the one named BounceSlower). You can see that the action in the movie with added in-between frames feels different from the action in the movie in which one keyframe directly follows another. The added frames slow the motion.

✔ Tip

■ Keep in mind that this example serves to illustrate a process. In most animations, you shouldn't overuse this technique. If you simply add many in-between frames, you'll slow the action too much and destroy the illusion of movement.

Figure 8.32 Select a frame; Ctrl-click (Mac) or right-click (Windows), and choose Insert Frame from the contextual menu (top); Flash inserts an in-between frame directly after the selected frame (bottom).

Figure 8.33 With in-between frames separating the initial keyframes, the first part of the animation moves at a slower pace than the second.

Onion Skin button — *Onion-skin markers*

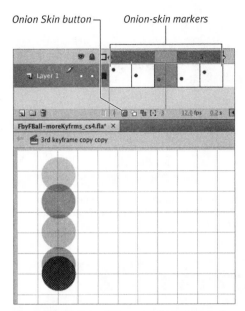

Figure 8.34 In Onion Skin mode, Flash displays the content of multiple frames but dims everything that's not on the current frame. The onion-skin markers in the Timeline indicate how many frames appear.

Onion-Skin Outlines button —

Figure 8.35 In Onion Skin Outlines mode, Flash displays the content of multiple frames, but it uses outlines for everything that's not in the current frame.

Using Onion Skinning

In frame-by-frame animation, you make incremental changes to the graphic elements in each keyframe. In the bouncing-ball animation, you must position the ball in each frame to make the smoothest movement. To make this task easier, Flash's onion-skinning feature displays the graphic elements of keyframes in context with the elements of surrounding frames.

Onion skinning displays dimmed or outline versions of the content of multiple selected frames. You determine how many frames Flash displays at once. The buttons for turning on and off the various types of onion skinning appear at the bottom of the Timeline, in the Timeline's Status bar.

To turn on onion skinning:

◆ In the Status bar of the Timeline, click the Onion Skin button.

The content of all the frames included in the onion-skin markers appears in a dimmed form (**Figure 8.34**). You can't edit the dimmed graphics—only the full-color graphics in the current frame.

To turn on outline onion skinning:

◆ In the Status bar of the Timeline, click the Onion Skin Outlines button.

The content of all the frames included in the onion-skin markers appears in outline form (**Figure 8.35**). You can't edit the outline graphics—only the solid graphics that appear in the current frame.

To adjust the number of frames included in onion skinning:

1. In the Status bar of the Timeline, click the Modify Onion Markers button.

   A pop-up menu appears, containing commands for setting the way the onion-skin markers work (**Figure 8.36**).

2. To see frames on either side of the current frame, do one of the following:

   ▲ To see two frames on either side of the current frame, choose Onion 2.

   ▲ To see five frames on either side of the current frame, choose Onion 5.

   ▲ To see all the frames in the movie, choose Onion All (**Figure 8.37**).

   Flash moves the onion-skin markers around in the Timeline as you move the playhead. Flash always includes onion skins (either solid or outline) for graphics in the selected number of frames before the current frame and after it.

✔ Tips

■ Flash doesn't show the contents of locked layers in onion-skin views.

■ Drag onion-skin markers in the Timeline to include more frames or fewer frames in the onion-skin view.

■ You can prevent the onion-skin markers from moving each time you select a new frame in the Timeline. Set the markers to encompass the frames you want to see together. From the Modify Onion Markers menu, choose Anchor Onion. As long as you keep selecting frames inside the anchored range, the anchored set of frames stays in Onion Skin mode.

Modify Onion Markers button

Figure 8.36 The Modify Onion Markers pop-up menu gives you control over the number of frames that appear as onion skins.

Figure 8.37 With Onion All chosen in the Modify Onion Markers menu, Flash extends the markers to enclose all the frames of the Timeline.

Objects available
for editing

Edit Multiple
Frames button

Figure 8.38 In Edit Multiple Frames mode, Flash displays and makes editable all the graphics in the frames that the onion-skin markers indicate. This feature makes it possible to move an animated graphic to a new location in every keyframe at the same time.

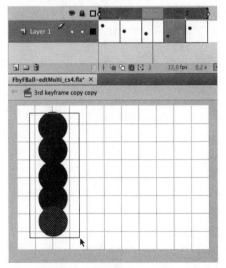

Figure 8.39 In Edit Multiple Frames mode, you can use the selection tool to select graphics in any of the frames enclosed in the onion-skin markers.

Editing Multiple Keyframes

If you decide to change the location of an animated element, you must change the element's location in every keyframe in which it appears. Repositioning the items one at a time is not only tedious but also dangerous. You may miss a keyframe, and you can easily get the animated elements out of alignment. Flash solves this problem by letting you move elements in multiple keyframes simultaneously. The same markers used for onion skinning apply to Edit Multiple Frames mode. You can edit any of the keyframes that fall within the range of frames set off by the markers.

Editing multiple keyframes is especially important for frame-by-frame animation, shape tweens, and classic tweens. For motion tweens, it's easy to reposition the tween target in every frame of the animation simply by moving the motion path (see Chapter 11).

To relocate animated graphics on the Stage:

1. Open or create a five-frame animation of a bouncing ball.

2. In the Timeline's Status bar, choose Edit Multiple Frames (**Figure 8.38**).

   Flash displays all graphics in all frames within the onion-skin markers and makes them editable.

3. From the Modify Onion Markers menu, choose Onion All.

   Now you can see the ball at each stage of its bounce, and you can edit each of these stages.

4. Using the selection tool, draw a selection rectangle that includes all the visible balls on the Stage (**Figure 8.39**).

continues on next page

5. Drag the selection to the opposite side of the Stage (**Figure 8.40**).

With just a few steps, you've relocated the bouncing ball. (Imagine how much more work it would have been to select each keyframe separately, move the circle for that frame, select the next keyframe, line up the circles precisely in the new location, and so on.)

✔ Tip

■ When you select Edit Multiple Frames, Flash no longer displays onion skinning for keyframes; onion skinning does appear for in-between frames with tweened content. If you find it confusing to view solid graphics in multiple keyframes, turn on Outline view in the layer-properties section of the Timeline (**Figure 8.41**).

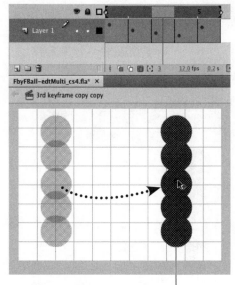

Outline previews the new location —
as you drag selected graphics

Figure 8.40 In Edit Multiple Frames mode, you can relocate an animated graphic completely, moving it in every keyframe with one action.

Figure 8.41 Turn on Outline mode to make it easier to work with graphics in multiple frames.

ANIMATION WITH CLASSIC TWEENING

In Chapter 8, you created a three-frame animation of a bouncing ball by changing the position of the ball graphic in each of the three keyframes. Animating movement and changes to shapes by hand (frame by frame) is labor-intensive. Adobe Flash CS4 Professional reduces the number of frames you must draw when you use a process called *tweening*.

Flash performs three types of tweening: classic tweening, shape tweening, and motion tweening. This chapter introduces classic tweening; Chapter 10, shape tweening; and Chapter 11, motion tweening. (Chapter 13 introduces another type of animation, inverse kinematics, which also creates a series of incremental changes to a structure composed of shapes or symbols.)

Classic and shape tweening both use keyframe spans to create animation. To set up the keyframe span, you place one version of a graphic element in an initial keyframe, and a second version in an ending keyframe. When you assign tweening to the keyframe span, Flash creates a series of images that accomplish the changes incrementally. The number of in-between frames determines the number of images in the series and the length of the animation. Motion tweening takes a different approach, using a single keyframe per sequence and using property keyframes to define changes to the graphic element.

A Note about Motion Tweening

Flash CS4 introduces a new type of tweening, motion tweening, that makes it easy to create and work with tweens. This *QuickStart Guide* covers classic tweening directly after frame-by-frame animation, because both depend on a series of keyframes, and therefore bear certain similarities. As you'll see in the tasks in this chapter, however, classic tweening reduces the number of keyframes you need to create in order to produce animation. Motion tweening reduces that number even more, making it possible to create animation with just one keyframe (see Chapter 10). There are specific animation tasks that you can accomplish only with classic tweening (see the sidebar "When to Use Classic Tweening," later in this chapter). If you don't need to do those tasks, you may be better off using motion tweening.

When to Use Classic Tweening

Tweening reduces the amount of labor involved in creating animation sequences. Instead of drawing the graphics for every frame of a movie, you create the essential frames—the keyframes—and let Flash do the redrawing. But each type of tween has different requirements and different strengths. Here are some things to consider about classic tweening and motion tweening (you'll learn more about the latter in Chapter 11).

Classic tweening requires symbols, so it's only appropriate to use when you will be animating changes in the properties of a symbol instance on the Stage. Such properties include the symbol's location on the Stage (position), the symbol's size (scale), whether the symbol changes its orientation to the Stage (rotation), and so on. Classic tweening doesn't allow you to change an element's outlines; for that, you need shape tweening (Chapter 10) or inverse kinematics (Chapter 13).

Motion tweening also involves working with symbols and changing their properties. How do you decide between classic and motion tweening? Classic tweening allows for some workflows often used by character animators. Because you set up initial and ending keyframes in classic tweening, you can map out a complete animation quickly by placing all the keyframes first and assigning classic tweening later, a process known as *blocking*. Classic tweening knits those segments together seamlessly, interpolating changes from one keyframe to the next and from that keyframe to the next, and so on. That's not the case for motion tweening. Each motion-tween span is an independent segment of animation, with a single keyframe. If you want the segments to link smoothly, you need to do a bit of extra work to make sure the position of a tweened object at the end of one span matches up correctly with its counterpart in the next tween span.

Another reason to use classic tweening is to take advantage of a graphic symbol's ability to display different frames of its Timeline on command. Character animators use this feature to turn multiframe graphic symbols into miniature libraries, building a set of facial expressions or gestures into a single symbol, then displaying just the one that's needed at any given time. (You'll learn about creating multiframe, animated, graphic symbols in Chapter 12.) Classic tweening's multiple-keyframe approach also lets you interpolate between two different color effects (one applied to the symbol instance in the initial keyframe of the tween, the other applied to the symbol instance at the end). In motion tweens, since each tween span has just one symbol instance, Flash can't interpolate changes to color effects.

Creating a Bouncing Ball with Classic Tweening

To create a classic tween, you must place the appropriate type of content in the keyframe that defines the beginning of the keyframe span and in the keyframe that marks the end of the span. You then tell Flash to create the classic tween. Flash can only create classic tweens from symbols. Flash can create the symbols for you, using the content of the active layer, but it's safest to create the symbols yourself (see the sidebar "Classic Tween Symbols: Best Practice"). You can use classic tweening to create the same bouncing ball you made in Chapter 8, by changing the position of the ball symbol.

Which Frames Contain Tweening?

As your road map of the movie, the Timeline provides visual cues about which frames contain tweens. For classic tweens and shape tweens, Flash draws an arrow across the keyframe span to indicate the presence of a tween (**Figure 9.1**). (Note that the arrow doesn't appear if you've set frames to Preview or Preview in Context.) Frames containing a dotted line are set to contain a classic tween or a shape tween, but something is wrong and Flash can't complete the tween. Such tweens are called *broken tweens*.

Figure 9.1 An arrow in a keyframe span indicates that the frames contain a proper tween sequence (top). A dotted line indicates that the keyframe span is set to tween, but there's a problem with the tween (bottom).

Color coding in the Timeline distinguishes different types of tweens. With Tinted Frames active (choose it from the Timeline's panel menu), Flash applies a shade of light bluish-purple (Mac) or bluish-gray (Windows) to the frames that contain a classic tween. If Tinted Frames is inactive, the frames are white (Mac) or patterned (Windows), and Flash changes the arrow that indicates the presence of a tween from black to red. Flash indicates shape tweens by tinting frames light green (if Tinted Frames is active) or by changing the tweening arrow to light green (if Tinted Frames is inactive). For motion tweens, Flash always highlights the tween span in light blue (see Chapter 11). For inverse kinematics armatures, Flash always highlights the pose span in olive green (see Chapter 13).

CLASSIC TWEENING

To prepare content for classic tweening:

1. In keyframe 1 of a new document, place an instance of a symbol that represents a ball near the top of the Stage (**Figure 9.2**).

   For example, use the oval tool to draw a circle shape, then convert it to a symbol (see Chapter 7) and name it MyBall. Flash could convert the shape for you, but it's best to do the conversion yourself (see the sidebar "Classic Tween Symbols: Best Practice").

2. ⌘-click (Mac) or Ctrl-click (Windows) frames 5 and 10 and press F6.

   Flash creates keyframes 5 and 10, duplicating keyframe 1. (To review creating keyframes, see Chapter 8). By changing the position of the ball in those keyframes, you tell Flash how to create the animation.

3. To set the ball's position for the low point of the bounce, do the following:

   ▲ In the Timeline, move the playhead to keyframe 5.

   ▲ On the Stage, drag the ball symbol to the bottom of the Stage.

Figure 9.2 To set up a traditional bouncing-ball with classic tweening, create the first keyframe, and position the ball symbol near the top of the Stage, at the top of its bounce.

Classic Tween Symbols: Best Practice

To create a classic tween, Flash must work with symbols. If you issue the command to create a classic tween when you've selected other types of graphic objects (merge-shapes, drawing-objects, primitive-shapes, groups, or text), Flash automatically converts the selection to a pair of symbols—one for the initial keyframe of the tween, the other for the ending keyframe. There's no warning dialog, Flash just puts generically named symbols (for example, Tween 1 and Tween 2) in the library and goes ahead with the tween. Unless you immediately rename the tween symbols something identifiable, it may be confusing should you need to go in and edit your tween later. Also, if you accidentally put more than one object on the layer you're using for the classic tween, Flash combines the objects to make one symbol instead of warning you that the tween can have only one object per layer (Flash would warn you if you tried to apply classic tweening to a layer with multiple symbols). For best results, before you apply tweening, convert the graphic element (or elements) you want to tween into a symbol.

Keyframes

Reposition symbol

Symbol in new position in each keyframe

Figure 9.3 The initial keyframes for a classic tween are similar to those of a frame-by-frame animation. The difference is that the content of the keyframe must be a symbol. To let Flash create the incremental changes to your symbol, you assign classic tweening to the keyframe span.

4. To set the ball's position for the rebound, do the following:

   ▲ Move the playhead to keyframe 10.

   ▲ Drag the symbol two-thirds of the way back up toward the original location.

You have just set up a frame-by-frame animation much like the one you created in Chapter 8, except that the keyframes are farther apart. In keyframe 1, the ball is at the top of its bounce; in keyframe 5, the ball is at the bottom of its bounce; and in keyframe 10, the ball is almost back to the top of its bounce (**Figure 9.3**). To have Flash interpolate the changes and create a smoother animation than in the frame-by-frame exercise, you need to tell Flash to apply tweening to the keyframe spans.

The Many Ways to Position Tweened Symbols

In the preceding task, you position a classic-tween symbol by dragging it directly on the Stage, but you could use the Property inspector or the Info panel to do the job instead. The trick is to make sure the symbol is selected. In step 3 of the task, for example, instead of moving the playhead to keyframe 5, you could select the keyframe in the Timeline, which also selects the contents of that frame on the Stage. You can access the Info panel and enter new values for the symbol's *x*- and *y*-coordinates to change the ball's position.

Although the Info panel recognizes a symbol selected this way, the Property inspector does not. When you select a keyframe in the Timeline, the Property inspector displays the properties of the frame itself, not its content (even though that content is selected on the Stage). To allow the Property inspector to focus on a classic-tween symbol, you must select that symbol directly—for example, by clicking it with the selection tool. You can then access the Property inspector and use the X and Y hot text in the Position and Size section to position the symbol on the Stage.

To apply classic tweening:

1. To apply classic tweening to the first half of the ball's bounce, in the Timeline, select any of the frames in the first keyframe span—1, 2, 3, or 4 (**Figure 9.4**).

   Flash automatically selects the ball symbol. To define a classic tween, the item to be tweened must be selected.

2. Choose Insert > Classic Tween (**Figure 9.5**).

   Flash defines frames 1–4 as a classic tween, updating the Timeline to give you information about the tween (**Figure 9.6**). (See the sidebar "Which Frames Contain Tweening?" earlier in this chapter.) These in-between frames no longer display the content of the preceding keyframe; instead they display the incrementally changed tween content that Flash creates. This tween content is shielded so you can't select it (clicking the tween content is just like clicking a blank area of the Stage). You can use the selection tool to drag classic tween content in an in-between frame, but doing so transforms that frame into a keyframe.

Figure 9.4 You can select any frame in a keyframe span to assign classic tweening.

Figure 9.5 To assign classic tweening, choose Insert > Classic Tween.

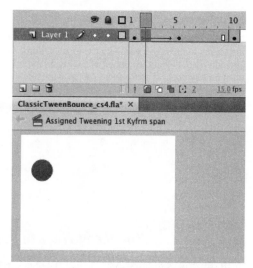

Figure 9.6 Flash adds information to the Timeline to indicate when frames contain classic tweens. Here, a blue tint and an arrow signify a completed classic tween.

CLASSIC TWEENING

Figure 9.7 With two motion-tween sequences, you can create a bouncing ball: one sequence shows the downward motion, and the other shows the rebound.

Range of frames being displayed as onion skins

Position of ball in the three in-between frames

Figure 9.8 Turn on onion skinning to preview the positions of a classically tweened symbol on the Stage.

3. To define the classic tween for the second half of the ball's bounce, in the Timeline, Ctrl-click (Mac) or right-click (Windows) any of the frames in the second keyframe span—5, 6, 7, 8, or 9—and choose Create Classic Tween from the contextual menu.

Flash creates the second half of the ball's bounce with another classic tween (**Figure 9.7**).

✔ Tips

■ When you choose Preview or Preview in Context from the Timeline's panel menu, the tweening arrow doesn't appear in the frames containing tweens. Nor can you see the incremental steps Flash creates for the tween. But if you turn on onion skinning, you can see the interpolated content for all the in-between frames in position on the Stage (**Figure 9.8**).

■ Oddly enough, although you can't select a symbol on an in-between frame of a classic tween, you can edit it. Double-clicking a symbol on an in-between frame opens that symbol in symbol-editing mode. And you must be careful when you double-click; if you drag the symbol on an in-between frame even a tiny bit, Flash creates a new keyframe.

■ In this simple example, the ball moves at a constant rate through each half of its bounce. If you want the ball to slow down as it reaches the top of its upward rebound, you could use easing to vary the rate of change in the ball's position. For a quick introduction to easing, see Chapter 12.

CLASSIC TWEENING

249

Adding Keyframes to Classic Tweens

After you have set up a classic tween, Flash creates new keyframes for you when you reposition a classic-tween symbol on an in-between frame. You can also add new keyframes by choosing Insert > Timeline > Keyframe.

To add keyframes by repositioning a classic-tween symbol:

1. Create a ten-frame classic tween of a bouncing ball, following the steps in the preceding task.

2. In the Timeline, select frame 3.

   On the Stage, you see the ball symbol in one of the in-between positions Flash created.

3. In the Tools panel, choose the selection tool.

4. Drag the ball to a new position—slightly to the right of its current position, for example.

   Flash inserts a new keyframe at frame 3 and splits the preceding five-frame tween into separate tweens (**Figure 9.9**). The new keyframe contains another instance of the ball symbol.

To add keyframes by command:

1. Continuing with the document from the preceding task, select frame 7 in the Timeline.

2. Choose Insert > Timeline > Keyframe.

   Flash creates a new keyframe in frame 7. A new instance of your symbol appears on the Stage in the position Flash created for it in that in-between frame. You can now change the symbol's position (or change other properties of the symbol).

In the selected frame, the symbol appears in its tweened position

Repositioning the symbol creates a new keyframe

Onion-skin view of other tween positions for the symbol

Figure 9.9 Repositioning the ball in an in-between frame that's part of a classic tween creates a new keyframe and a revision of the tweened frames.

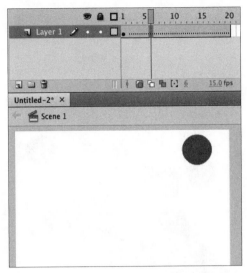

Figure 9.10 The dotted line in the Timeline indicates that these 20 frames contain a classic tween, but a broken one. There is no ending keyframe to define changes to the tween symbol.

Completed classic-tween segment

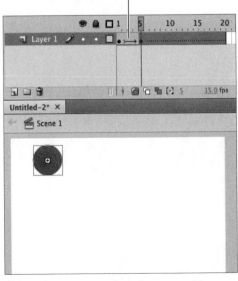

Figure 9.11 As you move the ball to new positions in different frames within the keyframe span set to classic tweening, Flash creates new keyframes and completes the tween segments between keyframes.

Moving Symbols in Straight Lines

In the preceding tasks, you created a well-behaved bouncing ball—one that moves up and down. To make one that bounces around like a crazy Ping-Pong ball, add more keyframes and place the ball symbol in various locations. The symbol moves in a straight line from one position to the next, but the effect is livelier. To get frenetic bouncing, move the symbol a great distance in a small number of in-between frames. To slow the action, move the symbol a short distance or use a larger number of in-between frames.

To move an item from point to point:

1. To set up an open-ended classic tween, in a new Flash document or on a new layer, do the following:
   ▲ In keyframe 1, place an instance of a symbol containing a graphic of a ball.
   ▲ In the Timeline, select frame 20, and choose Insert > Timeline > Frame. Flash creates a keyframe span by defining 19 in-between frames.
   ▲ In the Timeline, select any frame in the keyframe span (frames 1–20) and choose Insert > Classic Tween. Flash assigns classic tweening to the keyframe span, but the dotted line in the Timeline indicates that the tween isn't yet complete (**Figure 9.10**). You need to create keyframes that describe the ball's motion.

2. In the Timeline, position the playhead in frame 5.

3. On the Stage, drag the ball symbol to a new position.
   Flash creates a new keyframe in frame 5 and completes a classic tween for frames 1–4 (**Figure 9.11**).

continues on next page

4. Repeat this repositioning process (steps 2 and 3) for frames 10, 15, and 20.

You now have a ball that bounces around wildly (**Figure 9.12**).

5. To end the classic tween, select the last keyframe in the series.

6. Choose Insert > Remove Tween.

If you don't remove tweening from the last frame, any frames that you add after that will also be set to classic tween, which may create unexpected results.

✔ Tip

■ To add more frames, after step 4 select frame 30 or frame 40, then choose Insert > Timeline > Frame. Flash makes all the newly defined frames part of the classic tween. Now you can add keyframes by following the procedure described earlier in this task. Just be sure you end up with a keyframe as the last frame in the series. If you have more frames than you need, you can remove them.

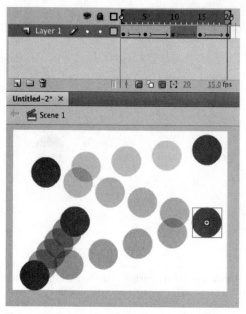

Figure 9.12 By stringing classic tweens together, you can animate a symbol that moves from point to point.

Figure 9.13 The first phase in creating a classic tween with a symbol that follows a path is to set up the classic tween with the symbol in its beginning and ending positions. In this phase, the symbol moves from the beginning to the end in a straight line. (Onion Skin mode and Edit Multiple Frames are selected to show all the tweened movement.)

Figure 9.14 When you choose Add Motion Guide Layer from the contextual menu, Flash adds a motion-guide layer with a default name (Guide: plus the name of your originally selected layer). Flash indents the original selected layer and links it to the motion-guide layer. Flash defines the linked layer as a guided layer.

Moving Symbols Along a Path

In the preceding task, you made a ball move all over the Stage in short, point-to-point hops. A ball does sometimes behave this way, but other things may require movements that are softer—trajectories that are arcs, not straight lines. You could achieve this effect by stringing together many point-to-point keyframes, but Flash's classic tweening offers a more efficient method: the *motion guide*. Motion guides describe the exact path an animated graphic-object takes. Note that if you don't have a special need to use a classic tween (see the sidebar "When to Use Classic Tweening," earlier in this chapter), motion tweening provides an even easier way to work with objects moving along a path (see Chapter 11).

To add a motion-guide layer:

1. In a new Flash document or on a new layer, create a ten-frame classic tween.

   In the first keyframe, place the symbol to be tweened in the top-left corner of the Stage. In the last frame, place the symbol in the bottom-right corner of the Stage. Your document should resemble **Figure 9.13**.

2. Select the layer that contains the symbol you want to move along a path.

3. Control-click (Mac) or right-click (Windows) the layer-name area and choose Add Classic Motion Guide from the contextual menu.

   Flash adds the classic motion-guide layer directly above the layer you clicked and gives it a default name of Guide, followed by the name of the layer you selected (**Figure 9.14**). The motion-guide icon appears next to the layer name. Flash also indents the layer you clicked, linking it to the motion-guide layer.

continues on next page

4. In the Tools panel, select a tool that creates merge-shape or drawing-object lines (strokes), such as the pencil tool.

5. In the Timeline, select keyframe 1 of the motion-guide layer.

6. Draw a line on the Stage showing the path you want the classically tweened symbol to take (**Figure 9.15**).

Lines on a motion-guide layer control the motion of classically tweened symbols on linked layers.

To connect tweened elements to a motion guide:

1. Continuing with the document from the preceding task, choose View > Snapping > Snap to Objects.

For Flash to move a classic-tween symbol along a motion guide, the transformation point of the symbol (which appears as a small white circle) must be centered on the line. The Snap to Objects setting helps you position the symbol correctly. (To learn more about the transformation point, see Chapters 4 and 7.)

2. In keyframe 1, using the selection tool, drag the classic-tween symbol by its transformation point to position it directly over the beginning of the motion guide.

As you drag, the snapping ring enlarges slightly when it approaches any snapping elements you have set. For example, with Snap to Objects active, the ring grows larger when the point you're dragging is centered over the motion guide.

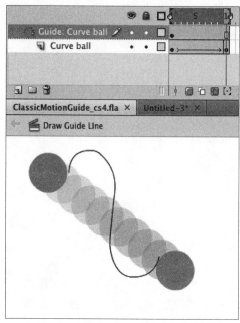

Figure 9.15 A line on a motion-guide layer acts as a path that controls the motion of a classic-tween symbol on a linked layer.

The Mystery of Motion Guides

A *motion guide* is a graphic you create on a special separate layer. The motion guide defines the path for a symbol to follow in a classic tween. One motion-guide layer can control classic-tween symbols on several layers. The motion-guide layer governs any layers linked to it. The linked layers are defined as guided layers in the Layer Properties dialog.

If you want different classic-tween symbols to follow different paths, create several motion-guide layers within a single Flash document. Each motion guide governs the actions of classic-tween symbols on its own set of linked layers.

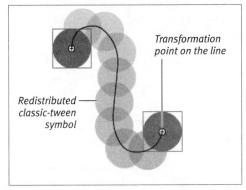

Figure 9.16 To follow the motion guide, each instance of the classic-tween symbol must have its transformation point sitting directly on the motion-guide line. (The transformation point appears as a small white circle.)

3. In keyframe 10, drag the classic-tween symbol to position its transformation point directly over the end of the motion guide.

Flash redraws the in-between frames so that the symbol follows the motion guide (**Figure 9.16**). Flash centers the classic-tween symbol over the motion guide in each in-between frame. In the final movie, Flash hides the guide.

✔ Tips

- After you draw the motion guide, lock the motion-guide layer to prevent yourself from editing the guide accidentally as you snap the classic-tween symbol to the guide.

- When you select the initial keyframe of a classic tween in the Timeline, the Tweening section of the Frame Property inspector contains a Snap check box; select it to have Flash help you center keyframe graphics over the end of the guide.

- You can use most of Flash's drawing tools—line, pencil, pen, oval, rectangle, polygon, polystar, and brush—to create a motion guide. For best results, the path should not be closed. If you use the rectangle or oval tools, use the eraser tool to create a small break in the path. The tools may be set to Merge Drawing or Object Drawing mode. The paths created by the oval- and rectangle-primitive tools, however, do not work as motion guides.

- To make two symbols move along two different paths, place each symbol in its own layer, and set up its classic tween animation. Then create a separate motion-guide layer (with a different motion-guide line) for each one.

MOVING SYMBOLS ALONG A PATH

About Motion Guides and Orient to Path

A ball is round and symmetrical; it looks natural following a motion guide whether it's a flat line or a complex curve. Other symbols may require rotation to appear natural as they move along the path created by the motion guide. You might want a living creature to face in the direction it's moving, rotating slightly to match the twists and turns of its path. If the path is a simple arc, rotating the symbol instances in the initial and ending keyframes of a classic tween to align with the motion guide is usually enough to make the movement seem natural, as Flash interpolates between the two positions. If the curve is complex—an *S* shape, for example—that change in orientation may not be enough (**Figure 9.17**). In Orient to Path mode, Flash forces a classic-tween symbol instance to rotate to preserve its orientation to the motion guide, through all its curves. To activate Orient to Path mode, in the Tweening section of the Frame Property inspector, select the Orient to Path check box (**Figure 9.18**).

Figure 9.17 The triangle has been rotated in the initial and ending keyframes to align with the motion guide, but without activating Orient to Path, that rotation doesn't give Flash enough information to keep the triangle aligned in the midsection of the curve (left). When Orient to Path is active, the arrow rotates to align better with the path at every frame (right).

Figure 9.18 For a classic tween, in the Tweening section of the Frame Property inspector, select Orient to Path. This forces Flash to rotate the classic-tween symbol to face the direction of movement.

Figure 9.19 To assign classic tweening to a keyframe span, select any frame in the span, then choose Insert > Classic Tween.

Figure 9.20 To make a classic-tween symbol grow in equal steps, in the Tweening section of the Frame Property inspector, select the Scale check box.

Animating Changes in Size

In classic tweening, you can animate changes to the size of a symbol from one keyframe to the next by changing the symbol's Horizontal Scale and/or Vertical Scale properties. To enable the symbol to grow or shrink in a classic tween, you must select the Scale check box in the Frame Property inspector.

To make a classic-tween symbol grow and shrink:

1. In a new Flash document or on a new layer, in keyframe 1, place a symbol instance on the Stage.

   (To review the creation and use of symbols, see Chapter 7.)

2. To create a keyframe that defines the end of a growing sequence, in the Timeline, select frame 5; then choose Insert > Timeline > Keyframe.

   Flash duplicates the symbol from keyframe 1 in the new keyframe.

3. Select any of the frames in the keyframe span (frame 1, 2, 3, or 4).

4. Choose Insert > Classic Tween (**Figure 9.19**).

   The classic-tween arrow and color coding now appear in the keyframe span.

5. With the frame you selected in step 3 still selected, access the Property inspector.

   The Frame Property inspector contains a Tweening section, with settings that apply to this segment of classic tweening.

6. In the Tweening section make sure the Scale check box is selected (it is selected by default) (**Figure 9.20**).

   continues on next page

When Scale is selected, Flash increases the size of the symbol instance in equal steps from keyframe 1 to keyframe 5. Otherwise, the symbol remains at its original size through all the frames of the keyframe span (frames 1–4) and suddenly increases to the larger size at the final keyframe (frame 5).

7. With the playhead in keyframe 5, select the symbol instance and make it bigger.

   (For detailed instructions on resizing graphics, see Chapter 4.)

8. To add the ending keyframe for a shrinking sequence, in the Timeline, select frame 10; then press F6.

   Flash duplicates the symbol from keyframe 5 in the new keyframe.

9. Select any of the frames in the keyframe span (frame 5, 6, 7, 8, or 9).

10. Choose Insert > Classic Tween.

    The classic-tween arrow and color coding now appear in the second keyframe span (frames 5–9). The Scale check box is already selected in the Tween section of the Frame Property inspector.

11. With the playhead in keyframe 10, select the symbol instance and make it smaller.

    Flash creates a tween that shrinks your graphic in five equal steps (**Figure 9.21**).

✔ Tip

■ As long as you don't change the settings in the Frame Property inspector, the Scale check box remains selected, and Flash updates the tween anytime you change the content in one of the keyframes in the sequence. You don't have to have the Frame Property inspector open to fine-tune the size of your scaling graphic.

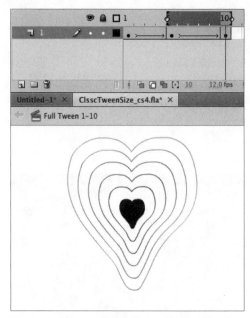

Figure 9.21 To tween a shrinking symbol in a classic tween, make it smaller in the ending keyframe of the sequence. Turn on Onion Skin mode to see the size of the symbol Flash creates for each in-between frame.

Figure 9.22 To prepare a rotational classic tween, in the keyframe that ends the sequence, rotate the item to its ending position.

Rotating and Spinning Graphics

In classic tweening, you can make a symbol spin by changing its Rotation property. When you create a classic tween for rotation, you must not only create beginning and ending keyframes (as you did for animating changes to position and size), you must also specify the direction of rotation, and the number of times to spin.

To rotate a symbol less than 360 degrees:

1. In a new Flash document or on a new layer, in keyframe 1, place a symbol instance on the Stage.

   You can create a new symbol or use an existing one; use a graphic that looks different at various stages of its rotation— for example, a triangle or an arrow. (To review symbol creation, see Chapter 7.)

2. In the Timeline, select frame 5, and choose Insert > Timeline > Keyframe.

   Flash duplicates the symbol from keyframe 1 in the new keyframe.

3. On the Stage, in keyframe 5, rotate the symbol instance 90 degrees clockwise (**Figure 9.22**).

   (For detailed instructions on rotating elements, see Chapter 4.)

continues on next page

4. In the Timeline, select any of the frames in the first keyframe span (frame 1, 2, 3, or 4).

5. Choose Insert > Classic Tween.

6. With the frame you selected in step 4 still selected, access the Frame Property inspector's Tweening section.

7. From the Rotate menu, choose one of the following options (**Figure 9.23**):

▲ The **Auto** option rotates the graphic in the direction that requires the smallest movement (**Figure 9.24**).

▲ **CW** rotates the graphic clockwise.

▲ **CCW** rotates the graphic counter-clockwise.

8. To rotate less then 360 degrees, click the Rotation Count hot text (to the right of the Rotate menu), enter 0, and press Enter.

Flash tweens the symbol so that it rotates around its transformation point. Each in-between frame shows the symbol rotated a little more.

Figure 9.23 The Rotate menu in the Tweening section of the Frame Property inspector lets you tell Flash the direction in which to rotate a symbol in a classic tween.

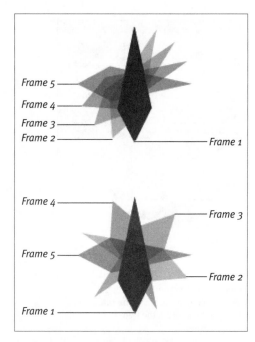

Figure 9.24 To create a classic tween that involves rotation, you can specify the direction of the rotation as clockwise or counterclockwise. You can also choose Auto to let Flash pick the direction that involves the smallest change, which allows Flash to create the smoothest motion. Compare the degree of change in each frame between rotating an arrow clockwise from 12 o'clock to 3 o'clock (top) versus rotating the arrow counterclockwise to reach the same position (bottom).

Figure 9.25 In the Frame Property inspector, you can set the number of times a classically tweened item should spin.

Figure 9.26 Compare a single rotation (top) with a double rotation (bottom) in the same number of frames.

To spin a symbol 360 degrees:

1. Follow steps 1 and 2 of the preceding task to create a five-frame sequence with identical keyframes in frame 1 and frame 5.

   You don't need to reposition your graphic, because the beginning frame and ending frame of a 360-degree spin should look exactly the same.

2. In the Timeline, select any of the frames in the first keyframe span (frame 1, 2, 3, or 4).

3. Choose Insert > Classic Tween and access the Frame Property inspector.

4. In the Tweening section, from the Rotate menu, choose a direction of rotation.

5. Select the Rotate Count hot text, to the right of the Rotate menu, and enter the number of rotations you want to use (**Figure 9.25**).

   The value you enter determines how Flash tweens the symbol. Flash creates new positions for the symbol to rotate it completely the given number of times in the span of frames. Flash tweens the symbol differently depending on the number of rotations you choose (**Figure 9.26**).

ROTATING AND SPINNING GRAPHICS

Animating Color Effects

When you use classic tweening to animate changes to symbol instances in keyframes, you can also tween changes in color, by applying a color effect to the symbol instance.

To change a symbol's color over time:

1. In a new Flash document, create a five-frame classic tween: In keyframe 1, place a symbol instance containing a red object on the Stage. In the Timeline, select frame 5, and choose Insert > Timeline > Keyframe. Select any of the frames in the first keyframe span (frame 1, 2, 3, or 4) and choose Insert > Classic Tween.

2. With keyframe 5 as the current frame, select the symbol and access the Property inspector.

3. To change the symbol's color, in the Color Effect section of the Property inspector, from the Style menu, choose new settings. (For detailed instructions on modifying symbol color, see Chapter 7.)

   Flash recolors the symbol in three transitional steps—one for each in-between frame (**Figure 9.27**).

4. To tween additional color changes, add tween segments.

   In the Timeline, select frame 10 and press F6 to duplicate the preceding keyframe. Select any of the frames in the second keyframe span (frame 5, 6, 7, 8, or 9) and choose Insert > Classic Tween. Select the symbol in frame 10 and repeat step 3.

✔ Tip

■ You can use classic-tweening to change a symbol's transparency (Alpha), making that symbol appear to fade in or out.

Figure 9.27 You can change the color of a symbol, as well as its position, in a classic tween. Flash creates transitional colors for each in-between frame.

ANIMATION WITH SHAPE TWEENING

When to Use Shape Tweening

Flash CS4 offers two laborsaving methods for animating changes to shapes: shape tweening and inverse kinematics (IK; see Chapter 13). Shape tweening lets you animate changes to the outline of a merge-shape or drawing-object. You can use a shape tween to modify a shape slightly—for example, to make a box bulge outward on one side—or to completely transform a shape—for example, to turn Cinderella's pumpkin into a coach. You have full control over the shape at key points in the transformation because you draw the shapes in the initial and ending keyframes and you can use shape hints to improve the transitions. But Flash's interpolation of the changes might still be unsatisfactory. Depending on the shapes involved, inverse kinematics (IK) might be a better choice. You can use IK to animate changes to the outline of a shape; the movement of the IK structure within the shape determines how the outline changes, and you can adjust the structure to help create the transitions you want.

Shape tweening in Adobe Flash CS4 Professional works much like classic tweening. You set up a keyframe span (the graphic content of the beginning and ending keyframes must be different in some way), then you define the keyframe span as a shape tween. Flash redraws the graphics for each in-between frame, making the incremental changes that transform the first shape into the final one. Shape tweens can animate changes to the path that defines the shape of a graphic element as well as to an element's size, color, location, and so on.

Flash can shape-tween more than one graphic on a layer, but the results can be unpredictable. When you have several shapes on a layer, there is no way to tell Flash which starting shape goes with which ending shape. By limiting yourself to a single shape tween on each layer, you can tell Flash exactly what to change.

Unless otherwise indicated, you can perform the tasks in this chapter using merge-shapes, drawing-objects, or primitive-shapes.

Creating a Bouncing Ball with Shape Tweening

Although shape tweens can animate changes in many properties of graphics—color, size, location—the distinguishing function of shape tweening is to transform one shape into another. You could use a shape tween to replicate the simple bouncing-ball animation you created in Chapters 8 and 9, but a better use of shape tweening for a bouncing ball is to flatten the ball as it strikes the ground.

To prepare content for shape-tweening:

1. In keyframe 1 of a new document, create a bouncing ball shape near the top of the Stage.

   Use the oval tool in either Merge mode or Object Drawing mode to draw a circle.

2. ⌘-click (Mac) or Ctrl-click (Windows) frames 5 and 10 and press F6.

   Flash creates keyframes 5 and 10, duplicating keyframe 1 (**Figure 10.1**). (To review creating keyframes, see Chapter 8).

3. In frame 5, select the ball and drag it to the bottom of the Stage, the low point of the bounce.

4. Using any of the techniques you learned in Chapter 4, reshape the circle, elongating it a bit sideways and flattening the bottom (**Figure 10.2**).

5. In frame 10, select the ball, and drag it to a position slightly above mid-Stage, almost back to the starting point.

✔ Tip

- In step 5, instead of dragging the ball to position it, you could select the ball shape, then use the Property inspector or Info panel to change the x- and/or y-coordinates for the shape's bounding box.

Figure 10.1 To begin setting up the bouncing ball as a shape tween, you create keyframes 1, 5, and 10, just as you did for classic tweens in the previous chapter. The ball must be a shape, not a symbol instance.

Figure 10.2 Changing the shape of the ball graphic in the keyframe representing the bottom of the bounce makes the movement appear more natural. The ball seems to respond to gravity by flattening on contact with something solid—say, the floor. (Turn on onion skinning to see the beginning and ending keyframes.)

Insert

Figure 10.3 To create the tween, choose Insert > Shape Tween.

Figure 10.4 When you select a keyframe span of a shape tween, the Tweening section of the Frame Property inspector displays the shape-tween settings. To determine how Flash handles changes to corners in your graphic as it changes shape, choose a setting from the Blend menu.

Figure 10.5 With onion skinning turned on, you can see the in-between frames Flash creates for the shape tween in the second keyframe span (the rebound). This animation looks similar to the bouncing ball created with a classic tween. In this case, the change in the object's shape creates the illusion of impact.

To apply shape tweening:

1. To define the shape tween for the first half of the ball's bounce, in the Timeline, select any of the frames in the first keyframe span (frame 1, 2, 3, or 4).

   Note that the ball is selected automatically. When you define a shape tween, the element to be tweened must be selected.

2. Choose Insert > Shape Tween (**Figure 10.3**).

   Flash creates a shape tween in frames 1–4 and color-codes those frames in the Timeline. With Tinted Frames active (choose it from the Timeline's panel menu), Flash applies a light green shade to the frames containing a shape tween. If Tinted Frames is inactive, the frames are white (Mac) or patterned (Windows), but Flash changes the arrow that indicates the presence of a tween from black to green.

3. In the Tweening section of the Frame Property inspector, from the Blend menu, choose either of the following options (**Figure 10.4**):

   ▲ Choose **Distributive** to smooth out the in-between shapes.

   ▲ Choose **Angular** to preserve sharp corners and straight lines as one shape transforms into another.

4. To define the shape tween for the second half of the ball's bounce, in the Timeline, select any of the frames in the second keyframe span (5, 6, 7, 8, or 9).

5. Repeat steps 2 and 3.

   Flash creates the second half of the ball's bounce with another shape tween (**Figure 10.5**).

Morphing Simple Lines and Fills

Flash can transform both fill shapes and lines (strokes). In this section, you try some shape-changing tasks with both types of shapes.

To transform an oval into a rectangle:

1. In a new Flash document or on a new layer, in frame 1, draw an outline oval on the Stage (**Figure 10.6**).

2. In the Timeline, select frame 5, and choose Insert > Timeline > Blank Keyframe.

   Flash creates a keyframe but removes all content from the Stage.

3. On the Stage, in frame 5, draw an outline rectangle (**Figure 10.7**).

   Don't worry about placing the rectangle in exactly the same location on the Stage as the oval; you'll adjust the position later.

4. In the Timeline, select any of the frames in the keyframe span (1, 2, 3, or 4).

5. Choose Insert > Shape Tween.

   Flash transforms the oval into the rectangle in three equal steps—one for each in-between frame (**Figure 10.8**).

6. To align the oval and rectangle, in the Timeline's Status bar, click the Onion Skin button or the Onion Skin Outlines button. Flash displays all the in-between frames.

7. In the Timeline, position the playhead in frame 1.

Figure 10.6 Draw an oval in the first keyframe of your shape tween.

Figure 10.7 Draw a rectangle in the second keyframe of your shape tween.

Figure 10.8 When you define frames 1–4 as shape tweens, Flash creates the three intermediate shapes that transform the oval into a rectangle. Turn on onion skinning to see the shapes for the in-between frames.

Figure 10.9 Use onion skinning to help position your keyframe shapes. Here, with frame 1 selected, you can drag the oval to center it within the rectangle (top). That makes the oval grow into a rectangle without moving anywhere else on the Stage (bottom).

Figure 10.10 Flash transforms a rectangle into a free-form brushstroke with shape tweening.

8. On the Stage, reposition the oval so that it aligns with the rectangle (**Figure 10.9**).

The oval transforms into a rectangle, remaining in one spot on the Stage.

To transform a rectangle into a free-form shape:

1. In a new Flash document or on a new layer, in frame 1, draw a rectangular fill on the Stage.

2. In the Timeline, select frame 5, and choose Insert > Timeline > Blank Keyframe.

3. On the Stage, in frame 5, use the brush tool to paint a free-form fill.

Don't make the fill too complex—just a blob or brushstroke with gentle curves.

4. In the Timeline, select any of the frames in the keyframe span (1, 2, 3, or 4).

5. Choose Insert > Shape Tween.

Flash transforms the rectangle into the free-form fill in three equal steps—one for each in-between frame (**Figure 10.10**).

Shape-Tweening Multiple Shapes

In classic tweening (Chapter 9) and motion tweening (Chapter 11), Flash limits you to one item per tween, meaning just one item per layer. In shape tweening, however, Flash can handle more than one shape on a layer. The drawback is that you may get some strange results. The simpler and fewer the shapes you use, the more reliable your multiple-shape tweens will be. For the most predictable results, limit yourself to one shape per layer.

You may want to keep both shapes on the same layer for a fill with an outline (stroke), however. As long as the transformation isn't too complicated, Flash can handle the two together.

To shape-tween fills with strokes (outlines):

1. Follow the steps in the preceding tasks to create a shape tween of an outline oval transforming into a rectangle.

2. Fill each shape with a different color.

   Flash tweens the fill and the stroke together and tweens the change in color (**Figure 10.11**).

Figure 10.11 Here, Flash transforms a shape with a stroke in five frames. The shape tween changes not only the graphic's shape, but also its color (from dark to light).

✔ Tips

- You can tween a disappearing act: Make the color of the stroke around a shape (or the shape, or both) get gradually lighter and lighter, until it finally disappears. Make the color of the final stroke (and/or shape) in the tween match the color of the background, or give it a fully transparent color (one with an alpha setting of 0 percent).

- To ensure that the item in the preceding tip does fully disappear (some low-color monitors may not display tint and alpha changes accurately), select the frame following the last keyframe of the tween sequence. Choose Insert > Timeline > Keyframe to duplicate the previous keyframe; then delete your disappearing stroke (or shape).

When Multiple-Shape Tweens on a Single Layer Go Bad

If you're shape-tweening stationary elements, you probably can get away with having several on the same layer. But if the elements move around much, Flash can get confused about which shape goes where. Although you may intend the paths of two shapes to cross, Flash creates the most direct route between the starting shape and the ending one. **Figure 10.12** illustrates the problem.

All objects on one layer

All objects on one layer

Light circle and arrow on one layer

Dark circle and arrow on another layer

Figure 10.12 Tweening multiple shapes whose paths don't cross in a single layer works fine. In the left-hand image, both objects are on the same layer, and the light circle transforms into the light arrow without a hitch. In the middle image, both objects are on the same layer, but Flash transforms the light circle into the dark arrow and the dark circle into the light arrow because that's the most direct path. If you want to create diagonal paths that cross, you must put each object on its own layer, as in the right-hand image.

Transforming a Simple Shape into a Complex Shape

The more complex the shape you tween, the more difficult it is for Flash to create the expected result. You can help Flash tween better by using *shape hints*—markers that let you identify points on the path of the original shape that correspond to points on the path of the final shape.

To shape-tween a more complex shape:

1. In a new Flash document, or on a new layer, create a five-frame shape tween using an oval.

   In the Timeline, in frame 1, draw an oval fill with no stroke. On the Stage select frame 5, and choose Insert > Timeline > Keyframe. Flash duplicates the contents of keyframe 1 in keyframe 5. In the Timeline, select any of the frames in the keyframe span (1, 2, 3, or 4) and choose Insert > Shape Tween.

2. Create the ending shape.

   In the Timeline, position the playhead in frame 5. Using the selection tool or subselection tool, drag four corner points in toward the center of the oval to create a flower shape. (For more detailed instructions on editing shapes, see Chapter 4.)

3. Play the movie to see the shape tween.

   Flash handles the tweening for this change well (**Figure 10.13**). It's fairly obvious which points of the oval should move in to create the petal shapes. If you modify the shape further, however, it becomes more difficult for Flash to know how to create the new shape. That's when you need to use shape hints.

Frame 1

Frame 2

Frame 3

Frame 4

Frame 5

Figure 10.13 Flash handles the tween from an oval to a simple flower shape without requiring shape hints.

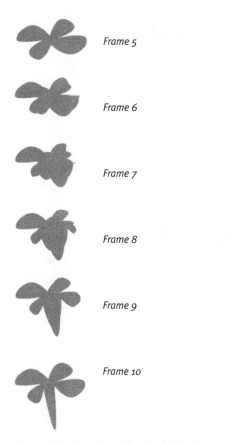

Frame 5

Frame 6

Frame 7

Frame 8

Frame 9

Frame 10

Figure 10.14 The addition of a stem to the flower overloads Flash's capability to create a smooth shape tween. Frames 7 and 8 are particularly bad.

Figure 10.15 Choose Modify > Shape > Add Shape Hint to activate markers that help Flash make connections between the original shape and the final shape of the tween.

To use shape hints:

1. Using the animation you created in the preceding task, add another shape-tween segment:

   In the Timeline, select frame 10, and choose Insert > Timeline > Keyframe. Flash duplicates the flower shape in a new keyframe. Select any frame in the keyframe span (5, 6, 7, 8, or 9) and choose Insert > Shape Tween.

2. In keyframe 10, edit the flower to add a stem.

   Reshape the flower's path with the selection tool or the pen and subselection tools, or add a stem with a brushstroke in the same color as the flower.

3. Play the movie.

   The addition of the stem to the flower makes it difficult for Flash to create a smooth tween that looks right (**Figure 10.14**).

4. To begin adding shape hints, position the playhead in keyframe 5 (the initial keyframe of this tweening sequence).

5. Choose Modify > Shape > Add Shape Hint, or press Shift-⌘-H (Mac) or Ctrl-Shift-H (Windows) (**Figure 10.15**).

   Flash places a shape hint—a small red circle labeled with a letter, starting with *a*—in the center of the object in the current frame. You need to reposition the shape hint to place it on a problem point on the shape's path.

   continues on next page

6. With the selection tool, drag the shape hint to a problem point on the edge of the shape.

   As you drag, Flash previews the hint's position with a circle icon; the circle gets darker and thicker when it connects with the path. Don't worry about getting the shape hint in exactly the right spot; just make sure it's on the path. You can fine-tune its position later.

7. Repeat steps 5 and 6 until you have placed shape hints on all the problem points of your shape in keyframe 5 (**Figure 10.16**).

   Each time you add a shape hint, you get another small red circle labeled with a letter. You can't place the hints at random; you must place them so they go in alphabetical order around the edge of the shape. (Flash does the best job when you place shape hints in counterclockwise order, starting in the upper-left corner of the shape, but you can also place them in clockwise order.)

8. In the Timeline, position the playhead in keyframe 10.

   Flash has already added shape hints to this frame; they all stack up in the center of the shape.

9. With the selection tool, drag each shape hint to its position on the path of the new shape.

   Keep them in the same order (counterclockwise or clockwise) you chose in step 7 (**Figure 10.17**). When the end-of-tween shape hint is sitting on a path, the hint changes from red to green; if you select the initial keyframe of the span, you can see that the associated beginning-of-tween hint has turned yellow.

10. To evaluate the improvement in tweening, play the movie.

Areas of change

Figure 10.16 Start adding shape hints in the first keyframe of a tween sequence. Flash places the hints in the center of the tweened object (top). You must drag the hints into position (middle). Distribute the hints in alphabetical order along the object's path, placing them on crucial points of change (bottom). Here, the three points with hints a, b, and c define the points from which the stem of the flower will grow.

Figure 10.17 To complete the placement of shape hints, select the second keyframe of your tween sequence. Flash stacks up hints corresponding to the ones you placed in the preceding keyframe (top). You must drag them into the correct final position (bottom).

Indent is incorrect

Frame 6

Frame 7

Indent improves

Frame 6

Frame 7

Stem tweens correctly

Frame 6

Frame 7

Figure 10.18 It can be difficult to match up points in the two keyframes exactly when you first place the shape hints. When you've positioned the hints in the beginning and ending keyframes of a sequence, turn on onion skinning to see where you need to adjust the placement of your hints. With the initial placement, Flash starts the stem growing with an indent at the bottom (top). Moving the points closer together improves the tween (middle). When the onion skins reveal a smooth tween, you're done (bottom).

11. To fine-tune the shape hints' positions, select one of the tween's keyframes, and turn on Onion Skin mode.

    Set the onion markers to include all the frames of the tween. Where the onion skins reveal rough spots in the tween, you may need to match the hint position better from the first keyframe to the last one (**Figure 10.18**). Repositioning the shape hints changes the in-between frames. You may need to adjust the shape hints in both keyframes. If you still can't get a smooth tween, try adding more shape hints.

✔ Tips

- To remove a single shape hint, make the initial keyframe the current frame. Select the shape hint you want to remove, and drag it out of the document window. Or, Control-click (Mac) or right-click (Windows) the shape hint, and choose Remove Hint.

- To remove all the hints at the same time, with the initial keyframe current, choose Modify > Shape > Remove All Hints. Or ⌘-click (Mac) or Ctrl-click (Windows) any shape hint, and choose Remove All Hints.

- If you can't create a smooth tween using shape hints alone, break the tween into smaller pieces by adding keyframes where the morphing gets off track. Then redraw the shapes for those frames yourself.

SIMPLE SHAPE INTO A COMPLEX SHAPE

Creating Shapes That Move As They Change

You can't create shape tweens that automatically follow a path, but you can move shapes around the Stage in straight lines. To do so, reposition the elements on the Stage from one keyframe to the next.

To shape-tween a moving graphic:

1. In a new Flash document or on a new layer, select frame 20, and choose Insert > Timeline > Frame.

   Flash adds blank in-between frames 2 through 20.

2. Select keyframe 1 and create some content to start the sequence; for example, draw a circular fill in the lower left corner of the Stage.

3. In the Timeline, select any frame in the span (frames 1–20).

   Note that you must click the frame to select it; you can't just position the playhead in the frame.

4. Choose Insert > Shape Tween.

   Flash defines the keyframe span as a shape tween. In the Timeline, a dotted line appears in the keyframe span, indicating that the tween is incomplete (**Figure 10.19**). Now you can add keyframes and shapes.

5. In the Timeline, insert a blank keyframe at frames 5, 10, 15, and 20.

   Flash creates four shape-tween sequences (**Figure 10.20**). For the moment, they're broken tweens because the keyframes are empty.

Figure 10.19 To save yourself numerous trips to the menu bar, you can assign the shape-tween property to a range of frames and add keyframes and shapes later. The initial keyframe must contain a shape, but the later keyframes can be blank.

Figure 10.20 When you insert keyframes into a long tween sequence, Flash breaks it into smaller tween sequences. Until you place content in the keyframes, the Timeline displays the dotted line in each span to indicate a broken tween.

Onion skinning on — Edit Multiple Frames

First half of the full tween sequence

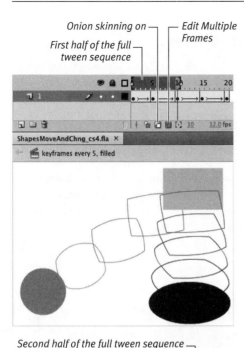

Second half of the full tween sequence

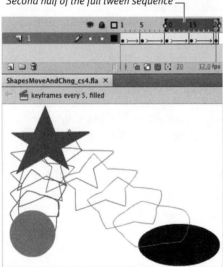

Figure 10.21 Place a different shape in a different location in each keyframe. Flash creates the intermediate steps necessary to transform the shapes and move them across the Stage. Play the movie or turn on onion skinning to examine the motion and shape changes in the in-between frames. (Here, Edit Multiple Frames is also on, making it easy to see the keyframe shapes.)

6. To complete the tween sequences, in each keyframe, draw a different shape; place each one in a different corner of the Stage.

In keyframe 5, for example, draw a rectangular fill in the top-right corner of the Stage. In keyframe 10, draw an oval in the bottom-right corner of the Stage. In keyframe 15, draw a star in the top-left corner of the Stage. And in keyframe 20, duplicate keyframe 1's circle in the bottom-left corner of the Stage. For extra variety, give each object a different color. As you add content to keyframes, Flash fills in the spans in the Timeline with tween arrows.

7. Play the movie.

You see a graphic that bounces around the Stage, morphing from one shape to the next (**Figure 10.21**).

The Pitfalls of Primitive Tweens

Although you can create shape tweens using oval- or rectangle-primitives, you're likely to find the animation Flash creates with them to be a bit disappointing. When you use a primitive's control points to change the primitive's path on the Stage, there is a sense of motion as the shape redraws itself. Drag the control point for the start or end angle of an oval-primitive, and the preview radius line rotates like the minute hand of a clock. As Flash redraws the shape, there is feeling of rotation, as if you're opening and closing a folding paper fan. In shape-tweening, Flash doesn't re-create that motion by animating the control points' movements; instead, working with the merge-shapes that lie at the foundation of the primitives, Flash transforms the initial shape into the final shape. You wind up with an oval, for example, that squeezes itself down into a pie wedge. Shape hints may help that transformation, but they won't create the feeling of rotation. If you decide to use shape hints with a primitive, you must deselect it. Otherwise the shape-hint choice is unavailable in the Modify > Shape submenu.

Moving Morphing Shapes Along a Curve

Tweened shapes can't automatically follow a curving path the way classic- and motion-tweened objects can, but you can make Flash do the work of creating the separate keyframes you need to make a shape that changes as it moves along a curved path. First, create your shape tween. In the Timeline, select the full range of frames in the tween sequence. Choose Modify > Timeline > Convert to Keyframes. Flash converts each in-between frame (with its transitional content) into a keyframe. Now you can position each keyframe shape anywhere you like. To map out a curved path to guide you in positioning each shape correctly, create a regular guide layer (see Chapter 6), and draw the path you want your morphing shape to follow. Choose View > Snapping > Snap to Objects. Reposition the shape in each keyframe. When you drag a shape close to the line on the guide layer, Flash snaps the shape to the line.

Alternatively, to animate a morphing shape that follows a path, create a shape tween, then save that animation as a movie-clip symbol (see Chapter 12). Use that symbol as the tween target in a motion tween, then edit the motion path to create the curves you want (see Chapter 11).

Animation with Motion Tweening

In a classic tween, you create animation by setting up a series of keyframes; each keyframe contains a separate instance of the symbol you want to animate. You manipulate each symbol individually to change its properties. Flash calculates any differences in the symbols' properties at each keyframe (position, size, rotation, and so on) and uses that information to create a series of images in which the symbol changes incrementally.

Motion tweens work somewhat differently. You set up a single keyframe, with a single symbol instance, then define a motion-tween span. Within that span property keyframes account for changes to the symbol's properties. Again, Flash animates the symbol instance—known as the *tween target* or *target instance*—by creating a series of images that change the tween target's properties over time.

A New Meaning for Motion Tween

The term *motion tweening* presents a challenge to anyone who has worked in previous versions of Flash. In Flash CS3 and earlier versions, motion tweening was the name for the style of animation that CS4 calls *classic tweening*. Here's the key to revising your vocabulary: motion tweening requires just one tween-span in the Timeline and one symbol instance on the Stage. Classic tweening requires one or more keyframe spans in the Timeline; each span begins and ends with a separate symbol instance on the Stage.

Understanding and Using Motion Tweens

To tap into the real power of motion tweening, think of the motion tween as one long animation with various properties changing independently at different times, instead of as a string of animation segments where all properties change together at key points.

A classic tween is something like walking down a path and encountering a set of similar yet different objects. At one spot there might be a white rectangular box, at another spot a red box, and at a third spot a red box that's been rotated. The animation would be a box that transforms from white to red, and rotates. Each point of change is a keyframe that you must fill with a whole new box, even if you only want to change one or two of its properties. Flash interpolates the changes between keyframes in a series of images corresponding to the number of frames in the keyframe span.

A motion tween is more like watching one object on a moving conveyor belt. You put the box on the moving belt; a few feet down the line, you dump a bucket of red paint over the box; a bit farther along, you poke the box with a stick to rotate it. In a motion tween, you don't need a new box at each point of change; you just need an instruction to change a specific property (or properties). Again, Flash interpolates the motion tween's property changes in a series of images; this time the number of images corresponds to the number of frames between property keyframes.

Motion tweening lets you reduce the number of keyframes and symbol instances in your movie. It's highly efficient, and Adobe recommends that you use it for most of your object-tweening needs. You should use motion tweening when you want to create a continuous segment of animation using a single tween object that changes properties. But use classic tweening when you want to block out the animation first with multiple segments using multiple keyframes—especially if you intend to use animated graphics symbols to create a library of character expressions for use in those keyframes.

You should also use motion tweening when you want precise control over individual properties and *easing*, a method of speeding or slowing changes to properties (see Chapter 12). (Use classic tweening if you want to apply different color effects to the tween object in different segments of the animation—for example, having the tween object change color in one segment, then change transparency in the next.) Use motion tweening also when you want to take advantage of motion presets to quickly create common animations, such as fly-ins or bounces, and when you want to animate objects that you've manipulated with Flash's 3D tools.

When you need to animate shapes, use shape tweening or frame-by-frame techniques; and when you need to animate articulated structures, use inverse kinematics (see Chapter 13).

Creating a Bouncing Ball with Motion Tweening

It's easy to do a version of the standard bouncing-ball animation with motion tweening. A motion tween uses a single instance of the ball. You place it in a tween span in the Timeline and tell Flash how to move that instance by adding position keyframes.

To set up a motion-tween:

1. Open a new Flash document.

   The document contains one layer and one keyframe (frame 1).

2. To preset the motion tween's duration, select the frame that marks your desired span length—for example, frame 10—and choose Insert > Timeline > Frame.

   Flash removes the dividers between frames and adds a hollow rectangle to frame 10, indicating a keyframe span.

3. In the Timeline, select keyframe 1.

4. Place an instance of a symbol that represents a ball near the top of the Stage.

   For example, use the oval tool to draw a circle shape, then convert it to a symbol (see Chapter 7) and name it MyBall.

5. To apply motion tweening to the target symbol, do either of the following:

   ▲ In the Timeline, select keyframe 1 (the one containing MyBall) or any frame in the keyframe span (frames 1–10). Flash selects the symbol on the Stage.

   or

   ▲ On the Stage, select the symbol you want to animate (MyBall). Flash selects the entire keyframe span in the Timeline.

   continues on next page

Motion-Tween Symbols: Best Practice

Flash can create motion tweens using symbols or text fields. If you attempt to apply motion tweening to other types of content, a dialog appears asking if you want Flash to convert the content to a symbol for you. If you answer yes, Flash creates the symbol with a generic name and carries out the motion tween. This is an improvement over Flash's automatic creation of symbols for classic tweens (where Flash just creates the symbol without any warning). Still, it's a good idea to decline Flash's automated conversion. Say no to the dialog and create your own symbol, so you can be sure it includes what you want it to include and you can give the symbol a meaningful name.

6. Choose Insert > Motion Tween (**Figure 11.1**).

Flash converts the keyframe span to a *tween span*, and identifies the layer as one containing motion tweening by adding a motion-tween icon before the layer name (**Figure 11.2**). Flash tints the frames of the span light blue. The tween target, MyBall, displays in all the frames of the span. To animate MyBall, you must add property keyframes within the tween span. The symbol in a motion tween is called the *tween target*.

✔ Tips

■ Defining a keyframe span (step 2 in the preceding task) is optional. If you apply motion tweening to a single keyframe, Flash creates a tween span with a default length (see the sidebar "How Flash Determines Tween-Span Length").

■ You can apply motion tweening directly to an object on the Stage (for best results, apply motion tweening only to a symbol or text field; see the sidebar "Motion-Tween Symbols: Best Practice"). Using the selection tool, Control-click (Mac) or right-click (Windows) the object to be tweened. From the contextual menu, choose Create Motion Tween.

■ Each motion tween is limited to one object. If you apply motion tweening directly to an object on the Stage and there are other objects on the same layer, Flash pulls the selected object out to a separate new layer to create the motion tween. Flash inserts additional new layers in the Timeline hierarchy as needed to preserve the stacking order of the objects.

End-of-span icon for keyframe spans

No end-of-span icon for tween spans

Figure 11.1 To create a motion-tween span of a specific length, first define a keyframe span in the Timeline (top). When you choose Insert > Motion Tween (middle), Flash converts that range of frames to a tween span (bottom). Otherwise, Flash decides how long the span should be, based on the specifics of the current Timeline.

Figure 11.2 Flash identifies layers containing a tween span in the Timeline by adding a motion-tween icon to the left of the layer name and tinting the tween span's frames light blue. (Tinted Frames need not be selected from the Timeline's panel menu; the motion-tween tint always appears.)

How Flash Determines Tween-Span Length

The Insert > Motion Tween command creates tween spans of different lengths depending on the arrangement of frames in the active layer. If you want Flash to create a tween span with a specific number of frames, you must first set up a keyframe span with that number of frames. **Figure 11.3** shows how Flash decides what length to make the tween span when you issue the Insert > Motion Tween command.

Before creating motion tween   **After creating motion tween**

Target symbol in keyframe 1 of layer with no other defined frames; Flash creates one-second tween span based on frame rate (at default of 24fps, tween span contains 24 frames)

Target symbol in keyframe span; Flash converts keyframe span to tween span (same number of frames)

Target symbol is last frame of layer with other defined frames; Flash creates 1-frame tween span

Figure 11.3 Flash's Insert > Motion Tween command creates tween spans of different lengths depending on how many frames and keyframes already exist in the layer.

Tweening One Symbol Among Many

A motion-tween span holds just one symbol (or text field) at a time. For simplicity, in this book you always apply motion tweening to a single symbol on its own layer. You can actually apply motion tweening to a selected object (or objects) on a layer with other objects.

Here's how it works. Select the target object(s), then choose Insert > Motion Tween. If the selection includes everything on the layer, Flash creates the tween span in that layer. If the layer contains objects that aren't part of the selection, Flash pulls the selected object(s) out to a new layer and creates the tween span there. The layer containing the tween span gets a special motion-tween icon (a series of squares). If the selection contains multiple objects on the same layer, or an object other than a symbol or text field, Flash must convert the selection to a symbol to create the tween span (see the sidebar "Motion-Tween Symbols: Best Practice," earlier in this chapter). If you select multiple symbols and/or text fields, each residing on its own layer, Flash creates a separate tween span for each selected object on its original layer.

To preserve the original stacking order of the selected object(s), Flash creates new layers. Any items that originally stacked below the selected object wind up on a layer below the layer containing the new tween span; any items that originally stacked above the selected object, wind up on a layer above the tween span.

To change the tween target's position for the downward bounce:

1. Continuing with the file from the preceding task, to set the tween target's position for the low point of the bounce, in the Timeline, position the playhead in frame 5.

2. Using the selection tool, drag the tween target (MyBall) to the bottom of the stage.

   In the Timeline, Flash adds a diamond icon to the tween span at frame 5. The diamond indicates a property keyframe—in this case a position keyframe (see the sidebar "About Property Keyframes"). The motion path for the tween appears on the Stage (**Figure 11.4**).

Figure 11.4 When you change the position of the tween target on the Stage (top), Flash adds a property keyframe, represented by a small diamond icon, to the current frame of the Timeline and creates a motion path on the Stage (bottom).

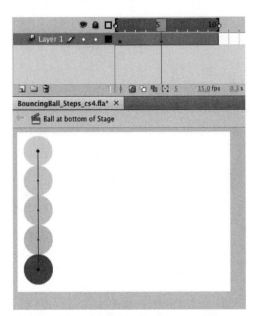

Figure 11.5 The motion path gives you some idea about the movement of the tween target in a motion tween, but it's also good to play the animation to see how it's working. Here, onion skinning allows you to see the interpolated changes to the tween target.

3. Choose Control > Play to see the animation.

The ball moves from the top of the Stage to the bottom in five frames, then sits at the bottom for five frames (**Figure 11.5**).

4. Save your document as a template for future use; name it DownBounceMaster.

Be sure to close the template document before moving on to the next task. (For detailed instructions about templates, see Chapter 1.)

✔ Tip

■ When a symbol is selected, you can change its position by changing its *x*- and *y*-coordinates in the Info panel or in the Position and Size section of the Property inspector. You may need to click the symbol to view its properties in the inspector. If you select the tween span, the symbol is also selected, but it's the span that has focus; properties of the motion tween appear in the inspector.

CREATING A MOTION TWEEN

About Property Keyframes

Flash's Motion Editor displays each tweenable property in a separate graph. By viewing the graph, you can see the exact values for tweened properties at every frame in a selected tween span. The Timeline is less precise. A diamond icon appears in a frame when you've assigned a value to a property in that frame. By assigning a value—for example by manipulating the tween target on the Stage, or by entering a value in the Motion Editor—you create a *property keyframe*.

The Timeline indicates the presence of one or more property keyframes with a diamond icon. You can set the Timeline to display these diamonds or to hide them (see the sidebar, "About Hiding Property Keyframes," later in this chapter). The Motion Editor displays curves for all tweenable properties; for example, in the Basic Motion section of the panel, you'll see separate curves for the horizontal and vertical positions of an object. The Timeline lumps the two into one property-keyframe type: *position.* The Timeline can display diamonds for six properties: Position, Scale, Skew, Rotation, Color, and Filter. For the tasks in this book, when talking about the Timeline, we refer to these general categories when mentioning the presence of a property keyframe. For example, frame 5 contains a *position keyframe* and a *rotation keyframe*. When talking about the Motion Editor, we refer to the specific property curves—for example, the X curve and the Rotation Z curve each have a property keyframe at frame 5.

To change the tween target's position for the upward bounce:

1. Using the DownBounceMaster template you created in the preceding task, open a new document.

2. To set the ball's position for the rebound, in the Timeline, click frame 10, and use the arrow keys to position the tween target two-thirds of the way back up toward the original position.

    When you click a frame within a tween span, the playhead moves to that frame, and the *entire* tween span highlights, indicating that the span is selected. Flash also selects and highlights the tween target on the Stage, making it ready for manipulating, either directly with the selection tool or through a panel setting. The position of the playhead within the tween span determines where Flash will add new property keyframes that represent the changes you'll make (**Figure 11.6**).

    Flash adds a second position keyframe to the tween span, at frame 10, and adds a new segment to the motion path on the Stage. In this case, the new segment lies directly over the original path.

3. Choose Control > Test Movie to preview the animation.

    The ball moves from the top of the Stage to the bottom, then rebounds almost back to the top. If you let the animation loop, the ball bounces continually.

4. Save the document as a template for future use; name it FullBounceMaster.

    Be sure to close the template document before moving on to the next task. (For detailed instructions about templates, see Chapter 1.)

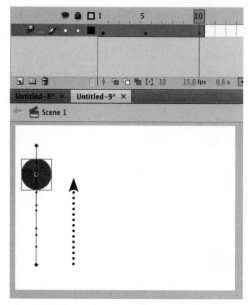

Figure 11.6 The position of the playhead in a selected tween span tells Flash where to add a property keyframe for any changes you make to the selected tween target.

✔ Tip

■ In this task you create the rebound by adding a second position keyframe. This method makes it easy to know that a change takes place at this point in the Timeline. The drawback to this method is that the motion path for the rebound lies directly on top of the motion path for the downward bounce; it can be difficult to manipulate the overlapping segments of the motion path. More-advanced animators can achieve the same result by adding easing to create the rebound motion. (For a quick introduction to easing, see Chapter 12.) You can see an example of this in the default motion preset named Bounce – Smoosh (see the sidebar "About Motion Presets").

The Mystery of Roving Keyframes

In animation, the number of frames used to create motion can affect how fast or slow the motion seems. An object that covers lots of ground in a few frames seems to move quickly. One that goes a short distance over many frames seems to move slowly.

When you resize a tween span in the Timeline, Flash redistributes the tween span's position keyframes to retain the proportions of fast and slow movement. Start with a 15-frame motion tween, add a position keyframe at frame 5, and move the ball 100 pixels to the right; add another position keyframe at frame 15, move the ball 50 pixels down. The movement to the right (the first third of the tween) seems faster than the movement down (the last two-thirds). Now stretch the span in the Timeline (see the tasks in "Modifying Tween Spans," later in this chapter) to 30 frames. That first position keyframe winds up at frame 9, preserving the feeling that the first third of the movement is faster than the rest.

As you tweak the animation in a motion tween, you may wind up with undesirable changes of speed. You can force Flash to redistribute position keyframes so that the speed is uniform by setting keyframes to *roving*. Roving keyframes relinquish their specific frame-number assignment, allowing Flash to distribute motion evenly across the tween span. In the example above, the ball moves 150 pixels total, over 15 frames. If you change the tween span to use roving keyframes, Flash redistributes the motion so the ball moves 10 pixels in each frame. The ball now starts moving down between frames 10 and 11 (**Figure 11.7**).

continues on next page

Figure 11.7 When you first activate roving keyframes for a span, Flash removes the position keyframes in the middle of the span, and places one property keyframe at the end so that motion is distributed evenly.

The Mystery of Roving Keyframes *continued*

While the span is set to roving keyframes, Flash redistributes any positional changes you make to the tween target, so the action stays at a constant rate. If you later change the tween span back to using to non-roving keyframes, Flash updates the Timeline with position keyframes that reflect the redistribution. In the 15-frame example, if you change the tween span to use non-roving keyframes again, Flash captures the redistribution by adding a position keyframe at frame 10.

To turn on roving keyframes from the Timeline, Control-click (Mac) or right-click (Windows) the tween span and from the contextual menu, choose Motion Path > Switch Keyframes to Roving. To turn off roving, access the contextual menu for the tween span and choose Motion Path > Switch Keyframes to Non-Roving. In the Motion Editor, you can set individual position keyframes to roving. Roving keyframes appear as dots instead of squares in the property curve. Control-click (Mac) or right-click (Windows) a control point in either the X or Y property curve and select Roving in the contextual menu. Flash changes the control points to dots in that frame for both the X and Y curves. To turn off roving, repeat the process and deselect Roving in the menu.

About Motion Presets

The *motion preset* is a form of reusable animation. A preset is basically a copy of a tween span with its motion path, property keyframes, and easing intact, just waiting to be assigned a tween target. The preset contains all the information about how the animated item moves, what properties change when, how long it takes to change, and so on. The only thing missing is the symbol.

To use a motion preset, access the Motion Presets panel (if it's closed, choose Window > Motion Presets). The panel looks something like a library panel: motion presets appear in hierarchical folders in a scrolling list; a window at the top previews the animation of a selected preset. Flash CS4 comes with a number of default presets; you can also save custom presets. Open the folder containing the desired preset, and choose a preset name. On the Stage, select the item you want to animate, then in the Motion Presets panel, click the Apply button. Flash turns the selected item into a tween target and creates a motion-tween layer and tween span, just as when you use the Insert > Motion Tween command. However, the motion preset creates not just the tween span but also all the property curves necessary to create the animation. When you click the Apply button, Flash begins the animation with the tween target at its current Stage position. To have the tween target go through its motion and end up at its current position, Shift-click Apply.

You can save your own motion tweens as presets. In the Timeline, select a tween span. In the Motion Presets panel, click the Save Selection As Preset button (the dog-eared page icon in the lower-left corner). Enter a name in the Save Preset As dialog and click OK. Flash adds your preset to the Custom folder in the panel.

The Mystery of Motion Paths

In a motion tween where the tween target changes position, Flash creates a *motion path*, which is a graphic representation of those changes in position. The motion path is an object, similar to a path you'd create with Flash's drawing tools, but with some important differences. A merge-shape or drawing-object Bézier path consists of anchor points with line segments and curves connecting them. A motion path is also a Bézier path, but it contains *frame points* representing the frames in the tween, as well as *control points* (similar to anchor points) representing the position keyframes in the tween (**Figure 11.8**).

In tween spans with up to 100 frames, there is one frame point for each frame in the span. To make tween spans with more than 100 frames easier to deal with, Flash displays evenly spaced small dots that represent a group of frames—for example, every fifth frame (the exact number of frames represented depends on the length of the tween span).

Initially, as you position the tween target, it moves in straight lines and the motion path consists only of straight-line segments. You can edit the motion path to create curves for the tween target to follow.

The motion path and tween target are separate objects, but they are linked together as part of a motion-tween object. You can delete the tween target or swap in a different symbol instance, and the motion path remains a part of the tween object, with all its control points intact, waiting to animate whatever symbol you place into the tween span. You can also swap one motion path for another.

Figure 11.8 In tween spans with up to 100 frames, frame dots—the small round dots in a motion path—represent the frames of the tween. Diamonds (control points) represent the initial keyframe and any position keyframes in the tween. In spans with more than 100 frames, the motion path displays evenly spaced small dots (bottom). To view control points in such large spans, you can select the motion path with the subselection tool. Moving the diamonds using the subselection tool changes the tween target's Stage location at the corresponding frame. You can also edit the motion path to create curves.

Working with Motion-Tween Paths

Any motion tween in which the tween target changes position contains a motion path. Whenever you change a tween target's position at a specific frame—either by manipulating the tween target on the Stage or by entering a new *x*- or *y*-coordinate for the target in a panel—Flash adds a control point to the path at that frame (see the sidebar "The Mystery of Motion Paths"). Initially, your position changes result in a motion path consisting of straight-line segments. To make a symbol follow a curve, you must edit the motion path. Editing a motion path is similar to editing a merge-shape or drawing-object path (see Chapter 4).

Figure 11.9 You can relocate an entire motion-tween animation on the Stage by dragging a selected motion path with the selection tool.

To reposition a motion path:

1. Select the motion path on the Stage.

   Using the selection tool, for example, click directly on the motion path.

2. To change the motion path's position, do any of the following:

   ▲ Using the selection tool, position the pointer over the path. When the selection modifier appears, drag the motion path to a new location (**Figure 11.9**).

   ▲ Use the arrow keys to move the selected path.

   ▲ Access the Motion Tween Property inspector, and in the Path section, use the X and Y hot text to enter new values for the *x*- and *y*-coordinates of the upper-left corner of the path's bounding box. The tween target is connected to the path; the entire animation sequence moves to the new location.

✔ Tips

■ For the tasks in this section, you'll need a motion tween to work on; unless otherwise instructed, use the DownBounceMaster template you created earlier in this chapter. For details on opening new documents from templates, see Chapter 1.

■ Depending on the particular motion path and tween target, it may be difficult to select just the path. You can select both the tween target and the path, for example, by drawing a selection rectangle that includes the path and the tween target. You're ready to drag the selection or move it using the arrow keys.

■ Note that if you select both the path and the tween target, the Property inspector doesn't display the Path section. The Position and Size section does appear, showing the properties of the entire selection. Changing the X and Y values moves the motion path. To see the properties of the motion path alone, deselect the tween target, leaving just the path selected.

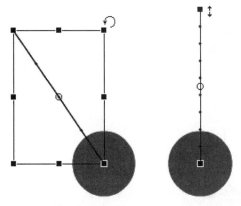

Figure 11.10 Flash's free-transform tool activates a transform box around a selected a motion-tween path (left). For horizontal or vertical paths, the path activates without a box (right). The tool works on the motion path as it would on any other object. Drag the handles to resize, rotate, or skew the bounding box containing the path.

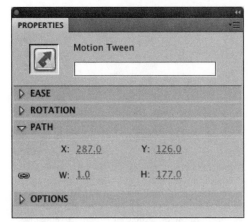

Figure 11.11 The Path section of the Motion Tween Property inspector contains hot text governing the properties of the motion path's bounding box. Changing values for W (width) and H (height) changes the width and height of the path's bounding box, thereby increasing or decreasing the path length.

To resize the path:

1. Select the motion path on the Stage.

2. In the Tools panel, select the free-transform tool.

   Flash activates a transform box for the motion path, just as it would for a regular path (**Figure 11.10**).

3. Using the techniques you learned in Chapter 4, manipulate the resize handles to change the length (and/or orientation) of the path.

   or

1. Select the tween span in the Timeline and access the Motion Tween Property inspector.

2. In the Path section, use the W and H hot text to enter new values for the width and height of the motion path's bounding box (**Figure 11.11**).

   Click the hot text to enter a precise value; drag the hot text's invisible slider to choose a value interactively.

✔ Tip

- You can also access the Path section of the Motion Tween Property inspector after selecting the motion path on the Stage.

WORKING WITH MOTION-TWEEN PATHS

To reshape a motion path by moving control points:

1. Using the FullBounceMaster template you created earlier in this chapter, open a new document.

   The motion path contains three control points, corresponding to the three position keyframes you created for the bouncing ball.

2. In the Tools panel, select the subselection tool (the hollow-arrow pointer).

3. On the Stage, position the hollow-arrow pointer over a control point (one of the large diamonds in the motion path)—for example, the point corresponding to the ball's final position (**Figure 11.12**).

   A hollow-square modifier appears next to the arrow when the tool is on a control point.

4. Drag the control point to a new location—for example, to the bottom-right corner of the Stage.

   Flash redraws the motion path as you drag.

5. Play through the movie.

   Now, instead of bouncing, the ball drops down and moves to the right.

✔ Tip

- When a solid-square modifier appears next to the hollow arrow, the subselection tool is over the path but not over a control point. Dragging with the solid-square modifier active moves the entire motion path.

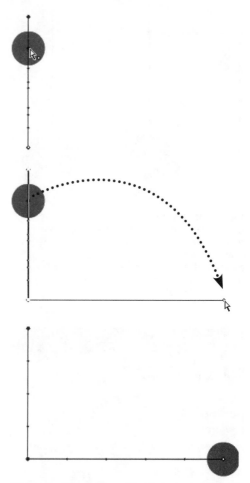

Figure 11.12 When you position the subselection tool over a control point in a motion path, a hollow-square modifier appears (top). Here the path for the rebound lies directly on top of the path for the downward bounce. You can drag the control point to reposition the tween target on the Stage at that frame (middle). Flash redraws the motion path when you release the mouse button (bottom). The new path makes the ball move down and to the right.

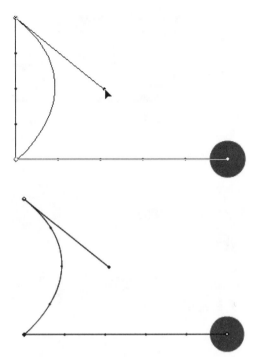

Figure 11.13 Use the subselection tool to Option-drag (Mac) or Alt-drag (Windows) Bézier handles from the control points in a motion path (top). Reposition the handles to transform a straight-line motion path into a curved one (bottom).

To transform a straight-line motion path to an arc:

1. Continuing with the file from the preceding task, in the Tools panel, select the subselection tool.

2. On the Stage, position the pointer over the motion path's initial control point.

   This control point corresponds to the keyframe at the beginning of the motion-tween span.

3. To extend Bézier handles for modifying the path, Option-drag (Mac) or Alt-drag (Windows) the control point.

   Drag in the direction you would like the curve to grow (**Figure 11.13**). Flash redraws the motion path, creating a curve.

✔ Tip

- To gain more control over the curve of the path—for example, making the ball follow an S curve—repeat step 3 for all the control points in the motion path and adjust the Bézier handles to achieve the desired curves.

Modify Motion Paths the Natural Way

You can modify a motion path with the selection tool. The technique is similar to one you learned for modifying lines with natural drawing tools in Chapter 4. Make sure the tween target and the motion path are deselected. Position the selection pointer over the motion path, between two control points. When the curve-point modifier appears, drag that segment of the motion path to create a curved segment. To further refine the curve, switch to the subselection tool and click a control point. Bézier handles extend from the two control points that define the curve segment.

Although the selection tool can transform the motion-path segment into an arc, it can't create angular changes to the path. When you edit a merge-shape or drawing-object path, you can Option-drag (Mac) or Alt-drag (Windows) to add new corner points, but this method doesn't add control points to a motion path. To add control points, you must add position keyframes (see the next task in this section, "To add control points to a motion path").

To add control points to a motion path:

1. Continuing with the file from the preceding task, in the Timeline click frame 3.

   The playhead moves to frame 3, and Flash selects the entire tween span.

2. Control-click (Mac) or right-click (Windows) frame 3.

3. From the contextual menu that appears, choose Insert Keyframe > Position (**Figure 11.14**).

   Flash adds a position keyframe to frame 3. A diamond icon appears in the Timeline, and a new control point appears in the middle of the motion path on the Stage. The tween target moves to that point on the motion path on the Stage.

4. Repeat step 3 to add as many control points as you like.

   You can use the techniques in the preceding tasks to reposition the new control point(s) or activate the Bézier handles to reshape each segment of the motion path.

To remove control points from a motion path:

1. Continuing with the file from the preceding task, in the Timeline ⌘-click (Mac) or Ctrl-click (Windows) frame 3.

   Flash selects frame 3. To select one frame of a tween span, you must use the modifier key (see the section "Modifying Tween Spans," later in this chapter).

2. Control-click (Mac) or right-click (Windows) frame 3.

3. Choose Clear Keyframe > Position from the contextual menu.

   Flash removes the position keyframe from the selected frame. If you select multiple frames, the Clear Keyframe command removes all keyframes of the selected type from all the selected frames.

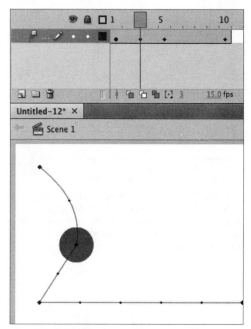

Figure 11.14 To add new control points to a motion path, you must create a new position keyframe. One way is to Control-click (Mac) or right-click (Windows) a selected frame within the tween span and choose Insert Keyframe > Position from the contextual menu (top). Flash adds a property-keyframe diamond icon to the Timeline (bottom).

Frame 5

Figure 11.15 There is a property-keyframe diamond in frame 5 of this Timeline, but the fifth dot in the motion path is just a small, frame dot. That means the diamond icon represents a property other than position. Here, onion skinning reveals that the tween target is rotating as well as moving to the right. The diamond represents a rotation keyframe.

■ To delete all position keyframes quickly, select the motion path and press the Delete key. Flash deletes the path and all its position keyframes. All other property keyframes remain, so, for example, the tween target might grow or rotate or change color, but it stays in one place while doing so. If you subsequently add a motion path to the span, those same property changes take place and the tween target moves along the new path.

✔ Tips

■ In the Timeline, the property keyframe's diamond icon gives you no clue as to what type of property (or properties) are changing at any given frame. If a diamond appears in the Timeline for a frame where you'd like a control point, but the motion path displays only a small, frame dot, you need to add a position keyframe (**Figure 11.15**).

■ In step 2, as long as the tween span is selected and the playhead is in frame 3, you can access the contextual menu by clicking anywhere in the span. Flash adds the new property keyframe in the same frame as the playhead. If the span is not selected when you access the menu, however, the playhead jumps to whatever frame you click. It's safest to click in the frame where you want to add the property keyframe.

■ Here's a quick way to add a position keyframe without actually changing the tween target's position in that frame. In the Timeline, position the playhead in the desired frame. Select the tween-target symbol on the Stage, press the up-arrow key, then press the down-arrow key. Flash adds a position keyframe to account for the change in the position property even though the tween-target symbol winds up in its original position.

■ You can also add a position keyframe using the Motion Editor (see "Motion Editor Basics," later in this chapter).

Orienting a Tween Target to a Curved Path

By default, a tween target keeps its original orientation to the Stage even when following a curving motion path. To create more natural movement, you can force a tween target to rotate to preserve its orientation to the motion path in each frame of a tween.

To orient a tween target to a curving path:

1. Create a ten-frame motion tween of a symbol that follows a curving path.

   Use the techniques you learned in the preceding section to create the curving motion path. For the symbol instance, use a graphic that's not circular; an arrow, a triangle, or an animal will show the effect clearly.

2. Turn on onion skinning to see how the tween target moves along the path without orientation (**Figure 11.16**).

3. In the Timeline, select the tween span and access the Motion Tween Property inspector.

4. In the Rotation section of the inspector, select the Orient to Path check box (**Figure 11.17**).

   Flash adds a rotation keyframe to every frame in the tween span, adjusting the degree of rotation in each frame to preserve the tween target's original alignment with the path.

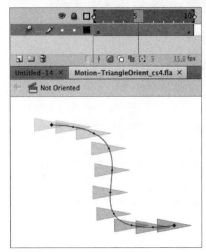

Figure 11.16 The Motion Tween Property inspector displays attributes of the tween. In the Rotation section, when the Orient to Path check box is deselected (top), the tween target maintains its original orientation to the Stage throughout the motion tween (bottom).

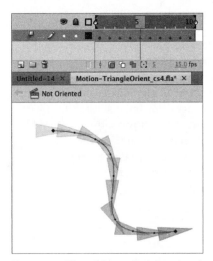

Figure 11.17 When Orient to Path is active, the tween target maintains its original alignment to the motion path throughout the motion tween. Flash adds a rotation keyframe to every frame of the tween span.

Figure 11.18 Whenever a motion-tween layer is the active layer, and the playhead is in a tween span, dragging a symbol from the library to the Stage (top) brings up a dialog asking if you want to replace the original tween target with the object you're dragging (bottom).

Swapping Tween Elements

Because Flash treats a motion tween as an object, it's easy to swap elements in and out of the tween span. You can replace the tween target with any other symbol while retaining all the property changes of the original tween. You can also change the motion path by pasting a different path into the tween span. The pasted path can be a motion path from another tween span, or a merge-shape or drawing-object path.

To swap a tween target:

1. Open a new document using the FullBounceMaster template you created in the previous section.

   It contains a ten-frame motion tween of a bouncing ball, using a symbol named MyBall.

2. Create a new symbol.

   For example, convert a square shape to a symbol named MySquare (for details about creating symbols, see Chapter 7).

3. Select the motion-tween span in the Timeline and access the Library panel.

   If it's not open, choose Window > Library.

4. Drag a copy of MySquare from the library to the Stage.

   A dialog appears asking if you want to replace the existing tween target (**Figure 11.18**).

continues on next page

5. Click OK.

Flash removes the original symbol (MyBall) from the tween and substitutes an instance of MySquare. The Tween span retains all its property keyframes. The tween target moves to the Stage position where you dragged the new symbol, and the motion path moves to match (**Figure 11.19**).

✔ Tips

■ Pasting a copied symbol instance to the Stage with the motion-tween span active also brings up the dialog asking if you want to replace the existing tween target. Depending on which Paste command you used, when you click OK, Flash pastes the symbol its original location or in the center of the Stage and moves the motion path to link up with the new tween target.

■ If the location of the tween is important, be sure to use the Edit > Paste in Place command.

■ To swap symbols and preserve the tween target's original stage position, select just the tween target on the Stage and use the Swap button in the Property inspector (see the section "Swapping One Symbol Instance for Another," in Chapter 7).

Figure 11.19 When you swap tween targets by dragging a new symbol to the Stage (top), the size and shape of motion path and the location of the frame dots and control points stay the same, but the path moves to hook up with the new symbol wherever you dragged it (bottom). Reposition the path if needed.

About Hiding Property Keyframes

By default the Timeline displays all six types of property keyframes. If you create property changes for individual properties in different frames, the Timeline may resemble a diamond bracelet, with property-keyframe markers in almost every frame. To reduce the clutter, you can choose which types of property keyframes appear in the Timeline. Click any frame in a motion-tween span and choose View Keyframes from the contextual menu; a submenu of all six property types, plus All and None, appears. You can select or deselect one property each time you access the menu. Once you deselect a type, Flash stops displaying that type in the Timeline. If your Timeline seems light on property keyframes, or you're trying to insert property keyframes using the contextual menu and not seeing the results in the Timeline, try choosing to view that property type again. (You can also verify the location of the property keyframes in the Motion Editor.)

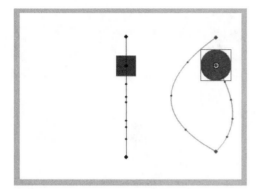

Figure 11.20 The Move Ball and Move Box motion tweens start out with similar motion paths. To practice swapping paths, modify one motion path to create a curve.

To swap a motion path:

1. Continuing with the document from the preceding task, add a new layer and create a second motion tween.

   Layer 1 already contains a motion tween that moves MySquare vertically. In layer 2, create a similar motion tween using the MyBall symbol. In the initial keyframe, for example, position MyBall near the upper right corner of the Stage; in frame 5, move MyBall to the bottom of the Stage; in frame 10, move the ball back near the top. Name the layers Move Ball and Move Box, to remind you which tween is on which layer.

2. Using the techniques you learned earlier in this chapter, modify the motion path in the tween span in the Move Ball layer to make a curved path (**Figure 11.20**).

3. In the Tools panel, choose the selection or subselection tool.

continues on next page

Drawing New Motion Paths

In addition to copying and pasting motion paths between motion spans, you can copy and paste a regular merge-shape or drawing-object path created with Flash's drawing tools (see Chapter 2). This swap option makes it possible to create motion paths using Flash's Bézier tools, which may be easier than editing a motion path to create curves. You simply draw a path, copy it, then paste it into a tween span. The pasted path becomes the new motion path. There are two things to keep in mind: you can't draw directly in a motion-tween span, and you can't use a closed path as a motion path.

To draw a new path for a motion tween, you must work in a keyframe that's not part of a motion-tween span. An easy way to do that is to add a new layer and work in the initial blank keyframe. Alternatively, you could open a new document and work there.

If you try to paste a closed path—for example, a circle—into a motion-tween span, a warning dialog informs you that a motion guide must have two end points. To work around this requirement, draw a circular stroke using the oval tool, then use the eraser tool to delete a tiny portion of the stroke. The path is now open, and you can use it to move a tween target around a circular path.

4. On the Stage, click directly on the motion path for MyBall and choose Edit > Copy.

Flash copies the motion path to the Clipboard.

5. To select the tween target to which you want to attach the new motion path (MySquare), do either of the following:

▲ On the Stage, click MySquare.

▲ In the Timeline, click the tween span in the Move Box layer.

6. Choose Edit > Paste in Center or Edit > Paste in Place.

Flash pastes the ball's motion path into the square's span, distributing the movement over the full length of the target span using roving keyframes. The pasted path has just two position keyframes: the initial keyframe and the last keyframe of the span (**Figure 11.21**).

7. Play through the animation.

MySquare and MyBall now trace the same path in different areas of the Stage, but the timing is different. MyBall reaches the lowest point of its curve at frame 5, where there's a position keyframe; MySquare reaches the same point somewhere between frames 6 and 7.

✔ Tips

■ To make two tween targets follow the exact same path, after you paste the path—while it's still selected—access the Path section of the Property inspector. Using the X and Y hot text, enter values that match those of the first tween's motion path. Flash positions the pasted motion path in the exact same Stage location as the copied path.

■ It doesn't matter whether you choose to paste the path in the center of the Stage or to paste it in place. The pasted path always links up to the target instance's transformation point.

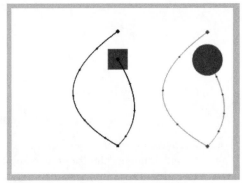

Figure 11.21 Pasting a motion path wipes out any position keyframes in the middle of the target span. Flash creates one position keyframe in the last frame of the span and spreads the animation over the whole span. In this example, the original path in the Move Box layer has a position keyframe at frame 5 (top). After you paste the copied path, that position keyframe disappears (bottom). Note that Flash doesn't change the starting position of the selected tween target; Flash positions the path to connect with the target's transformation point. The shape and size of the motion path determine the ending position of the tween target.

Figure 11.22 The properties that you can animate using a Motion Tween appear in the Motion Editor. While the Timeline indicates points of change to one or more properties by adding a diamond icon to the frame (top), that icon isn't very informative. The Motion Editor gives you specific information about what properties are changing and offers precise control over those changes (bottom).

Figure 11.23 To view more or fewer graphs in the Motion Editor, click the triangle next to the category name to toggle between collapsed and expanded views. To keep the workspace manageable, collapse the categories you're not working on.

Motion Editor Basics

Flash's Motion Editor is a complex and powerful tool that presents information about motion-tween animation in a graphical form. The horizontal axis of the graph represents frame numbers (or in essence, time); the vertical axis represents the value of the property being graphed. Editing the graphs changes the animation. Motion Editor is a bit of a misnomer since it controls not only the position of the tween target (which creates the motion), but various other tweenable properties as well. Many of the sophisticated techniques this panel offers are beyond the scope of a *Visual Quickstart Guide,* but using the Motion Editor to create simple animation is a good way to start. First familiarize yourself with the mechanics of the panel.

To view property curves:

1. Access the Motion Editor.

   If the panel isn't open, choose Window > Motion Editor.

2. To display the property curves for a motion tween, do one of the following:

   ▲ In the Timeline, select the tween span or any frame in the span.

   ▲ On the Stage, select the motion path.

   ▲ On the Stage, select the tween target.

   The graphs for the tweenable properties appear in the Motion Editor (**Figure 11.22**). The panel groups properties into categories: Basic Motion, Transformation, Color Effect, Filters, and Eases.

3. To expand or collapse a category, click the triangle to the left of the category name.

   The category toggles between its expanded and collapsed states (**Figure 11.23**).

✔ Tips

- Some of the properties in the Color Effects and Filters categories can't be graphed as curves; such properties appear in the Graph column as property keyframes on a gray line. Tint Color in Color Effects is one example: there is no "redness" value that Flash could graph along the vertical axis. Tint Amount, which does have a corresponding value (a percentage), gets its own row with a graph in the Tint subcategory of the Motion Editor.

- The arrow keys act as shortcuts for navigating the Motion Editor's many rows. To move up and down the rows, use the up- and down-arrow keys. Flash selects the next row in turn, if the next row is the main category row; and it's in collapsed mode, it stays collapsed. If the next row is a property within an expanded category, Flash selects the row and enlarges it. The right- and left-arrow keys also let you navigate the panel's rows; these keys open collapsed categories as you navigate.

Motion Editor vs. Timeline

The fundamental tool for working with frame-by-frame animation and shape and classic tweening is the Timeline (with its layers and frames). The keyframes displayed in the Timeline give you information about where the key points of change occur. Motion tweens are also Timeline based, but they give you the power to control changes to properties individually. That means there can be many more key points of change to track in an animation segment. The Timeline presents a limited amount of information about what type of change is happening at any given frame (and a limited amount of control over those changes). To see more detail, and gain full control over the property keyframes in a motion-tween span, you must use the Motion Editor. **Figure 11.24** gives an overview of the panel's elements.

continues on next page

Motion Editor vs. Timeline *continued*

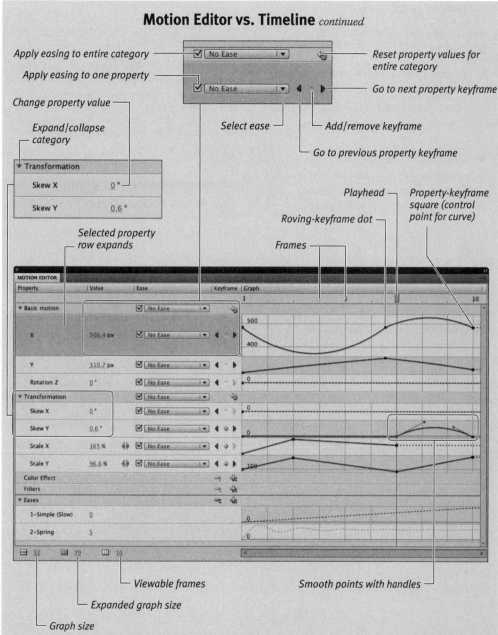

Apply easing to entire category — Reset property values for entire category

Apply easing to one property — Go to next property keyframe

Change property value

Select ease — Add/remove keyframe

Expand/collapse category

Go to previous property keyframe

▼ Transformation

Skew X — 0°

Skew Y — 0.6°

Playhead — Property-keyframe square (control point for curve)

Selected property row expands

Roving-keyframe dot

Frames

MOTION EDITOR

| Property | Value | Ease | Keyframe | Graph |

▼ Basic motion — No Ease

X — 506.4 px — No Ease

Y — 310.7 px — No Ease

Rotation Z — 0° — No Ease

▼ Transformation — No Ease

Skew X — 0° — No Ease

Skew Y — 0.6° — No Ease

Scale X — 165% — No Ease

Scale Y — 96.6% — No Ease

Color Effect

Filters

▼ Eases

1-Simple (Slow) — 0

2-Spring — 5

32   79   10

Viewable frames

Smooth points with handles

Expanded graph size

Graph size

Figure 11.24 The Motion Editor contains its own version of the Timeline with its own playhead. The Motion Editor shows you information for just one motion-tween span at a time. Each tweenable property has its own row. If the property can be graphed as a curve, the row contains a graph with Bézier curves representing the changes to that property within the selected motion-tween span. Property keyframes appear in the graph as control points (black squares) defining the shape of the curve. The horizontal axis of the graph represents time/frame numbers; the vertical axis represents the value of the property being graphed.

MOTION EDITOR VS. TIMELINE

To customize graph views:

1. Access the Motion Editor and select a tween span.

2. To set the size of the rows containing the property graphs, do either of the following:

   ▲ To set the minimum row height for all properties, use the Graph Size hot text.

   ▲ To determine how much a row enlarges when you select it, set the Expanded Graph Size hot text to the desired row height in pixels (**Figure 11.25**).

3. To see more (or fewer) frames in the panel, use the Viewable Frames hot text to set the number of frames displayed (**Figure 11.26**).

   Unlike the Timeline, which displays all the frames in a layer, the Motion Editor only shows the frames of the selected tween span. The maximum value for Viewable Frames is the number of frames in the span.

✔ Tip

■ To set Viewable Frames to show all the frames in a span quickly, enter a number that's bound to exceed the number of frames in the span—for example, 99,999. Flash changes the value to the actual number of frames, and sizes the graph accordingly.

— Set minimum row height

— Set expanded row height

Figure 11.25 Hot-text controls in the Motion Editor let you set the size of the rows and thereby, the size of the graphs. Clicking anywhere in the gray area of the row to the left of the graph expands the row to the current maximum setting.

— Viewable Frames hot text

— Viewable Frames hot text

Figure 11.26 The Motion Editor can display one frame of the selected tween span, several frames (top), or all the frames in the span (bottom). Use the Viewable Frames hot text to set the number of frames that appear in the Graph column.

Figure 11.27 To position the playhead in the Motion Editor, click a tick mark for the frame location you want, or drag the playhead to the frame.

No property keyframe at frame 4

Property keyframe at frame 4

Figure 11.28 When the current frame has no property keyframe, the Add or Remove Keyframe button is ghostly gray and quite hard to see (top). When the frame has a property keyframe, the button turns yellow. Property keyframes in the graph appear as black squares (or dots if the keyframe is set to roving).

To add keyframes to a property curve:

1. In the Graph column of the Motion Editor, position the playhead in the desired frame (**Figure 11.27**).

   You can drag the Motion Editor playhead to a new location or click directly on the frame number or a tick mark above the graphs.

2. In the row containing the property curve you want to change, click the Add or Remove Keyframe button (**Figure 11.28**).

   When the current frame of the property curve lacks a keyframe, the button is a barely visible gray diamond. Clicking it adds a property keyframe (represented by a black square) to the graph. Flash connects the property keyframes with a solid line. When the current frame contains a property keyframe, the button turns yellow and is easier to see.

To remove keyframes from a property curve:

◆ Repeat steps 1 and 2 of the preceding task, this time positioning the Motion Editor's playhead in a frame that contains a property keyframe.

   Flash removes the black square from the graph and redraws the curve segment.

To navigate the property keyframes:

◆ To move the Motion Editor's playhead from one property keyframe to the next in a property curve, click the Go to Previous/Next buttons (the right- and left-facing triangles on either side of the Add or Remove Keyframe button in the row containing the desired property curve).

✔ Tips

■ Instead of using the Add or Remove Keyframe button, you can Control-click (Mac) or right-click (Windows) the property curve itself at any frame and choose Add Keyframe from the Contextual menu.

■ Holding down the #-key (Mac) or Ctrl-key (Windows) and positioning the pointer over the property curve, changes the pointer to a pen icon with a plus sign. Click the graph to add a new control point (**Figure 11.29**).

■ Remember that Flash updates the Motion Editor graphs whenever you change the tween target's properties by any method; the Motion Editor need not be open. If, for example, the playhead is sitting in a frame that lacks property keyframes for X and Y positions, and you move the tween target either by dragging it on the Stage or by changing its *x*- and/or *y*-coordinates in the Property inspector or Info panel, Flash adds property keyframes to the X and Y graphs in the Motion Editor.

■ When you Control-click (Mac) or right-click (Windows) directly on a property keyframe in a property curve, the contextual menu includes the choice Remove Keyframe (**Figure 11.30**).

■ Holding down the ⌘-key (Mac) or Ctrl-key (Windows) and positioning the pointer over a control point in a property curve changes the pointer to a pen icon with a minus sign. Click the control point to remove it.

■ You can remove all property keyframes from all the graphs in a category by clicking the Reset Values button (the return-arrow icon) in the main category row of the Motion Editor.

Figure 11.29 Within the Motion Editor graph, holding down the #-key (Mac) or Ctrl-key (Windows) turns the pointer into a pen icon with a plus sign, similar to the add–anchor-point tool for drawing paths. Click a frame to add a new control point (property keyframe) to the property curve.

Figure 11.30 Control-click (Mac) or right-click (Windows) a property keyframe in the Motion Editor to access the contextual menu. Choosing Remove Keyframe removes the control point you clicked (removing the property keyframe) and redraws the curve.

Figure 11.31 Create a motion tween for working with the Motion Editor. Here, a star symbol is the tween target for a 24-frame motion tween.

Figure 11.32 When you select a tween span in the Timeline (top), the Motion Editor displays the properties of that motion tween (bottom). For a two-dimensional tween, the Basic Motion category contains graphs for three properties: X (horizontal position), Y (vertical position), and Rotation Z (the degree of rotation applied to the tween target).

Adding More Motion

The tasks in the first section of this chapter showed you how use motion tweening to create the standard bouncing-ball animation. For those tasks, you dragged the tween target (the symbol named MyBall) on the Stage to add position keyframes to the motion-tween span. You can also use the Motion Editor to add position keyframes and assign values for the x- and y-coordinates of the tween target.

To create motion by adding position keyframes in the Motion Editor:

1. Open a new Flash document (with default settings) and create a 24-frame motion tween.

   The Timeline has one layer with a blank keyframe at frame 1. Create a symbol containing a star shape; name the symbol MyStar. In keyframe 1, place an instance of MyStar on the Stage. With MyStar selected, access the Position and Size section of the Property inspector, and use the X and Y hot text to position the symbol at the upper-left corner of the Stage. For example, set X and Y to 50 pixels. Choose Insert > Motion Tween. Flash creates a default motion-tween span 24 frames long. Your document should look something like **Figure 11.31**.

2. With the tween span selected in the Timeline, access the Motion Editor's Basic Motion category (**Figure 11.32**).

   If the panel is closed, choose Window > Motion Editor. If necessary, click the triangle to the left of the category name to view its graphs.

continues on next page

3. In the Graph column, position the Motion Editor's playhead at frame 5 (**Figure 11.33**).

   You may need to scroll the graph to see frame 5. The graph contains a black square representing the initial keyframe at frame 1. The dotted lines in the Basic Motion graphs indicate the initial keyframe; the dotted line indicates that the tween span contains no position or rotation keyframes that create movement.

Figure 11.33 To add a property keyframe to a specific frame, you need to position the playhead in that frame in the Graph column of the Motion Editor.

4. In the X row, click the Add or Remove Keyframe button.

   Flash adds a property keyframe to both the X (horizontal position) and Y (vertical position) graphs at frame 5 (the current frame) and thus completes the first segment of the two property curves, changing the dotted line to a solid black line (**Figure 11.34**).

5. To move the tween target to the right, use the X hot text to increase the value for the horizontal position from 50 to 500.

   Flash redraws the property curve (**Figure 11.35**). When the document's units of measure are set to pixels, changing the X value from 50 to 500 moves the tween target 450 pixels to the right.

6. To move the tween target downward, repeat steps 3–5 for frame 15, this time using the Y hot text to increase the value for the vertical position from 50 to 300.

   When the document's units of measure are set to pixels, changing the Y value from 50 to 300 moves the tween target 250 pixels toward the bottom of the Stage.

7. To move the tween target diagonally, repeat steps 3 and 4 for frame 20, then use the X and Y hot text to set new values for the horizontal and vertical positions.

   Setting both values to 100, for example, moves the tween target diagonally back toward the upper left corner of the Stage.

Figure 11.34 After you add a property keyframe, a new control point appears in the property curve. Adding a property keyframe to the X curve (horizontal position) simultaneously adds one to the same frame of the Y curve (vertical position). Flash links the X and Y values because they translate to x- and y-coordinates for the tween target's transformation point.

Figure 11.35 Changing the value for a control point in the X row moves the tween target on the Stage. Flash updates the motion path on the Stage and completes a segment of the X and Y property curves in the Motion Editor.

Figure 11.36 The X and Y property curves in the Motion Editor show all the points of change in the tween target's position. The motion path on the Stage shows the same thing; the larger points in the path are the equivalent of the property keyframes in the curves.

Figure 11.37 Removing a property keyframe from the X (or Y) property curve removes a control point from the motion path on the Stage. Flash redraws the motion path and the property curves.

8. Repeat steps 3–5 for frame 10, this time setting the X value to 350 and the Y value to 250.

Flash adds property keyframes to the X and Y graphs, updates their curves, and updates the motion path on the Stage (**Figure 11.36**). You can refine the animation by adding (or removing) property keyframes at any point in the curve; you can add a property keyframe within an existing curve segment (between property keyframes), or add a property keyframe in the dotted-line section of the graph to create a new curve segment.

✔ Tip

- In step 6, using a higher value to position a symbol lower on the Stage may seem counterintuitive (especially if you're using the Y hot text interactively—dragging down in the hot text moves the symbol up on the Stage). It's all due to the way Flash tracks elements (see the sidebar "How Flash Tracks Elements," in Chapter 4).

To edit motion by removing position keyframes in the Motion Editor:

1. Continuing with the file from the preceding task, position the Motion Editor's playhead in frame 10.

2. In either the X or Y row, click the yellow Add or Remove Keyframe button.

Flash removes the black square from both graphs, redraws the X and Y curves in the Motion Editor, and redraws the motion path on the Stage (**Figure 11.37**). The curves and motion path return to the way they were before you completed step 8 in the preceding task.

3. Save this document as a template and call it MovingStarMaster.

Animating Other Property Changes

You can use the Motion Editor to add property keyframes for all the properties that you can animate with motion tweens. The process is similar to adding property keyframes for Stage position. The specific settings and graphs are different. In the following tasks, you'll create some basic property keyframes to animate changes in size, rotation, and color.

Figure 11.38 You can use the Rotation Z hot text in the Motion Editor to add a bit of spin to the tween target.

To rotate the tween target:

1. Using the MovingStarMaster template you created in the preceding task, open a new document, select the tween span, and access the Basic Motion section of the Motion Editor.

   If necessary, click the triangle to the left of the category name to view its graphs.

2. Position the Motion Editor's playhead in frame 5.

3. Use the Rotation Z hot text to enter the degree of rotation.

   For this task, enter 90 degrees. Positive values create clockwise rotation; negative values, counterclockwise.

   Flash adds a property keyframe to the Rotation Z graph and updates the curve (**Figure 11.38**).

Manipulating Tween Targets to Add Property Keyframes

In Chapter 9, you placed symbol instances in keyframes on either end of a keyframe span to create a classic tween. You then changed the properties of the symbols by manipulating the symbol instances directly—for example, using the free-transform tool to change a symbol's size. You can also use those techniques in motion tweening. Whenever you manipulate a tween target on the Stage, Flash translates your changes into property keyframes. You saw Flash add position keyframes to the Timeline when you created the bouncing ball earlier in this chapter. The technique works for any property that you can tween in a motion tween. Flash creates property keyframes in both the Timeline and the Motion Editor in response to your changes to the Tween target on the Stage. For example, open a new document using the BounceDownMaster template. Position the playhead at frame 7. Using the free-transform tool, change the size of the tween target (MyBall). Flash adds a scale keyframe to frame 5 in the Timeline and adds a property keyframe to frame 7 of the property curves for Scale X and/or Scale Y in the Motion Editor.

Figure 11.39 Onion skinning reveals that the tween target rotates in five steps when you add a property keyframe at frame 5 of the Rotation curve in the Motion Editor.

4. Scrub through the animation by moving the playhead one frame at a time.

   The star rotates 90 degrees in five steps (frames 1–5) (**Figure 11.39**). It retains its rotated position for the rest of the tween.

5. Save this document as a template, name it RotateStarMaster.

✔ Tip

■ In the preceding task, the star stops rotating at frame 5. If you want the star to begin rotating again in later frames, you need to add more rotation keyframes. If you want the star to rotate continuously throughout the tween to reach 90 degrees, place the rotation keyframe at the end of the tween span, or apply the rotation to the entire tween span via the Motion Tween Property inspector (see the sidebar "The Mystery of Autorotation in Motion Tweens").

A Note About Editing Motion

Often, the easiest way to create and edit the movement of a tween target is to drag the target instance on the Stage. Dragging creates a new position keyframe at the current frame automatically; dragging lets you interactively check and adjust the tween target's position and relationship to other elements. If you need to position a tween target precisely, you can enter *x*- and *y*-coordinates for the tween target's registration point using the Property inspector, the Info panel, or the Motion Editor. Which method is best? In part, it depends on your working style. But there's another issue to be aware of. The behind-the-scenes math that the Motion Editor uses to calculate and draw the motion path works somewhat differently than the math in all the other methods. Using the hot text and graphs in the Basic Motion section of the Motion Editor can have unexpected results for the motion path on the Stage. And as a practical matter, the graphs in the Motion Editor are small and difficult to deal with in comparison with the motion path on the Stage. The tasks in this section show you how to use the Motion Editor by adding keyframes and changing the X and Y hot-text values to move the tween target in straight lines around the Stage. To move a tween target in more complex ways, and to edit the motion path once you've created the keyframes you want, it's best to work directly with the tween target and motion path on the Stage, or to use the Property inspector or Info panel to enter specific *x*- and *y*-coordinate values.

To change a tween target's scale:

1. Repeat steps 1 and 2 of the preceding task. This time, access the Transformation section of the Motion Editor.

2. To change the size of the tween target, access the Scale X and Scale Y rows and do either of the following:

   ▲ To preserve the tween target's aspect ratio, set the Link Values icon to its linked mode (the closed-link icon) (**Figure 11.40**). If necessary, click the icon to change modes. Then use the Scale X or Scale Y hot text to enter a new percentage. In linked mode, changing one value automatically changes the other by the same amount. Larger values increase the size of the tween target; smaller values reduce it.

   ▲ To change the tween target's vertical and horizontal dimensions independently, set the Link Values icon to its unlinked mode (the broken-link icon). Then use the Scale X or Scale Y hot text to enter new percentages independently.

Scale width and height independently

Link width and height

Figure 11.40 The Link Values icon in the Scale rows of the Motion Editor works just like the constrain icon in the Transform panel. When the chain link is broken, you can change the X and Y values independently. When the chain is closed, changing one value changes the other as well, preserving the tween target's aspect ratio.

The Mystery of Autorotation in Motion Tweens

For the tasks in this section, you rotate the motion-tween target by creating rotation keyframes in the Motion Editor. You must specify a precise degree of rotation, using negative values to rotate the tween target counterclockwise and positive ones to rotate it clockwise. When you created classic tweens (see Chapter 9), you let Flash automatically spin objects by entering values in the Rotate section in the Tweening area of the Frame Property inspector. The technique also works for a motion-tween target. Select the tween span in the Timeline to see the properties of the motion tween. In the Rotation section of the Motion Property inspector use the Rotation Amount and Additional Rotation hot text to set the number of times the tween target rotates (set Rotation Count to 0 if you want the target to rotate less than 360 degrees). There's just one little quirk to keep in mind: when you create rotation for the tween target via the Property inspector, Flash spreads the rotation out over the entire tween span. Even when you specifically select a single frame earlier in the tween span, Flash adds the rotation keyframe to the last frame in the current span. If you want the rotation to end at an earlier frame, you can select the rotation keyframe and drag it from the last frame of the tween span to the desired frame (see "Modifying Tween Spans," later in this chapter).

Figure 11.41 Onion skinning reveals the interpolated steps that change the tween target's size when you add a property keyframe to the Scale X curve in the Motion Editor. With Link Values active, a Scale X value of 70 percent shrinks the star while keeping its aspect ratio.

3. Play through the animation.

The star moves around the Stage. By the time it reaches the halfway point of its horizontal motion (at frame 5), the star has changed to the new size you specified in step 3 (**Figure 11.41**). Note that it keeps this new size for the remainder of the animation, or until you add another scale keyframe. The position keyframes that exist at frames 15 and 20 have no effect on the size of the star.

✔ Tip

■ The graphs for the skew property are also located in the Transformation section of the Motion Editor and work similarly. Add new keyframes to the Skew X and/or Skew Y graphs. Then use the Skew X hot text to change the horizontal skew of the tween target. Use the Skew Y hot text to change the vertical skew. Skew values are always set independently.

A Note about Rotation and 3D Tweening

In preceding task, you learn about rotation in two dimensions (rotation along the z-axis). When you create a motion tween, Flash also lets you create rotation in three-dimensional space (rotation along the x-, y-, and z-axes). To access those properties, you need to Control-click (Mac) or right-click (Windows) a motion-tween span in the Timeline and choose 3D Tween from the contextual menu. The additional rotation properties appear in the Basic Motion section of the Motion Editor. Animated 3D rotations are beyond the scope of a *Visual Quickstart Guide*. If you'd like to learn more, check out *Flash CS4 Professional Advanced for Windows and Macintosh: Visual QuickPro Guide*, by Russell Chun (Peachpit Press, 2008).

To change a tween target's color:

1. Continuing with the file from the preceding task, with the tween target (MyStar) selected on the Stage, in the Graph column of the Motion Editor, position the playhead in frame 12.

2. In the Color Effect row, from the Add Color menu (the plus-sign icon), choose the desired effect (**Figure 11.42**).

   The Add Color menu offers the same effects you learned about for modifying symbol instances in Chapter 7. For this task, choose Tint, a new subcategory in the Color Effect section of the Motion Editor. Rows and graphs for Tint Color and Tint Amount appear in the Tint subcategory.

3. To assign a new color to the tween target, do the following:

   ▲ In the Tint Color row, click the color control and choose a color from the pop-up swatch set.

   ▲ Use the Tint Amount hot text to determine how much of the tint to apply to the tween target. For this example, choose 90 percent.

4. Play through the animation.

   Flash changes MyStar from its original color to its new color in 12 steps (**Figure 11.43**). MyStar keeps its new color for the rest of the tween.

Figure 11.42 Click the Add Color menu (the plus sign) in the Motion Editor's Color Effect row, then choose a color effect to apply to your tween target (top). The Tint effect property curves appear: Tint Color and Tint Amount (bottom).

Figure 11.43 By adding a property keyframe at frame 12 of the Tint and Amount curves, you set up the star to change color over the first 12 frames.

ANIMATING OTHER PROPERTY CHANGES

About Editing Curves in the Motion Editor

The graphs in the Motion Editor show changes to each property as a Bézier-style curve. The horizontal axis of the graph shows frame numbers (time); the vertical axis shows the property values. You can edit most property curves inside the Motion Editor in ways similar to those you learned for editing Bézier paths (Chapter 4). The exceptions are the X and Y property curves that define the motion path. Curves do appear in the Motion Editor for the X and Y properties, but you can only edit them by editing the motion path on the Stage.

The terminology for property curves differs a bit from that for Bézier paths. In a property curve, each property keyframe appears as a *control point* that defines the curve (like an anchor point in a Bézier path). As you change a property in various frames of a motion tween, Flash adds control points to that property curve. Initially, each control point is a corner point, and the curve consists of straight line segments. You can convert the control points to *smooth points* (similar to curve points in a Bézier path), then use a smooth point's handles to shape the curve on either side of the control point. You can drag control points horizontally, moving the property keyframe to a new frame in the tween, and you can drag control points vertically, to adjust the value of the property.

As you drag a control point in the graph, a tool tip appears showing the frame number and current value of the point. To stop viewing the tool tips, Control-click (Mac) or right-click (Windows) in the Graph column, but not on the curve or control point itself; and from the contextual menu, deselect Show Tooltips.

Here are some ways you can edit the curves of a property in the Motion Editor (**Figure 11.44** on the next page).

To select a control point, click it. Flash highlights the point in green. To select multiple points in one property curve, Shift-click each point. To deselect a point, Shift-click it.

To move a control point to a different frame number, drag it in the graph.

To change the control point's value (the value of the property), drag the control point up or down. The graph scrolls as you drag. This can be hard to work with when the Motion Editor is set to a small size. To make the graphs easier to work with, make the Motion Editor a floating panel and resize it to be fairly large (see Chapter 1).

To transform a corner point to a smooth point, Control-click (Mac) or right-click (Windows) the control point and choose Smooth, Smooth Left, or Smooth Right from the contextual menu. The options available in the menu depend on the configuration of the property graph (if you select the control point in frame 1, for example, the left-side options aren't available). Smooth adds handles to both sides of the point, Smooth Left adds a handle to the left, and Smooth Right adds a handle to the right. Manipulating a handle adjusts the curve on that side of the control point. Whenever you select a smooth point, its handles appear. By adjusting the curve, you tell Flash how quickly to apply the change to that property. The steeper the curve, the faster the change takes place.

continues on next page

About Editing Curves in the Motion Editor *continued*

To transform a smooth point to a corner point, Control-click (Mac) or right-click
(Windows) the point and choose Corner Point, Linear Left, or Linear Right from the contextual menu. Again, the options in the menu depend on the configuration of the property graph.
Corner Point removes the handles from both sides of the control point; Linear Left removes
the left-side handle; Linear Right removes the right-side handle.

Click to select control points; Shift-click to deselect

Selected control points highlight in green

Option-drag (Mac) or Alt-drag (Windows) to access handles to manipulate curve

Drag control point to reposition, drag horizontally to move to new frame, drag vertically to change property value; tool tip shows value

Control-click (Mac) or right-click (Windows) a control point; choose a new point type from the contextual menu

Figure 11.44 You can edit most of the property curves directly in the Motion Editor's Graph column. You can
add and remove control points and create smooth points to adjust the property curves, adding subtlety to
the changes in your animation. Steeper curves translate to faster changes; flatter curves translate to more
gradual changes.

Figure 11.45 Flash tints motion-tween spans light blue. Click any frame in a motion-tween span (top) to select the entire span (bottom). A darker highlight indicates the selection.

Begin drag

End drag

Figure 11.46 To select a range of frames within a tween span, ⌘-drag (Mac) or Ctrl-drag (Windows) through the desired frames in the Timeline.

Modifying Tween Spans

Selecting and manipulating the frames of a tween span in the Timeline is similar to working with frames in keyframe spans when you've set Preferences to span-based selection style (see Chapter 8). But there are a few twists. (Note that the Preferences setting has no effect on tween spans.) No matter which frame you click in a tween span, Flash selects the entire span. Dragging the first or last frame expands (or reduces) the motion tween as an object; Flash adjusts the position of any property keyframes within the tween span to spread the animation out (or squeeze it down) to fit the new span proportionally. You must use a modifier key to select individual frames or to expand the span by adding in-between frames at the end without redistributing the existing property keyframes.

To select the entire tween span:

◆ Click any frame within the tween span. Flash selects the entire span and highlights it (**Figure 11.45**).

To select one frame in a tween span:

◆ In the Timeline, ⌘-click (Mac) or Ctrl-click (Windows) the desired frame. Flash highlights the selected frame.

To select multiple frames in tween spans:

◆ In the Timeline, ⌘-drag (Mac) or Ctrl-drag (Windows) through all the frames you want to select (**Figure 11.46**).

To resize a tween span:

1. Position the pointer over the last frame in the tween span.

   The icon changes to a double-arrow.

2. To change the span's size, do either of the following:

   To lengthen the span, drag to the right.

   Flash treats the span and the animation it contains as an object, and redistributes property keyframes within the span proportionally (**Figure 11.47**).

   or

   To shorten the span, drag to the left.

✔ Tips

- You can't select a range of frames by ⌘-clicking (Mac) or Ctrl-clicking (Windows) the first frame and then Shift-⌘-clicking (Mac) or Shift-Ctrl-clicking (Windows) the last frame (as you can in a keyframe span with span-based selection mode). Always ⌘-drag (Mac) or Ctrl-drag (Windows) to select a range of frames within a tween span.

- You can also resize a tween span by dragging the first frame in the span.

- Increasing the size of the span eats into or deletes other spans or keyframes on the same layer, just as it does with keyframe spans (see Chapter 8). Reducing the size of the span creates new empty keyframe spans.

Original span · *Ready to resize*

Drag right to enlarge

Resized span, with redistributed property keyframe

Figure 11.47 Resizing a tween span by dragging doesn't merely add frames to or remove frames from the end of the span. The animation contained in the tween span expands or contracts as an object. Flash redistributes the property keyframes to preserve the proportions of the tween. The original tween span has a property keyframe roughly at midspan, and so does the resized span. Flash does its best to maintain the relative positions of the property keyframes within the span. In the original span, 4 frames come before the property keyframe and 5 come after it. When you double the length of the span, Flash doubles the number of frames before the property keyframe to 8; that leaves 11 frames that come after. That's slightly more than double, but necessary to fill out the 20 frames.

Shift-dragging to the left...

Clips off the end of the span

Figure 11.48 Shift-drag the end of a tween span to resize it without redistributing its property keyframes. Shift-drag to the right to add in-between frames at the end of the span. Shift-drag to the left to clip off the end of the span.

To extend or trim the end of a tween span:

1. Position the pointer over the last frame in the tween span.

   The double-arrow pointer appears.

2. To change the end of the span, do either of the following:

   ▲ To add in-between frames at the end of the span, Shift-drag to the right.

   or

   ▲ To remove frames from the end of the span, Shift-drag to the left.

   Flash resizes the tween span (**Figure 11.48**). If you drag over property keyframes, Flash does not reposition them within the remaining span; instead Flash cuts the property keyframes along with the in-between frames.

✔ Tip

■ You can also add in-between frames to extend the span. Select a protoframe, then choose Insert > Timeline > Frame (or press F5). Flash extends the tween span to the selected frame. If you select frames within the span and press F5, Flash increases the size of the span by adding that number of in-between frames. Where Flash adds the frames depends on the precise location of your selection in relation to any property keyframes.

To shorten a tween span by removing internal frames:

1. Select one or more contiguous frames within the tween span.

2. Choose Edit > Timeline > Remove Frames.

   Flash deletes the frames, removing any property keyframes that fall within the selection, and shortens the tween span by the number of frames selected (**Figure 11.49**).

✔ Tip

■ The contextual menu for tween spans also contains a Remove Frames command.

To cut frames out of a tween span:

1. Select one or more contiguous frames within a tween span.

2. Choose Edit > Timeline > Cut Frames.

   Flash converts the selection to an empty keyframe span with a blank initial keyframe. Other frames in the selection become in-between frames. Flash converts any frames that follow the selection to a second tween span based on the original tween target, with all the properties that had been applied at that frame (**Figure 11.50**).

✔ Tip

■ You can split or combine tween spans. To divide a span, Control-click (Mac) or right-click (Windows) to select the frame at which the span should split. From the contextual menu choose Split Motion. To combine spans, in the Timeline, Shift-click one or more contiguous tween spans in a layer. Control-click (Mac) or right-click (Windows) any of the selected frames, and from the contextual menu choose Join Motions. Flash creates a single tween span using the tween target from the earliest span.

Original span with selected frames

New span with frames removed

Figure 11.49 The Edit > Timeline > Remove Frames command shortens the tween span by removing the selected frames, including any property keyframes in the selection.

Original span with selected frames

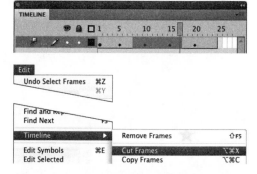

New span; cut frames leave empty keyframe span

Figure 11.50 When you cut selected frames from a tween span (instead of removing them), Flash transforms them to an empty keyframe span. If you cut frames midspan, the empty keyframe span winds up in the middle. The remaining frames from the original tween span become a second tween span.

Figure 11.51 Drag a selected motion-tween span in the Timeline to move it within one layer, or to move it to a different layer. The results vary depending on the elements in the layer. Dragging a tween span to the right into a second tween span (A) creates a new keyframe span in the first span and squeezes the initial keyframe of the second span as far as possible to the right into a shortened span (B). Dragging a tween span to the left (C) shortens the preceding span (D). Dragging a tween span so that it completely covers another span (E) replaces the covered span and its contents with the dragged span (F).

To move tween spans using drag and drop:

◆ Select the span and drag it to the right or left within the layer.

Flash repositions the span. Depending on the particular configuration of elements in the layer, Flash resizes other spans, removes their content, and/or creates blank keyframe spans in the original tween span's location (**Figure 11.51**). If you drag a tween span so that it completely covers another keyframe or span, Flash deletes the covered item. Flash creates an empty keyframe span at the end of the layer to retain the layer's original number of defined frames.

✔ Tips

■ You can drag a tween span to a different layer.

■ Option-dragging a tween span creates a copy of the span, which you can place elsewhere on the same layer or on a different layer.

■ You can also drag and drop one or more property keyframes within a tween span. ⌘-click (Mac) or Ctrl-click (Windows) to select the frame containing the property-keyframe diamond you want to move (or ⌘- or Ctrl-drag to select a range of frames with multiple diamonds) and position the pointer over the selection. When a hollow-square modifier appears next to the arrow icon, drag the selection to a new position in the Timeline. Remember that each diamond icon may represent more than one property. Dragging a selection repositions the property keyframes for all the properties associated with each diamond.

To remove property keyframes:

1. To remove one type of property keyframe from a single frame, ⌘-click (Mac) or Ctrl-click (Windows) the frame to select it.

2. To access the contextual menu for frames, Control-click (Mac) or right-click (Windows) the selected frame.

3. Choose Clear Keyframe.

4. From the submenu that appears, choose one of the following:

   ▲ To remove one category of property keyframes at a time, choose a type: Position, Scale, Skew, Rotation, Color, or Filter.

   ▲ To remove all categories simultaneously, choose All (**Figure 11.52**).

   Flash removes the property keyframe(s) from the selection in the Timeline, updates the property curve in the Motion Editor, and updates the tween target and/or motion path on the Stage.

✔ Tips

- When working with the Timeline, if you want to remove more than one category of property keyframes but preserve some, you must repeat the preceding task, choosing a different category each time.

- To remove all the property keyframes from curves in a single Motion Editor category simultaneously, click the Reset button in the main category row.

- Be careful when using the contextual menu's Clear Keyframe commands, however, as they remove all the property keyframes of a selected type from all selected frames. If you select the entire span, the commands delete all property keyframes of the selected type throughout the span.

Figure 11.52 To remove a property keyframe, select one or more frames in the Timeline and access the contextual menu for frames. Choose Clear Keyframe and choose a property type from the submenu. Flash removes all property keyframes of that type from all selected frames. To remove all property keyframes of all types from the selected frames, choose All.

Figure 11.53 Choose Edit > Timeline > Copy Frames to make a copy of a selected tween span. You can then paste the tween into another layer, or elsewhere in the same layer, to reuse the motion.

✔ Tips

■ You can reuse just part of a tween. If your selection includes just in-between frames, Flash creates a new initial keyframe when it pastes the copied frames. The tween target has the properties it had in the first selected frame. If the target was in the middle of turning from red to blue, for example, in the pasted tween, the tween target starts out with the same purple color it had in the first frame of the selection.

■ If you paste a motion-tween span into a layer containing classic or shape tweens, Flash creates a keyframe span the length of the copied tween span. The span consists of a keyframe containing the tween target in its original form, followed by plain in-between frames.

Copying Frames and Properties

You can reuse all or part of a motion tween by copying and pasting frames from the tween span into other frames in the Timeline. The frames receiving the copied frames can be part of an existing span or be blank. Similarly, you can copy properties and paste them into a frame within an existing motion-tween span.

To copy and paste a complete motion tween:

1. To select the motion tween, in the Timeline, click any frame in the tween span.

2. Choose Edit > Timeline > Copy Frames (**Figure 11.53**).

3. In the Timeline, do one of the following:

   ▲ Create a new layer and select its initial blank keyframe or one of its protoframes.

   ▲ Add a new blank keyframe to the end of an existing layer containing a motion tween, and select it.

   ▲ Select a protoframe at the end of a layer containing other motion tween(s).

   ▲ Select a frame or range of frames within an existing tween span.

4. Choose Edit > Timeline > Paste Frames. Flash pastes a tween span with the same content and property changes. The initial keyframe of the pasted tween is in the selected frame, and the pasted span extends for the same number of frames as the original. If you paste frames into the middle of another tween span; Flash divides that span and may overwrite some of it. If you add to a protoframe following a tween span, Flash extends the preceding span with in-between frames; no redistribution of property keyframes occurs.

To copy and paste property keyframes:

1. Open a new document using the RotateStarMaster template, which you created earlier in this chapter.

2. Add a new layer; in keyframe 1, place a different symbol instance in the lower-left corner of the Stage—say, a square named MySquare—and choose Insert > Motion Tween.

   Flash creates another motion tween; currently the tween span contains no property keyframes. Name the layers according to their contents, Star and Square.

3. In the Timeline, in the Star layer, ⌘-click (Mac) or Ctrl-click (Windows) frame 17 to select it.

   Flash can only copy properties from one frame at a time.

4. Control-click (Mac) or right-click (Windows) the selected frame, and from the contextual menu, choose Copy Properties (**Figure 11.54**).

5. Repeat steps 3 and 4, this time selecting frame 5 in the Square layer and choosing Paste Properties from the contextual menu.

   Flash creates a new property keyframe in frame 5 of the Square layer, using the property settings that existed at frame 17 of the Star layer. MySquare moves to the right side of the Stage (to the same position MyStar has at frame 17) and rotates 90 degrees (**Figure 11.55**).

✔ Tip

■ The Copy Properties command captures property values for all the property types that exist for the selected tween target at the frame where you copy. The Paste Properties command, however, only pastes properties that already exist in the tween you're pasting to.

Figure 11.54 To copy properties, you must select a single frame in the motion-tween span. Control-click (Mac) or right-click (Windows) the selected frame and choose Copy Properties from the contextual menu. The selected frame can be the initial keyframe, a property keyframe, or an in-between frame.

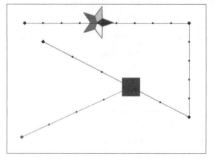

Figure 11.55 The properties of the star in frame 17 (top) have been copied and then pasted onto the square at frame 5 (bottom).

The Insert > Keyframe Conundrum

When creating classic tweens and shape tweens, going to the menu bar and choosing Insert > Timeline > Keyframe (or pressing F6) is a great timesaver that you'll use often. It allows you to duplicate the preceding keyframe quickly to create tween segments. By habit, you might reach for F6 while working in a motion tween, but train yourself to pause first to evaluate your needs.

There is only one true keyframe in each motion-tween span; it's the first frame of the span. All the other "keyframes" are property keyframes controlling changes to individual properties. (Just to add to the confusion, the contextual menu for tween spans contains the command Insert > Keyframe; the submenu makes it clear that you're actually inserting property keyframes.) Pressing F6 within a tween span creates *property* keyframes for every property that exists at that point (**Figure 11.56**).

continues on next page

Figure 11.56 The Motion Editor makes it easy to see what's happening when you evoke the Insert > Keyframe command for a motion tween. Select a motion-tween span that has lots of property changes of different types (top). Access the Motion Editor. Position the playhead at an in-between frame and press F6. Flash adds a new control point to every graph (bottom).

The Insert > Keyframe Conundrum *continued*

Four of the properties represented by diamond-shaped property keyframes in the Timeline—Position, Scale, Skew, and Rotation—are always present in the initial keyframe of the tween span. You don't see diamonds because that keyframe uses a solid-bullet icon. But if you open the Basic Motion and Transformation sections of the Motion Editor, you will see a property keyframe at the beginning of each curve, even before you make changes to any property. These properties allow Flash to describe the tween target. At a minimum, pressing F6 creates property keyframes for all these properties. The Color and Filter properties (found in the Color Effect and Filters sections of the Motion Editor) work differently; you must add them to the tween. If they are in effect, pressing F6 also creates their property keyframes.

If you need to change every property at one point, then creating all those control points simultaneously is helpful. Often, however, you just wind up with excess control points whose value doesn't change. Extra control points may make it harder to edit the property curves to create subtle changes. You can move an excess control point to a different frame where that property should change, but that's a tedious process for long animations, where a tween span may contain dozens or hundreds of frames.

Property Keyframe Mysteries: Insert vs. Convert

In Chapter 8, you learned about the differences between using the Insert and Convert commands to add keyframes to the Timeline. Similar principals govern when you use the Insert > Timeline > Keyframe or Modify > Timeline > Convert to Keyframe commands within a tween span, but there are a few twists. Remember that in tween spans, these commands add property keyframes, not true keyframes (see the sidebar "The Insert > Keyframe Conundrum").

The Insert command adds a property keyframe only in the frame where the playhead is, no matter how many frames of the tween span are selected. The Modify command adds a property keyframe in multiple selected frames, but only if they are a subset of the frames in the tween span. When the entire tween span is selected, the Modify command adds a property keyframe only in the frame where the playhead is.

MORE-COMPLEX ANIMATION TASKS

12

You've learned to manipulate shapes and symbols, animating them one at a time, in a single layer, but Adobe Flash CS4 Professional is capable of handling much more complicated animation tasks. To create complex animated movies, you'll need to work with multiple shapes or symbols and multiple layers. You may even want to use multiple scenes to organize long animations. In this chapter, you learn to work with multiple layers in the Timeline, stack animations on the various layers to create more-complex movement, and save animations as reusable elements for easy manipulation—either as animated graphic symbols or as movie-clip symbols. With these techniques, you can really start to bring your animations to life.

A Note About Scenes

A Flash project requiring lots of animation may include hundreds of frames. You can break the animation into smaller chunks by creating scenes. When you publish a movie from a regular Flash document, the scenes play back in order unless you use the interactivity features to provide instructions for playing the scenes in a different order.

Scene basics. To add a new scene, choose Insert > Scene. To select a scene to edit, in the Edit bar, click the Edit Scene button and select a scene from the pop-up menu (**Figure 12.1**). You can also use Flash's Scene panel to see what scenes exist in your movie, select a scene to edit, create new scenes, duplicate scenes, delete scenes, and reorganize them (**Figure 12.2**). To access the Scene panel, choose Window > Other Panels > Scene.

Figure 12.1 The Edit bar displays the name of the current scene. Choose a scene from the Edit Scene pop-up menu to switch scenes quickly.

Figure 12.2 The Scene panel lists all the scenes in a movie. It also provides buttons for adding, duplicating, and deleting scenes.

The pitfalls of using scenes. Scenes in Flash are tools for organizing content during authoring; they don't exist at runtime. When you create a Flash document, each scene acts like a self-contained movie, but when you publish the file, Flash links the scenes into one continuous set of frames. (Imagine a document with two scenes: scene 1 has frames numbered 1–10, and scene 2 has frames numbered 1–10. The published file winds up with frames numbered 1–20.)

The fact that each scene is, in a sense, a new beginning can make it difficult to keep the continuity of actions between scenes. For movies with interactivity that requires variables, scenes may be inappropriate. In such cases, you may need to stick to a single long movie or use separate movies or separate movie clips within one movie to organize your animation. The fact that scenes don't exist in the published movie presents other problems. For example, you must be careful to avoid using identical frame labels in multiple scenes. Otherwise, interactivities that rely on those frame labels to locate and display the appropriate frame will not work.

Figure 12.3 To deselect all frames quickly, click in the number area above the frames, or in the gray area below the layers in the Timeline.

Manipulating Frames in Multiple Layers

As your animation gets more complex, you'll need to add layers to your document. You can perform editing operations on selected frames and layers, for example, by copying, cutting, and pasting frames across multiple layers. You can also insert frames, keyframes, and blank keyframes into selected keyframe spans, tween spans, and layers.

To select frames in several layers:

1. Create a practice document containing multiple layers and tweens (see the sidebar "Layers to Play With").

2. To deselect all frames, in the Timeline, click in a blank area of the Timeline (**Figure 12.3**).

    Deselecting frames prevents you from accidentally moving selected frames or adding them to a selection.

continues on next page

Layers to Play With

To practice working with frames and layers, create a document with four layers, each with 20 defined frames. Add content that helps you see what's going on. Use the text tool, for example, to place the frame number in every other frame of layer 1 and to place a text block with the layer name in layers 2, 3, and 4. Set up a motion tween by selecting frame 1 in layer 4 and choosing Insert > Motion Tween. Set up a classic tween by selecting frame 10 in layer 3, choosing Insert > Timeline > Keyframe, then selecting any frame in the preceding keyframe span (frames 1–9) and choosing Insert > Classic Tween.

3. To draw a selection rectangle in the Timeline, do one of the following:

▲ In frame-based selection mode, to begin with a frame that is outside a motion-tween span, drag diagonally from the first frame through all the desired frames (**Figure 12.4**).

▲ In span-based selection mode, to begin with a frame that is outside a motion-tween span, ⌘-drag (Mac) or Ctrl-drag (Windows) to select a range of frames.

▲ In either selection style, to begin with a frame that is part of a motion-tween span, ⌘-drag (Mac) or Ctrl-drag (Windows) to select a range of frames.

Flash highlights the selected frames as you drag.

✔ Tips

■ You can define a selection rectangle by clicking instead of dragging. In span-based selection mode (or to begin with a frame that's part of a motion-tween span), add the appropriate modifier key—⌘ (Mac) or Ctrl (Windows) when you click and Shift-click. In frame-based selection mode, starting with a frame outside a motion-tween span, click and then Shift-click diagonally opposite corners of an imaginary rectangle to highlight the fames. Flash highlights all the frames in the rectangle that you've defined (**Figure 12.5**).

■ You can't use the click/Shift-click method if your selection would end with a frame set to motion tweening; you'd just wind up selecting the ending frame.

Drag to opposite corner

Begin selection

Figure 12.4 In frame-based selection mode, when beginning a selection outside a motion-tween span, simply drag across frames and layers to select frames. For example, in layer 1, drag from frame 4 diagonally up and to the right till you reach frame 15 in layer 4. In span-based mode, ⌘-drag (Mac) or Ctrl-drag (Windows). If you're selecting only motion-tweened frames, or you want to start your selection within a motion-tween span, use the span-based method.

With one corner selected

Prepare to click the opposite corner

After Shift-clicking with modifier key

Figure 12.5 You can select frames without dragging. In span-based selection mode—or to begin the selection inside a motion-tween span—⌘-click (Mac) or Ctrl-click (Windows) one frame, and then Shift-⌘-click (Mac) or Ctrl-Shift-click (Windows) another frame to define a selection block. In frame-based selection mode—or to begin the selection outside a motion-tween span—click one corner of the block, then Shift-click the opposite corner (the ending frame must be outside a motion-tween span).

Figure 12.6 You must use the Edit > Timeline > Copy Frames command to copy selected frames. The standard copy command won't work.

To copy selected frames:

1. Continuing with the practice document from the preceding exercise, select frames 5–10 in all four layers.

2. Choose Edit > Timeline > Copy Frames (**Figure 12.6**).

   Flash copies the frames and layer information to the Clipboard.

To replace the content of frames with a multiple-layer selection:

1. Continuing with the document from the preceding task, select frames 15–20 on all four layers.

2. Choose Edit > Timeline > Paste Frames.

   Flash pastes the copied frames 5–10 into frames 15–20 in each of the four layers (**Figure 12.7**). The numbers on the Stage in layer 1 now start over with the number 5 at frame 15, 7 at frame 17, and 9 at frame 19. Flash created a new keyframe in frame 15 of layer 2, a new classic-tween keyframe span in layer 3, and a new motion-tween span in layer 4.

Frames selected

Frames pasted

Figure 12.7 Pasting copied frames into existing frames replaces their content. Here, the content copied from keyframe 9 winds up in keyframe 19 and continues to show in frame 20, where the playhead is.

MANIPULATING FRAMES IN MULTIPLE LAYERS

To paste a multiple-layer selection into blank frames:

1. Continuing with the document from the preceding task, select frame 21 on all four layers.

2. Choose Edit > Timeline > Paste Frames.

   Flash pastes the copied frames 5–10 into protoframes 21–26 in each of the four layers (**Figure 12.8**). Layer 1 now displays the number 5 at frame 21, 7 at frame 23, and 9 at frame 25. Flash created a new keyframe in frame 21 of layer 2, a new classic-tween keyframe span in layer 3, and a new motion-tween span in layer 4

✔ Tip

- You can also paste a multiple-layer selection into a new document, scene, or layer. By default, the document, scene, or layer starts with a blank keyframe in frame 1. Select that keyframe and choose Edit > Timeline > Paste Frames. Flash adds layers to accommodate the copied frames and layers.

Figure 12.8 Pasting a multiple-layer, multiple-frame selection at the end of a set of defined frames (top) extends the Timeline to accommodate the new frames and layers (bottom).

Figure 12.9 To animate several symbols simultaneously with classic or motion tweening, each symbol must be on a separate layer. Descriptive layer names help you keep track of what goes where.

Animating on Multiple Layers

To animate multiple objects simultaneously with classic or motion tweens, you must put each object on a separate layer. Flash restricts you to just one object per tween for motion tweens and classic tweens. Shape tweens allow you to work with more than one shape per tween, but it's usually best to stick with just one. The tasks in this section introduce you to tweening items on multiple layers simultaneously.

Working with multiple-layer classic tweens

For the tasks in this section, you'll combine three simple classic tweens on three layers, to create a game of Ping-Pong. The first step is to create the symbols and layers. One layer contains a Ping-Pong ball symbol; the other layers each contain a paddle symbol.

To set up the graphics layers:

1. Open a new Flash document, and add two new layers.

2. Rename the layers.

   To help keep track of the elements, name the top layer Ball, the next layer 1st Paddle, and the bottom layer 2nd Paddle.

3. Create the graphics as symbols (see Chapter 7).

   Create a symbol named PingPongBall containing an appropriate graphic element (for example, use the oval tool to draw a circular fill). Create two symbols—1stPaddle and 2ndPaddle—each containing a paddle graphic (for example, use the rectangle tool to draw a rectangular fill). Place each symbol in the layer that has the same name. Your file should look like **Figure 12.9**.

continues on next page

ANIMATING ON MULTIPLE LAYERS

4. Save the file as a template named PingPongSetupMaster.

Be sure to close the template file before continuing (for details about saving documents as templates, see Chapter 1). You can use the same initial graphic setup to create a classic-tween or motion-tween version of the Ping-Pong animation.

To set up a classic tween in all layers with one command:

1. Using the PingPongSetupMaster template you created in the preceding task, open a new document.

2. In the Timeline, select keyframe 1 in all three layers.

3. Choose Insert > Classic Tween (**Figure 12.10**).

Flash sets all three frames to be classic tweens.

4. In the Timeline, select frame 20 in all three layers.

5. Choose Insert > Timeline > Frame.

Flash extends the classic tween through frame 20 on all three layers. A dotted line across the frames indicates that the tween is incomplete (**Figure 12.11**). To make the ball and paddles move around the Stage, you must complete the classic-tween sequences, by adding keyframes and repositioning the symbol instance in each one.

Figure 12.10 With frames selected on multiple layers (top), choosing Insert > Classic Tween (bottom) sets up classic tweens on all the layers.

Figure 12.11 The frames on all three layers have been set to classic tweening, but the tweens are broken, as indicated by the dotted lines. You must add keyframes and content.

ANIMATING ON MULTIPLE LAYERS

Figure 12.12 Moving a symbol in a frame that's defined as part of a classic tween causes Flash to make the layer containing the symbol the active layer. Flash creates a keyframe in that layer for the symbol's new position, thus completing one tween sequence.

Figure 12.13 As you reposition the paddle, Flash selects frames 5–20; but the completed tween segment appears correctly in frames 1–4.

To rough out the movement— classic tweening:

1. Continuing with the file from the preceding task, in the Timeline, position the playhead in frame 5.

2. On the Stage, drag the ball to the approximate location where it should connect with one of the paddles for the first hit.

   Ball becomes the active layer. In frame 5, Flash creates a new keyframe containing another instance of the PingPongBall symbol in its new location (**Figure 12.12**). Flash completes the tween in the first keyframe span (frames 1–4) of the Ball layer, which displays the completed-tween arrow. The broken-tween line remains in all the other frames.

3. On the Stage, reposition the first paddle so that it connects with the ball for the first hit.

   Flash makes 1st Paddle the active layer and creates a new keyframe (in frame 5) containing another instance of the 1stPaddle symbol in its new location (**Figure 12.13**).

4. In the Timeline, position the playhead in frame 10.

continues on next page

ANIMATING ON MULTIPLE LAYERS

5. On the Stage, drag the ball to the approximate location where you want it to connect with a paddle for the second hit.

Flash makes Ball the active layer and creates a keyframe (in frame 10) containing another instance of the PingPongBall symbol in its new location. Flash completes the classic tween between keyframe 5 and keyframe 10 of the Ball layer.

6. On the Stage, reposition the second paddle so that it connects with the ball for the second hit.

Flash makes 2nd Paddle the active layer and creates a keyframe (in frame 10) containing another instance of the 2ndPaddle symbol in its new location (**Figure 12.14**).

7. Repeat steps 1–6, creating keyframes 15 and 20 to make the ball connect with each paddle one more time.

8. Play the movie to see the animation in action.

✔ Tip

■ Currently, all layers in this Flash document are set to be classic tweens. If you add more frames later, they will also be set to classic tweening. To completely end the tweening sequences, you need to remove the tween from the last keyframe in each layer. Select the final keyframes and choose Insert > Remove Tween.

Figure 12.14 Moving an element in another frame creates another tween. Here, the paddle on the right side appears to move more slowly than the paddle on the left side, because Flash is creating a ten-frame tween for the right paddle, which moves a short distance. The left paddle tweens in five frames and moves a greater distance. (Here, onion skinning is turned on to make the tweened shapes visible.)

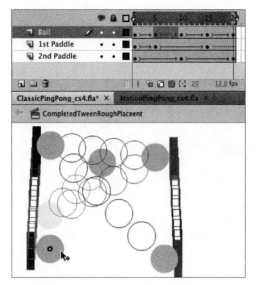

Figure 12.15 You can easily fine-tune the location of objects in classic tweens by turning on Onion Skin Outlines and Edit Multiple Frames. Here, the paddle on the right doesn't move in a straight line. If you want it to do so, reposition the paddle graphics in the first and final frames so that one lies directly above the other; then reposition the ball so that it comes into contact with both paddles.

To fine-tune the movement—classic tweening:

1. Continuing with the file from the preceding task, in the Status bar, click the Onion Skin Outlines button and the Edit Multiple Frames button to activate these modes.

Position the onion handles to cover all 20 frames or choose Onion All. With Edit Multiple Frames active, the symbol instances in keyframes appear as solid objects; the interpolated tween graphics appear as onion outlines.

2. Reposition the symbol instances as necessary to fine-tune the motion (**Figure 12.15**).

For example, using the selection tool, drag a symbol instance on the Stage. Or select the instance and use the X and Y hot text in the Position and Size section of the Property inspector to change the symbols' x- and y-coordinates.

✔ Tips

■ After you define a keyframe span as a classic tween, any slight change you make to the tweened symbol instance on an in-between frame causes Flash to create a new keyframe. Even clicking and holding more than a second or two causes Flash to insert a keyframe. So that you don't change objects' positions or create new keyframes accidentally, lock or hide the layers that you're not working on.

■ Motion tweens are not as delicate as classic tweens; you can click and hold on a tween target on an in-between frame without fear of accidentally creating a property keyframe. Still, once you've positioned elements as you want them on a layer, locking it is a good idea to prevent unintended changes.

Working with multiple-layer motion tweens

For the tasks in this layer, you'll combine three simple motion tweens on three layers, to create a game of Ping-Pong much like the classic-tween animation you created in the preceding section. As in that animation, one layer contains the ball; the other layers each contain a paddle.

To set up a motion tween in all layers with one command:

1. Using the PingPongSetupMaster template you created in "To set up the graphics layers," earlier in this section, open a new document.

2. To define the length of the motion tween, in the Timeline, select frame 20 in all three layers.

3. Choose Insert > Timeline > Frame.

   Flash defines in-between frames 2–20 in all layers. Frame 20 is selected in all three layers.

4. Choose Insert > Motion tween.

   Flash creates a 20-frame motion-tween span in each layer (**Figure 12.16**). Frame 1 of each layer is a keyframe containing the span's tween target (in the top layer, for example, it's an instance of the PingPongBall symbol). To make the symbols move around the Stage, you must add position keyframes to each tween span. You can do this by repositioning the tween targets at specific frames.

Figure 12.16 When one frame is selected in keyframe spans on multiple layers, choosing Insert > Motion Tween converts all the spans to tween spans. You can see that the ending rectangle of the keyframe span disappears.

Figure 12.17 Dragging a symbol on the Stage in a motion tween adds a position keyframe at the current frame and creates a motion path.

Figure 12.18 By repositioning all of the tween targets in the appropriate frames, you create the same type of Ping-Pong animation in a motion tween that you created earlier in a classic tween.

To rough out the movement— motion tweening:

1. Continuing with the file from the preceding task, in the Timeline, position the playhead in frame 5.

   The method you used to create keyframes within a classic tween, also works to create position keyframes in a tween span. Dragging a symbol to a new location on the Stage creates a new position keyframe in the Timeline at the current frame (the one where the playhead is located).

2. On the Stage, drag the ball to the approximate location where it should connect with one of the paddles for the first hit.

   Ball becomes the active layer. In frame 5, Flash creates a position keyframe. Note that no other property changes exist currently for this frame. Flash creates a motion path from the ball's original location to its new location in frame 5 (**Figure 12.17**).

3. Follow steps 3–8 of "To rough out the movement—classic tweening," in the preceding section.

   Reposition the tween targets PingPongBall, 1stPaddle, and 2ndPaddle on the Stage in frames 5, 10, 15, and 20.

   Flash adds position keyframes and extends the motion path for each tween target after you move it (**Figure 12.18**).

To fine-tune the movement— motion tweening:

1. Continuing with the file from the preceding task, to view and manipulate the motion paths of multiple tween targets simultaneously, do the following:

   ▲ In the Tools panel, choose the selection or subselection tool.

   ▲ On the Stage, click any motion path. The Motion Tween Property inspector displays properties for motion tweening.

   ▲ From the Property inspector's panel menu, choose Always Show Motion Paths (**Figure 12.19**).

   Viewing multiple motion paths gives you access to every motion path (and every control point), not just the path whose tween span is active. Viewing all the paths together gives you some context for adjusting the target symbols' relative positions on the Stage.

Figure 12.19 To see motion paths for all the tween targets simultaneously, select any motion path on the Stage. Access the Property inspector and choose Always Show Motion Paths from the panel menu (top). Now, when the playhead is at a frame where multiple layers contain tween spans, Flash displays a motion path for each span whose layer is visible in the Timeline (bottom). (To view just the path of the tween span in the active layer where the playhead is located, deselect Always Show Motion Paths.)

Figure 12.20 The PingPongBall and 1stPaddle tweens each have a position keyframe in frame 5; their tween targets appear on the Stage as solid objects centered over the control point for frame 5. The 2ndPaddle tween has no position keyframe at frame 5; its tween target appears on the Stage as a solid object centered over the frame point for frame 5. When you drag PingPongBall, Flash moves the control point in the motion path. If no position keyframe exists for that target in the current frame, when you drag the tween target, Flash adds a position keyframe to the current frame.

2. To adjust a tween target's position at a specific frame, do the following:

▲ Position the playhead in the desired frame in the Timeline or Motion Editor. Each tween target appears on its motion path at the associated frame point or control point. To adjust the tween target at an existing position keyframe, move the playhead to a frame that has a position-keyframe diamond in the Timeline or a property keyframe in the X and Y property curves in the Motion Editor.

▲ In the Tools panel, choose the selection tool.

▲ Drag the tween target to a new location on the Stage (**Figure 12.20**). Note that if there is currently no position keyframe for the target you drag, Flash creates a new one.

continues on next page

3. To adjust all tween targets in context, at any position keyframe, do the following:

   ▲ In the Status bar, click the Onion Skin Outlines button to activate onion skinning. Position the onion handles to cover the tween span or choose Onion All. The onion outlines show you how the tween targets relate to one another as they follow their motion paths.

   ▲ In the Tools panel, choose the subselection tool.

   ▲ Drag any control point on the Stage. Flash previews the new motion path as you drag (there is no preview for a tween target's onion outline, however). Release the mouse button and Flash redraws the motion path and the outlines (**Figure 12.21**).

✔ Tips

- In step 1, to access the Motion Tween Property inspector, you could select a tween span in the Timeline instead of selecting a motion path on the Stage.

- With Edit Multiple Frames active, Flash displays the content of all the keyframes within the onion markers. When positioning graphics on multiple layers for classic tweening, you need to have Edit Multiple Frames active to see (and manipulate) the symbol instances in all the keyframes of the tween simultaneously. With motion tweening, that's unnecessary and may be confusing. Each motion tween has just one keyframe, the one at the beginning of the tween span. Even when the playhead is in a property keyframe later in the tween span, the solid symbol always appears at the initial control point of the motion path.

Figure 12.21 To get more context for adjusting the position of multiple motion tweens, turn on onion skinning. You can then use the subselection tool to reposition any control point in any visible motion path. You don't need to position the playhead in a specific frame, and you can't accidentally add new position keyframes.

Tweening Text

You can use the multiple-layer tween idea to animate individual characters within a piece of text. After you create the text that you want to animate, select it and choose Modify > Break Apart. That command places each character in its own text field. Next, with each character of the text selected, choose Modify > Timeline > Distribute to Layers. Each character winds up on its own layer. Now use any of the animating techniques you learned in Chapters 8 (frame by frame), 9 (classic tween), and 11 (motion tween), to animate the individual text characters (**Figure 12.22**).

To transform the shapes of the letters, you need to use shape tweening. That means converting the letters from editable text elements to editable graphics. Select one or more text fields containing individual letters, and choose Modify > Break Apart. The letterforms look the same, but now they're raw shapes that you can modify with the drawing tools and use in shape tweens. When you select one of the letters on the Stage, the selection-highlight dots reveal that it's a separate merge-shape. Shape-tweening letters can get pretty complex. Remember to use shape hints to help Flash make the transition between shapes correctly (see Chapter 10).

Text distributed to layers

Broken-apart text; one character per text field

Each letter is a separate motion tween

Figure 12.22 Using Flash's Modify > Break Apart command in conjunction with the Modify > Timeline > Distribute to Layers command, you can set up tweens quickly to animate individual text characters. Each letter in this animated text is a motion tween.

Working with multiple-layer shape tweens

An important thing to remember about complex shape tweens is that Flash deals most reliably with a single shape tween on a layer. In the following tasks, you create a multipart, multilayer graphic, and you shape-tween the whole package simultaneously.

To create shape tweens on separate layers:

1. Open a Flash document, and add two new layers.

2. Rename the layers Top Flame, Middle Flame, and Bottom Flame.

   Naming the layers helps you keep track of the objects and their locations.

3. Create the shapes.

   On the Stage, use the oval tool to create three concentric oval shapes without strokes. In the Bottom Flame layer, create a large oval; in the Middle Flame layer, create a medium oval and center it over the first oval; in the Top Flame layer, create a small oval and center it over the medium oval. Give each oval a different color. Your file should look something like **Figure 12.23**.

Figure 12.23 Create each part of a multiple-element shape tween on a separate layer. Name the layers to help you track what goes where.

ANIMATING ON MULTIPLE LAYERS

When Should One Element Span Several Layers?

Often, an element that you think of as a single entity consists of several shapes in Flash. A candle flame is a good example. To simulate the flickering of a lighted candle, you might create a flame with three shades of orange and then animate changes in the flame shape and colors.

It's natural to keep drawing each piece of the flame in one layer, especially if you're creating merge-shapes and want to see the interaction of the shapes immediately. Unfortunately, Flash has trouble tweening multiple shapes (both merge-shapes and drawing-objects) on a single layer. You're better off creating a rough version of each piece in a separate layer and then fine-tuning that version. Or, create your shapes in one layer, but then select them and choose Insert > Timeline > Distribute to Layers to place them on separate layers. That way, Flash has to tween only one shape per layer, and the result will be cleaner.

Figure 12.24 When your selection contains frames from multiple keyframe spans, you can assign shape-tweening to those keyframe spans simultaneously. Access the contextual menu for frames, for example, and choose Create Shape Tween.

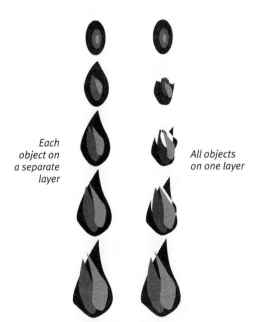

Each object on a separate layer

All objects on one layer

Figure 12.25 No matter whether you use merge-shapes or drawing objects, if you put the three flames on separate layers (left), Flash does a reasonable job of tweening even when you don't add shape hints. With all three flame shapes on a single layer (right), Flash has difficulty creating the tweens.

4. Select frame 5 in all three layers.

5. Choose Insert > Timeline > Keyframe.
   Flash creates a keyframe with the same content as keyframe 1 for each layer.

6. In the Timeline, select any of the frames in the keyframe 1 span (1, 2, 3, or 4) in all three layers.

7. Control-click (Mac) or right-click (Windows) the selected frames and choose Create Shape Tween from the contextual menu.
   Flash creates shape tweens in frames 1–4 on all three layers (**Figure 12.24**). To create flickering flames, you need to reshape the ovals in keyframe 5.

8. In the Timeline, position the playhead in keyframe 5.

9. On the Stage, edit the ovals to create flame shapes.

10. Play the movie to see the animation in action.
    Flash handles the shape-tweening of each layer separately. For comparison, try creating the oval and flame shapes on a single layer and then shape-tweening them (**Figure 12.25**).

11. Click the Onion Skin Outlines and Edit Multiple Frames buttons to activate these modes; then reshape the flame objects as necessary to fine-tune the motion.

ANIMATING ON MULTIPLE LAYERS

Reversing Animation

Sometimes, you can save effort by creating just half the animation you need and letting Flash do the rest of the work. Think of the candle flame that grows and shrinks. The shrinking phase is the reverse of the growing phase. You can make a copy of the growing-flame animation and then have Flash reverse it. The technique for reversing animation is the same for shape tweens and classic tweens; you can reverse the animation of motion tweens in a variety of ways.

To reverse the animation created with key-frame spans (classic and shape tweening), simply swap the order in which the keyframes appear in the Timeline, then Flash interpolates the changes between those elements, and the animation "runs in reverse." There are two ways to reverse the animation in motion tweens: reverse the direction that the tween target takes as it moves along the motion path, and reverse the order in which all prop-erty changes take place (see the sidebar "The Mystery of Motion Reversal").

To reverse the frame order for shape (or classic) keyframe spans:

1. Open the document you created in the preceding section.

   This movie spans five frames on three layers. The first keyframe shows the flame as three concentric oval shapes; the final keyframe shows the flame in a taller, flick-ering configuration.

2. In the Timeline, select all five frames on all three layers.

3. In one of the selected frames, Control-click (Mac) or right-click (Windows) to access the contextual menu for frames, then choose Copy Frames (**Figure 12.26**).

Figure 12.26 The contextual menu for frames lets you copy all selected frames with a single command.

Figure 12.27 After you paste the copied selection, the second tween sequence starts with the oval flame (left) and ends with the tall, flickering flame (right).

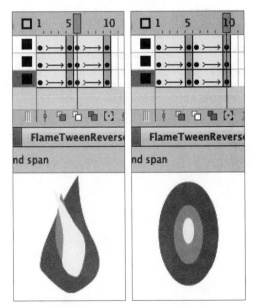

Figure 12.28 After you reverse the frames, the second tween sequence starts with the flickering flame (left) and ends with the oval flame (right).

4. In the Timeline, select frame 6 in all three layers.

5. In one of the selected frames, Control-click (Mac) or right-click (Windows) to access the contextual menu for frames, and choose Paste Frames.

   Your movie now contains two back-to-back animation sequences of the growing flame (**Figure 12.27**).

6. In the Timeline, select frames 6–10 on all three layers.

7. Choose Modify > Timeline > Reverse Frames.

   Flash reverses the tween in the second sequence so that the flame starts out tall and flickery, and winds up in its original oval configuration in the final keyframe (**Figure 12.28**).

✔ Tips

- Because the technique in the preceding task reverses the order in which keyframes appear in the Timeline, you can also use it to reverse the direction for animation you create using frame-by-frame techniques. Select the full range of keyframes, then choose Modify > Timeline > Reverse Frames.

- In the preceding task, you wind up with back-to-back duplicate keyframes (frames 5 and 6 both contain the tall flame). You can convert the duplicate to an in-between frame, adding it to either of the tween segments. To add it to the first tween segment, select frame 5 in all three layers (to add it to the second segment, select frame 6 in all layers), ⌘-click (Mac) or Ctrl-click (Windows) the selected frames, and from the contextual menu, choose Clear Keyframe.

REVERSING ANIMATION

To reverse the direction of motion for motion tweens:

1. Using the RotateStarMaster template you created in Chapter 11, open a new document.

   The file contains a 24-frame animation of a star that moves to three different spots on the Stage and rotates. (To review using templates, see Chapter 1.)

2. In the Timeline, add a new layer, and name the layers to identify them.

   Name the layer containing the motion tween Original Path; name the new layer Reversed Path. It's helpful to compare the original motion tween with the reversed version on separate layers.

3. To duplicate the motion tween, Option-(Mac) or Alt- (Windows) drag the tween span from the Original Path layer to frames 1–24 of the Reversed Path layer.

   The tween targets and motion paths stack right on top of one another.

4. On the Stage, drag the topmost motion path to a new location on the Stage. Separating the paths makes it easier to compare the motion. Your document should look something like **Figure 12.29**.

5. In the Timeline, in the Reversed Path layer, Control-click (Mac) or right-click (Windows) the tween span.

6. From the contextual menu, choose Motion Path > Reverse Path (**Figure 12.30**).

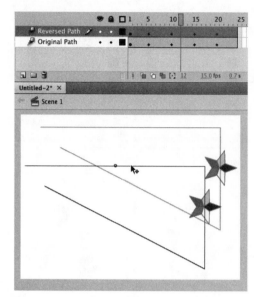

Figure 12.29 To make it easier to compare duplicated motion tweens, drag the topmost motion path to a different area of the Stage.

Figure 12.30 To change the direction of motion in a motion tween, Control-click (Mac) or right-click (Windows) a tween span and choose Motion Path > Reverse Path from the contextual menu.

REVERSING ANIMATION

Original motion tween

Reversed path

Figure 12.31 The Motion Editor makes it clear what happens when you choose the Motion Path > Reverse Path command: Flash flips the direction of the X and Y property curves.

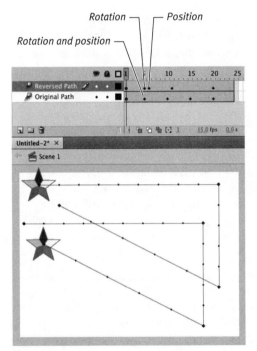

Figure 12.32 When you reverse a motion tween by using the Motion Path > Reverse Path command, Flash flips the X and Y property curves, resulting in new locations for property-keyframe diamonds in the Timeline.

Flash reverses the path by reversing the graphs for the X and Y property curves in the Basic Motion section of the Motion Editor (**Figure 12.31**).

7. Play through the animation.

The two stars start from opposite ends of the motion path and move in opposite directions. That's the result of reversing the property curves for X and Y. The Reverse Paths command has no effect on any other property curves. Both stars complete their rotation at frame 5. Note that when you apply the Reverse Path command to complex tweens, Flash may redistribute position keyframes in the Timeline, while keeping other property keyframes in their original locations (**Figure 12.32**).

8. To compare the tweens, play through the movie.

The two tween targets start at opposite ends of the motion path and move in opposite directions. Both complete their rotation by the time they hit frame 5.

✔ Tip

- Another way to reverse the direction of motion is to flip the motion path itself. For example, select the motion path on the Stage, then choose Modify > Transform > Flip Horizontal (or Flip Vertical). You can also use the free-transform tool to flip the direction of the path.

REVERSING ANIMATION

347

To reverse the order of all property keyframes:

1. Open a document containing a motion tween.

2. In the Timeline, Control-click (Mac) or right-click (Windows) the tween span.

3. From the contextual menu, choose Reverse Keyframes.

   Flash reverses the graphs for all of the property curves in the Motion Editor (see the sidebar "The Mystery of Motion Reversal").

✔ Tip

■ Using the Reverse Keyframes command may have unexpected results when you apply it to tweens where some property curves lack a property keyframe in the final frame of the tween span. That's because in reversing the property curves, Flash ignores any in-between frames that come at the end of the Motion Editor graph (the dotted-line portion of the property curve). To force Flash to flip the entire graph, you can add a property keyframe to the last frame of the tween.

Combining Tweening with Frame-by-Frame Techniques

Especially with shape tweening, you can't always rely on Flash to create in-between frames that capture the exact movement you want. You can combine Flash's tweening with your own frame-by-frame efforts, however, letting Flash do the work when it can, then using keyframe animation to refine the movement. Flash helps with the process by letting you convert the intangible in-between frames of a tween to keyframes that you can edit and refine yourself. The conversion process differs depending on the type of tweening.

Shape and classic tweens. For shape tweens and classic tweens, you can select one or more frames in the keyframe span and choose Modify > Timeline > Convert to Keyframes. Flash converts each selected frame to a keyframe containing a new shape or a new instance of the tweened symbol. A new instance has all the properties that were applied to the symbol at that in-between frame. Note that when converting in-between frames of a shape tween to keyframes, Flash always creates the new shapes as merge-shapes (even if the shapes in the preceding keyframe are drawing-objects or primitive-shapes). This could result in unexpected consequences if your shapes are on a single layer. It's another reason to make sure your shapes are on separate layers for tweened animation.

Motion tweens and inverse kinematics (IK). For motion tweens, Control-click (Mac) or right-click (Windows) anywhere in the tween span and choose Convert to Frame by Frame Animation from the contextual menu. Flash converts every frame in the span (whether selected or not) to a keyframe containing a new instance of the tween target. This new instance has all the properties that were applied to the tween target at that in-between frame of the motion tween. If you choose Modify > Timeline > Convert to Keyframes when one or more frames of a motion tween are selected, Flash adds property keyframes to the current frame (see the sidebar "The Insert > Keyframe Conundrum," in the section "Copying Frames and Properties," in Chapter 11). For pose spans created by inverse kinematics (IK), you also use the contextual menu's Convert to Frame by Frame Animation command; the Convert to Keyframes command creates a new pose, not a new keyframe (see Chapter 13).

The Mystery of Motion Reversal

Imagine animating a small red square that moves from left to right, doubles in size, and turns blue. You can reverse it in two ways: you can reverse the path to move a small red square from right to left (where it doubles in size and turns blue), or you can reverse the keyframes to move a large blue square from right to left (where it turns red and shrinks to half its size). The results are straightforward for a simple animation with just a few changes, especially if the changes take place in just two keyframes, one at the beginning of the tween span and one at the end. But if changes take place throughout the tween, and there are property keyframes in the middle of the tween span, Flash must decide exactly where to make the desired changes. The results can be complex and somewhat unexpected, especially when viewed in the Timeline.

To reverse motion tweening, Flash simply flips the property curve that appears in the Motion Editor graph. When you choose Motion Path > Reverse Path, Flash flips the X and Y curves in the Basic Motion section; when you choose Reverse Keyframes, Flash flips all the property curves.

Reversing a tween span that ends with in-between frames (where the property curve is a dotted line in the Motion Editor graph) can be especially confusing. Flash treats the curve from the first control point (the span's initial keyframe) to the last control point as an object and flips that. Flash excludes any in-between frames at the end of the tween span (where the property curve is a dotted line). This may make position keyframes appear in seemingly unexpected places in the Timeline when you reverse the animation (**Figure 12.33**).

Timeline

Figure 12.33 When you use the Motion Path > Reverse Keyframes command, the number of property-keyframe diamonds in the Timeline may appear to increase. That's because one diamond can represent multiple properties. The Motion Editor shows what happens.

Motion Editor

Original

— Frame 8

Reversed Path

— Frame 8

Reversed Keyframes

— Frame 10

Saving Animations As Symbols

In Chapter 7, you learned to save work for reuse and keep file sizes small by using symbols. Flash lets you do the same thing with entire multiple-frame, multiple-layer animation sequences. You can save such sequences either as an animated graphic symbol or as a movie-clip symbol. You can use these symbols repeatedly with a much smaller hit on file size than if you simply re-created the animation by using graphic-symbol instances within separate animations. Additionally, for complex animations, symbols help keep down the number of frames and layers that you have to deal with.

To convert an animation to a graphic symbol:

1. Open a multiple-layer animation, such as the three-layer, 20-frame animation created earlier in the chapter.

2. In the Timeline, select all frames in all layers (**Figure 12.34**).

3. Choose Edit > Timeline > Copy Frames.

4. Choose Insert > New Symbol, or press ⌘-F8 (Mac) or Ctrl-F8 (Windows).

   The Create New Symbol dialog appears (**Figure 12.35**).

5. In the Create New Symbol dialog, type a name for your symbol.

6. From the Type menu, choose Graphic as the symbol type.

7. Click OK.

   Flash creates a new symbol in the library and switches you to symbol-editing mode for that symbol.

   The name of your symbol appears in the Edit bar. The default Timeline for your new symbol consists of one layer and a blank keyframe at frame 1.

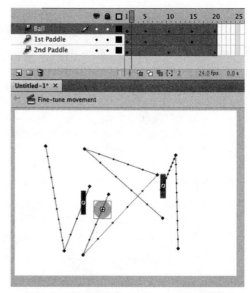

Figure 12.34 To convert an existing animation to a symbol, first select all the frames and layers that make up the animation sequence. (This example uses the Ping-Pong animation created in the section "Working with Multiple-Layer Motion Tweens," earlier in this chapter.)

Figure 12.35 You set a new symbol's type in the Create New Symbol dialog. Movie clips operate from their own independent Timeline. Animated graphic symbols play in sync with the main movie that contains them. One frame in the main movie's Timeline displays one frame of the graphic symbol's Timeline.

Symbol being edited

Registration crosshair

Current scene

All frames of animation pasted into Timeline

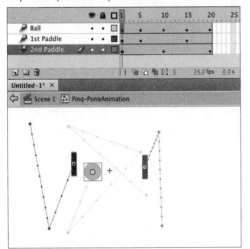

Figure 12.36 When you create a new symbol, Flash switches to symbol-editing mode, making the new symbol's Timeline available for editing (top). You must paste all the frames of your animation into the symbol's Timeline to create the animated symbol (bottom).

Figure 12.37 Selecting Movie Clip in the Type section of the Create New Symbol dialog defines a symbol that has an independent Timeline. The entire movie-clip symbol runs in a single frame of the main movie.

8. In the symbol Timeline, select keyframe 1, and choose Edit > Timeline > Paste Frames.

Flash pastes the frames and layers that you copied from the original movie into the Timeline for the symbol (**Figure 12.36**). If you want to make any adjustments in the animation sequence, you can do so at this point.

9. To return to document-editing mode, choose Edit > Edit Document.

To convert an animation to a movie-clip symbol:

◆ Follow the steps in the preceding task, but this time, in step 6, choose Movie Clip as the symbol type (**Figure 12.37**).

✔ Tip

■ To make a movie clip that contains exactly the same frames as an existing animated graphic symbol, you can duplicate that symbol and change its type. Select the animated graphic symbol in the Library panel. From the panel menu, choose Duplicate. The Duplicate Symbol dialog appears, allowing you to rename the symbol and set its type to Movie Clip.

Symbols Reduce Layer Buildup

In general, for tweened animations, you need to place each object on a separate layer. To animate a person, for example, create separate layers for the head, the torso, each arm, and each leg. For complex motion, you might even create separate layers for the eyes, mouth, fingers, and toes. Add some other elements to this character's environment, and you wind up dealing with many layers.

Turning an animation sequence into a symbol in effect collapses all those layers into one object. The process is a bit like grouping, but for Timeline layers instead of shapes. On the Stage, the symbol exists on a single layer, but that layer contains all the layers of the original animation.

How Do Animated Graphic Symbols Differ from Movie-Clip Symbols?

Flash provides for two kinds of animated symbols: graphic symbols and movie clips. The difference is a bit subtle and hard to grasp at first. An animated graphic symbol is tied to the Timeline of any movie in which you place the symbol, whereas a movie-clip symbol runs on its own independent Timeline. When the playhead stops moving in the main Timeline, an animated graphic symbol stops playing, but a movie-clip symbol continues to play.

Think of the frames of an animated graphic symbol as a tray of slides and a movie-clip symbol as a film loop. The animated graphic symbol projects its slides, one per frame, in lockstep with the frames of its hosting movie: to see the next frame of the symbol, you move to the next frame in the hosting movie. Like a tray of slides, an animated graphic symbol has no sound track. If you use sounds in an animated graphic symbol, those sounds don't play when you place the symbol into the main Timeline. If you've attached ActionScript 1.0 or 2.0 to buttons in your animated graphic symbol, that interactivity survives when you place the symbol into the main Timeline (although any actions that control the Timeline affect the Timeline of the hosting movie, not the graphic symbol itself, potentially creating confusion).

Any ActionScript 3.0 that you've placed in frames on the Timeline of the graphic symbol will not publish; ActionScript 3.0 frame actions that are nested within symbols inside the animated graphic symbol survive, but may also control a different Timeline than you expect, depending on how you set them up. Other types of interactivity do not survive the process of being turned into a graphic symbol. (To learn more about ActionScript 3.0 and interactivity, see Chapter 15.)

A movie-clip symbol can project all its frames one after another, over and over, in a single frame of the hosting movie. Movie clips do have a sound track and do retain their interactivity. (To learn more about sound, see Chapter 17. For interactivity, see Chapters 14 and 15.)

One more thing to know about the two symbol types is that movie clips, because they run on their own Timeline, don't appear as animations in the Flash authoring environment. You see only the first frame of the movie as a static element on the Stage. Animated graphic symbols, which use the same Timeline as the main movie, display their animation in the authoring environment.

Figure 12.38 Select the animated graphic symbol you want to use, and then drag a copy to your Flash document to place an instance on the Stage.

Figure 12.39 When you drag an instance of the animated graphic symbol to the Stage, you see the symbol's first frame with its graphics selected. You must add frames to allow the full animation of the symbol to play in the main movie.

Using Animated Graphic Symbols

To put an animated graphic symbol to work, you must place an instance of it in your main movie. The layer of the movie where you place the symbol must have enough frames to display the symbol. You can use instances of an animated graphic symbol just as you would any other symbol—combine it with other graphics on a layer; use it in a classic tween or motion tween; modify its color, size, and rotation; and so on.

To place an instance of an animated graphic symbol:

1. Follow the steps in "To convert an animation to a graphic symbol," earlier in this chapter.

2. Choose Insert > Scene.

   Flash adds a new scene. The Timeline has one layer with a blank keyframe in frame 1. The Stage is empty.

   Adding a new scene gives you a blank Stage to work with and makes it easy to compare the two animations: the original (created directly in the main movie Timeline) and the instance of the graphic symbol placed in the movie.

3. Access the Library panel and select the Ping-PongAnimation symbol.

   The first frame of the animation appears in the preview window (**Figure 12.38**).

4. Drag a copy of the symbol to the Stage.

   Flash places the symbol in keyframe 1. You can see only the first frame of the animation (**Figure 12.39**). The animation is 20 frames long, so you must add at least 20 frames to view the symbol in its entirety.

continues on next page

5. In the Timeline, select frame 20, and choose Insert > Timeline > Frame.

6. Play the movie.

Now Flash can display each frame of the animated graphic symbol in a frame of the movie. Frame 2 of the symbol appears in frame 2 of the movie, frame 5 of the symbol appears in frame 5 of the movie, and so on (**Figure 12.40**). If the layer containing the animated–graphic-symbol instance in the main Timeline has fewer frames than the symbol requires, Flash truncates the symbol. If the layer has more frames than the symbol requires, Flash starts playing the graphic symbol over again to fill those extra frames.

✔ Tips

■ By default, Flash loops the animation of graphic symbols. To prevent looping of a selected symbol instance, in the Looping section of the Property inspector, from the Options menu, choose Play Once.

■ To display just one frame of the animated graphic symbol, from the Options menu, choose Single Frame, then enter the desired frame number in the First field.

■ Character animators can take advantage of this feature to create a miniature library of symbols within a symbol. Each frame of an animated graphic symbol holds a different version of a feature—for example, an eye. Frame 1 contains an open eye; frame 2, that same eye half closed; frame 3, the eye fully closed. To animate a character's eye movements, you set up a classic tween using the animated graphic symbol, then set each keyframe of the classic tween to show the appropriate eye position.

Figure 12.40 Frames 1–20 are just regular defined frames, they haven't been assigned any kind of tweening, but they still display animation. Flash displays 20 frames of the animated graphic symbol that you placed in keyframe 1. It's as though the symbol is a tray of slides, and Flash is projecting one image per frame in the main movie. If the main movie is longer than the slide show, Flash starts the slide show over.

Sidebar (left margin, vertical): **USING ANIMATED GRAPHIC SYMBOLS**

Figure 12.41 Drag an instance of your movie clip from the Library panel to the Stage (top). Flash places the instance in keyframe 1 (bottom).

Using Movie-Clip Symbols

You put movie-clip symbols to work by placing an instance of a symbol on the Stage in your Flash document. Unlike animated graphic symbols, movie-clip symbols have their own Timeline. A movie clip plays continuously, like a little film loop, in a single frame of the main movie. As long as the movie contains no other instructions that stop the clip from playing—a blank keyframe in the Timeline for the layer containing the movie clip, for example—the clip continues to loop.

As you work on your Flash document, you can see only the first frame of a movie clip. To view the animation of the movie-clip symbol in context with all the other elements of your movie, you must export the movie (by choosing one of the test modes, for example). You can preview the animation of the movie-clip symbol by itself in the Library panel.

To place an instance of a movie clip:

1. Follow the steps in "To convert an animation to a movie-clip symbol," earlier in this chapter.

2. Choose Insert > Scene.

   Flash creates a new scene and displays its Timeline: a single layer with a blank keyframe in frame 1. The Stage is empty.

3. Access the Library panel and select the Ping-PongClip symbol.

   The first frame of the animation appears in the preview window.

4. Drag a copy of the selected symbol to the Stage.

   Flash places the symbol in keyframe 1 (**Figure 12.41**). You don't need to add any more frames to accommodate the animation, but you must export the movie to see the animation.

To view the movie-clip animation in context:

1. Continuing with the movie you created in the preceding task, choose Control > Test Scene (**Figure 12.42**).

   Flash exports the movie to a Flash Player format file, adding the name of the scene and the .swf extension to the filename and using the current publishing settings for all the export options. (For more information on publishing settings, see Chapter 18.) During export, Flash displays the Exporting SWF Movie dialog, which contains a progress bar and a Stop (Mac) or Cancel (Windows) button for canceling the operation (**Figure 12.43**).

   When it finishes exporting the movie, Flash opens the SWF file in Flash Player so you can see the movie in action (**Figure 12.44**).

2. When you've seen enough of the movie in test mode, click the movie window's Close button (Mac) or Close box (Windows) to exit Flash Player.

Figure 12.42 Choose Control > Test Scene to preview the animation of just one scene in a movie.

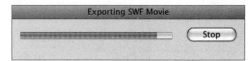

Figure 12.43 The Exporting SWF Movie dialog contains a progress bar and a button for canceling the export.

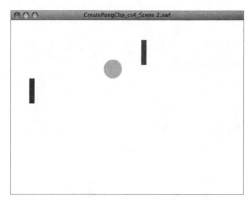

Figure 12.44 Flash Player displays your movie in a regular window. To exit the Player, close the window.

Using Easing

In the classic-tween and shape-tween bouncing-ball examples, a single keyframe span contains the downward bounce. You can add frames to the keyframe span, making the downward bounce take longer, but the movement still happens at a constant rate. Similarly for motion tweens, the changes from one property keyframe to the next happen at a constant rate. Easing allows you to vary that rate, making changes start slowly and finish rapidly and vice versa. By setting an Ease value in the Property inspector, you can control the rate of change for all properties within a keyframe span (for classic or shape tweens) or tween span (for motion tweens). (You can also set easing between IK poses in the Property inspector.) To gain control over the rate of change for specific properties and frames, you need to apply custom easing (see the sidebar "About Custom Easing").

Using Custom Easing to Create Motion

You can use custom easing values (see the sidebar "About Custom Easing," later in this chapter) to create variations on the general motion of a tweened symbol whether it's in a classic tween or a motion tween. To create movement through easing, you must adjust easing values to apply different percentages of a property change at different frames of the animation. Imagine, for example, a tween that moves an oval from one side of the Stage to the other in 20 frames. Now apply easing to the X (horizontal position) curve. If, for example, you set the easing curve so that frame 5 carries out 100 percent of the horizontal change and frame 10 carries out just 50 percent, the oval moves to the right side of the Stage at frame 5, back to mid-Stage at frame 10, then back to the right side at frame 20. To see this technique in action, check out the canned animation named Wave that comes in the Motion Presets panel (in the Default Presets folder). Wave uses easing in the Y (vertical position) property curve to make the tween target move up and down repeatedly, although the curve has just three y-position keyframes.

To apply easing to the span:

1. Create a ten-frame tween and access the Property inspector.

   You can use classic, shape, or motion tweening to create the tween.

2. In the Timeline, select the tween by doing the following:

   ▲ For classic and shape tweens, select any frame in the keyframe span.

   ▲ For motion tweens, select any frame in the tween span.

3. To make the animation start slowly (ease in), do one of the following:

   ▲ For classic and shape tweens, in the Tweening section of the Frame Property inspector, use the Ease hot text to enter a negative value.

   ▲ For motion tweens, in the Ease section of the Motion Tween Property inspector, use the Ease hot text to enter a negative number.

   The word *in* appears next to the hot text value (**Figure 12.45**). Easing in makes the animation start slowly and speed up toward the end. The lower the Ease value, the greater the rate of acceleration.

Classic tween   *Motion tween*

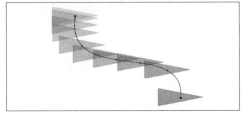

Figure 12.45 A negative Ease value makes changes in the initial frames of the tween smaller and changes toward the end larger. The animation seems to start slowly and then speed up.

USING EASING

Classic tween   Motion tween

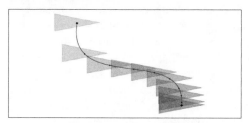

Figure 12.46 A positive Ease value makes changes at the end of the animation smaller and changes in the initial frames larger. The animation seems to start quickly and then slow down.

Classic tween   Motion tween

Figure 12.47 With an Ease value of 0, Flash distributes the tweening changes evenly across the in-between frames. The effect is that of animation moving at a constant rate.

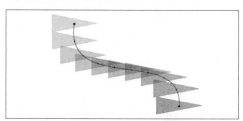

4. To make the animation start quickly and decelerate (ease out), do one of the following:

▲ For classic and shape tweens, in the Tweening section of the Frame Property inspector, use the Ease hot text to enter a positive number (**Figure 12.46**).

▲ For motion tweens, in the Ease section of the Motion Tween Property inspector, use the Ease hot text to enter a positive number.

The word *out* appears next to the hot-text value. Easing out makes the animation start quickly and slow down toward the end. The higher the Ease value, the greater the rate of deceleration.

✔ Tip

■ An Ease value of 0 causes Flash to display the whole animation at a constant rate (**Figure 12.47**).

About Custom Easing

You can create custom easing for classic tweens and motion tweens, but not for shape tweens or IK poses. For classic tweens, custom easing is the only way to control the speed of individual property changes within a single keyframe span. For motion tweens, you can use the Motion Editor to create separate easing curves for each property. These advanced techniques are beyond the scope of a *Visual QuickStart Guide,* but here's a brief look at how to access the controls.

Classic easing. To create custom easing for a classic tween, select any frame in the keyframe span. In the Tweening section of the Frame Property inspector, click the Edit Easing button (the pencil icon), to the right of the Ease hot text. The Custom Ease In/Ease Out dialog appears (**Figure 12.48**). The dialog shows the selected tween's changes over time on a graph; the horizontal axis represents each frame in the tween; the vertical axis represents the amount of change. You can edit the graph similar to the way you'd edit a Bézier path. Click the line (or curve) to add control points, then position the Bézier handles. You can ease all properties simultaneously or set specific easing values for five properties: Position, Rotation, Scale, Color, and Filters. Choose specific properties from the Property menu.

Figure 12.48 For classic tweens, click the Edit Easing button (the pencil icon) in the Tweening section of the Frame Property inspector (top) to access the Custom Ease In/Ease Out dialog (bottom). Custom easing lets you control easing precisely, frame by frame, by creating a curve that defines the rate of change in each frame. Click anywhere on the line (or curve) to add a new control point with handles. Without easing, the rate is constant, starting at 0 percent in the first frame of the tween and reaching 100 percent in the last frame of the tween.

About Custom Easing *continued*

Motion easing. You create custom easing for motion tweens in the Motion Editor. There you'll find a special Eases category. To view and work with an easing curve in the Motion Editor, you must bring the ease into the Eases category (select it from the Add Ease menu, the plus-sign button). A row with a graph for that ease appears in the Eases category. Flash comes with a number of preset easing curves for common situations, such as Simple, Start and Stop, and Bounce. To create a custom easing curve, choose Custom from the Add Ease menu. Flash adds a new row with a graph for your custom easing curve (**Figure 12.49**).

To apply an easing curve to a property—either a preset curve, or one of your own devising— you must choose the easing curve from the Easing menu in the row for the property you want to control. The Easing menu in each row lists all the easing curves currently available in the Eases category. If you don't see the curve you want in a specific Easing menu, you need to add the curve to the Eases category.

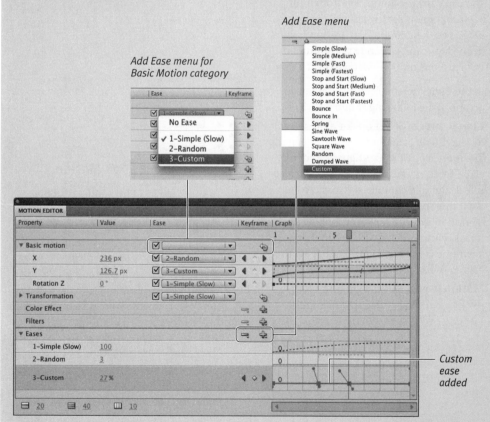

Figure 12.49 The Motion Editor's Eases category is the place to create custom easing curves. To begin the process, click the Add Ease menu (the plus sign) in the Eases row and choose Custom. You can then modify the graph in the Custom row. To apply the custom curve to a property curve, select the custom easing curve from the Easing menu in the row of the property you want to control.

Re-creating Classic and Motion Tweens

Flash offers three commands that will help you reduce repetitive animation work. Copy Motion, Paste Motion, and Paste Motion Special streamline the process of animating multiple objects that go through the same "motions."

To copy motion:

1. Create a single-layer animation using either classic tweening (Chapter 9) or motion tweening (Chapter 11).

   You can copy the animation from multiple keyframe spans set to classic tweening, so long as the keyframe spans are contiguous in one layer. You can copy the animation from just one motion-tween span at a time.

2. In the Timeline, to select the animation, do one of the following (**Figure 12.50**):

   Classic tween. Select one or more frames in a keyframe span set to classic tweening. The frames must be contiguous and must all be set to classic tweening. You can also select multiple contiguous classic-tween keyframe spans to copy the full range of motion. Do not, however, include the final keyframe of a classic tween if that keyframe is not highlighted as having the classic-tween property.

   Motion tween. Select a single motion-tween span. Flash can copy the motion of just one tween span at a time.

Figure 12.50 To copy a classic or motion tween, in the Timeline, select one or more frames in one classic tween's keyframe span or in contiguous spans (top) or in one motion tween's tween span (bottom).

About Copy Motion

Flash's Copy Motion command copies information that defines a classic-tween or motion-tween sequence: changes to a tweened object's properties (such as position, rotation, scale); duration of the tween (the number of frames it takes); and other tween settings (such as Easing). The Paste Motion command lets you apply that information to a different object (let's call it the *tween object*) to change its properties in the same way, over the same number of frames, using the same Tween settings. The Paste Motion Special command lets you apply changes to the tween object's properties selectively. The Copy Motion As ActionScript 3.0 command translates motion-tween animation to ActionScript 3.0–generated animation.

Figure 12.51 The Edit > Timeline > Copy Motion command copies the properties that define a tween or tweens in a selected set of frames.

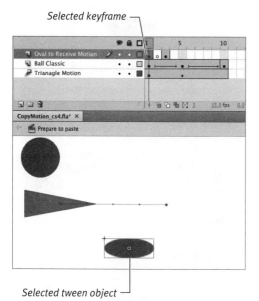

Selected keyframe ⏤

Selected tween object ⏤

Figure 12.52 To apply the copied motion tween to a new tween object, select the symbol on the Stage (or select its keyframe in the Timeline).

3. Choose Edit > Timeline > Copy Motion (**Figure 12.51**).

Flash copies the changes in properties that define the tween for each selected (or partially selected) span. For classic tweens, the properties Flash copies are x-position, y-position, horizontal scale, vertical scale, rotation and skew, color, filters, and blend mode. For motion tweens, Flash copies all the properties of the tween that you can access via the Motion Editor.

To apply copied motion to a different tween object:

1. To select the tween object that will reenact the copied motion, do one of the following:

▲ On the Stage, select the object to which you want to apply the copied motion (**Figure 12.52**).

or

▲ In the Timeline, select a keyframe containing the tween object to which you want to apply the copied motion.

With both selection methods, the new tween object must be one that can be tweened in the same way as the original tween object. (A merge-shape, for example, can't be used in classic tweening or motion tweening.) For best results, apply the copied motion only to a tween object that's isolated on its own layer.

continues on next page

2. Choose Edit > Timeline > Paste Motion.

For classic tweens, Flash inserts into the Timeline the same number of keyframe spans (with the same number of frames and keyframes) as you copied. For motion tweens, Flash inserts a tween span of the same length, and with the same property keyframes, as the tween span you copied. The target keyframe you selected and all subsequent frames get pushed out to later frames in the Timeline (**Figure 12.53**).

3. Play the movie.

The tween object to which you applied the copied classic-tween or motion-tween property changes now moves and transforms in the same way the original tween object did.

✔ Tips

■ You don't have to paste all the properties for a copied classic tween. To paste properties selectively, follow step 1 in the preceding task to select the classic tween. Then choose Edit > Timeline > Paste Motion Special. The Paste Motion Special dialog appears. To apply individual tween properties, select any of the following check boxes: X position, Y position, Horizontal Scale, Vertical Scale, Rotation and Skew, Color, Filters, and Blend Mode. When pasting a copied motion tween, the Paste Motion Special command is not available, but you have complete control over the properties in the pasted motion tween via the Motion Editor.

■ You can also copy classic-tween and motion-tween properties in a form that can be pasted into the Actions panel or an ActionScript file. Flash translates the animation you created using graphics tools and classic or motion tweening into animation created by ActionScript. You'll learn more about the Copy Motion As ActionScript 3.0 command in Chapter 15.

Copied span

Motion pasted

Figure 12.53 The Paste Motion command pastes the tween sequence(s) of the copied motion into the Timeline for the selected tween object. The command preserves any existing unselected frames and keyframes in the Timeline, pushing them to later frames.

INTRO TO INVERSE KINEMATICS

13

Inverse kinematics (IK) is a method of animating objects and shapes that relies on a structure—called an *armature*. An IK armature works something like a skeleton, with multiple linked segments called *bones*. Once you set up the structure, you can manipulate it to create various configurations, or *poses*. Imagine manipulating a human skeleton; if you raise the hand and bring it in toward the torso, the forearm also raises, and the elbow bends. Similarly, if you move one bone in an IK armature, connected bones move in response. Flash interpolates changes between poses to create animation. While the process of creating natural-looking movement with IK animation is complex and far beyond the scope of a *Visual QuickStart Guide*, the tasks in this chapter introduce you to creating armatures and poses using Flash's IK tools.

You can connect Flash's IK bones in a linear structure (like the bones in a human arm), have bones branch from one spot (like the hands of an analog clock), or combine both styles. You can use IK armatures to link multiple symbol instances, governing the relationships between the elements and controlling the ways they can move in relation to one another. You can also use IK armatures within a single shape, controlling the way the shape's outline changes.

When to Use Inverse Kinematics

Flash's inverse-kinematics tools enable you to animate natural motion without redrawing lots of shapes or repositioning multiple symbols. You create armatures—skeleton-like structures that govern relationships between symbol instances or control the way a shape's outline changes over time. Moving one bone in the armature affects other connected bones to reconfigure the entire structure. Use IK when you want to animate symbols that have a permanent relationship—for example, the parts of a person or creature that can only bend in certain ways or the parts of an engine or machine that move in predictable, constrained ways, like pistons, cogs, and flywheels. Another reason to use IK is to create shapes with moving, transforming outlines, where the changes can be controlled by an internal structure, such as a wiggling worm, or blade of grass that bends in the wind.

Using Armatures to Connect Symbols

When you use IK armatures to connect two or more symbol instances, the whole structure moves together, something like a marionette puppet. You can link symbol instances in linear or branching fashion or use a combination, where one or more branches extend in linear fashion. In a simplified cartoon body, for example, you might have three bones branching from the base of the character's neck; one connects to the head, a second connects to the right shoulder, a third to the left shoulder. Each shoulder bone could connect in linear fashion to bones for the upper arm, forearm, and hand. For the tasks in this section, you'll create a linear armature. (Because you can also use IK armatures with shapes, make sure that any artwork you're planning to connect in symbol form has in fact been converted into symbols before you start linking with the IK bone tool.)

About IK Drawing Preferences

When an IK bone connects two symbol instances, the ends of the bone (its head and tail) create points around which the attached symbol instances rotate. A symbol instance has its own point of rotation, the transformation point. How do the two work together? There are two styles. Flash can set the transformation point wherever you create a head/tail point, or you can have Flash force the bone to start or end at the symbol instance's existing transformation point. By default, when you click with the bone tool to create a bone's head, or release the mouse button to create the bone's tail, Flash moves the transformation point to the spot where you clicked or released. To change the setting, choose Flash (Mac) or Edit (Windows) > Preferences. In the Preferences dialog, choose Drawing from the category list. To have Flash retain the current transformation point, in the IK Bone Tool section, deselect the Auto Set Transformation Point check box (**Figure 13.1**). Now when you create IK bones, the head (or tail) point snaps to the existing transformation point of the symbol instance. The tasks in this chapter use the default style.

Figure 13.1 In the Drawing category of the Preferences dialog, in the IK Bone Tool section, deselect the Auto Set Transformation Point check box to have Flash preserve the transformation points of the symbol instances as you create IK bones. The head or tail of the bone snaps to the existing transformation point when you add a bone to the symbol instance.

Figure 13.2 The first step in creating an IK animation with symbol instances is to place instances on the Stage. Place the symbol instances into the relative positions they should have in the animated character or element that you're creating.

Figure 13.3 To begin connecting symbols into an IK armature, select the bone tool. The pointer becomes a black bone with a plus sign.

Figure 13.4 When the pointer is over a symbol instance, the pointer's bone and plus sign change to white, indicating that you can begin creating an IK bone. Click and drag to begin drawing the first bone. When you use Flash's default IK drawing style, position the pointer where you want the symbol instance's transformation point (the point of rotation) to be. Flash moves the transformation point to the spot you click.

Figure 13.5 As long as the pointer is within the symbol instance where you placed the head of an IK bone, the pointer is black with a No-symbol modifier, indicating that you can't end the bone.

To link symbol instances in a linear armature:

1. Create the symbol, or symbols, that you want to animate with a linear IK structure.

   For this task, you'll link multiple instances of one symbol to form a chain that can curl up or down from one end. Use the oval tool to create an oval shape and convert it to a symbol named myOval (see Chapter 7).

2. Place instances of the symbol(s) on the Stage and arrange them in the desired relative positions (**Figure 13.2**).

   For this task, use four instances of myOval lined up horizontally.

3. In the Tools panel, click the current IK tool, and from the submenu, select the bone tool (or press X) (**Figure 13.3**).

   The pointer changes to a small black bone with a plus-sign modifier, indicating that you are ready to begin placing bones.

4. To begin drawing the first bone in the chain (the *parent bone*), position the pointer over the first symbol instance (**Figure 13.4**).

   The pointer changes to a white bone with a plus-sign modifier, indicating that you are within a symbol where you can start a bone.

5. Click and drag to connect with the second symbol instance in the chain.

   Flash starts creating the bone; the point you click becomes the bone's head. As you drag, the pointer changes to a black bone with an international No symbol, a circle with a slash (**Figure 13.5**). This pointer indicates that you are within the symbol instance containing the head of the bone; the tail of the bone must be in a different instance.

continues on next page

6. To complete the first bone (to create the *tail* point), position the pointer within the second symbol instance and release the mouse button.

As it moves into the area of a different symbol instance, the pointer changes to a white bone and plus sign, indicating that you can complete the IK bone (**Figure 13.6**). The second instance can overlap the first symbol instance or be separate.

When you release the mouse button, Flash draws a bone connecting the two symbol instances and pulls them out of their current layer(s) and into a new layer, called a *pose layer*. Flash gives the pose layer a default name (see the sidebar "About Pose Layers") and gives the symbol instances default names, identifying them as IK nodes (see the sidebar "The Mystery of IK Instance Naming").

7. To begin drawing the second bone in the chain (a *child* bone), position the pointer over the tail of the first bone you created.

The bone pointer changes from black to white, indicating that you're ready to add another bone.

Original Timeline

End parent bone

Layer created after bone completion

Some content remains in layer 1

Completed parent bone

Figure 13.6 When the pointer enters the area of a symbol instance other than the one you clicked to create the IK bone's head, the pointer turns white and a plus-sign modifier appears. You can release the mouse button to place the tail of the bone (the second point of rotation). When the bone is complete, Flash pulls the connected symbol instances into a special armature layer in the Timeline.

Bone Views

The default graphic representation of an IK bone is a bulky item, especially if you're using it with small, delicate artwork. After creating the first IK bone in an armature, you can view bones in an outline form or as a single line. To change the look of the bones, select the armature, for example, by selecting the pose span in the Timeline. In the Property inspector, in the Options section, from the Style menu, choose Wire (the outline form), Solid (the default, triangular form), or Line (a 1-pixel line).

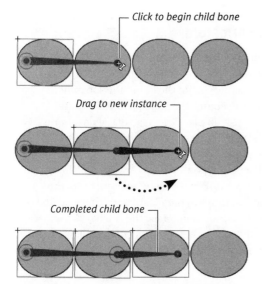

Click to begin child bone

Drag to new instance

Completed child bone

Figure 13.7 To connect a child bone, position the pointer over the tail of the parent bone. Then click and drag.

All content pulled into armature layer

Figure 13.8 As you complete more bones, Flash pulls the newly connected symbol instances into the same armature layer with the others.

8. Click and drag to connect with the third symbol instance.

Flash completes the second bone and pulls the third symbol instance into the armature layer (**Figure 13.7**).

9. Repeat steps 7 and 8 to add bones connecting the third and fourth symbol instances (**Figure 13.8**).

Flash completes the third bone and pulls the fourth symbol instance into the armature layer. You're ready to manipulate the armature and create poses (see "Working with Poses," later in this chapter).

✔ Tips

■ In step 5, the spot you click becomes the head of the first bone in a chain of bones. Take a moment to consider the placement of the head. In an IK arm, the head of the parent bone corresponds to a shoulder joint. If you plan to overlap the upper arm with the character's torso, then you'd probably want to place the joint in that area of overlap. If the upper arm will sit next to the torso, but not overlap it, you might want to place the joint closer to the edge of the upper-arm symbol.

■ Note that in the four-node chain you created in the preceding task, there are just three bones. The number of bones in a linear armature is always one less than the number of nodes in that armature.

■ You don't need to be precise in positioning the head of a child bone. Whenever the pointer is within the area of the node containing the parent's tail point, the pointer changes to the white bone with a plus sign. Clicking anywhere within the node automatically connects to the tail point in that node.

USING ARMATURES TO CONNECT SYMBOLS

Anatomy of an Armature

A linear armature contains a chain of bones in a hierarchical structure (**Figure 13.9**). The first bone is known as the *parent;* all the bones that extend from it are known as *child* bones. The spot you click to begin drawing a bone becomes the *head* of the bone. The spot where you release the mouse button to complete the bone becomes the *tail.* In a linear armature, the bones link head-to-tail. After you create one bone, you place the head of the next bone directly over the tail of the preceding bone. The head and tail are both points of rotation, or *joints,* and they coincide with the transformation points of the symbol instances in which they reside. By default, Flash relocates the transformation point whenever you click the bone tool within a symbol instance, placing the transformation point right where you place the head of the bone. (You can change that Preferences setting so that Flash snaps the head and tail points to the symbol instances' existing transformation points; see the sidebar "About IK Drawing Preferences," earlier in this chapter.) By default, the head and tail points allow bones to rotate through 360 degrees, like the hands of an analog clock.

continues on next page

Figure 13.9 In a linear armature, Flash highlights each head point with a circle. When you join multiple symbols in an armature, the first child bone starts at the tail of the parent bone; that point is also the head of the child bone.

Anatomy of an Armature *continued*

You can control movement at a head point in various ways: you can allow full rotation (the default), prevent rotation completely, or limit rotation to create a joint that bends in one direction, like an elbow or a knee; you can prevent (the default), allow, or limit horizontal and vertical movement (known as *x*- and *y-translation*). You cannot control movement at a tail point. In a linear armature, most of the joints containing a tail point also contain a head point; you can constrain the joint by constraining the head. The symbol instance that comes at the end of the armature chain, however, contains a tail point that stands on its own. The final symbol instance in an IK chain can always rotate 360 degrees around its transformation point.

Branching armatures do not have a hierarchical structure: all the bones branch from a single spot—known as the *root* of the branches—and are known as *sibling* bones (**Figure 13.10**). The location of the head joint is the same for all siblings. Although the bones are separate, their head joints must have identical rotation and translation settings. Flash handles that automatically.

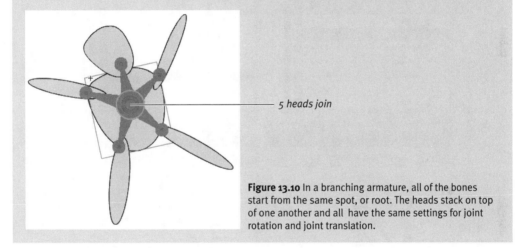

5 heads join

Figure 13.10 In a branching armature, all of the bones start from the same spot, or root. The heads stack on top of one another and all have the same settings for joint rotation and joint translation.

The Mystery of IK Instance Naming

When you create an IK armature by connecting symbol instances, Flash gives each instance—or *node*—a default instance name, starting with ikNode_0, ikNode_1, and so on. Each bone also gets a default instance name, starting with ikBoneName_1, ikBoneName_2, and so on. Note that this means the numbers for nodes and bones will always differ by 1: the bone whose head attaches to ikNode_0 is ikBoneName_1, the bone whose head attaches to ikNode_1 is ikBoneName_2, and so on. When you create an IK armature within a shape, there are no nodes, but the bones get the same style of default instance name.

About Pose Layers

When you connect the first two symbol instances of an IK chain with the bone tool, Flash pulls the instances into a new layer, known as a *pose layer*. (Flash gives the pose layer a default name—for example, Armature_1.) Flash places the pose layer directly above the layer that originally held the symbol instance that now contains the bone's tail (**Figure 13.11**). As you continue to add symbol instances to the chain, Flash pulls each new addition into the existing pose layer; each added IK node stacks above the nodes already on the pose layer.

When you first create an IK armature, the pose layer consists of a one-frame pose span, tinted olive green, containing a diamond icon. The diamond indicates the presence of an IK armature in a particular configuration, or *pose*. You can define more frames to extend the span or drag to extend the span, then add poses at later frames to create motion over time (see the section "Working with Poses," later in this chapter).

Figure 13.11 Each number on the Stage is a symbol instance that started out on its own layer. Connecting the 2 to the 5 (left) creates the armature layer above the layer that contained the 5 originally. Connecting the 5 to the 2 (right) creates the armature layer above the layer that contained the 2. Within the pose layer, the IK nodes stack in the order in which you connected them (connecting the 5 to the 2 puts the 2 at the top of the stack). Each IK node you connect with child bones goes to the top of the stack. The stacking order of other elements in the Timeline is unaffected.

Click to start parent bone

Drag to extend bone ●●●●●●●●●➤

Release to complete bone

Figure 13.12 Adding bones within a shape is very similar to adding bones between symbol instances, except that all the bones stay within the same shape.

Creating IK Shapes

An IK armature inside a shape works something like a hand in a sock puppet. The armature can be linear or branching or a combination of the two styles. The steps for creating the chain or branches are quite similar to those for connecting symbols. The difference is that you place all the bones within a single shape. You can use a merge-shape, drawing-object, or primitive-shape, with or without a stroke. Once you add IK bones to the shape, Flash converts it to a new type of shape, an *IK shape*.

To combine linear and branching armatures inside a shape:

1. Using Flash's drawing tools, on the Stage, create a shape to which you want to add an internal armature structure.

   For this task, draw a rounded rectangle, making it fairly long and narrow (see Chapter 2). You'll create an armature that has two linear chains that branch from a central point, allowing the shape to curl up or down from either end, the way a worm might wriggle from either end, or the way that the arms extending from the torso of a cartoon character might bend up or down.

2. In the Tools panel, select the bone tool.

3. To begin drawing the first bone in the chain (the parent bone), position the pointer over the shape.

4. Click at the spot where you want the armature to start—for example, the center of the rectangle (**Figure 13.12**).

   Flash places the head of the parent bone. The head and tail points of each bone create points of rotation (places where the shape can bend). The shape as a whole pivots around the head of the parent bone in the chain.

continues on next page

5. To complete the bone, drag to the first spot where your shape should be able to bend, then release the mouse button.

For this example, plan to place three bones in each half of the rectangle. Flash pulls the shape into a new pose layer and converts the shape to an IK shape.

6. To add the second bone in the chain, position the pointer over the tail of the first bone you created, and click.

To add a bone to the armature within a shape, the pointer must be directly over the bone you're adding to. The black No pointer changes to the white–plus-sign pointer when you're directly over the tail (or head) of an existing bone. Flash places the second bone's head.

7. To complete the second bone, drag to the spot where the bone should end, and release the mouse button.

8. Repeat steps 6 and 7 to create the third bone, this time starting at the tail of the second bone.

9. To create another IK chain that branches from the first, position the pointer over the head of the parent bone you created in steps 4 and 5.

10. To begin drawing the first bone (parent) of the second branch, click and drag in a different direction from the parent bone in the existing chain (**Figure 13.13**).

For this example, drag to the left.

11. Repeat steps 6 and 7 to create a three-bone chain in the left side of the rect-angle (**Figure 13.14**).

You're ready to manipulate the armature and create poses (see "Working with Poses," the next section in this chapter).

Click to start branching bone

Drag to extend bone

Release to complete bone

Figure 13.13 To begin the branching bone, position the pointer over the head of the parent bone in the existing chain, then drag to the left.

2nd branch   *1st branch*

Figure 13.14 Your finished shape has two branches that start from the center of the shape. Each branch then continues with a linear chain of IK bones. This arrangement allows the two halves of the rectangle to curve independently, thus creating more-complex poses.

Figure 13.15 No matter what type of shape you start out with, once you place an IK bone within the shape, it becomes a special type of object called an IK shape. Here, the rounded rectangle started as a merge shape, as shown in the Property inspector (top); after adding a bone, the Property inspector reveals it is an IK shape (bottom).

✔ Tips

■ In the preceding task, you created two branches from the same root. You can also create branches farther down the chain. Just begin drawing a new bone by clicking the head of any bone in the chain. In an IK shape, drag the first bone in the new branch in a different direction within the shape. In an armature connecting nodes, drag the first bone in the new branch to a symbol instance that's not yet part of the armature.

■ As soon as you've placed a bone within a shape, Flash changes the shape's type. Check the Property inspector; as you add the bones, the name at the top changes—for example, from Shape to IK Shape (**Figure 13.15**). The registration point of an IK shape is at its center.

■ Before you start creating bones, consider how many you'll need to be able to bend the shape to create the poses you need. The more bones you create, the more varied and refined the movements you'll be able to create with new poses. But more bones can also make it trickier to maneuver the IK shape.

Working with Poses

When you first create an armature, the pose layer contains a pose span with one pose frame (the frame with the diamond icon). Similar to keyframes, pose frames mark key points of change that enable Flash to create IK animation. Each pose frame acts a bit like a property keyframe in a motion tween, giving Flash information about the position and rotation of each element in the armature. Flash creates a series of images that interpolate the changes required to transform the armature from one pose to the next. The property settings for the bones, and the way you set up the armature, restrict how the elements can move. To create IK animation, you must extend the pose span, add poses at the desired frames, select the armature to view and activate the bones, and manipulate the armature to put the elements into poses. To reposition the elements within the selected armature, use the selection tool.

Putting an Armature Through Its Paces

To edit an armature—to change the arrangement of IK nodes, to change the length of a bone, or change the number of bones—you must make sure the pose span contains just its initial pose. Although Flash sometimes lets you make some edits when there are multiple poses, the resulting IK animation will not work properly.

To avoid the extra work of setting up poses, then having to delete them if you run into a problem, it's helpful to try manipulating your armature in lots of different ways before creating the real poses for your animation. Give the armature a good workout, dragging the bones around to create all the positions you want to animate.

You could manipulate the armature in the initial frame of the pose span, before adding new poses or extending the span. If you do find a problem, however, it can be difficult to get the underlying shape or symbol instances back to the precise starting arrangement. To make it easy to revert to the original pose quickly, extend the pose span by a small number, say, five frames; position the playhead at the end of the span; and start manipulating the armature to see how the pieces move together. Flash adds a pose at the current frame. Continue putting the armature through its poses, until you find a problem, or until you're sure everything is OK. If it turns out that you need to edit the armature, you just remove that one pose. The first frame of the pose span contains the original pose with the symbol instances or shape arranged in the original position. Now you can edit the armature as you like and test again.

Figure 13.16 To extend a pose span, position the pointer over the black bar at the right side of the pose span (top). When the double-arrow pointer appears, drag the end of the span to the desired frame (middle). Flash extends the pose span and selects it (bottom).

Figure 13.17 Access the contextual menu in a pose span and choose Insert Pose (top) to add a diamond-shaped pose icon to the current frame (bottom). (Note that when the playhead is in the pose frame, the diamond looks more like a dot. Move the playhead and you'll see a diamond just like the one in the span's first frame.)

To define the pose span's length:

◆ Do either of the following:

▲ In the pose layer in the Timeline, position the pointer over the black bar at the outside edge of frame 1 and drag to extend the pose span to the desired frame (**Figure 13.16**).

or

▲ Click the frame that should mark the end of the span and choose Insert > Timeline > Frame.

Flash extends the olive-green highlight of the pose span through the selected frame.

To create a new pose frame via Timeline command:

◆ In the Timeline, within the armature layer, Control-click (Mac) or right-click (Windows) the desired frame and choose Insert Pose from the contextual menu (**Figure 13.17**).

If you click a frame inside the pose span, Flash adds a diamond-shaped pose icon to that frame. If you click a protoframe following the existing pose span, Flash extends the pose span to the frame you click and adds the diamond icon. You can now manipulate the IK armature to the desired configuration.

✔ Tip

■ You can also create a new pose by manipulating an armature on the Stage, analogous to the way you can add new keyframes to classic tweens or new property keyframes to motion tweens by manipulating symbol instances on the Stage within the defined span containing the tween. You simply click the desired frame within the pose span or position the playhead at the desired frame. Then use the selection tool to manipulate the armature on the Stage. Flash adds a diamond icon representing a pose to the current frame.

WORKING WITH POSES

To select an armature:

◆ Using the selection or subselection tool, do either of the following:

▲ For an armature connecting IK nodes, click any node (any connected symbol instance).

or

▲ For an armature within an IK shape, click anywhere within the shape.

Flash selects the IK nodes or IK shape and makes the bones visible (**Figure 13.18**). Icons indicating range of motion appear at each joint.

To manipulate the armature to create a pose:

1. In the Timeline, position the playhead in the desired frame in a pose span.

2. Select the armature you want to pose.

3. Using the selection tool, position the pointer over a bone.

A black bone icon appears next to the arrow pointer, indicating that you're ready to manipulate the armature (**Figure 13.19**).

4. To activate a bone for rotating, click it.

Flash highlights it in a different color than the other bones in the armature.

Click to select IK shape

IK shape and armature selected

Click to select IK node

IK node and armature selected

Range-of-motion icons, full rotation

Figure 13.18 Clicking an IK shape or an IK node with the selection tool activates the bones of the armature so that you can manipulate them to create poses.

Figure 13.19 To interact with a specific bone, click it with the selection tool, then drag it to position it. The bone rotates around its head. Other bones and nodes move in response if their joint settings allow for movement.

WORKING WITH POSES

IK shape

Figure 13.20 To manipulate an armature, you use the selection tool. You can drag bones and nodes to position them and reconfigure the armature. In an IK shape, dragging the bones changes the contours of the shape.

Figure 13.21 You can also manipulate an IK armature by dragging nodes with the selection tool. The final node in an IK armature rotates freely when you drag that node.

5. To reposition the selected bone, drag it (**Figure 13.20**).

The bone rotates and/or moves, and the armature changes in response to your manipulation. The precise ways that the structure can move depend on the settings you've created for each bone in the Property inspector (see the sidebar "Move Those Bones"). If the bone is in an armature connecting IK nodes, the node containing the head moves along with the bone.

6. To reposition an IK node, drag directly on the symbol instance (**Figure 13.21**).

If the IK node contains the head of a bone, the symbol instance and that bone rotate around the head point (the transformation point) according to the settings for that bone. If the IK node contains just a tail (that is, if the IK node is the last element in a linear armature), the node rotates around the tail point.

✔ Tips

■ You don't have to select an individual bone to drag it; you can simply click and drag a bone in one step. Selecting the bone first highlights it and lets you see that you are working with the right portion of your armature.

■ As you manipulate an armature to reach new poses, remember that Flash is not recording the action. You need to create poses at key positions for your IK elements so that Flash can interpolate between poses to create the movement you want. For example, just because you rotated a bone clockwise to reach a certain position doesn't mean Flash chooses that direction when it creates the animation. You may need intermediate poses to ensure that things move in the ways you intend.

To remove a pose from the pose span:

1. Position the playhead at the frame containing the pose.

2. Control-click (Mac) or right-click (Windows) the frame containing the diamond icon.

3. From the contextual menu, choose Clear Pose (**Figure 13.22**).

✔ Tips

- You can position the playhead by clicking the frame containing the pose diamond. Flash selects the entire pose span, but when you access the contextual menu for the frame containing the pose, the Clear Pose command removes just the pose in that frame.

- You can't remove the pose from the first frame of a pose span, but you can remove multiple poses in subsequent fames with one command. ⌘-drag (Mac) or Ctrl-drag (Windows) to select a subset of frames that includes the poses you want to eliminate but that excludes the initial pose. When you access the contextual menu from any frame in the selection, the Clear Pose command removes all poses from the selection. If you drag-select the entire pose span, or click an in-between frame to select the whole span, then access the contextual menu, the Clear Pose command is disabled.

Figure 13.22 Control-click (Mac) or right-click (Windows) a pose frame to access the contextual menu. Choose Clear Pose to remove that pose from the span.

Move Those Bones

Dragging a highlighted bone causes it to rotate around its head; moving the highlighted bone can also push on any bones that are higher up the chain, causing them to rotate as well. When a bone is set to allow x- and/or y-translation, you can also drag the bone along those axes. Any constraints you've put in place on how each bone rotates will govern the ways you can interact with the bones as you drag them on the Stage. As you manipulate a highlighted bone, any child bones that are located lower in the hierarchy simply come along for the ride, retaining their current orientation with respect to their parent bone(s).

Manipulating Pose Spans in the Timeline

The mechanics of manipulating pose spans in the Timeline is quite similar to that for manipulating tween spans for motion tweens (see Chapter 11). A major difference is that a pose span must stay on its own special armature layer: you can't copy or move a pose span to a different layer, nor can you add other content to the layer containing a pose span.

Like a tween span, a pose span is an object, and clicking any frame within the span selects the entire span. To select a single frame in a pose span, ⌘-click (Mac) or Ctrl-click (Windows) the frame. To select a range of frames, ⌘-drag (Mac) or Ctrl-drag (Windows) through the desired frames. To move the span within the layer so that the animation starts at a different frame, select the span and drag it. When you drag the span, Flash creates blank keyframes as needed. For example, if you created the IK armature in frame 1 of the Timeline, then drag the pose span to the right, Flash creates a blank keyframe at frame 1. To enlarge the pose span proportionally (to lengthen the IK animation but preserve the relative timing of the pose changes), drag the last frame of the pose span to the right; Flash redistributes the pose-frame diamonds. To reduce the span proportionally, drag the last frame to the left. To extend the end of the pose span, adding in-between frames after the final pose frame, Shift-drag the last frame of the span to the right; to clip frames off the end of the span, Shift-drag the last frame to the left.

You can also copy and paste poses. Select a frame containing a pose-frame diamond; Control-click (Mac) or right-click (Windows) the selected frame and choose Copy Pose from the contextual menu. Select the frame where you want to repeat the pose, access the contextual menu again, and choose Paste Pose.

Encapsulating IK in Symbols

To get the fullest value from your IK animations, you may want to incorporate them into symbols that can be animated with tweening. You might, for example, create a wiggly worm using an IK shape, put that animation into a movie-clip symbol, then use an instance of the worm symbol in a motion tween. The motion tween can make the constantly wiggling worm wander around the Stage, change size or color, and so on. To convert an IK animation to a symbol, select the IK shape or all of the IK nodes (selecting the pose span in the Timeline automatically selects all the IK elements). Choose Modify > Convert to Symbol, or on the Stage, Control-click (Mac) or right-click (Windows) the selected IK shape or any of the selected IK nodes, and from the contextual menu, choose Convert to Symbol. In the Convert to Symbol dialog that appears, you can name the symbol and choose its type, library location, and so on (see Chapter 7).

Author-Time IK vs. Runtime IK

Do you want to be able to set poses for armatures during authoring to create animation? Or do you want to let your audience drag and manipulate IK elements to change their positions interactively as they view your Flash movie?

To do the moving yourself during authoring and have Flash play back the movement at runtime, select the armature layer, the pose span, or any frame within the pose span, and access the IK Armature Property inspector. In the Options section, from the Type menu, choose Authortime (**Figure 13.23**). (Authortime is the default setting.) To simply set up an armature that your target audience can play with, choose Runtime. (Note that more-advanced Flash users can control IK armatures using ActionScript. To be controlled by scripting, the armature must be set to Runtime, and must contain just the initial pose in the pose span.)

Figure 13.23 To use IK armatures to create poses during authoring and have them play back as animation in your published movie, select a pose span and choose Authortime from the Type menu in the Options section of the IK Armature Property inspector. To allow the end user to play with the IK armature, posing elements while interacting with the published movie, choose Runtime. Flash's default Type setting is Authortime.

Constraining IK Motion

You can limit the way IK bones move. You can allow or prevent a bone from rotating, for example, to control the way a character can bend its arms and legs. You can also allow or prevent movement along a bone's x-axis (x-translation) and/or y-axis (y-translation). The axes in this case refer not to the x- and y-axes of the Stage, but to the axes of the bone instance (see the sidebar "Translating the Direction of Translation"). Enabling translation for the parent bone in an armature allows the entire armature to move around on the Stage. Enabling translation for a child bone allows that bone to move closer to its parent or farther away. Moving a child bone along its x- and/or y-axis within an armature in an IK shape can make the shape expand and contract. Making such movements in an armature connecting IK nodes can help you to create mechanisms with moving parts.

The methods for enabling and constraining rotation and translation with IK nodes and IK shapes is similar. The tasks below work with IK nodes. Try experimenting with enabling and constraining the motion of bones within a shape once you've completed the tasks with nodes.

Translating the Direction of Translation

Although x- and y-translation deals with movement along the horizontal and vertical axes, the axes in question are not the axes of the Stage. This can be confusing at first. Each bone instance has its own x-axis and y-axis; the orientation of the axes depends on a variety of factors, including the bone's original orientation to the Stage, the bone's original orientation to its parent bone, whether the bone is in an IK shape or is connecting IK nodes, and whether or not the bone has been rotated from its original position. The easiest way to tell where the axes of a bone are, and what directions they cover, is to select the bone and look at the range-of-motion icon at its head (see the sidebar "The Mysterious Range-of-Motion Icons"). When translation is enabled for the selected bone, the icon includes double-headed arrows for unconstrained x- and y-translation, I-beams for constrained translation. The arrows (or I-beams) indicate the directions in which the head point of the bone can move.

To constrain rotation at a bone's head:

1. Create a simple IK armature that uses two bones to connect three symbol instances in a horizontal chain.

   This task uses three instances of a symbol containing a rectangle.

2. Using the selection tool, select the armature containing the bone you want to constrain.

3. Click the parent bone, the first bone in the chain, and access the Property inspector.

   The selected bone highlights, and its properties appear in the inspector (**Figure 13.24**).

4. With the parent bone selected, in the Joint: Rotation section of the Property inspector, select the Enable check box (it is selected by default).

   When joint rotation is enabled, the selected bone can rotate through 360 degrees around its head. To restrict that movement, you must constrain the rotation.

5. Select the Constrain check box.

   Flash assigns default constrain values: Minimum –45 degrees, Maximum 45 degrees (**Figure 13.25**).

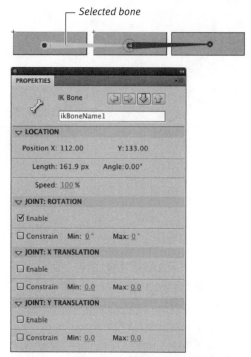

Selected bone

Figure 13.24 Selecting a bone in an armature reveals its properties in the Property inspector. By default, joint rotation is enabled. You can manipulate the selected bone by dragging it with the selection tool; you can rotate the bone 360 degrees around the head point. The rest of the armature follows along. By default, joint translation is disabled. The head of the bone cannot move from its current x-/y-coordinate.

Figure 13.25 When you select the Constrain check box in the Joint: Rotation section of the Property inspector, Flash creates Min and Max values of –45 and 45 degrees for the selected bone (top). The range-of-motion icon depicts the motion available to the bone (bottom).

Bone in original position

Range of motion

After rotating bone on Stage

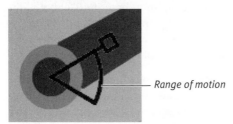

Range of motion

Figure 13.26 As you drag a bone whose rotation is constrained, the lever moves within the range-of-motion icon's arc. Once the lever reaches the edge of the arc, you can't rotate the bone farther in that direction. Note that after you reposition a bone on the Stage, Flash changes the bone's Min and Max values in the Joint: Rotation section of the Property inspector. The new values correlate to the bone's current orientation on the Stage. The total degrees of rotation available, however, are the same as those you entered. (Occasionally, the total differs by a degree or two due to mathematical rounding as Flash calculates Stage positions for the elements).

6. Using the Min and Max hot text, enter rotation values in the following ways:

   ▲ To allow rotation counterclockwise from the current starting position, using the Min hot text, enter a negative value. The lower the value, the greater the range of motion allowed.

   ▲ To allow rotation clockwise from the current starting position, using the Max hot text, enter a positive value. The higher the value, the greater the range of motion allowed.

   Click the hot text to enter a precise value; drag the hot text's invisible slider to choose a value interactively. A range-of-motion icon appears at the head of the selected bone; the icon's arc and lever indicate how far the bone can rotate (see the sidebar "The Mysterious Range-of-Motion Icons").

7. Repeat steps 3–6 for the second bone (the child bone).

8. Extend the pose span to frame 5 and position the playhead there.

9. In the Tools panel, choose the selection tool.

10. Manipulate the bones to see their range of motion.

    As you drag a bone, watch the range-of-motion icon at its head; the lever moves in concert with the bone within the defined arc. When the lever hits the edge of the arc, you have reached the end of allowable rotation; the bone can rotate no farther in that direction (**Figure 13.26**).

CONSTRAINING IK MOTION

✔ Tips

- To get a feel for how the constrain settings work, try disabling rotation for the parent bone and setting the child bone's Min to −30 and Max to 30. Now try to reposition the armature by dragging the bones and boxes with the selection tool. The first box doesn't rotate, the second box rotates a little (through 60 degrees), and the third box rotates a full 360 degrees. Now try reversing the settings, disabling rotation for the child bone. The first and second boxes rotate as a unit around the head of the parent bone (the unit can rotate only 60 degrees), and the third box still rotates 360 degrees.

- You can turn the constrain setting on and off. In the example above, imagine that you wanted the first and second boxes to move as a unit, but to be at a 90-degree angle to one another. You could position the boxes as desired, then activate the constrain setting and set the value to 0. The first two boxes can rotate around the head of the first bone in the chain, but always maintain their "bent" configuration. If you later decide that should be a 45-degree angle, deselect the Constrain check box, reposition the elements, then select Constrain again and set the Min and Max values.

- Because the constrain settings affect the head joint of the bone they apply to, you cannot constrain the rotation of the last symbol in a chain. But there are cases where you might want to constrain that element. Imagine, for example, a simplified cartoon arm consisting of three ovals—upper arm, forearm, and hand. You don't want the hand to be able to spin 360 degrees like a propeller on a plane. The only way to constrain it is to find a way to make it not the final symbol in the chain. Create a small symbol that has no graphic content. Place an instance of the empty symbol next to the hand. Then connect the hand to the empty symbol instance. No one will see the empty instance, but now you can constrain the hand.

- When the Enable check box is selected for Joint: Rotation, entering 0 for both Min and Max prevents rotation entirely, but the quickest way to prevent rotation is to deselect the Enable check box.

- Constrain settings apply throughout the IK pose span. You cannot create different constraints for the same joint in individual pose frames.

The Mysterious Range-of-Motion Icons

At the head of each IK bone, range-of-motion icons indicate the ways in which that joint can move (**Figure 13.27**).

When rotation is enabled and unconstrained, the icon is a circle around the head joint. When rotation is constrained, the circle changes to an arc with a lever inside. The lever represents the bone, and the arc indicates the range through which the bone can move. Unfortunately, the lever is not always parallel to the bone itself, which means you must use your imagination and spatial reasoning to convert the arc-and-lever image to the actual angles you want the bone to move through on the Stage. The orientation of the icon depends on a variety of factors, including whether the bone is a parent or a child, the parent bone's original orientation to the Stage, the child bone's original orientation to its parent, whether the bone is in an IK shape or is connecting IK nodes, and whether or not the bone has been rotated from its original position. The best way to get a feel for the way the icon works is to play with a few bones and try out the constrain settings. Manipulate the bones to see how the arc and lever work together in the range-of-motion icon to restrain the rotation of the bone on the Stage.

When x- or y-translation is enabled for a bone, the range-of-motion icon includes lines representing the x- and y-axes of the bone. For unlimited motion, the line is a double-headed arrow. When motion is constrained, the line changes to an I-beam shape, with the end posts of the I showing how far the bone's head can move in each direction.

There are no range-of-motion icons at the tail of the last bone in chain. That joint is always unconstrained.

Rotation enabled, unconstrained

Rotation enabled, constrained

X-translation enabled, unconstrained

X-translation enabled, constrained

Y-translation enabled, unconstrained

Y-translation enabled, constrained

Figure 13.27 A variety of icons appear at the head of a bone to indicate the range of motion allowed for the bone. Circular icons (complete circles or pie-wedge arcs) correspond to rotational motion; linear icons (double-headed arrows or I-beams) correspond to x- and y-translation.

To allow *x*-axis translation of the armature as a whole (via the parent bone):

1. Follow steps 1–3 in the preceding task.

2. To disable rotation of the selected parent bone, in the Joint: Rotation section of the Property inspector, deselect the Enable check box.

   This step is optional but useful. When rotation is enabled for a bone, the bone's *x*-axis changes orientation as the bone rotates. You may begin dragging the bone horizontally, for example, and wind up rotating the bone slightly in the process. The *x*-axis that started out horizontal in relation to the Stage is now at an angle. If you keep dragging, you'll be moving the armature diagonally in relation to the Stage, not horizontally. Turning off rotation, at least temporarily, makes it easier to set the *x*-axis position of the bone.

3. To allow the entire armature to move along the bone's *x*-axis, with the parent bone selected, select the Enable check box (it is deselected by default) in the Joint: X Translation section of the Property inspector.

   When *x*-translation is enabled, the selected bone's head can move along the bone's *x*-axis. A double-arrow range-of-motion icon appears at the selected bone's head. To restrict how far the head can move along the bone's *x*-axis, you must constrain the translation.

Negative arm of x-axis   Positive arm of x-axis

Figure 13.28 To allow movement of an IK bone's head along the bone's x-axis, select the Enable check box in the Joint: X Translation section of the Property inspector, then select Constrain and set Min and Max values. Min values allow movement along the negative arm of the bone's x-axis; Max values allow movement along the positive arm. When the bone's x-axis parallels that of the Stage, as in this figure, the Min value allows the bone's head to move to the left from the current starting position; the Max value allows the bone's head to move to the right. For bones with axes that don't align to the axes of the Stage, the terms *left* and *right* don't really apply. Select a bone to view its range-of-motion icon. The linear portions of the icon represent the bone's axes for translation.

4. In the Joint: X Translation section of the Property inspector, select the Constrain check box.

   Flash assigns default constrain values (**Figure 13.28**). With the document set to use pixels, the defaults are Min –50 pixels, Max 50 pixels. The range-of-motion icon changes from a double-headed arrow to a horizontal I-beam. The end posts of the icon indicate the limits of how the head can move.

5. Use the Min and Max hot text to enter the desired values in the following ways:

   ▲ To allow movement along the negative arm of the bone's x-axis, using the Min hot text, enter a negative value. The lower the value, the farther the bone's head can move in that direction.

   ▲ To allow movement along the positive arm of the bone's x-axis, using the Max hot text, enter a positive value. The higher the value, the farther the bone's head can move in that direction.

6. Create a few poses, repositioning the parent bone on the Stage in each one, then play through the animation.

   The three boxes maintain a constant distance from one another as the whole set moves side to side.

✔ Tips

■ The Min and Max values for *x*- and *y*-translation are relative. When you reposition the bone on the Stage, the Min and Max values in the Property inspector change. The total number of pixels in the range stays the same, however.

■ No matter what units of measure you set in Document Properties, Flash uses pixels in the Min and Max values for x- and y-translation. To avoid confusion, when working with IK animation, set up the document to use pixels (see Chapter 1).

CONSTRAINING IK MOTION

To allow *y*-axis translation of the armature as a whole (via the parent bone):

◆ Continuing with the armature from the preceding task, repeat steps 3–5. This time choose the Enable and/or Constrain check boxes in the Joint: Y Translation section of the Property inspector (**Figure 13.29**).

Selecting the Enable check box in the Joint: Y Translation section allows the selected bone unrestricted movement along its *y*-axis. The range-of-motion icon appears as a double arrow. When you select the Constrain check box, the icon changes to an I-beam. The Min hot text controls movement along the negative arm of the bone's *y*-axis; the Max hot text controls movement along the positive arm of the bone's *y*-axis.

Figure 13.29 To allow movement of an IK bone's head along its y-axis, select Enable in the Joint: Y Translation section of the Property inspector, then select Constrain and set Min and Max values. Min values allow movement along the negative arm of the bone's y-axis; Max values allow movement along the positive arm. When the bone's y-axis parallels that of the Stage, as in this figure, the Min value allows the bone's head to move upward from the current starting position; the Max value allows the bone's head to move downward. For bones with axes that don't align to the axes of the Stage, the terms *upward* and *downward* don't really apply. Select a bone to view its range-of-motion icon. The linear portions of the icon represent the bone's axes for translation.

Drag farther from parent

Drag closer to parent

Figure 13.30 By allowing x- and y-translation for the child bone, you can drag it along its x- and y-axes. As the child's head gets farther from its parent's head, the parent bone gets longer. As the child's head gets closer to its parent's head, the parent bone gets shorter.

To allow *x*- and *y*-axis translation of individual child bones:

1. Continuing with the three-node armature from the preceding tasks, select the child bone (the second bone in the chain) and disable rotation for that bone.

   To make the bones easier to work with, in the Joint: Rotation section of the Property inspector, deselect the Enable check box.

2. To enable the head of the selected child bone to move farther from (or closer to) the head of its parent (the preceding bone), do either of the following:

   ▲ To allow movement along the bone's *x*-axis, in the Joint: X Translation section of the Property inspector, select the Enable check box. To limit the range of movement, select the Constrain check box and use the Min and Max hot text to enter the desired values.

   or

   ▲ To allow movement along the bone's *y*-axis, in the Joint: Y Translation section of the Property inspector, select the Enable check box. To limit the range of movement, select the Constrain check box and use the Min and Max hot text to enter the desired values.

3. Using the selection tool, drag the selected child bone to reposition it.

   As the child's head gets farther from the parent's head, the parent bone gets longer; as the child's head gets closer to the parent's head, the parent bone gets shorter (**Figure 13.30**).

4. Create a few poses with the child at different distances from the parent, and play through the animation. The first two boxes move closer and farther apart; the third box maintains a constant distance from the second box.

Editing IK Elements

An armature isn't set in stone once you've created and posed it. The thing to remember about editing armatures is that you must remove any poses that you've created before you start making changes. Otherwise, you'll get some strange results. When a pose span contains just one pose, you can edit the armature in a variety of ways. You can change the position of head and tail joints in IK nodes, reposition IK nodes relative to one another, remove bones and nodes, and add bones and nodes. You can change, add, and remove bones inside an IK shape; change bone length; and edit the path of an IK shape. You can also control which bones affect which portions of an IK shape's path, by using the bind tool.

To reposition a bone's head/tail within an IK node:

1. To select a node whose head or tail you want to adjust, using the selection or subselection tool, click the node.

2. In the Tools panel, choose the free-transform tool.

   Flash activates the transform box of the selected symbol instance and highlights the transformation point as a white circle. The head and tail points are located at the transformation point of an IK node.

3. Position the pointer over the transformation point.

   A chain-link modifier appears next to the pointer, indicating that you can reposition the transformation point.

4. Drag the transformation point to a new location within the IK node (**Figure 13.31**).

   The white circle representing the transformation point moves to the new location. Flash also moves the head and/or tail points associated with that transformation point.

Original

Ready to reposition transformation point

Drag transformation point

Transformation point relocated

Head relocated

Figure 13.31 Use the free-transform tool to change the location of the head or tail in an IK node by dragging the symbol instance's transformation point. The IK bones are not visible while you use the free-transform tool, but behind the scenes, Flash also moves the head and/or tail points associated with that transformation point. Select the armature to see the bones in their new position.

Original armature

Reposition IK node

Revised armature

Figure 13.32 You can relocate a selected node (or multiple selected nodes) by Option-dragging or ⌘-dragging (Mac) or Alt-dragging (Windows) the selection. As you Option-drag (Mac) or Alt-drag (Windows), the IK bones disappear; Flash redraws the bones when you release the mouse button. If you drag with the other modifier key, the bones remain visible in their original locations until you release the mouse button.

Original armature

Reposition joint

Revised armature

Figure 13.33 Use the subselection tool to change the length of a bone within a selected IK shape. Drag the head or tail point to change the length of the bone.

To reposition IK nodes:

◆ Using the selection tool, Option-drag or ⌘-drag (Mac) or Alt-drag or Ctrl-drag (Windows) one node (or multiple selected nodes).

Reposition the selected node (or nodes) and release the mouse button (**Figure 13.32**).

To change bone length in IK Shapes:

1. In the Tools panel, choose the subselection tool.

2. Position the pointer over a head or tail point.

3. Drag the head or tail to a new location within the IK shape, and release the mouse button.

Flash redraws the bones on either side of the point you drag (**Figure 13.33**).

To edit an IK shape's path:

1. To view the bones, select the armature in an IK shape.

2. Using the subselection tool, click the edge of the selected IK shape.

If the shape has a stroke, click the stroke; otherwise, click at the edge of the shape. Flash activates the shape's Bézier path in blue, displaying control points as hollow blue squares.

3. To activate handles for a control point, click that point.

Flash activates the point and its handles, displaying them as three hollow red squares connected by lines. The central square represents the control point on the path; the outer squares work as Bézier-style handles.

continues on next page

EDITING IK ELEMENTS

4. To change the path of the IK shape, do any of the following (**Figure 13.34**):

- ▲ To relocate the control point, drag the middle red square.

- ▲ To reshape the curve, drag an outer red square to reposition the handles, as you would with Bézier paths (see Chapter 4).

- ▲ To delete the selected point, press Delete.

- ▲ To add a new point, click an area of the path that currently lacks a control point.

✔ Tips

■ Adding control points is tricky; it's easy to accidentally activate the handles of a nearby control point instead. Try changing the magnification of the Stage and keep clicking in slightly different areas of the path.

■ You can also use the regular Bézier add–anchor-point tool to add control points to an IK shape.

A

B

C

D

Figure 13.34 Click the outline of an IK shape with the subselection tool to activate control points for the shape's path (A). Click a control point directly to select it; it highlights with three red squares (B). Drag the central square to relocate the control point (C); drag a side square to reshape the curve as if using a Bézier handle (D).

About the Bind Tool

To control the way an IK shape redraws when you create poses, Flash connects (or *binds*) the control points of the shape to one or more bones in the armature. When you reposition a bone, Flash repositions the control points that bind to that bone and redraws the path of the IK shape accordingly. You can edit those connections with the bind tool, which is located in the Tools panel, in a submenu together with the bone tool. First, select the armature using the selection or subselection tool. Next, choose the bind tool and click a bone to select it. Flash highlights the selected bone with a red line, and highlights in yellow all the points that bind to the bone. A point that binds only to the selected bone appears as a yellow square. A point that binds to multiple bones, including the selected bone, appears as a yellow triangle (**Figure 13.35**).

continues on next page

Figure 13.35 The bind tool shows you which points on the path of an IK shape are controlled by which bones. Click a bone with the bind tool to see its connections. The bone highlights with a red line; control points that are bound to the bone highlight in yellow. Squares indicate points that are bound just to the selected bone. Triangles indicate points that are bound to the selected bone and to at least one other bone.

ABOUT THE BIND TOOL

About the Bind Tool *continued*

To break a connection to the selected bone, using the bind tool, Option-click (Mac) or Ctrl-click (Windows) the yellow square or triangle; the highlight disappears, and the binding is broken (**Figure 13.36**). (To unbind multiple points, using the bind tool with the modifier key, drag a selection rectangle around the points.) To bind an unconnected control point (a blue square) to the selected bone, using the bind tool, Shift-click the control point. (To bind multiple points, using the bind tool, Shift-drag a selection rectangle around the points.)

Selected points to unbind

Points no longer bound

Figure 13.36 To unbind points, Option-click (Mac) or Ctrl-click (Windows) the yellow square or triangle. To unbind multiple points, using the bind tool with the modifier key, drag a selection rectangle around the points.

Reposition bone

Shape no longer changes

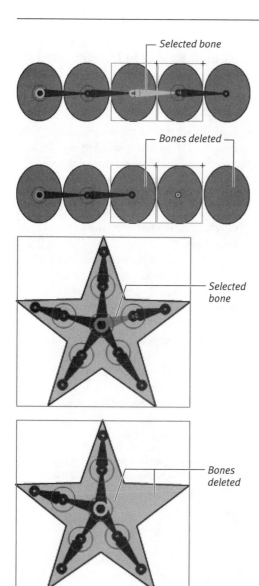

Figure 13.37 To remove a bone from an armature, select the bone and press Delete. Flash removes that bone and any children attached to it.

To remove individual bones:

1. In the Tools panel, choose the selection or subselection tool.

2. Click any of the IK nodes in an armature.

   or

   Click the IK shape that contains an armature.

3. To select a bone to be removed, click it.

   The selected bone highlights in different color than the other bones in the armature.

4. Press Delete.

   Flash removes the selected bone (**Figure 13.37**). In a linear armature, Flash also deletes all child bones connected to the selected bone. The disconnected nodes remain on the pose layer.

✔ Tip

- Removing a bone from an IK node does not restore the symbol instance's original transformation point. The transformation point remains where the head/tail point was in the IK node.

EDITING IK ELEMENTS

To remove an entire armature:

1. In the Timeline, Control-click (Mac) or right-click (Windows) the pose span.

2. From the contextual menu, choose Remove Armature.

   Flash deletes all the bones on the Stage and converts the pose span to a keyframe span in the Timeline. The symbol instances (or the shape) become the content of the initial keyframe, and the remaining frames become in-between frames.

✔ Tip

- You can also remove an armature from a selected IK shape by choosing Modify > Break Apart. Flash removes all the IK bones and returns the shape to its original form. The shape remains on the Armature layer. The Modify > Break Apart command also removes all the bones in an armature from a set of linked IK nodes, with one twist: any selected symbol instance gets converted to its underlying shape(s), just as it would with the normal Break Apart command. If you select the armature by clicking one node, that symbol instance converts to a shape; the others remain symbols. If you select the armature by choosing Edit > Select All or by dragging a selection rectangle around all the nodes, all the symbol instances convert to shapes.

About Easing in IK Animation

As in tweening, in IK animation you can make movement accelerate or decelerate by using easing. The procedure is similar to that for applying easing (see Chapter 11) to classic and shape tweens, except that the easing occurs between poses, not keyframes. Here's a quick overview. In the Timeline, click the pose where you'd like easing to start taking effect. IK easing begins in the selected pose frame (the one with the diamond) and affects the in-between frames up to the next pose frame. If you prefer, you can simply click the span between poses to apply the ease (easing starts in the pose frame that comes first). In the Easing section of the IK Armature Property inspector, from the Type menu, select a style of easing (**Figure 13.38**). Use the Strength hot text to determine how aggressive the acceleration or deceleration is. You cannot create custom eases for IK animations.

Figure 13.38 To add easing to IK animation, select a pose frame in the Timeline (or select a frame between poses). Access the Property inspector, and from the Type menu in the Ease section, choose a style.

BUILDING BUTTONS FOR INTERACTIVITY

The Mystery of Button Symbols

Buttons are short interactive movies that allow changes to occur when the user moves the pointer over an area of the screen. When you create a symbol and select Button as the symbol type, Flash sets up a Timeline with four frames. You create keyframes and graphics for the first three frames to display the button in three common states: Up, Over, and Down. A keyframe in the fourth frame defines the active area of the button. You can include movie clips within each keyframe of a button to create buttons that are fully animated, and you can create scripts that activate buttons to give your viewers more control of the movie.

The Up keyframe shows graphics that end users see when the pointer lies outside the button's active area. The Over keyframe shows what the user sees when the pointer rolls over the button; additional visual changes let the user know the button is live. The Down keyframe shows how the button looks when the user clicks it and the Hit keyframe defines the area where mouse movements trigger the button.

After you master Flash CS4 Professional's drawing and animating tools, you can create movies that play from beginning to end. But Flash does more than make animated movies; it creates interactive environments that transform viewers into users. To move your Flash movie into the realm of interactive experience, you must add interface elements that give users control. The most common interface element is a button. Buttons have two levels of interactivity: first, responding to user input with visual feedback—for example, changing color when the pointer enters the button area; second, carrying out tasks—for example, switching to a new scene when a user clicks the button.

Flash comes with a number of predefined user-interface elements, including button symbols and button components. For these elements, built-in coding takes care of the first level of button interactivity, responding to mouse movements with visual feedback. To achieve the second level of interactivity— making buttons respond in new ways and carry out tasks—requires scripting. You'll learn some simple ways to do that in Chapter 15.

In this chapter, you learn to set up the first level of interactivity using button symbols and button components. You also learn to set up a movie-clip symbol that can act as a visually responsive button.

Creating a Basic Button Symbol

A button is a Flash movie clip with different keyframes that represent the button in all its possible states. The button symbol has three button-state frames—Up, Over, Down—plus one frame for defining the active button area. To create the most basic button symbol, choose a simple shape and place it in the keyframe for each state; change the shape's color or add or modify internal elements for the various states. When you complete all four keyframes, your button is ready to use. Return to document-editing mode, and drag an instance of the button symbol from the Library panel to the Stage.

To create a button symbol:

1. Open a Flash document to which you want to add buttons.

2. Choose Insert > New Symbol, or press ⌘-F8 (Mac) or Ctrl-F8 (Windows) (**Figure 14.1**).

   The Create New Symbol dialog appears.

3. Type a name in the Name field (for example, MyBasicButton), choose Button in the Type section, and click OK (**Figure 14.2**).

   Flash creates a new symbol in the Library panel and returns you to the Timeline and Stage in symbol-editing mode. The Timeline contains the four frames that define the button: Up, Over, Down, and Hit.

   By default, the Up frame contains a keyframe (**Figure 14.3**). You must add keyframes to the Over, Down, and Hit frames and place the graphic elements in each keyframe of the button. To give users feedback about the button—so they can tell when they're on a live button and sense the difference when they click it— use a different graphic in each keyframe.

Figure 14.1 Choosing Insert > New Symbol is the first step in creating a button.

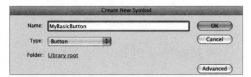

Figure 14.2 To make a button, create a new symbol and choose Button as the type in the Create New Symbol dialog. You also name the button here.

Figure 14.3 The Timeline for every button symbol contains four frames: Up, Over, Down, and Hit. Flash automatically puts a keyframe in the Up frame of a new button symbol.

Registration crosshair marks the center of the symbol's Stage

Figure 14.4 When a button is waiting for your viewer to notice and interact with it, Flash displays the contents of the Up keyframe.

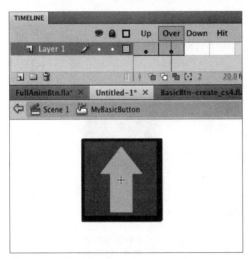

Figure 14.5 When the viewer's pointer rolls or pauses over the button, Flash displays the contents of the Over keyframe.

To create the Up state:

1. Using the file from the preceding task, in the Timeline, select the Up keyframe.

2. On the Stage, create a new graphic or place a graphic symbol (**Figure 14.4**).

   This graphic element becomes the button as it's sitting onstage in your movie, waiting for someone to click it. The crosshair in the middle of the Stage in symbol-editing mode becomes the registration point for the symbol.

To create the Over state:

1. Using the file from the preceding task, in the Timeline, select the Over frame.

2. Choose Insert > Timeline > Keyframe.

   Flash duplicates the Up keyframe. Now you can make minor changes in the Up graphic to convert it to an Over graphic. Enlarge an element within the button, for example (**Figure 14.5**). Duplicating the preceding keyframe makes it easy to align all your button elements so they don't appear to jump around as they change states.

To create the Down state:

1. Using the file from the preceding task, in the Timeline, select the Down frame.

2. Choose Insert > Timeline > Keyframe.

   Flash duplicates the Over keyframe. Now you can make minor changes to convert the Over graphic to a Down graphic. Change the button color, for example, and reverse the shadow effect so the button looks indented (**Figure 14.6**).

   After you create graphics for the three states of your button, you need to define the active area of the button.

To create the Hit state:

1. Using the file from the preceding task, in the Timeline, select the Hit frame.

2. Choose Insert > Timeline > Keyframe.

   Flash duplicates the Down keyframe. When you use a graphic with the same shape and size for all three phases of your button, you can safely use a copy of any previous keyframe as the Hit-frame graphic.

3. If you want, use the paint-bucket and ink-bottle tools to fill the Hit-frame graphic with a single color (**Figure 14.7**).

   This step isn't required, but it helps remind you that this graphic isn't one that viewers of your movie will see.

4. Choose Edit > Edit Document, or click the Back button in the Edit bar.

   Flash returns you to the main Timeline. Now you can use the button symbol in your movie just as you would use any other symbol.

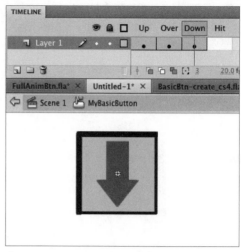

Figure 14.6 When the viewer clicks the button, Flash displays the contents of the Down keyframe.

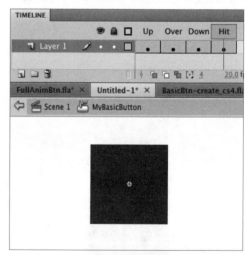

Figure 14.7 The graphic in the Hit keyframe doesn't need to be a fully detailed image of the button in any state; it just needs to be a silhouette of the button shape. Flash uses that shape to define the active button area. This Hit keyframe contains a copy of the Down keyframe that has been filled with dark gray.

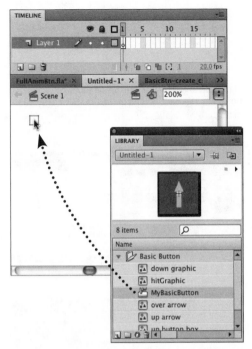

Figure 14.8 To incorporate the button symbol into your Flash movie, drag an instance of the button from the Library panel to the Stage.

Figure 14.9 By default, in document-editing mode, button-symbol instances on the Stage display just the Up keyframe. To see the different states as the pointer interacts with a button during authoring, choose Control > Enable Simple Buttons.

To place the newly created button in your movie:

◆ Continuing with the file from the preceding task, drag an instance of the button MyBasicButton from the Library panel to the Stage (**Figure 14.8**).

You can modify the instance to change its size, rotation, and color. (For more information on modifying symbol instances, see Chapter 7.)

✔ Tips

■ To create a consistent look on a Web site, you may want to use a set of buttons over and over. You can even reuse buttons in several projects with only slight changes. To save time, devote one document to buttons, and always create your button symbols there. Then you can copy a button from this master button file to your current Flash document and tweak the button there.

■ Fill the graphics in the Hit keyframe with a bright color that you won't use elsewhere in your movie, to create a visual cue that you're in the Hit keyframe of a button, in symbol-editing mode.

■ You can preview the Up, Over, and Down states of your button by selecting the button in the Library panel and then clicking the Play button in the preview window. Flash displays each frame in turn.

To preview button states on the Stage:

◆ Choose Control > Enable Simple Buttons (**Figure 14.9**).

Flash displays the Up, Over, and Down states as you move the pointer over the button and click. Remember, with buttons enabled, you can't select them or work with them. To turn off Enable Simple Buttons mode, choose Control > Enable Simple Buttons again.

Creating Shape-Changing Button Symbols

Button graphics can emulate real-world switches or toggles. In a game, you can disguise buttons as part of the scenery—making the blinking eye of a character a button, for example. When the Up, Over, and Down keyframes of your button symbol contain graphics of different shapes and sizes, however, you need to create a graphic for the Hit state that covers all of the other states.

To create Up, Over, and Down states with various graphics:

1. Open a Flash document and choose Insert > New Symbol.

   The Create New Symbol dialog appears.

2. Enter a name in the Name field (for example, AnimatedBtn), choose Button in the Type section, and click OK (**Figure 14.10**).

   Flash creates a new symbol in the Library panel and returns you to the Timeline and Stage in symbol-editing mode.

3. In the Timeline, select the Over, Down, and Hit frames.

4. Control-click (Mac) or right-click (Windows) the selected frames and choose Convert to Blank Keyframes from the menu (**Figure 14.11**).

5. With the Up keyframe selected in the Timeline, on the Stage, create a new graphic, or place an instance of the graphic symbol that you want to use for the button's Up state.

6. Repeat step 6 for the Over and Down keyframes.

   For this task, use graphics that have different shapes—a circle, a star, and a double-headed arrow, for example.

Figure 14.10 Name your button symbol and choose Button as the symbol type in the Create New Symbol dialog.

Figure 14.11 With the Over, Down, and Hit frames of a button symbol selected, Control-click (Mac) or right-click (Windows) to access the contextual menu and choose Convert to Blank Keyframes. Flash adds blank keyframes to all the selected frames.

Onion-skin outlines

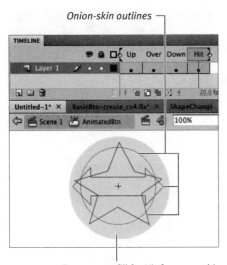

Transparent fill for Hit-frame graphic

Figure 14.12 The silhouette in the Hit keyframe needs to encompass all possible button areas in all three button modes. For example, if you duplicate only the circle as the graphic for the Hit keyframe for this button, you exclude the tips of the star. As the user moves the pointer over the tips, the button returns to its Over phase; the user can't click the tips to activate the button. If you duplicate only the star, the user may roll over several areas of the circle and never discover that it's a button.

Figure 14.13 By copying the graphic in each of the button states and using the Paste in Place command to place them in the Hit keyframe, you wind up with a perfectly positioned silhouette that incorporates all the possible button areas.

To create the Hit state for graphics of various shapes:

1. Using the file you created in the preceding task, in the Timeline, select the Hit keyframe.

2. To create the graphic that defines the button's active area, do either of the following:

   ▲ Draw a simple geometric shape large enough to cover all areas of the button. Turn on onion skinning so you can see exactly what you need to cover (**Figure 14.12**).

   ▲ Use Flash's Edit > Copy and Edit > Paste in Place commands to copy the graphic elements from the first three keyframes of the button and paste them into the Hit keyframe of the button one by one. The graphics stack up in the Hit keyframe, occupying the exact area needed to cover the button in any phase of its operation (**Figure 14.13**).

3. Return to editing the document, for example, by choosing Edit > Edit Document. You're ready to place an instance of the button on the Stage and test it out by choosing Control > Test Movie.

✔ Tip

■ Use a transparent color (one with an alpha value less than 100 percent) for the graphic in the Hit keyframe. In Onion Skin mode the Up, Down, and Over graphics show through the Hit graphic, making it easy to see how to position or size the graphic in the Hit keyframe to cover the graphics in the other keyframes.

Creating Fully Animated Button Symbols

The button symbols you created in the preceding tasks are animated in the sense that they change as the user interacts with them. Flash also lets you create button symbols that are fully animated—a glowing light bulb, for example, or a little ladybug that jumps up and down, saying, "Click me!" The trick to making fully animated buttons is placing movie clips in the keyframes of your button. Because the movie clips play in their own Timeline, animated buttons remain animated even when you pause the main movie.

To animate a rollover button:

1. Open a Flash document to which you want to add buttons.

2. Choose Insert > New Symbol.
   The Create New Symbol dialog appears.

3. Name your button (for example, FullAnimBtn), choose Button in the Type section, and click OK.

4. In the Timeline, select the Over, Down, and Hit frames of the button, and choose Modify > Timeline > Convert to Blank Keyframes.
   Flash creates blank keyframes for the button's Over, Down, and Hit frames.

5. In the Timeline, select the Up keyframe, and place an instance of a movie-clip symbol on the Stage. For this example, the Up-keyframe clip contains a spinning pentagon (**Figure 14.14**).

6. In the Timeline, select the Over keyframe, and place an instance of a movie-clip symbol on the Stage.
   In this example, the Over-keyframe clip contains a pentagon that turns into a star (**Figure 14.15**).

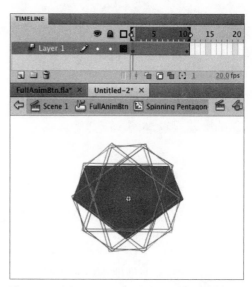

Figure 14.14 Placing an animated symbol in the Up keyframe of a button symbol makes that animation appear when the button is in the Up state. Here, onion skinning in symbol-editing mode reveals all the frames of a spinning-pentagon animation created with a motion tween.

Figure 14.15 With an animated symbol in the Over keyframe of a button, that animation appears when the pointer rolls or rests over the button area. Here, the Preview mode of the Timeline shows the frame-by-frame animation of a pentagon shape that turns into a star.

Figure 14.16 With an animated symbol in the Down keyframe of a button, the animation plays when the viewer clicks inside the button area. Here, onion skinning in symbol-editing mode reveals all the frames of a shooting-star created with classic tweening.

Figure 14.17 When you're creating a graphic for a Hit keyframe, use onion skinning to see the initial keyframe of the movie clip in each button frame. Here, the graphic in the Hit keyframe is a transparent fill, which also helps you position the graphic to cover the graphics in the other keyframes.

7. Repeat step 6 for the Down keyframe.

For this example, the Down-keyframe clip contains a star that flies apart (**Figure 14.16**).

8. In the Timeline, select the Hit keyframe, and create a graphic that covers all the button areas for the three button states (Up, Over, and Down).

A large oval works well for this purpose (**Figure 14.17**). This graphic creates an active button area that's larger than the spinning pentagon. As your viewer's pointer nears the spinning graphic during playback, the button switches to Over mode. In Over mode, the oval is big enough to encompass all points of the star, and in Down mode, the user can let the pointer drift a fair amount and still be within the confines of the button.

9. Return to document-editing mode (for example, by clicking the name of the current scene in the Edit bar).

10. Drag a copy of the FullAnimBtn symbol from the Library panel to the Stage.

✔ Tips

■ You can place a movie-clip instance in the Hit keyframe of your button, but only the visible content from the clip's first frame determines the hit area.

■ With buttons enabled, in document-editing mode, Flash previews the animation of the Up, Over, and Down keyframes of your button symbol.

Using Button Components

The elements that make up the user interface (UI) of an application are the little things that let users interact with your content: menus, check boxes, scroll bars, and so on. Flash's button symbols are one type of UI element, with built-in scripting for simple behavior (displaying the common button states) and looks that you can freely define. However, Flash also offers a more complete set of UI elements in the form of *components* (see the sidebar "The Mystery of Components"). You can modify both the behavior and the graphics of Flash components. Flash's button components have more built-in scripting to govern behavior, and they offer predefined graphics that help create a consistent look and feel for your Flash creations. To put a component to use, you place an instance of it in your Flash document.

To place an instance of the button component:

1. Open a Flash document to which you'd like to add a button component.

2. Access the following panels: Components, Component Inspector, Library, and the Property inspector.

   These panels are all found under the Window menu.

3. If necessary, in the Components panel, expand the list of user-interface components (**Figure 14.18**).

   Click the triangle (Mac) or the minus or plus sign (Windows) to the left of the name User Interface to toggle between the list's expanded and collapsed views.

Figure 14.18 The Components panel lists all the default components that come with Flash. There are two categories of components for ActionScript 3.0: User Interface and Video. Buttons are found under User Interface. To expand or collapse the list, click the minus or plus sign (Windows) or triangle (Mac) to the left of the title User Interface.

Figure 14.19 A component is a special form of movie clip. When you drag a Button component from the Components panel to the Stage, the button becomes an asset (its type is Component) in the Library panel of that document.

Figure 14.20 During authoring, each component instance appears on the Stage showing its first frame, using the current parameter settings. As you drag, you see the ghosted original as you would for any other object on the Stage. To preview all the states of the component, use one of the test modes—for example, choose Control > Test Movie.

4. Drag an instance of the button component to the Stage.

Flash adds the button component and a folder named Component Assets to the document's library (**Figure 14.19**).

✔ Tip

■ Components work similarly to other library assets (for more about working with library assets, see Chapter 7). A confusing apparent similarity is that you can rename a component in the Library panel by double-clicking its name (Button) to activate a text field and typing a new name. It's unadvisable to do so, however. You can change the name of the master component, but on the Stage the component instance still bears the name Label. Moreover, if you bring another copy of the original button component into the same document, the two components will have the same linkage ID, which may create problems when using the components in your published movie.

To preview the component instance:

◆ To view all the parameters and button states of a button component, choose Control > Test Movie.

During authoring, the button component on the Stage displays the Up state created by the component's current parameter settings (**Figure 14.20**). To view a fully enabled button component, you must view it in Flash Player. (Choose Control > Test Movie.)

Modifying Button Components

The Component Inspector offers seven modifiable parameters for the button component. The tasks below work with two of them: changing the button's label and setting the button to work as a toggle.

To modify button-component dimensions:

1. Continuing with the file you used in the preceding task, on the Stage, select the instance of Button.

2. In the Position and Size section of the Property inspector, use the W and H hot text to enter new values for width and height (**Figure 14.21**).

   By default, Flash links the width and height values; the chain-link icon appears in its closed form. Linking the dimensions preserves the component's aspect ratio (the ratio of width to height) when you enter new values. For this task, click the chain-link icon to unlink the values. Then use the hot text to enter values that create a square button. For example, click the H hot text, enter a value of 100 to match the current W value, and press Enter to confirm the new value.

   The button's dimensions change according to the value(s) you enter (**Figure 14.22**). The bounding box of the button defines the active area of the button. As you change the dimensions, Flash automatically changes the hit area for the button component to match.

Figure 14.21 To change the dimensions of a button-component instance, access the Position and Size section of the Property inspector. Use the W and H hot text to enter new width and height values.

Aspect ratio locked   Aspect ratio unlocked

Figure 14.22 You can change the rectangular Button component to a square by entering the same value for width and height (here it's 100 pixels). To change the aspect ratio (the ratio of width to height), make sure the chain-link icon appears in its broken form. When the chain link is closed, Flash preserves the component's original aspect ratio; entering a new height changes the value for width accordingly. When the chain link is broken, you can set the width and height values independently.

✔ Tips

■ There are other ways to resize the button component. You can select the component instance and resize it using the Transform panel or the free-transform tool. Alternatively, you can enter new width and height values in the Info panel.

■ You can rotate or skew a button component with the free-transform tool or Info panel. You should know, however, that Flash creates the button's label text using device fonts, which can't be rotated or skewed. If you rotate or skew a button component, its label text disappears.

■ You can position a selected button component precisely by entering x- and y-coordinate values in the Info panel or in the Position and Size section of the Property inspector.

The Mystery of Components

Flash's components are predefined user-interface elements with built-in graphics and coding that make them easy to use. Adobe designed components to work together to give an application or a Web site a consistent look and feel. Components depend on ActionScript to carry out their intended behavior. Flash CS4 offers two types of components: those that work with ActionScript versions 1.0 and 2.0, and those that work with version 3.0.

Flash stores components in the *Components panel,* a sort of library of components. The Components panel displays different items depending on which version of ActionScript is selected in the Publish Settings dialog of the current Flash document. When you create a new Flash File (ActionScript 3.0) document, it is set to work with the 3.0 components, and those are the only components that appear in the Components panel. (To learn about Publish Settings and switching ActionScript versions for your document, see Chapter 18.)

A component is actually a sophisticated, scripted movie-clip symbol. The ActionScript 1.0 and 2.0 components are a special type of movie clip called a *compiled clip.* ActionScript 3.0's video components are also compiled clips, but the 3.0 user-interface components are really just regular movie clips whose look you can easily modify. See the sidebar "The Mystery of ActionScript 3.0 Component Skins," later in this chapter. (It is also possible to modify the look of compiled clips, but the process is somewhat complex and beyond the scope of this book.)

Flash lets you modify certain properties of a component—for example, the label of the button component—by changing parameters in the Component Inspector.

Advanced Flash users can use ActionScript to make components communicate with one another and to change the components on the fly at runtime, but even someone new to scripting can use simple components to add interactivity to a project.

Advanced scripters can also create their own components and share them with other Flash users. One source for new components is the Adobe Exchange portion of the Adobe Web site. As third-party components become available, you can add them to your Components panel for easy access.

MODIFYING BUTTON COMPONENTS

To modify button-component labels:

1. Continuing with the file you used in the preceding task, on the Stage, select the instance of Button.

2. Access the Component Inspector.

   The panel has three sections: Parameters, Bindings, and Schema.

3. If Parameters isn't active, click the Parameters button (Mac) or tab (Windows) to view the component's parameters.

   The panel displays a two-column table (**Figure 14.23**). The first column contains the parameter names; the second column contains the value for each parameter.

4. To modify the text that appears on your button instance, in the row for label, click the value Label.

   Flash activates the text field and selects the name; enter a new name, such as testComponent (**Figure 14.24**).

5. Press Enter, or click outside the active text field.

   With Flash's default settings, the new label text appears within the button-component instance (**Figure 14.25**). Be forewarned, if your text is wider than the button instance, Flash will truncate the text to make it fit within the visible button area.

Figure 14.23 The Component Inspector displays all the parameters of the button component that you can modify during authoring.

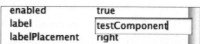

Figure 14.24 In the Component Inspector click the value field in the Label row to activate text entry (top). Type your new label text (bottom), then press Enter to confirm the new label.

Figure 14.25 When you change the button-component instance's Label parameter in the Component Inspector, Flash previews your new label text in the instance on the Stage.

Figure 14.26 When you select the Toggle value in the Parameters section of the Component Inspector, you can access a menu for choosing a value of true or false.

Figure 14.27 When the button-component instance has a Toggle value of true, it acts as a toggle button. Here the button-component instances are viewed in Test-Movie mode. The button on the left is deselected, and the one on the right is selected.

To set the button component to act as a toggle:

1. Select an instance of a button component on the Stage.

2. In the Component Inspector, set the Toggle value to true (**Figure 14.26**). Click anywhere in the row labeled Toggle, to activate the value pop-up menu. Click the value field to open the menu and select true. The button now acts as a toggle, so repeated clicks turn the button on and off (**Figure 14.27**).

✔ Tips

- The Parameters section of the Component Inspector also contains a field for the button component's Selected value (the choices are true and false). Use the Selected value to set a toggle button's initial state (true sets the button to be selected initially; false sets the button to be deselected initially).

- To open the Value pop-up menu quickly, double-click the value in the Toggle row.

MODIFYING BUTTON COMPONENTS

413

The Mystery of ActionScript 3.0 Component Skins

You can edit ActionScript 3.0's User Interface components the way you would edit any movie-clip symbol. Let's look at the Button component as an example.

When you drag an instance of the button component to the Stage, Flash adds the master button component and a Component Assets folder to the library of your document. Inside the assets folder is a subfolder containing the component's *skins*. The subfolder for the button component, named ButtonSkins, contains all the symbols that make up the button component's states. You can modify these underlying symbols, as you would any symbol, to change the look of the component. To modify each skin symbol directly, double-click it in the library; Flash opens the symbol in symbol-editing mode. Alternatively, you can double-click a component instance on the Stage to gain access to all of that component's skins in symbol-editing mode. The top layer of the component symbol's Timeline is labeled assets. Keyframe 2 of the asset layer contains a symbol that itself contains all the skins that make up the look of the component—in this case, the button states (**Figure 14.28**). Double-click any of the skins to edit it.

To change a button component's look yet retain a consistent, user-friendly button, you will probably need to modify every skin that relates to the button component. You may also need to modify other components if you plan to use them within the same application or Web site as your modified button component. The changes you make to the component's skins will affect every instance of the component in your movie.

Figure 14.28 Double-clicking a component instance on the Stage opens the master component's skins for editing. The skin symbols are found in keyframe 2 of the assets layer of the master component.

Figure 14.29 The first step in making a movie clip that acts like a button is creating a new symbol. Choose Insert > New Symbol, then set the symbol type to Movie Clip and enter a name in the Create New Symbol dialog.

Figure 14.30 When you set up the movie-clip button, it's a good idea to create a separate layer for the actions, text, and graphic elements in the movie clip's Timeline.

Why Make Movie-Clip Buttons?

Flash's button symbols make it easy to create buttons quickly, but they limit you to just three states: Up, Over, and Down. Sometimes you'd like a button to have more states than that. The best interface designs use elements consistently. That way, users know what options are available to them and always know where to find the interface elements for carrying out a task. Think of a typical slide show with a Next button. Ideally, the button is always present in the same location. When you view the last slide, the Next button is inactive (and looks inactive).

When you make your own movie-clip buttons, you can create as many states as you like.

Creating Movie-Clip Buttons

Flash's button symbols have built-in rules about how the button displays its three states in response to the user's mouse movements. You can take control of that functionality yourself and also create a button that has more than three states by making your own movie-clip button. In the following tasks, you learn to assemble artwork in the Timeline of the movie clip to create a button with four states: Up, Over, Down, and Disabled. To give the movie-clip button even the first level of interactivity—to make the movie clip respond to mouse movements by displaying different states—you must attach ActionScript. You learn to do that in Chapter 15.

To create the button states:

1. In a Flash document where you'd like to use buttons that are movie-clip symbols, choose Insert > New Symbol.

   The Create New Symbol dialog appears.

2. Type a name for your symbol, MovieClipBtn; choose Movie Clip as your symbol type; and click OK (**Figure 14.29**).

   Flash switches to symbol-editing mode. In the Timeline you see one layer, with a keyframe in frame 1.

3. Add two new layers to the Timeline, for a total of three layers.

   Each layer holds a different type of information for your button (**Figure 14.30**). The top layer holds ActionScript that tells the movie-clip button what to do; name this layer Actions. The second layer holds text identifying each keyframe that represents a button state; name this layer Labels. The bottom layer holds the graphic elements that give the button its look in each state; name this layer ButtonGraphics.

   continues on next page

CREATING MOVIE-CLIP BUTTONS

4. In the Timeline, for all three layers, insert keyframes in frames 4, 7, and 10 (**Figure 14.31**).

The layers that you added already had keyframes at frame 1. You need to add three more keyframes to accommodate all four button states: Up, Over, Down, and Disabled. Spacing out the keyframes makes them easier to deal with and lets you view the frame labels that you create in the following task.

5. In the ButtonGraphics layer, select keyframe 1; using the oval tool, draw an oval centered over the registration mark on the Stage.

This graphic represents the button's Up state. Give the oval a red fill and a black stroke. Make the stroke fairly wide so the graphic looks more buttonlike.

6. Select the oval, and choose Edit > Copy.

7. Select keyframe 4 in the ButtonGraphics layer, and choose Edit > Paste in Place.

This graphic represents the button's Over state. Change the fill color to green.

8. Repeat step 7 for keyframes 7 and 10.

In keyframe 7, change the oval fill to blue, to represent the Down state. In keyframe 10, change the fill to a light gray and the stroke to a dark gray, to represent the button in its Disabled state (**Figure 14.32**).

✔ Tip

■ There is no need to create a Hit-state keyframe for a movie-clip button. When you add the appropriate ActionScript (see Chapter 15), Flash uses the graphic element(s) in the frames of your movie clip that are displayed as button states to define the hit area.

Figure 14.31 A movie-clip button needs a keyframe for each button state. Creating longer keyframe spans helps you organize the layers visually and makes room for frame labels.

Figure 14.32 With Preview selected as your frame-viewing mode, the Timeline displays all the button-state graphics you've placed in the keyframes of the movie-clip button symbol. Use shades of gray for the graphics in the frame that represents the Disabled state. (For clarity, since this book can't show you colors, the Disabled-state graphic contains an X.)

Figure 14.33 Using the button state as the name for a selected keyframe reminds you what's in the frame, and you can use ActionScript to find a frame by label name. In the Label section of the Property inspector, enter the button-state description in the Name field.

Figure 14.34 A red flag in a keyframe indicates that the frame has a label name. If there are enough in-between frames following the keyframe, Flash displays the frame label as well as the flag (here frames have been added at the end of the sequence to make the Disabled label visible). The labeled keyframes in this movie-clip symbol indicate which button state the keyframe represents.

To assign frame labels to button-state keyframes:

1. Continuing with the file you created in the preceding task, in the Labels layer of the Timeline, select keyframe 1.

2. Click the Name field in the Label section of the Property inspector to activate the field, then type the name of the button state (_up), and press Enter to confirm the name (**Figure 14.33**).

   The Type menu (located beneath the Name field) tells Flash how to interpret the text in the Name field. Keep the default setting Name. When you finish typing the label, Flash places a red-flag icon and the label text in any keyframe that has a Name label (**Figure 14.34**).

3. Repeat steps 2 and 3 for keyframes 4, 7, and 10, entering the names _over, _down, and Disabled.

   Why use keyframe labels? A label reminds you what's in the keyframe. More important, you can use ActionScript to find a frame by label name and then display that frame. You'll use this technique to create the button's visual feedback in response to mouse movements (see Chapter 15).

4. Return to document-editing mode; for example, click the Back button in the Edit bar.

continues on next page

5. Drag an instance of the `MovieClipBtn` symbol to the Stage.

This movie clip is ready to be scripted to act like a button and to carry out whatever tasks you set for it with ActionScript. You'll learn to complete the button's interactivity in Chapter 15. To check out your button states, click the Play button in the symbol preview in the Library panel, or choose Control > Test Movie to play the symbol instance. Flash moves through the keyframes and displays each button state in turn.

6. Save this document for use in Chapter 15. Call it MyOwnBtn.fla.

✔ Tips

■ When you use the labels `_up`, `_down`, and `_over` in your movie clip, ActionScript recognizes these labels as button states and you will do minimal scripting to get the button to work (see Chapter 15). To make a more flexible button (for example, one that responds differently to different mouse movements), use other labels. You can use MyUp, MyOver, MyDown, MyDragOut, and so on.

■ Another way to add a reminder about what a keyframe does is to add a comment. To enter a frame comment, select the keyframe; in the Name field in the Label section of the Property inspector, type two slashes (//) followed by your comment text (**Figure 14.35**). Frame labels and frame comments are mutually exclusive: each keyframe can have one or the other. To work around that limitation, add separate layers for comments and labels. Place keyframes in both layers, and then add comments to one layer and labels to the other, as needed.

■ Instead of typing two slashes, just type the comment text. From the Type pop-up menu, choose Comment. Flash adds the slashes for you.

Figure 14.35 The Name field in the Label section of the Property inspector can also be used to create comments for a selected keyframe. Enter two slashes in the field to begin comment text, or choose Comment from the Type menu. Comments appear in the Timeline in the keyframe span; long comments are cut off by the next keyframe in the layer.

The Mystery of Frame-Label Naming

Flash is sensitive about names. Frame-label names become part of target paths in ActionScripting; therefore, certain characters that have special meaning in scripting—slashes, equals signs, plus signs, and so on—are off-limits for labeling frames. To be safe, use only letters, numbers, and underscore characters. Don't even use spaces to make word divisions in frame labels; use capitalization and the underscore character instead.

Basic
Interactivity

ActionScript Versions

Flash CS4 contains two flavors of ActionScript—version 2.0 (which also includes 1.0) and 3.0. ActionScript 3.0 differs significantly from the previous versions, and you cannot mix versions within one Flash creation. So which version should you use?

ActionScript (AS) 2.0 has some advantages over 3.0 for beginners who need to create only simple interactive content. AS 2.0 lets you think about interactivity in a concrete way and attach scripts to buttons and other objects directly. But ActionScript 3.0 has its own advantages. It standardizes the procedures for scripting, making it easier to transfer knowledge from one area of scripting to another. Because AS 3.0 will be the standard going forward, this book focuses exclusively on version 3.0.

To create scripts that use AS 3.0, you must set your Flash document's publish settings to AS 3.0. (You can do that when you create the document initially or in the Publish Settings dialog. You'll learn more about publishing in Chapter 18.)

Adobe Flash CS4 Professional includes a complete scripting language, ActionScript, that you can use to create complex, interactive Web sites for e-learning, e-commerce, and other Internet applications. But teaching ActionScript and scripting in detail is beyond the scope of this book. However, it is possible to create scripts for a number of common tasks without much difficulty. In this chapter you will use ActionScript 3.0 to add basic interactivity to your Flash content. To create scripts, you will enter code in meaningful segments. Some characters—such as opening and closing braces—act as a team to enclose code; both characters must be present for the script to work. To help create accurate code, you will first enter such characters as a pair, then add the code that belongs inside. You will also revise and add to scripts as you go. Other scripting help in this book comes from script figures, which show completed segments of code. For context, when a script figure illustrates specific steps in a task, the text that you enter for those steps appears in boldface; text that is already present from earlier steps appears in regular type. Full scripts are available the book's companion Web site; for directions to download them, please see the Introduction, page xviii.

Touring the Actions Panel

The Actions panel has three work areas: the Script pane, the Actions Toolbox, and the Script Navigator. To access the panel, choose Window > Actions or press Option-F9 (Mac) or F9 (Windows).

The Script pane is a text window where you assemble scripts. You can enter actions into the pane manually (it acts like a text editor); and you can also add actions from the Actions Toolbox or the Add pop-up menu. (To access the Add menu, click the plus sign in the toolbar above the Script pane.) You can import scripts or pieces of script from an external file, such as one created with a stand-alone text editor.

The Mystery of ActionScripting

A *script* is a series of commands, or statements, that makes Flash perform tasks at runtime—that is, when a published Flash (SWF) file runs in Flash Player for your end users to view (see Chapter 18).

Creating ActionScript basically means writing text. In Flash's default workflow you write scripts in the Script pane of the Actions panel, and Flash stores them as part of the FLA file. You can also save scripts as separate ActionScript files (files with the extension .*as*), and instruct Flash to include them only when publishing. When you save scripts externally, you have the option to edit them in any external text editor.

The Actions panel's Script Assist mode helps you enter code in the Script pane. For beginners, the word *assist* sounds attractive, but the feature requires some knowledge of scripting. Script Assist lets you create code by choosing check boxes or menu items and entering text in special fields. Script Assist ensures that your ActionScript code has the correct syntax (see the sidebar "The Mystery of ActionScript Syntax," later in this chapter). To use Script Assist, however, you must already know the kind of statements you need to create an interaction.

Previous versions of Flash tried to provide scripting assistance with Behaviors, which create the underlying code for a task you want to accomplish, such as linking to a Web site. The code created by Behaviors is incompatible with ActionScript 3.0. Hence the Behaviors panel is disabled when you choose ActionScript 3.0 as the scripting language for your document.

The best way to create interactivity in Flash is to write the necessary scripts on your own. As scary as this proposition may seem to those who have never scripted before, it is actually less work than learning how to use the tools that Flash provides to help you write code. The exercises in this book create scripts that carry out simple tasks in Flash, such as setting up buttons that start and stop playback of a movie. These techniques are inappropriate for developing an online store or a complex e-learning course. But they may be all you need to let your end users start, stop, and replay an animated cartoon; select a favorite scene to view; or link to a Web page. And with any luck, they'll whet your appetite for learning more about ActionScript.

The Actions Toolbox contains most of the words (actions) that make up the ActionScript language. These pieces of code appear in hierarchical lists; click one of the folder-like icons to view the contents of a category. Double-click an action to add it to the Script pane. You can also drag items from the Actions Toolbox to the Script pane. (The list of ActionScript actions also appears in the Add menu.)

The Script Navigator helps you locate and maneuver through the scripts in your movie. This feature is most useful when you've used a large number of frame scripts in keyframes throughout the Timeline. **Figure 15.1** shows the elements of the Actions panel.

Figure 15.1 The Actions panel has three main areas: the Actions Toolbox, where you can choose actions; the Script Navigator, where Flash displays the elements in your movie that have scripts attached; and the Script pane, where Flash assembles the ActionScript.

Customizing the Actions Panel

You can modify the way the Actions panel displays to suit your taste or convenience. For example, you can resize the panel and its panes or collapse panes completely. You can customize the way scripts appear by choosing settings for font and size; highlighting script elements in different colors; and controlling the number of spaces Flash uses to indent with each tab you type. You can also turn code hints on or off.

To set preferences for the Actions panel:

1. Choose Flash > Preferences (Mac) or Edit Preferences (Windows).

   or

   From the panel menu in the top-right corner of the Actions panel, choose Preferences.

   The Preferences dialog appears.

2. In the Category list, choose ActionScript.

   The settings for working with statements in the Script pane of the Actions panel appear in the main window of the Preferences dialog (**Figure 15.2**).

3. To get scripting help from code hints, in the Editing section, select the Code Hints check box (**Figure 15.3**).

   Move the Delay slider to set the amount of time Flash waits before displaying the hint as you type directly in the Script pane.

Figure 15.2 In the Preferences dialog, choose the ActionScript category to access settings for customizing the way Flash displays your scripts.

Figure 15.3 To have Flash display code hints, select the Code Hints check box. To make hints appear more quickly, drag the Delay slider farther to the left.

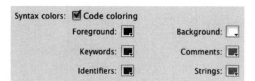

Figure 15.4 Activate syntax coloring by selecting the Code Coloring check box in the Syntax Colors section of the Preferences dialog's ActionScript category. Change the colors to make more of a distinction between scripting "words," to get a feel for ActionScript's parts of speech.

✔ Tips

- Flash's default settings for keywords and identifiers are similar shades of blue. Try setting them to wildly different colors— say, pink and orange. This technique will help you learn to recognize these different parts of ActionScript speech as they're used in the scripts you create.

- Code hints work like tool tips within the Actions panel when Script Assist isn't active. With code hints turned on, you can make the Actions panel display certain types of scripting information in a tool-tip–type box or drop-down menu. Position the insertion point to the right of a dot (a period character) or an opening parenthesis in the Script pane, and then click the Show Code Hints button. If you enable code hints in the ActionScript Preferences, the hints appear automatically when you type a period, a colon, or an opening parenthesis in the right context.

4. To choose the font for writing scripts, in the Font section, do the following:
   - ▲ From the pop-up menu of installed fonts, choose a font.
   - ▲ From the pop-up menu of sizes, choose a font size.

   The Actions panel can display scripts in text as small as 8 points and as large as 72 points.

5. To color-code script items, in the Syntax Colors section, select the Code Coloring check box (**Figure 15.4**).

   Using a color control to access a pop-up set of swatches, choose a new color for any of the following:

   Foreground. The basic text color for your scripts.

   Keywords. Words reserved for special purposes in ActionScript.

   Identifiers. The names of things—such as objects, variables, and functions—that are built into ActionScript.

   Background. The color against which your script displays in the Script pane.

   Comments. Text that Flash ignores when it reads the script, used to make notes about what's going on in the script.

   Strings. Series of characters (letters, numbers, and punctuation marks) that are enclosed within quotation marks.

6. Click OK.

   Flash applies your preferences settings immediately.

What Is Interactivity?

By default, a published Flash file plays through its scenes and frames sequentially. The movie opens with scene 1, plays all those frames in order, moves to scene 2, plays those frames, and so on. Sometimes that's appropriate; sometimes it's not.

Imagine an online training course where you want the same five frames of general instructions to appear before each section of the course. You can make those frames a separate scene and then duplicate the scene so it appears repeatedly between other scenes containing the training sections. But duplicating scenes increases file size, slows the performance of your published course, and makes it harder to edit later. A more efficient method is to create one scene containing the instructions and direct Flash to repeat that scene when each training section ends. Also, you may want the users taking your course to interact with the content: clicking buttons, dragging elements, or entering text to answer quiz questions, for example. And you may want the course to interact with the user, summarizing the quiz score. These are examples of interactivity in Flash.

To achieve this type of interactivity, you must create a script that directs the playback of your published Flash content, using ActionScript.

Two Styles of Scripting

ActionScript 3.0 lets you work in two scripting styles: you can create scripts that rely on *frame actions* and scripts that rely on *custom classes*. Each style stores the ActionScript code differently. For the tasks in this book, you'll create frame-action scripts, where code is attached to keyframes and stored in the FLA file. Scripts that rely on custom classes require that you create the code in external AS files.

You create frame actions by selecting a keyframe, then opening the Actions panel and entering the script. In the exported movie, when the playhead reaches the keyframe that contains the script, Flash carries out the script's instructions. These instructions might be to control the Timeline directly (for example, pausing playback of the movie), to set up interactivity for buttons (for example, telling Flash what to do when someone clicks a particular button), or to change the properties of objects located in that keyframe (for example, to move a symbol instance across the Stage).

Scripting with custom classes is similar to using symbols in the library. Creating or even editing classes is beyond the scope of this book. Yet by doing the tasks in earlier chapters, you have already interacted with some of Flash's built-in classes, such as `SimpleButton` and `MovieClip`. Advanced scripters can create and edit custom classes using the ActionScript editor or an external text editor.

Figure 15.5 Keyframes that contain actions display the letter *a* in the Timeline.

Figure 15.6 When you assign actions to many layers (top), it's harder to find them, and you may accidentally assign actions to the same frame number on different layers. Adding a separate layer for actions (bottom) makes it easy to find them all and to see whether a certain frame contains an action.

■ It's useful to create separate layers for labels and sounds as well as for actions. Keeping these three types of layers together at the top of the Timeline makes it easy to find the nongraphical information they contain.

Organizing Frame Actions

A little letter *a* in the Timeline indicates a keyframe that has actions attached (**Figure 15.5**). Can you imagine scrolling through dozens—or hundreds—of layers, looking for the letter *a* when you want to edit the actions in your document? That's a recipe for eyestrain. And more than that, it's a recipe for disaster if you need (or someone else needs) to change the ActionScript later; it's difficult to remember (or guess) where the frame actions are lurking. It's a good idea to put all your frame actions in their own layer.

Restricting frame actions to their own layer also prevents you from accidentally putting actions in keyframes in two different layers for the same frame number, which can cause problems if you reorder the layers.

To create a separate layer for frame actions:

1. Open a Flash document.

2. In the Timeline, add a new layer.

    (For detailed instructions on adding layers, see Chapter 6.)

3. Rename the layer Actions.

4. Drag the layer to the top of the Timeline.

    Keeping the Actions layer near the top of the Timeline makes it easier to find actions when you need to modify or add to them (**Figure 15.6**).

✔ Tips

■ To prevent yourself from adding graphic elements to the Actions layer accidentally, lock it (by clicking the bullet in the padlock column). Locking keeps you from making changes in the elements on the Stage for that layer, but it doesn't prevent you from adding actions to keyframes.

Adding Frame Actions

Some of the most basic scripting tasks involve controlling movie playback: making your movie stop and start and jump from place to place. By default, a movie begins running at playback; you can change that in the Publish Settings (see Chapter 18), but you can also do it with actions.

To make your first script in Flash, set up a multiframe document that has identifying text in each frame. Then add a `stop` action to keyframe 1, to make the movie pause on the first frame at playback. Save this file as a template for use in other scripting tasks.

To set up a document for testing frame actions:

1. Create a Flash document with two layers: Actions and Frames.

2. In the Actions layer, add in-between frames in frames 2–5; there is a keyframe in the first frame by default.

3. In the Frames layer, create keyframes in frames 2–5; there is a keyframe in the first frame by default.

4. On the Stage, for each keyframe, add text that identifies the frame number (Frame 1, Frame 2, and so on).

   Your document should look like **Figure 15.7**.

To begin scripting by adding comments:

1. Continuing with the document you created in the preceding task, in the Actions layer, select keyframe 1.

2. Access the Actions panel. (If the panel isn't open, choose Window > Actions.)

   The name Actions-Frame appears in the title bar of the Actions panel.

Figure 15.7 To test frame actions—actions that instruct Flash to move to a specific frame or to start and stop playback—it's useful to have a document that identifies each frame. That way, you can see the results of your scripts easily.

Figure 15.8 Open the panel menu in the Actions panel to make sure that line numbering and word wrap are active (if not, select them to activate them). Visible line numbers make it easier to keep your place while scripting; word wrap makes it easier to view scripts, as it forces them to stay within the visible Script pane area.

Figure 15.9 The toolbar of the Actions panel contains a number of tools for working with scripts, including Script Assist. Deselect the Script Assist button to close the Script Assist window so that you can type directly in the Script pane.

3. From the panel menu, in the upper-right corner of the Actions-Frame panel, make sure Line Numbers has a check mark indicating it's active (the default setting) (**Figure 15.8**). If Line Numbers is inactive, select it.

Visible line numbers make it easier to keep your place as you script.

4. From the panel menu, make sure Word Wrap has a check mark indicating it's active. If Word Wrap is inactive, select it.

Word Wrap forces the lines of your script to break to fit within the Script pane. Such line breaks aren't meaningful in the script itself; the ActionScript syntax tells Flash where the meaningful divisions in script text occur (see the sidebar "The Mystery of ActionScript Syntax," later in this chapter).

5. In the toolbar above the Script pane of the Actions-Frame panel, make sure that Script Assist is inactive (**Figure 15.9**). If necessary, click the Script Assist button to close the Script Assist window.

6. In the toolbar, click the Apply Line Comment button.

Flash adds two slashes (//) to line 1 of the Script pane. The blinking I-beam cursor appears at the end of the line.

continues on next page

ADDING FRAME ACTIONS

7. Type Pause the movie on frame 1 (**Figure 15.10**).

Your comment is added to the Script pane. With word wrap turned on, Flash wraps your text to fit in the Script pane; in the real script, the comment is just one line.

To set the movie to pause at playback:

1. Continuing with the document you created in the preceding task, position the cursor at the end of line 1 (your comment line), and press Enter.

Flash creates line 2 in the Script pane.

2. To add an action that pauses the Timeline, type stop();

The new action appears in line 2 in the Script pane; the word *stop* is highlighted in blue (**Figure 15.11**).

3. Save the document as a template for future use; name it FrameActionsMaster.

(For detailed instructions about saving documents as templates, see Chapter 1.)

4. Close the document.

Figure 15.10 The two slashes indicate the beginning of a comment. When you add a comment using the Insert Line Comment button, Flash adds slashes to the script automatically.

Figure 15.11 The stop(); action in line 2 sets the movie to be paused at runtime.

ADDING FRAME ACTIONS

About Comment Lines

The double slash is known as a *comment delimiter;* the delimiter sets the boundaries of a comment within a script. Flash ignores any text between the two slashes and the next paragraph return for the purposes of scripting. When compiling the script for playback, Flash leaves that text out of the final file, so your comments do not increase the SWF file size. It's a good idea to write notes about your script to remind yourself what you intend the script to do. Comments also help anyone who needs to modify your script later.

For long comments, a *multiline delimiter* excludes everything between the opening and closing delimiters from the script. Click the Apply Block Comment button in the toolbar above the Script pane to add a multiline comment to your script. A multiline comment begins with a slash followed by an asterisk (/*) and ends with an asterisk followed by a slash (*/).

When you're testing long scripts or trying different ways to achieve your scripting task, it can be useful to temporarily remove part of the script to see what happens. Comment delimiters let you do this quickly without deleting any code. If you want to block out a large section of the script temporarily, use the /* and */ delimiters.

The Mystery of ActionScript Syntax

ActionScript has its own rules, which are analogous to the rules of grammar and spelling in English. These rules, called *syntax*, govern such things as word order, capitalization, and punctuation of action statements. The following list briefly describes six crucial ActionScript punctuation marks that you'll use in writing scripts.

Dot (.). ActionScript uses *dot syntax*, meaning that periods act as links between objects and the *properties* (characteristics) and *methods* (behaviors) applied to them. In the statement

```
myClip.nextFrame();
```

the *dot* (the period) links the object (a movie-clip named `myClip`) with the method (`next-Frame`) that moves the playhead to the next frame in the Timeline. ActionScript also uses the dot in target paths (see the sidebar "The Mystery of Target Paths," later in this chapter).

Semicolon (;). A semicolon indicates the end of a statement. The semicolon isn't required—Flash interprets the end of the line of statements correctly without it—but including it is good scripting practice. The semicolon also acts as a required separator in some action statements.

Colon (:). When you first set up a variable (a container for content that changes), a colon separates the text that is the name of a variable from the text that defines what type of variable it is.

```
var myName:String;
```

A colon also separates the name of a method from its type.

Braces ({}). Braces set off ActionScript statements that belong together. For example, a set of actions that are supposed to take place after `function greeting()` must be set off by braces. Note that the action statements within braces can require their own beginning and ending braces. The opening and closing braces must pair up evenly. Pay close attention to where you're adding statements and braces within the Script pane to ensure that you group the actions as you intend.

Parentheses (()). Parentheses group the arguments that apply to a particular statement—defining the scene and frame in a `goto` action, for example. Parentheses also let you group operations, such as mathematical calculations, so that they take place in the right order.

Brackets ([]). Scripting frequently involves working with *arrays*, lists of similar elements. Placing a list inside brackets defines it as an array.

Programming Buttons with Frame Scripts

As you learned in the previous chapter, Flash's button symbols and button components have certain actions built in. By default, when you move the mouse into the button area, Flash jumps to the Over frame; when you click the button, Flash takes you to the Down frame. To make the button carry out a task or to refine the way a button responds to a user's mouse movements, you attach ActionScript to a keyframe and target an instance of a button symbol or button component.

To add a button to be controlled by a frame script:

1. Using the FrameActionsMaster template you created earlier in this chapter, open a new document (for details on opening new documents from templates, see Chapter 1).

2. In the Timeline, add a new layer anywhere below the Actions layer; name the new layer Buttons.

   Frame 1 of the new layer is a keyframe; frames 2–5 are in-between frames. Any items you place on this layer will be visible throughout the five-frame movie (**Figure 15.12**).

3. With the Buttons layer selected, place an instance of a button symbol on the Stage (**Figure 15.13**).

   Follow the techniques in Chapter 14 to create a new button symbol, or use one from the Common Library of buttons. (To access this library, choose Window > Common Libraries > Buttons.) Drag a button-symbol instance from the library to the Stage.

Figure 15.12 To practice with button actions, create a movie with identifying text and separate layers for buttons and actions. Add in-between frames as needed so that all the layers are the same length.

Figure 15.13 In-between frames extend the Buttons layer to the match the length of the other layers; the button symbol in keyframe 1 will be visible throughout the movie, although the identifying text from the Frames layer will change.

Figure 15.14 Select the button symbol on the Stage, and enter a name in the Instance Name field in the Property inspector.

4. To name the button instance, access the Property inspector and type a name in the Instance name field—for example, `enterBtn` (**Figure 15.14**).

For ActionScript to control a symbol, the symbol must have a unique instance name.

5. Save your file (for example, by choosing File > Save).

The Mechanics of Code Hints

How do code hints work? As you type text in the Script pane of the Actions panel, Flash tries to guess what you're about to script and help you out. Let's look at an example:

In line 1 of your script you enter the comment

`// SimpleButton startLesson;`

In subsequent lines of the script, whenever you type that instance name (`startLesson`) followed by a period (.), a code-hint window opens listing the actions and properties available for button symbols (**Figure 15.15**).

You can use the window's scroll bars (or the up- and down-arrow keys on your keyboard) to navigate the list of actions and properties. Select the item you want and press Enter to add it to your script. Or you can continue typing to have Flash autocomplete your code: the code-hint window narrows in on an action or property according to the letters you type. When the action or property you want is highlighted, press Enter. Flash autocompletes that piece of code in your script. You can override autocompleting by continuing to type manually in the Script pane, but autocompleting helps you avoid typos and speeds the coding process.

continues on next page

Figure 15.15 When your script contains a comment line associating an instance name with a type of object (here, line 1), a code-hint window opens whenever you type a period (.) following that instance name in the Script pane (top). As you continue typing characters, the code-hint window attempts to autocomplete your code (bottom).

✔ Tip

- Scripting is a complex process, often involving trial and error. As you create scripts, you may wish you could go back to a point where you know everything works. The Save As command makes that easier. Once you've set up your objects on the Stage and you're ready to add code, choose File > Save As. Each time you complete a segment of code that works the way you want, choose Save As again. Add a number, a letter, or an abbreviated description to the filename to make it easy to identify which version contains which completed work.

The Mechanics of Code Hints *continued*

When you use code hints to automate entry of an action that requires a parameter, Flash automatically adds an open parenthesis to your script and brings up another type of code hint, a *parameter hint* (**Figure 15.16**). (If you override autocompleting, the parameter hint appears after you type an opening parenthesis in the Script pane.) The parameter hint, which acts something like a tool tip, displays all possible parameters for the action you just entered. Parameter hints don't autocomplete code in the Script pane, but they can help you remember which parameters you need. Sometimes the same action is available for different objects; for example, Buttons and MovieClips have addEventListener. In that case, you can use the Previous and Next arrows on the left side of the window to scroll through the parameter hints until they match the object you script. Parameter hints also help you see which category folder in the Actions Toolbox contains the code you're looking for; each parameter hint begins with the path to the category folder containing the action you entered.

If you close a code-hint window by accident, or you later want to change your selection, you can open the window by placing your cursor to the right of a period or open parenthesis and clicking the Code Hint button in the toolbar above the Script pane. You can also use the keyboard shortcut Option-spacebar (Mac) or Ctrl-spacebar (Windows).

Figure 15.16 The parameter hint appears after you type an open parenthesis (or after you use code hints to automate adding an action or property that takes a parameter). If there are multiple parameter possibilities, use the Previous and Next buttons to scroll the list.

Figure 15.17 A code-hint comment needs a separate line in the Script pane. Position the cursor at the very end of line 2, press Enter, and Flash moves the cursor to line 3, where you can start entering the comment code.

Script 15.1 Defining a code-hint comment.

```
1  //Pause the movie on frame 1
2  stop();
3  // code-hint comments
4  // SimpleButton enterBtn;
```

Wide Scripts—Narrow Columns

A single line of ActionScript can be quite long. You can resize the Script pane of Flash's Actions panel so that a lot of code fits on one line, but we can't resize the columns in this book. That means for longer lines of code, the text has to wrap. In the Script figures, such as Script 15.2, the line numbers make it clear where you should type a return to begin a new line. In the numbered steps of a task, we'll use a small right arrow to indicate code that runs over to a new line simply because the column is too narrow. You would enter the following code, for example, as a single line of script, pressing the Return key only after the word *void*.

```
function handleClick
→ ( pEvent:MouseEvent ):void
```

To control a button using a frame script:

1. Continuing with the file that you created in the preceding task, make sure that the Actions panel is open and that code hints are enabled in Preferences (see the section "Customizing the Actions Panel," earlier in this chapter).

2. In the Actions layer, select keyframe 1.

   The Script pane of the Actions panel displays the code you already created; line 1 displays a comment; line 2 displays the stop(); action.

3. To add a code-hint comment, do the following:

   ▲ To start a new line, place the cursor at the end of line 2—after the stop(); action—and press Enter. Flash adds line 3 to the Script pane (**Figure 15.17**).

   ▲ In lines 3 and 4 type

   ```
   // code-hint comments
   // SimpleButton enterBtn;
   ```

   If you named the button instance something other than enterBtn, type that name instead. (**Script 15.1**).

4. To create the event-handler function, do the following:

   ▲ With the cursor at the end of line 4, press Enter to create a new line.

   ▲ In lines 5–8 type

   ```
   // event handlers
   function handleClick(
   → pEvent:MouseEvent ):void
   {
   }
   ```

   continues on next page

After you type the colon (:), a code-hint window opens. When the code you're entering highlights, press Enter to complete the word, or keep typing to complete it manually. The code inside the parentheses, called a *parameter*, provides information about where the event comes from (pEvent) and what kind of event it is (MouseEvent); a colon separates these two pieces of information (**Script 15.2**). (To learn more about the construction of functions, see "The Mystery of Functions," later in this chapter).

5. To make sure the event is triggered by enterBtn:

▲ Position the pointer at the end of line 7 (after the opening brace), and press Enter to create a new line 8.

Flash indents line 8 in the Script pane to visually remind you that this code is inside the braces and is part of the function.

▲ In lines 8–10 type

```
if( pEvent.target == enterBtn )
{
}
```

After you type the opening parenthesis, a code-hint window opens; just keep typing. You have just created what's known as a *conditional statement* (see the sidebar "The Mystery of the If Statement," later in this chapter). Flash executes the code within the braces only if the specified condition is met. In this case you are checking whether the event's target matches the button instance you want to control with your script (enterBtn) (**Script 15.3**).

Script 15.2 Defining the event handler.

```
3   // code-hint comments
4   // SimpleButton enterBtn;
5   // event handlers
6   function handleClick( pEvent:MouseEvent
    ):void
7   {
8   }
```

Script 15.3 Making sure the event was triggered by enterBtn.

```
6   function handleClick( pEvent:MouseEvent
    ):void
7   {
8     if( pEvent.target == enterBtn )
9     {
10    }
11  }
```

Script 15.4 The completed event handler.

```
1  //Pause the movie on frame 1
2  stop();
3  // code-hint comments
4  // SimpleButton enterBtn;
5  // event handlers
6  function handleClick( pEvent:MouseEvent
   ):void
7  {
8    if( pEvent.target == enterBtn )
9    {
10       // handle the event
11       nextFrame();
12   }
13 }
```

Figure 15.18 As you enter code in the Script pane, the code-hint window offers possible code items you might want. When the item you want appears highlighted, press Enter, and it gets added to the Script pane.

6. Position the pointer at the end of line 9 (after the opening brace), press Enter to create a new line, and then in lines 10 and 11 type

`// handle the event`

`nextFrame();`

Flash uses double indents in lines 10 and 11 to visually remind you that this code is inside the braces and is part of the `if` statement.

The `nextFrame();` action will advance the playhead by one frame (**Script 15.4**).

7. To start registering the event, do the following:

Place the cursor at the end of line 13, and press Enter to create a new line, and then in lines 14 and 15 type

`// register events`

`enterBtn.addEventListener();`

After you type the period, a code-hint window opens showing a list of action statements (**Figure 15.18**). As you type more characters, the statements in the list that start with those characters highlight; after you type *ad*, the statement `addEventListener` highlights. Press Enter (or double-click the statement) as soon as the desired statement highlights. Flash adds `addEventListener(` to the script and opens another code-hint window. Ignore the second window and type `);` to complete the statement.

continues on next page

8. To finish registering the event, do the following:

▲ In line 15, position the cursor within the parenthesis.

▲ Then type

```
MouseEvent.CLICK, handleClick
```

The code `MouseEvent.CLICK` tells Flash which of the possible button events you want your event handler to listen for (see the sidebar "Anatomy of a MouseEvent").

The code `handleClick` points to the event-handler function you created in the preceding steps; it must match what you typed after the keyword function in line 6.

You just programmed your first button event. The completed script should look like **Script 15.5.** It's time to see your work in action.

9. Select Control > Test Movie.

Flash publishes the movie and opens the SWF file in Flash Player. You see the text *Frame 1* and a button. Click the button, and the text *Frame 2* appears. Flash has moved the playhead to frame 2 in response to your clicking the button, just as you requested via ActionScript. Each click of the button moves the playhead forward one frame until the playhead reaches frame 5.

10. Save your document as a template for use throughout this chapter, and name it ButtonActionsMaster.

(For detailed instructions about saving documents as templates, see Chapter 1.)

11. Close the document.

Script 15.5 The completed frame script for controlling a button (this script becomes part of the ButtonActionsMaster template).

```
1  //Pause the movie on frame 1
2  stop();
3  // code-hint comments
4  // SimpleButton enterBtn;
5  // event handlers
6  function handleClick( pEvent:MouseEvent
   ):void
7  {
8    if( pEvent.target == enterBtn )
9    {
10     // handle the event
11     nextFrame();
12   }
13 }
14 // register events
15 enterBtn.addEventListener( MouseEvent.CLICK,
   handleClick );
```

Anatomy of a MouseEvent

There are several ways users can interact with a button in a Flash movie. They can move the mouse into and out of the active area of a button, they can click and release inside the active area, they can click inside the active area and, while still holding down the mouse button, roll outside the area, and so on. The code `MouseEvent.CLICK` describes one specific button event. The `MouseEvent` part tells Flash that the event to watch for is generated by an input device (like a mouse or a graphics pen); the `CLICK` part tells Flash to notice when the user presses and then releases inside the active area of a button.

✔ Tips

- If you don't get the expected result when you test the movie, close the test-movie window and access the Compiler Errors panel; if it's not open, choose Window > Compiler Errors (**Figure 15.19**). If it shows any errors, make sure the code you entered exactly matches Script 15.5, and then try again. Keep a particular eye out for periods, colons, semicolons, braces, and parentheses. For more details about testing your scripting work, see the section "Previewing Actions at Work," later in this chapter.

- The code-hint window doesn't stop you from typing, but it ensures that the actions you enter are spelled correctly. When the code-hint window appears, you can continue entering text by hand.

- You just created a template with a script for programming buttons. You can use this script over and over again, modifying it to meet different situations as needed.

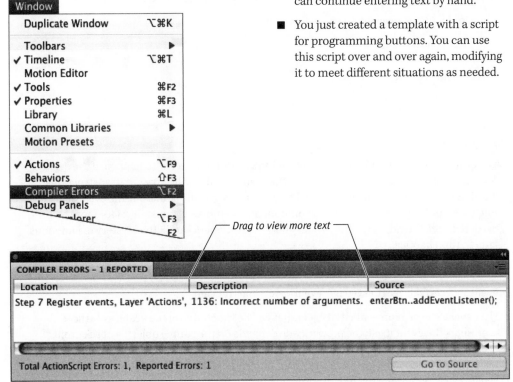

Figure 15.19 In document-editing mode, choose Window > Compiler Errors to open the Compiler Errors panel. The panel alerts you to problems in your script. Although the panel is resizable, the text within each column doesn't wrap; you may need to resize the columns to see the full error message.

PROGRAMMING BUTTONS WITH FRAME SCRIPTS

The Mystery of Event Handlers

In ActionScript as in English, the term *event* refers to something that happens, such as a user clicking a button. An *event handler* is a specific type of action statement, called a *function*, that describes what should happen in your Flash creation when a specific event occurs.

Events can be generated by humans or by the internal workings of your Flash creations. This chapter focuses on *user interactions*, events generated by people viewing and using your Flash content. (Some common user events are clicking a button, entering text, or clicking a check box.) Events not generated by users also affect the way a Flash movie runs, and you can write scripts that respond to such events. (Some common nonuser events are a movie finishing loading onto the user's computer or the playhead advancing to the next frame.)

Scripting for Interactivity

To make your Flash creation respond to a specific user interaction (event), you must create a script that does two things: *register to receive the event* created by that interaction and *handle the event*. Handling an event means creating a routine for Flash to use only after the event takes place—the *event handler*. Registering an event means writing a script that connects the object that triggers the event (for example, a button) with the event handler.

Code for handling an event takes the following format:

```
function handleEvent( event )
{
  if( event.target == eventSource )
  {
    // handle event...
  }
}
```

The event-handler function named handleEvent waits for an event to happen. If the event is triggered by the specified eventSource, the event handler will carry out its instructions. handleEvent represents the name you'll create for this specific situation. The eventSource might be a button instance, a button component, or a movie-clip instance (for more technical details, see the sidebars "The Mystery of the If Statement" and "The Mystery of Functions," later in this chapter).

Code for registering for an event takes the following format:

```
eventSource.addEventListener( eventName, handleEvent );
```

Here eventSource represents the object that will be the source of the event. eventName represents the event itself; the precise code depends on the source object; a click event, for example, can be generated by a button instance. (The code eventName represents actions for the objects you'll work with in this chapter and are built into ActionScript 3.0.) Finally, handleEvent represents the function you created for handling the event.

The Mystery of Instance Names and Code Hints

The name of an *instance* of an object on the Stage is an identifier that may wind up as part of a script. To prevent scripting problems, make sure instance names contain no spaces or characters that have special meaning in ActionScript—for example, avoid slashes or the equals sign. To be safe, use only letters, numbers, and underscore characters. Ideally, instance names should start with a lowercase letter.

When you name instances of button symbols, movie-clip symbols, and text fields, you can give Flash extra information about the object being named. Flash uses that information to assist you—giving you *code hints* as you type in the Actions panel.

There are two ways to activate the code-hint feature for specific objects. One is to name instances with an identifying suffix. To name button instances to take advantage of code hints, use the suffix _btn; for movie clips use _mc; and for text fields use _txt.

The other way is to add a comment line that creates a connection between an *identifier* (a script element that describes the type of object) and the instance name you've created for that object on the Stage. To add a comment line that identifies the instance, in the Script pane, insert two slashes, then the identifier for the type of object, then the instance name you've created for the object. For example, the comment lines

```
// SimpleButton startLesson;
// MovieClip circle;
// TextField message;
```

identify a button instance named startLesson, a movie-clip instance named circle, and a text field named message.

The tasks in this chapter use the comment-line method, as it is the preferred convention in AS 3.0.

The Mystery of the If Statement

Often when you create Flash content, you want one thing to happen under certain conditions, and something else to happen if those conditions aren't met. Your script needs to take different paths depending on the state of affairs.

One way to accomplish this is by using the *if statement*, which takes this format:

```
if( condition )
{
  action();
}
```

Here's a real-world example:

```
if( numLives == 0 )
{
  gotoAndStop( "gameOver" );
}
```

An if statement consists of the keyword if, followed by an opening parenthesis, then a condition that is either true or false, a closing parenthesis, and then a list of statements between braces. These statements execute only if the condition is true.

A condition could be a comparison. You might, for example, compare two items to see if they are equal or if the first is greater than the second. To script a comparison, you use an *operator* (a symbol or symbols) that describes the comparison. In ActionScript, the operator used to check for equality consists of two equal signs (==). ActionScript uses a single equals sign (=) to assign a value (for example, to say a rectangle's width is 1 inch), never to compare.

The most common, and important, comparison operators are as follows:

> greater than

>= greater than or equal to

< less than

<= less than or equal to

!= not equal to

When you check for a condition, you may want to run one block of code when the condition is met, and a different block of code when it's not. You could write two separate if statements or use an if-else statement. If-else statements take the format

```
if( condition )
{
  // code
}
else
{
  // other code
}
```

Finally, it is also possible to link up multiple conditions in an if-else-if-else statement using the following format:

```
if( foodInFridge )
{
  // eat at home
}
else if( haveMoney )
{
  // go out
}
else
{
  // call a friend
}
```

The Mystery of Functions

A *function* groups a number of actions together under a single name. When the function name appears in a script, Flash executes that group of actions. The basic format looks like this:

```
function functionName():Type
{
  // function code
}
```

The code block always starts with the *keyword* `function`. Next comes the function's name, represented here by `functionName`. (You get to create your function name; make it descriptive.) Immediately following the function's name is a pair of parentheses.

Next comes a colon (`:`), which separates the function's name from its *type*. In this example, the code for type is represented by `Type`. The type defines what kind of result the function will have. To understand the purpose of type, imagine a restaurant-tip calculator; it needs to come up with numbers in the result (as opposed to letters, for example). A tip-calculator function would have `Number` as the type. The most common type for functions, however, is `void`, meaning "there is no result." Actions that control Timeline playback, for example, have `void` as the type.

The braces (`{}`) enclose code that describes what the function actually does. Flash carries out the instructions within those braces only when certain conditions are met; in our example, this is when a user clicks the calculate-tip button.

Quite often, a function needs more information to operate; parameters convey that information. The tip-calculator function needs to know the cost of the meal. When you set up a function that requires parameters, the format changes slightly:

```
function functionName( param:Type, nextParam:Type ):Type
{
  // code
}
```

When a function has multiple parameters, the parameter names still go between the parentheses after the function name, but you must separate the names with commas.

Each parameter also has a type, just as the function has one.

Previewing Actions at Work

To see your scripts in action, you need to view the movie in Flash Player. You can do this by publishing the movie (see Chapter 18) or by using one of the test modes. *Test mode* is an abbreviated form of publishing a movie while still working in the authoring environment. To preview and test your scripts safely, follow a three-step procedure: (1) save your work; (2) check the script's syntax; and (3) test the movie.

To check the script's syntax:

1. With the document containing your script open, select the keyframe with the script you want to check, to view it in the Script pane of the Actions panel.

2. In the toolbar above the Script pane, click the Check Syntax button (the check mark icon), or press ⌘-T (Mac) or Ctrl-T (Windows) (**Figure 15.20**).

   Flash runs its compiler (see the sidebar "What Is a Compiler?" to check the selected code for errors of syntax (see the sidebar "The Mystery of ActionScript Syntax," earlier in this chapter). Flash displays a syntax-check-results dialog, with an OK button. If there are errors, Flash also opens the Compiler Errors panel.

Check Syntax button

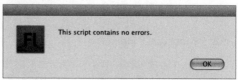

Figure 15.20 Click the Check Syntax button in the Actions panel to have Flash help you find syntax errors in your code. A dialog appears to let you know whether the script contains errors or not.

What Is a Compiler?

ActionScript is a computer language that lets scripters write instructions for the Flash Player to execute. Although it takes time to learn the language, humans can read it. A computer's CPU, however, works only with 0's and 1's; it can't read ActionScript directly. A *compiler* translates code written in a computer language into instructions that the processing unit can read. In the case of Flash, ActionScript is translated into compact byte-code that Flash Player understands.

Basic Interactivity

Figure 15.21 When the syntax check finds errors, a dialog informs you, and the Compiler Errors panel opens showing details about the errors in your script. Select the error in the panel and click the Go to Source button to go directly to the error in the Script pane of the Actions panel.

3. If the selected code contains no errors, click OK to close the syntax-check-results dialog.

or

If the selected code contains errors, click OK to close the syntax-check-results dialog, and do any of the following:

▲ Visually review the code in the Script pane and correct the errors you find.

▲ In the Compiler Errors panel, select the error and click the Go to Source button (**Figure 15.21**). Flash opens the Actions panel and highlights the line where the error occurred. Correct the error and repeat step 2.

Flash generally refuses to run scripts with errors; you need to correct them before you move on.

✔ Tips

■ Common scripting errors include missing, misplaced, or doubled commas, colons, parentheses, braces, and semicolons. Paired items, such as parentheses and braces, must have equal numbers of opening and closing elements, and they must be nested correctly (see the sidebar "The Mystery of ActionScript Syntax," earlier in this chapter).

■ A script that produces no errors doesn't necessarily do what you want it to do. The syntax check determines if your script follows the rules, but the compiler doesn't check the logic, and doesn't know what you intended the script to do.

To test scripts:

◆ Choose Control > Test Movie (or Control > Test Scene) (**Figure 15.22**).

Flash exports the movie (or scene) to a Flash Player file, adding the .swf extension (or the scene name plus the .swf extension) to the filename and using the current Publish settings. (For more information on Publish Settings, see Chapter 18.) During export, Flash displays the Exporting SWF Movie dialog, which contains a progress bar and a button for canceling the operation.

When it finishes exporting the movie, Flash opens the SWF file in Flash Player so you see the movie in action. The buttons and movie clips in the test window are all live, so you can see how they interact with the viewer's mouse actions. Any scripts you've created will run.

When you finish testing, exit the Player by clicking the movie window's close button (Mac) or close box (Windows). Flash returns you to the document-editing environment.

✔ Tips

■ Sometimes even when a script comes through the syntax check without errors, it has errors that show up when you test the movie. Flash opens the Compiler Errors panel as soon as it encounters one of these *runtime errors*. Runtime errors may occur, for example, when you try to target an object that doesn't exist; let's say you typed enerBtn as the instance name instead of enterBtn. The script still follows the syntax rules, but fails to find the instance when it runs.

Figure 15.22 To test the full animation and interactivity of ActionScript scripts, you must export your movie—for example, by choosing Control > Test Movie.

■ When you choose Control > Test Scene, Flash appends the scene name and the .swf extension to the file, when it creates the Player file. This situation can make the filename exceed the number of allowable characters. If Test Movie worked fine with your file, but Test Scene brings up the warning dialog, try shortening the scene name.

■ To test the interactivity of a symbol—for example, a movie clip—choose Control > Test Scene while you are working on the symbol in symbol-editing mode. Flash publishes just the symbol and the items nested within that symbol.

Figure 15.23 When you select a frame that contains actions, the script for that frame appears in the Actions panel.

Script 15.6 Adding the trace action to the event handler.

```
6  function handleClick( pEvent:MouseEvent
   ):void
7  {
8    if( pEvent.target == enterBtn )
9    {
10     // handle the event
11     nextFrame();
12     trace( "Click! New frame: " +
       currentFrame );
13   }
14 }
```

Modifying and Extending Button Scripts

When it comes to scripting, the first steps are often the most difficult; subsequent steps expand on what you've already learned. Earlier, you set up a frame script that controls a button on the Stage. In this section, that script becomes a stepping stone to creating different kinds of interactivity.

To create multiple actions in an event handler:

1. Using the ButtonActionsMaster template you created in the section "Programming Buttons with Frame Scripts," earlier in this chapter, open a new document.

   ButtonActionsMaster creates a five-frame document with identifying text for each frame, and one button instance. It also contains a stop action in keyframe 1, and a script that activates the button for interactivity.

2. In the Timeline, in the Actions layer, select keyframe 1 (**Figure 15.23**).

   Flash displays the script in the Script pane of the Actions panel. If the panel is not currently visible, access it, for example, by choosing Window > Actions.

3. To have Flash print a message in the Output window, position the cursor at the end of line 11, press Enter, and in the new line 12 type

   ```
   trace( "Click! New frame: " +
   → currentFrame );
   ```

   Make sure you enter this code before the closing brace (}) in line 13. Lines 12 and 13 of your code should look like **Script 15.6**.

continues on next page

The block of code that makes up the event handler now contains two statements. The `nextFrame` statement moves the playhead to the next frame. The `trace` statement tells Flash to print a message to the Output window. (Here, Flash builds the message out of the words inside the quotes plus the number of the frame where the playhead is currently.)

4. Save the document and give it a descriptive name, such as EventHandlerMultipleActions.

5. Check the script's syntax.

   For details about trouble-shooting syntax errors, see "Previewing Actions at Work," earlier in this chapter.

6. Choose Control > Test Movie.

   Your movie opens in a Flash Player window. Each time you click the button, the words *Click! New frame:* appear in the Output panel, followed by the current frame number (**Figure 15.24**). If the Output window isn't visible, Flash opens it for you.

To send the playhead to a specific frame:

1. To use the script created in the previous task as a building block, create a new copy of the document EventHandlerMultiple-Actions by choosing File > Save As.

   Give the copy a descriptive name, such as GoToFrame.

2. In the Timeline, select keyframe 1 of the Actions layer.

   The script you created earlier appears in the Script pane of the Actions panel.

Before clicking the button

After clicking the button

Figure 15.24 When you test a movie, the Output window displays your trace messages. For this movie, clicking the button creates a trace message.

Script 15.7 Sending the playhead to a frame number.

```
 6  function handleClick( pEvent:MouseEvent
    ):void
 7  {
 8    if( pEvent.target == enterBtn )
 9    {
10      // handle the event
11      gotoAndStop( 5 );
12      trace( :Click! New frame: " +
        currentFrame );
13    }
14  }
```

Figure 15.25 A Labels layer lets you make notes about what's happening in different frames right in the Timeline. To avoid accidentally placing graphic content on the Stage in the Labels layer, lock it. You can still add keyframes and labels to a locked layer.

3. In the Script pane, in line 11, select the code

   nextFrame();

   and replace it with

   gotoAndStop(5);

   Be sure to keep the code's original indentation. Instead of moving the playhead forward one frame at a time, the gotoAndStop action tells the playhead to jump to the frame number specified in parentheses.

4. Preview the action.

   Save the file, check the syntax (line 11 of the script should match **Script 15.7**), correct any errors, then test the movie (see "Previewing Actions at Work").

   Your movie opens in a Flash Player window. When you click the button, the movie jumps to frame 5, and the message in the Output window confirms it.

To create a frame label:

1. Create a copy of the previous task's document (GoToFrame), for example by choosing File > Save As.

   Give the copy a descriptive name, such as CreateFrameLabel.

2. In the Timeline, create a new layer above the Actions layer, name it Labels, and lock it (**Figure 15.25**).

   Having the Labels layer at the top helps you organize the Timeline; you can use labels to indicate the sections of your Movie.

continues on next page

3. Select frame 3 of the Labels layer and insert a blank keyframe, for example by choosing Insert > Timeline > Blank Keyframe.

4. With the new blank keyframe selected, access the Frame Property inspector; in the Label section, in the Name field, enter myLabel (**Figure 15.26**).

To confirm the label, press Enter or click outside the field. In the Timeline a little red flag appears in keyframe 3 of the Labels layer. Flash displays as much of your label as there's room for in the key-frame span (**Figure 15.27**).

5. Position the playhead in frame 5, but don't select a frame.

6. Insert enough in-between frames (for example, by pressing F5) to make the span large enough to display the full label.

Frame labels help you organize your Timeline. They are most effective when you can read them in the Timeline, rather than having to check the Property inspector.

Figure 15.26 Enter frame-label text in the Name field of the Frame Property inspector's Label section.

Figure 15.27 Frame labels appear truncated if the keyframe span is too short to display the full text (top). To gain the full benefit of using frame labels as visual aids, expand the span by adding in-between frames (bottom).

Script 15.8 Sending the playhead to a frame label.

```
6 function handleClick( pEvent:MouseEvent
  ):void
7 {
8   if( pEvent.target == enterBtn )
9   {
10    // handle the event
11    gotoAndStop( "myLabel" );
12    trace( "Click! New frame: " +
      currentFrame );
13  }
14 }
```

To send the playhead to a frame label:

1. Continuing with the file from the preceding task, select keyframe 1 in the Actions layer, and access the Actions panel.

   Your script appears in the Script pane.

2. In the Script pane, in line 11, select the code

   gotoAndStop(5);

   and replace it with

   gotoAndStop("myLabel");

   Be sure to keep the original indentation. With the gotoAndstop action, you can have the playhead go to a frame number or to a frame label.

3. Preview the action.

   Save the file, check the syntax (line 11 of your script should match **Script 15.8**), correct any errors, then test the movie (see "Previewing Actions at Work").

   Your movie opens in a Flash Player window. When you click the button, the movie jumps to the frame that bears the label myLabel.

✔ Tip

- In the preceding task, you made the playhead move to a specific frame and stop playback. You can also make the playhead jump to a specific frame and resume playback from there. In step 2, replace line 11's gotoAndStop action with gotoAndPlay.

Targeting Frame Labels

When using a gotoAndStop or gotoAndPlay action, you can enter a frame number or a frame label. There's an advantage to using frame labels. If you ever add or remove frames from the type of movie-clip button you learned to create in Chapter 14, the frame numbers for the button states may change. If they do, you must go back into the script to update the frame numbers. If you target the frame by label, you never need to update the script to accommodate changes to frame numbers.

Choosing Events

As users interact with a button, their mouse movements trigger various events. Releasing the mouse button while still over the button's active area triggers the `click` event. Rolling over and out of a button area triggers other events. To make a button react to these events, you must change your script to register for the desired event instead of `click`.

To handle an event when rolling over a button:

1. Open a new document using the ButtonActionsMaster template you created earlier in this chapter.

   Save the document using the name ButtonEvents.fla.

2. In the Actions layer, select frame 1 and access the Actions panel.

   The template's script appears in the Script pane.

3. In line 15, select the text

   `MouseEvent.CLICK`

   and replace it by typing

   `MouseEvent.ROLL_OVER`

4. Preview the action.

   Save the file, check the syntax (lines 14 and 15 of your code should match **Script 15.9**), correct any errors, then test the movie (see "Previewing Actions at Work").

   Your movie opens in a Flash Player window. Each time you roll over the button (move the pointer into the button's active area), the playhead moves one frame forward. Nothing happens when you click, other than the button showing the Down frame.

Script 15.9 Switching from a click event to a rollover event.

```
14  // register events
15  enterBtn.addEventListener(
      MouseEvent.ROLL_OVER, handleClick );
```

Script 15.10 Registering for the rollout event.

```
14  // register events
15  enterBtn.addEventListener(
      MouseEvent.ROLL_OUT, handleClick );
```

✔ Tips

■ A faster way to replace the event is to delete the code `.CLICK` and retype the period to trigger the code-hint window. You can then select `ROLL_OVER` from the list and press Enter. You could also just delete `CLICK`, position the cursor after the period, and press the Code Hint button in the toolbar above the Script pane.

■ In the preceding task, the event handler is still called `handleClick`. It would be more meaningful to rename it `handleRollOver`; just make sure you change it in both lines 6 and 15.

■ If you want the script to react when rolling out of the button instead of over, in line 15, select the text `MouseEvent.ROLL_OVER`, and replace it by typing `MouseEvent.ROLL_OUT` (**Script 15.10**).

Script 15.11 Adding the second event handler.

```
11      nextFrame();
12   }
13 }
14 function handleRollOver( pEvent:MouseEvent
   ):void
15 {
16   if( pEvent.target == enterBtn )
17   {
18     // handle the event
19     gotoAndStop( 2 );
20   }
21 }
22 // register events
```

To receive multiple events for a button:

1. Open a new document using the ButtonActionsMaster template you created earlier in this chapter.

   Save the document using the name ButtonMultiEvents.fla.

2. In the Timeline, in the Actions layer, select keyframe 1 and access the Actions panel.

   The template's script appears in the Script pane.

3. To define a second event handler, do the following:

   ▲ Place the cursor at the end of line 13 (after the closing brace) and press Enter to begin a new code block (the code that was originally on lines 14 and 15 moves down).

   ▲ In lines 14–21 type

   ```
   function handleRollOver(
   → pEvent:MouseEvent ):void
   {
     if( pEvent.target == enterBtn )
     {
       // handle the event
       gotoAndStop( 2 );
     }
   }
   ```

   Lines 14–21 should match **Script 15.11**.

   continues on next page

4. To register for the rollOver event, place the cursor at the end of line 23, press Enter to create a new line (24), and type

enterBtn.addEventListener(
→ MouseEvent.ROLL_OVER,
→ handleRollOver);

To receive multiple events from one button, you need to register for each event separately. You want the script to receive both events but react differently for each one. Defining a new event-handler function is a way to accomplish that (**Script 15.12**).

5. Preview the action.

Save the file, check the syntax (the complete script for the multi-event button should match **Script 15.13**), correct any errors, then test the movie (see "Previewing Actions at Work").

Your movie opens in a Flash Player window. Whenever you roll the pointer over the button, the playhead jumps to frame 2, and when you click the button, the playhead moves to the next frame.

Script 15.12 Pay attention to the second event (rollover).

```
22  // register events
23  enterBtn.addEventListener(
    MouseEvent.CLICK, handleClick );
24  enterBtn.addEventListener(
    MouseEvent.ROLL_OVER, handleRollOver );
```

Script 15.13 The completed multi-event script.

```
1   //Pause the movie on frame 1
2   stop();
3   // code-hint comments
4   // SimpleButton enterBtn;
5   // event handlers
6   function handleClick( pEvent:MouseEvent
    ):void
7   {
8     if( pEvent.target == enterBtn )
9     {
10      // handle the event
11      nextFrame();
12    }
13  }
14  function handleRollOver( pEvent:MouseEvent
    ):void
15  {
16    if( pEvent.target == enterBtn )
17    {
18      // handle the event
19      gotoAndStop( 2 );
20    }
21  }
22  // register events
23  enterBtn.addEventListener(
    MouseEvent.CLICK, handleClick );
24  enterBtn.addEventListener(
    MouseEvent.ROLL_OVER, handleRollOver );
```

The Mystery of Mouse Events

Button symbols and movie-clip symbols are both in a group of Flash objects called *interactive objects*. Users interacting with any of the objects via an input device such as a mouse or a graphics pen can trigger the same events—known as *mouse events*. (Button components, despite having the word *button* in the name, are actually a special type of movie clip.)

All interactive objects have a whopping 19 events built in; 9 of them are mouse events. Each of them is part of Flash and has a predefined functionality. This means you can't rename them or change how they work. The following list shows the generic name of an event—for example, `click`—followed in parentheses by the ActionScript constant that refers to that event—for example, (`MouseEvent.CLICK`).

`click` (`MouseEvent.CLICK`) occurs when a user presses and then releases the mouse button while over the active area of a button or movie clip (an interactive object).

`rollOver` (`MouseEvent.ROLL_OVER`) occurs when the user moves the pointer over the active area of the interactive object. Once a user has triggered a `rollOver`, the `rollOver` event can't be triggered again until there has been a `rollOut` event.

`rollOut` (`MouseEvent.ROLL_OUT`) occurs when a user has moved the pointer into the active area of an interactive object and then moves the pointer out of the active area.

`mouseMove` (`MouseEvent.MOUSE_MOVE`) occurs whenever a user moves the pointer within the active area of an interactive object.

`doubleClick` (`MouseEvent.DOUBLE_CLICK`) occurs when a user clicks twice in rapid succession over the active area of an interactive object. This event is new to ActionScript 3.0. To use this event in your scripts, the `doubleClickEnabled` property of the button or movie clip needs to be set to `true`. (You must create a line in the script with the code `myBtn.doubleClickEnabled = true;`.)

The first three events in the list—`click`, `rollOver`, and `rollOut`—are the most common ones, and should be all you need for the vast majority of your button scripting tasks. The other two, `mouseMove` and `doubleClick`, give you a glimpse at what else is possible.

Button Components

Flash contains a selection of ready-made user interface (UI) elements. They can be found in the Components panel and include items such as RadioButton and ComboBox (for drop-down menus). Scripting the click-interactivity for button components and regular button symbols is similar.

To add a button component to your movie:

1. Open a new document using the ButtonActionsMaster template you created earlier in this chapter.

   Save the document using the name ButtonComponent.fla.

2. In the Timeline, in the Buttons layer, select keyframe 1.

3. Access the Components panel and, from the User Interface category, choose Button.

   If the panel isn't visible, choose Window > Components.

4. Drag an instance of the button component onto the Stage (**Figure 15.28**).

5. Select the button-component instance on the Stage and access the Property inspector.

6. In the Instance Name field, enter a name for the button-component instance—for example, myComponent (**Figure 15.29**).

   You are now ready to create a script that makes the component carry out a task.

✔ Tip

■ You can modify a component's appearance by editing its skin (see Chapter 14 for details).

Figure 15.28 Drag an instance of the button component from the Components panel to the Stage to add it to your movie.

Figure 15.29 To target a component with ActionScript, you must give it an instance name. Note that the Object Type menu in the Property inspector reveals that the Button component is actually a type of movie clip.

Script 15.14 Adding the code-hint comment for the button component.

```
3   // code-hint comments
4   // SimpleButton enterBtn;
5   // Button myComponent;
6   // event handlers
```

Script 15.15 The event handler for the button component.

```
12      nextFrame();
13    }
14  }
15  function handleComponent( pEvent:MouseEvent
    ):void
16  {
17    if( pEvent.target == myComponent )
18    {
19      // handle the event
20      enterBtn.visible = false;
21    }
22  }
```

To script a button component's interactivity:

1. Continuing with the file from the preceding task, select keyframe 1 in the Actions layer and access the Actions panel.

   The template's script appears in the Script pane.

2. To enable code hints for the component instance, place the cursor at the end of line 4 and press Enter to create a new line 5, then type

   ```
   // Button myComponent;
   ```

   A button component is more complex than a regular button, and enabling full code hints for components makes scripting them easier (**Script 15.14**).

3. To create the event handler for the component, do the following:
   ▲ Place the cursor at the end of line 14 (after the closing brace) and press Enter to begin a new code block.
   ▲ In lines 15–22, type
   ```
   function handleComponent(
   → pEvent:MouseEvent ):void
   {
     if( pEvent.target ==
     → myComponent )
     {
       // handle the event
       enterBtn.visible = false;
     }
   }
   ```

   The code should match **Script 15.15**. Instead of moving the playhead to a new frame, this event handler hides the enterBtn.

   continues on next page

4. With the cursor at the end of line 24 (after the semicolon), press Enter to create a new line and in line 25 type

```
myComponent.addEventListener(
→ MouseEvent.CLICK,
→ handleComponent );
```

The code should match **Script 15.16**.

5. Preview the action.

Save the file, check the syntax (the full script should match **Script 15.17**), correct any errors, then test the movie (see "Previewing Actions at Work").

Your movie opens in a Flash Player window. When you click the button component (named Label), Flash hides the button symbol (named Enter). Clicking the button symbol still advances the Timeline as you originally scripted it to do.

Script 15.16 Listening to the click event of the button component.

```
23  // register events
24  enterBtn.addEventListener(
    MouseEvent.CLICK, handleClick );
25  myComponent.addEventListener(
    MouseEvent.CLICK, handleComponent );
```

Script 15.17 Scripting a button component.

```
 1  //Pause the movie on frame 1
 2  stop();
 3  // code-hint comments
 4  // SimpleButton enterBtn;
 5  // Button myComponent;
 6  // event handlers
 7  function handleClick( pEvent:MouseEvent
    ):void
 8  {
 9    if( pEvent.target == enterBtn )
10    {
11      // handle the event
12      nextFrame();
13    }
14  }
15  function handleComponent( pEvent:MouseEvent
    ):void
16  {
17    if( pEvent.target == myComponent )
18    {
19      // handle the event
20      enterBtn.visible = false;
21    }
22  }
23  // register events
24  enterBtn.addEventListener(
    MouseEvent.CLICK, handleClick );
25  myComponent.addEventListener(
    MouseEvent.CLICK, handleComponent );
```

Selected instance —

— New instance name

Figure 15.30 To create an additional button quickly , duplicate the button instance, then modify the script. Be sure to give the duplicate a different instance name. You can later swap out the symbol with matching graphics.

Using One Event Handler for Multiple Events

Earlier in this chapter, you created individual event handlers for multiple events. Another way to deal with multiple events is to use one event handler with a parameter. With this technique, you create a script that examines the pEvent parameter that you've defined as part of the event-handler function to react differently for each button.

To add another button to be scripted:

1. Open a new document using the ButtonActionsMaster template you created earlier in this chapter.

   This document has one button instance—named enterBtn—on the Stage.
   Save the document using the name MultiEventsOneHandler.fla.

2. Select the enterBtn instance and choose Edit > Duplicate to create a new instance of the button (**Figure 15.30**).

   Position the duplicate so that it doesn't overlap the original button.

3. Access the Property inspector, and enter prevBtn in the Instance Name field.

   Now you have two buttons on the Stage that can be scripted to use the same event handler.

To script the second button:

1. Continuing with the file from the preceding task, in the Timeline, in the Actions layer, select keyframe 1 and access the Actions panel.

   continues on next page

2. To create a code-hint comment for the second button (`prevBtn`), in the Action panel's Script pane, place the cursor at the end of line 4 and press Enter to create a new line 5, then type

```
// SimpleButton prevBtn;
```

(See **Script 15.18**.)

3. Place the cursor at the end of line 13 —after the closing brace (})—and press Enter to create a new line.

Be sure to place the cursor after the correct closing brace. The brace in line 13 closes the `if` statement, while the brace in line 14 closes the function.

4. To update the event handler for two buttons, in lines 14–17, type

```
else if( pEvent.target == prevBtn )
{
    // handle the prevBtn event
    prevFrame();
}
```

This code extends the `if` statement to check for a second condition if the first condition is not met. The object of interest here is `prevBtn`. If `prevBtn` triggered the event, the script sends the playhead to the previous frame (**Script 15.19**).

5. To register for the `click` event of the `prevBtn`, place the cursor at the end of line 21, press Enter to create a new line (22), then type

```
prevBtn.addEventListener(
⇢ MouseEvent.CLICK, handleClick );
```

6. Preview the action.

Save the file, check the syntax (lines 3–22 should match **Script 15.20**, correct any errors), then test the movie (see "Previewing Actions at Work"). Your movie opens in a Flash Player window.

Clicking the `enterBtn` button advances the playhead one frame. Clicking the `prevBtn` sends the playhead back one frame.

Script 15.18 Adding the code-hint comment for the second button.

```
3  // code-hint comments
4  // SimpleButton enterBtn;
5  // SimpleButton prevBtn;
6  // event handlers
```

Script 15.19 The interaction for the second button.

```
12       nextFrame();
13     }
14     else if( pEvent.target == prevBtn )
15     {
16        // handle the prevBtn event
17        prevFrame();
18     }
19  }
```

Script 15.20 A single event handler for two buttons.

```
3  // code-hint comments
4  // SimpleButton enterBtn;
5  // SimpleButton prevBtn;
6  // event handlers
7  function handleClick( pEvent:MouseEvent
   ):void
8  {
9     if( pEvent.target == enterBtn )
10    {
11       // handle the event
12       nextFrame();
13    }
14    else if( pEvent.target == prevBtn )
15    {
16       // handle the prevBtn event
17       prevFrame();
18    }
19 }
20 // register events
21 enterBtn.addEventListener(MouseEvent.CLICK,
   handleClick );
22 prevBtn.addEventListener( MouseEvent.CLICK,
   handleClick );
```

Figure 15.31 This movie-clip symbol has keyframes for four button states: the standard three—Up, Over, and Down—plus a fourth, Disabled. Each keyframe has an appropriate frame label.

Figure 15.32 To prevent the movie-clip button from displaying its frames as an animation, you need to add a stop action to the Timeline of the button itself. Add it to frame 1 of the Actions layer.

Scripting Movie Clips to Act As Buttons

Flash's button symbols provide the most basic visual requirements for a button, giving you the options for different looks in the Up, Over, and Down states. Sometimes, however, you may need additional states. In a slide show, for example, the Next button should be disabled (and should look disabled) when you are viewing the last slide.

In Chapter 14 you learned how to set up a movie-clip symbol for use as a button that has a disabled state. In the following task you learn to program that symbol to work as a button.

To enable button behavior for the movie-clip button:

1. Open the file named MyOwnBtn.fla that you created in Chapter 14, in the section "Creating Movie-Clip Buttons."

   This document contains a movie-clip symbol called MoveClipBtn.

2. On the Stage, double-click the instance of the MovieClipBtn symbol to enter symbol-editing mode.

   The symbol's Timeline has three layers—Actions, Labels, and ButtonGraphics. The symbol has keyframes labeled _up, _over, _down, and Disabled, and graphics that make each state obvious (**Figure 15.31**).

3. In the symbol's Timeline, select keyframe 1 in the Actions layer (**Figure 15.32**).

continues on next page

4. To pause the movie-clip button, in the Script pane of the Actions panel, in line 1, type

`stop();`

By default, movie clips play at runtime. While that makes sense for animations, a button should stay in its Up state until the user interacts with it.

5. With the cursor at the end of line 1, press Enter to create a new line.

6. To activate button behavior for the movie clip, in line 2, type

`buttonMode = true;`

Until you do that, the movie clip doesn't know it's supposed to act like a button, despite the special frame labels you used.

7. Save your document, check the syntax of your code (your script should match **Script 15.21**), then select Control > Test Movie.

As it rolls over the movie-clip button, the pointer changes to a hand, and the playhead goes to the movie-clip's _over frame (**Figure 15.33**). When you press the mouse button, the playhead goes to the _down frame—just as it does for a regular button.

8. Close the test-movie window and navigate back to the main Timeline—for example, by choosing Edit > Edit Document.

Script 15.21 The code to activate button behavior.

```
1  stop();
2  buttonMode = true;
```

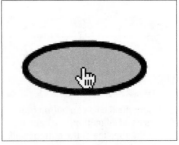

Figure 15.33 By labeling the frames of your movie-clip button _up, _over, and _down, you can take advantage of built-in ActionScript to give users feedback about the button. Adding the `buttonMode = true;` statement to the button's script tells Flash to change the pointer to the hand icon when it moves over the graphic content in a frame with one of those labels.

Figure 15.34 To target the movie-clip button, you must name the instance in the Property inspector's Instance Name field.

Script 15.22 A descriptive comment, pausing the Timeline, and defining the code-hint comment.

```
1  // Scripting a movie-clip button
2  stop();
3  // code-hint comments
4  // MovieClip myBtn;
```

To add a mouse event–handler that displays the disabled state:

1. Continuing with the file from the previous task, select the `MovieClipBtn` instance on the Stage and access the Property inspector.

2. In the Instance Name field, enter a name—for example, `myBtn` (**Figure 15.34**).

3. In the Timeline of the document, create a new layer above the existing layer; name the new layer Actions.

   With multiple layers in the Timeline, it's a good idea to name them all. Give the layer containing the movie-clip button a name—for example, `MC Button`.

4. Select keyframe 1 in the Actions layer, and access the Actions panel.

5. In the Script pane, in line 1, to document your script, type `//` followed by a description, and press Enter to create a new line.

   Adding a comment such as `// Scripting a movie-clip button` reminds you (and informs others) of what you intend your script to do.

6. With the cursor in line 2, type `stop();` to pause the movie, then press Enter to create a new line.

7. To create a code-hint comment, in lines 3 and 4, type

   `// code-hint comments`

   `// MovieClip myBtn;`

   This comment activates code hints by telling Flash that the instance `myBtn` is a `MovieClip` object (**Script 15.22**).

8. With the cursor at the end of line 4, press Enter to begin a new block of code.

continues on next page

9. To define the event handler, in lines 5–13, type

```
// event handlers
function handleClick
→ ( pEvent:MouseEvent ):void
{
  if( pEvent.target == myBtn )
  {
    myBtn.enabled = false;
    myBtn.gotoAndStop( "Disabled" );
  }
}
```

Line 6 defines the event handler. Line 8 makes sure the event was triggered by the button instance you intend, myBtn. Line 10 prevents the button from receiving anymore mouse events by setting the movie-clip instance's enabled property to false. Line 11 sends the playhead to the Disabled frame of the movie-clip (without the code in line 10 the playhead would go back to the _up frame as soon as the user rolled out of the active movie-clip area) (**Script 15.23**).

10. To register for the click event, with the cursor at the end of line 13, press Enter to create a new line; in new lines 14 and 15 type

```
// register events
myBtn.addEventListener(
→ MouseEvent.CLICK, handleClick );
```

11. Save your document, check the syntax of your code (your script should match **Script 15.24**), then select Control > Test Movie.

Your movie opens in a Flash Player window. The movie-clip button displays the Over state. When you click the button, the playhead moves to the Down label. As soon as you let go of the mouse button, the playhead moves to the Disabled frame, and the movie-clip button no longer reacts to the mouse.

Script 15.23 Adding the event handler.

```
4  // MovieClip myBtn;
5  // event handlers
6  function handleClick( pEvent:MouseEvent
   ):void
7  {
8    if( pEvent.target == myBtn )
9    {
10     myBtn.enabled = false;
11     myBtn.gotoAndStop( "Disabled" );
12   }
13 }
```

Script 15.24 The completed movie-clip button script.

```
1  // Scripting a movie-clip button
2  stop();
3  // code-hint comments
4  // MovieClip myBtn;
5  // event handlers
6  function handleClick( pEvent:MouseEvent
   ):void
7  {
8    if( pEvent.target == myBtn )
9    {
10     myBtn.enabled = false;
11     myBtn.gotoAndStop( "Disabled" );
12   }
13 }
14 // register events
15 myBtn.addEventListener( MouseEvent.CLICK,
   handleClick );
```

✔ Tip

■ The procedure for scripting interactive buttons and movie-clip buttons is identical. If you start a project using buttons, and later realize you need more functionality, you don't have to start over. Replace the buttons with movie-clip buttons using the same instance names, and your code will still work. You can then add movie-clip–specific scripts to display additional states, as shown in the preceding task.

Using Buttons to Control Timelines

Most Flash creations employ a mixture of interface objects: button symbols, button components, and movie clips. You can script a button (or button component) to start and stop the playback of a movie clip, or make the playhead jump to a specific frame in a movie clip. The key is to specify the correct target path.

The Mystery of Target Paths

All Flash creations have a certain amount of structural complexity. Even a simple movie like the one created with ButtonActionsMaster has a hierarchy of nested objects. (The Timeline you see when you open a Flash document in the authoring environment is actually a movie-clip object, so any objects on this main Timeline are considered nested objects.) But the structure gets really complex when you nest interactive objects inside other interactive objects—a button inside a movie clip, a movie clip inside a movie clip, a button inside a movie clip inside a movie clip, and so on.

A nested object is known as a *child object,* and the object containing that child is known as the *parent object.* As long as each parent and child has an instance name, it doesn't matter how complex the family relationship gets. You can create a script that manipulates any of the nested objects. The key is to identify the target object's place in the hierarchy of Timelines using a *target path.*

There are two types of target paths: *relative* and *absolute.* A relative target path starts with the target object and describes its relationship to other Timelines in the hierarchy—indicating, for example, that the target is me, or it's one level above me; or it's within me, one level down. An absolute target path starts with the highest-level Timeline and works its way down the hierarchy until it reaches the target object.

Just to complicate things, however, ActionScript 3.0 introduces a new type of interactive object, the *sprite.* A sprite is similar to a movie clip, but it has no Timeline and no frames. All of the animation and interactivity of a sprite happens because of scripting. Sprites can also be nested and have hierarchical relationships. And you use target paths to identify them. When you write target paths, you need to distinguish between sprite objects and Timeline-based objects (movie clips) by using the code `as sprite` or `as movieClip`—as shown in the examples below. (In this book, we work only with Timeline-based objects.)

continues on next page

To make a button stop movie-clip playback:

1. Open a new ActionScript 3.0 Flash document, add layers to create a three-layer document, and do the following:

   ▲ Name the top layer Actions.

   ▲ Name the second layer Buttons. In that layer, place a button-symbol instance at the upper-left corner of the Stage.

   ▲ Name the third layer MovieClips. In that layer, at the center of the Stage, place a movie-clip instance containing animation (for example, a simple classic tween or motion tween of a geometric shape that rotates and shrinks).

   ▲ Save the file and name it pauseClipControl.fla.

2. To prepare the instances for scripting, do the following:

   ▲ Access the Property inspector.

   ▲ Select the button, and in the Instance Name field, enter controlBtn.

   ▲ Select the movie clip, and in the Instance Name field, enter animMc.

3. In the Actions layer, select frame 1 and access the Actions panel.

4. To comment your script and pause the main Timeline at startup, in the Script pane of the Actions panel, in lines 1 and 2, type

```
// Controlling a movie clip with a
→ button
stop();
```

The Mystery of Target Paths *continued*

To start a relative target path, simply type the instance name of the object you want to target, such as *animMc*.

A relative path isn't restricted to looking at objects contained within the current Timeline. You can also go one or more levels up or down. This is where the concept of parent and child comes into play. Let's say you have a button with an instance name of *controlBtn* on the main Timeline where you've placed *animMc*. In the Timeline of *animMc*, you could write

```
(parent as MovieClip).controlBtn
```

This path directs ActionScript to go one level up to the parent Timeline, the one containing *animMc* (in this example, it's the main Timeline) and access the instance named *controlBtn*. (Whenever you use the code *parent* you must distinguish between sprites and movie clips.)

To target child objects, use dot syntax (place a period between the parent object and its child). To direct ActionScript to go down a level to access a movie-clip instance named *starMc* that's nested within *animMc*, the relative path would be *animMc.starMc*.

Optionally, you can start a relative target path with the code *this*. For example, *this.animMc.starMc* is the same as *animMc.starMc*.

An absolute path always starts at the main Timeline, which is also known as *root*. The format of an absolute target path for *starMC* looks like this:

```
(root as MovieClip).animMc.starMc.
```

(Whenever you use the code *root* you must distinguish between sprites and movie clips.)

Script 15.25 Commented script that pauses the Timeline, and defines code-hint comments.

```
1  // Controlling a movie clip with a button
2  stop();
3  // code-hint comments
4  // SimpleButton controlBtn;
5  // MovieClip animMc;
```

Script 15.26 Defining the event handler that checks for the event source.

```
5  // MovieClip animMc;
6  // event handler
7  function handleClick( pEvent:MouseEvent
   ):void
8  {
9    if( pEvent.target == controlBtn )
10   {
11     // handle event
12   }
13 }
```

Script 15.27 Registering the click event of controlBtn.

```
14 // register events
15 controlBtn.addEventListener(
   MouseEvent.CLICK, handleClick );
```

5. To enable code hints for the instances on the Stage, in lines 3–5 type the following code-hint comments (**Script 15.25**):

```
// code-hint comments
// SimpleButton controlBtn;
// MovieClip animMc;
```

6. To define an event handler that verifies the event source, in lines 6–13 type

```
// event handler
function handleClick(
→ pEvent:MouseEvent ):void
{
  if( pEvent.target == controlBtn )
  {
    // handle event
  }
}
```

This defines an event handler that makes sure the event is triggered by controlBtn (**Script 15.26**).

7. To register for the controlBtn's click event, in lines 14 and 15 type

```
// register events
controlBtn.addEventListener(
→ MouseEvent.CLICK, handleClick );
```

The main Timeline now receives the click event of the controlBtn, and you are ready to direct Flash to take control of the movie-clip instance animMc (**Script 15.27**).

continues on next page

8. Place the cursor at the end of line 11, press Enter to create a new line 12, and type

`animMc`

This is a relative target path: this script now aims from the main Timeline (where the script is located) to the `animMc` instance.

9. With the cursor at the end of line 12, directly after the target path, type

`.stop();`

This `stop` action attached to the target path tells Flash to pause playback of the movie-clip instance named `animMc`.

10. Preview the action.

Save the file, check the syntax (the code should match **Script 15.28**), correct any errors, then test the movie (see "Previewing Actions at Work").

In the Flash Player window, the animation plays in a continuous loop. When you click the button, the animation pauses.

Script 15.28 The completed script to pause a clip when a button is clicked.

```
1  // Controlling a movie clip with a button
2  stop();
3  // code-hint comments
4  // SimpleButton controlBtn;
5  // MovieClip animMc;
6  // event handler
7  function handleClick( pEvent:MouseEvent
   ):void
8  {
9    if( pEvent.target == controlBtn )
10   {
11     // handle event
12     animMc.stop();
13   }
14 }
15 // register events
16 controlBtn.addEventListener(
   MouseEvent.CLICK, handleClick );
```

The Pitfalls of Insert Target Path

The toolbar above the Script pane in the Actions panel displays an Insert Target Path button (the small crosshair icon). Click the button and Flash opens a dialog named Insert Target Path. This dialog ought to be a really helpful tool for both understanding the Timeline hierarchy and creating accurate target paths. Unfortunately, this feature didn't weather the transition to ActionScript 3.0 very well.

To make it short, the Insert Path dialog will in most cases create a broken target path. You can use it to get an understanding of the movie-clip hierarchy in your Flash creation, yet you're better off creating your target paths manually.

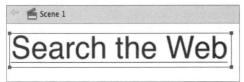

Figure 15.35 You can turn text into a live link for accessing Web pages. Select the text on the Stage (top). In the Options section of the Property inspector, type a URL in the Link field (middle). Flash creates a live link in the published Flash movie. Live-link text appears underlined in the authoring environment (bottom).

Figure 15.36 The Target menu specifies how Flash should open the link's URL in a browser window.

Linking to Other Web Pages

Flash gives you two ways to open new files by linking to URLs. You can select text on the Stage and turn it into a live link by entering a URL in the Link field in the Options section of the Text (Tool) Property inspector. You can also use ActionScript to instruct Flash Player to open a URL. Both techniques let you open the new file in a different browser window or different frame of the current window.

To create a text link to a URL:

1. On the Stage, select the text that you want to be a link.

   You can select individual letters or words using the text tool or select an entire text field using the selection tool.

2. Access the Options section of the Property inspector, and enter the desired URL in the Link field (**Figure 15.35**).

3. To choose a method for displaying the specified URL in the browser window, from the Target pop-up menu, choose one of the following (**Figure 15.36**):

   _blank opens the URL in a new browser window.

   _parent opens the URL in the parent of the current frame.

   _self opens the URL in same frame of the browser window as that of the content being currently viewed.

   _top opens the URL in the top-level frame of the current browser window.

   continues on next page

When you open the published HTML file from you hard drive and click the link to another Web site, you may get security errors (see the sidebar "A Note About Flash Player 10's Security," in Chapter 18). For links to work properly, you need to put the published files on a Web server.

4. Choose Control > Test Movie to try out your live link text.

When you move the pointer over the text, the pointing-finger cursor appears (**Figure 15.37**); when you click the text, Flash opens the URL in the specified form of browser window.

To script a button that opens a Web page:

1. Open a new document using the ButtonActionsMaster template you created earlier in this chapter, and save it as LinkBtn.fla.

   The Timeline has three layers—Actions, Buttons, and Frames.

2. To create the button that opens a new Web page, do the following:

   ▲ In the Timeline, select frame 5 of the Buttons layer, and insert a blank keyframe (for example, by choosing Insert > Timeline > Blank Keyframe).

   ▲ With keyframe 5 of the Buttons layer selected, drag an instance of a button symbol to the Stage, and access the Property inspector.

   ▲ With the button instance selected on the Stage, in the Instance Name field, enter an instance name, such as linkBtn.

Figure 15.37 The underlined text (top) is a live link created in the Property inspector. In the published movie (bottom), the text is not underlined, and the hand pointer appears when you move the pointer into the text field.

Script 15.29 Defining an event handler that checks for the event source.

```
1  // SimpleButton linkBtn;
2  function handleLink( pEvent:MouseEvent
   ):void
3  {
4    if( pEvent.target == linkBtn )
5    {
6    }
7  }
```

Script 15.30 Registering for the click event.

```
6    }
7  }
8  linkBtn.addEventListener( MouseEvent.CLICK,
   handleLink );
```

3. In the Timeline select keyframe 5 of the Actions layer, insert a blank keyframe, and access the Actions panel.

   In previous tasks you've always created scripts in keyframe 1 that start working with objects in frame 1. One way to create a script that relates to objects in a later frame is to add a blank keyframe in the Actions layer at that frame to hold the script.

4. To create a code-hint comment, in the Script pane of the Actions panel, in line 1 type

   ```
   // SimpleButton linkBtn;
   ```

5. To create the event handler that checks for the event source, do the following:

   ▲ With the cursor at the end of line 1, press Enter to begin a new code block.

   ▲ In lines 2–7, type

   ```
   function handleLink(
   → pEvent:MouseEvent ):void
   {
     if( pEvent.target == linkBtn )
     {
     }
   }
   ```

   The code so far should match **Script 15.29**.

6. To register for the click event, with the cursor at the end of line 7 (after the closing brace), press Enter to begin line 8, and type

   ```
   linkBtn.addEventListener(
   → MouseEvent.CLICK, handleLink );
   ```

   The code should match **Script 15.30**.

continues on next page

LINKING TO OTHER WEB PAGES

7. To create the network request, do the following:

▲ Place the cursor at the end of line 5 (after the opening brace) and press Enter to create a new line.

▲ In line 6, type

```
var request:URLRequest =
→ new URLRequest( "http://
→ www.google.com" );
```

Replace the link to Google with the URL you want to link to. In ActionScript 3.0, you need to create a URLRequest object with the URL to make any kind of external connection. Here the URLRequest is then stored in a custom variable called request.

8. To create the code that tells Flash to execute the link, with the cursor at the end of line 6 (after the semicolon), press Enter to begin line 7 and type

```
navigateToURL( request, "_blank" );
```

The parameter _blank is the same method for opening a browser window that you chose from a menu in step 3 of the first task in this section, "To create a text link to a URL." To use a different method, use the code _self, _parent, or _top; but be aware that you may need to create new security settings for those methods (for more details, see the sidebar "A Note About Flash Player 10's Security Settings," in Chapter 18).

9. Preview the action.

Save the file, check the syntax (the code should match **Script 15.31**), correct any errors, then test the movie (see "Previewing Actions at Work").

The first button that appears is one that you scripted as part of the template document. Clicking this button advances the movie to the next frame. Click this button until you reach frame 5. Clicking the button in frame 5 makes the default browser open a new window or tab with the URL you specified.

Script 15.31 Making a button link to another Web page.

```
1  // SimpleButton linkBtn;
2  function handleLink( pEvent:MouseEvent
   ):void
3  {
4    if( pEvent.target == linkBtn )
5    {
6      var request:URLRequest = new
       URLRequest( "http://www.google.com" );
7      navigateToURL( request, "_blank" );
8    }
9  }
10 linkBtn.addEventListener( MouseEvent.CLICK,
   handleLink );
```

✔ Tip

■ You don't always have to create scripts in a blank keyframe. Often the Actions layer's keyframe already exists, with script for controlling another button instance. You can simply add the new script to the end of the existing script. In the preceding exercise, for example, try adding the Web-page button to keyframe 1. Create the script at the end of the script that was already in the ButtonActionsMaster document. The line numbers will be different, but the button should work just fine.

Copy motion of first keyframe span

Copy motion of first and second keyframe spans

Final keyframe has no highlight, leave it deselected

Figure 15.38 To copy the motion of a classic tween, you need only copy one frame that's set with the classic tween property. With Tinted Frames active (choose it from the Timeline's panel menu), the bluish-purple (Mac) or bluish-gray (Windows) highlight indicates which frames are set to classic tweening. Don't include the keyframe at the end of the keyframe span if it has no classic-tween highlight.

Transforming Timeline Animation into Code

Ever since Flash added scripting capabilities in version 4, ActionScript programmers have created motion with code. But trying to script reusable animated effects based on a graphic designer's carefully choreographed tweening and keyframe animation was a grueling process of trial and error.

Flash's Copy Motion As ActionScript 3.0 command lets you capture classic tweens and motion tweens with code. In the Timeline, you select a single motion-tween span, or one or more contiguous keyframe spans of a classic tween, copy the tween as ActionScript, then simply paste that code into your script.

To copy motion from the Timeline:

1. Open a new Flash file (ActionScript 3.0), create a new movie-clip symbol with a shape in it such as a star, and name it Star.

2. Place an instance of the Star symbol on the Stage, and animate it using either classic-tweening or motion-tweening techniques (see Chapters 9, 11, and 12).

3. In the Timeline, to select the animation do one of the following:

   ▲ Select one or more frames of the classic tween. The frames must be contiguous and must all be set to classic tweening. You can select multiple contiguous classic-tween keyframe spans to copy the full range of motion. Do not, however, select the final keyframe of a classic tween if that keyframe is not highlighted as having the classic tween property (**Figure 15.38**).

   ▲ Select a single motion-tween span. Flash can create code for just one motion tween at a time.

continues on next page

4. Choose Edit > Timeline > Copy Motion As ActionScript 3.0 (**Figure 15.39**).

For classic tweens, a dialog named Prompt appears. For motion tweens, Flash creates the code immediately.

5. To complete the code for classic tweens, do the following:

▲ In the Prompt dialog, enter the instance name of the movie-clip symbol (or button) that you want to animate— for example, ovalMc (**Figure 15.40**). This instance doesn't have to exist yet, but to animate an object with the copied motion, you'll need to give the object this instance name.

▲ Click OK.

Flash translates all animation created by the selected tween(s) into ActionScript 3.0 code and places that code on the Clipboard, ready to paste into a script.

To paste the copied motion as ActionScript:

1. Open a new Flash file (ActionScript 3.0), and create a movie-clip symbol with a shape in it such as an oval, and name it Oval.

This is the symbol you want to animate.

2. Place an instance of Oval on the stage, and give it the instance name ovalMc.

3. Create a new layer and name it Actions.

4. With frame 1 in the Actions layer selected, access the Actions panel.

Figure 15.39 To translate Timeline animation into ActionScript, select the animation keyframes in the Timeline, then choose Edit > Timeline > Copy Motion As ActionScript 3.0.

Figure 15.40 When you copy the motion of a classic tween, Flash opens the Prompt dialog. Use the dialog to specify the name of the instance to which you want to apply the copied motion code.

XML begins

```
<Motion duration="5" xmlns="fl.motion.*"
```

```
</Motion>;
```

XML ends

Figure 15.41 The code derived from a classic tween is complex, but don't let it scare you. You don't have to edit it, just use it. You can also experiment with changing the XML code or, eventually, with modifying the ActionScript code.

5. To pause the movie at runtime, in the Script pane, in line 1, type `stop();`.

Pausing the movie is optional, but it lets you see that the motion is created by ActionScript, not by Timeline animation.

6. With the cursor at the end of line 1 (after the semicolon), press Enter to begin a new line.

7. With the cursor in line 2, Control-click (Mac) or right-click (Windows) and choose Paste.

Flash pastes the translation of the tween you copied. The translation for a classic tween is different from the translation for a motion tween. For a classic tween, you enter the instance name of the target object during the copy process (using the Prompt dialog). The script is complete once you paste it (**Figure 15.41**). For a motion tween, you need to add the instance name directly to the script.

To identify the tween target in pasted motion-tween code:

1. Follow the steps in the preceding tasks to copy the animation of a motion tween and paste it into the Actions panel.

2. In the Actions panel, scroll to the end of the pasted script.

    The script ends with a closing brace (}) on the last line (**Figure 15.42**). The line before that is a comment line containing a piece of code that you must to add to the script.

3. In the second to the last line, delete the two initial slashes.

    The two slashes turn the text into a comment that Flash ignores. Removing the slashes tells Flash to treat the line as part of the script.

4. Replace the placeholder text <instance name goes here> with the name of your movie-clip instance, ovalMc.

    Flash now uses the script to animate ovalMc. The number that follows the instance name in the code indicates the number of times Flash should repeat the animation. A setting of 0 tells Flash to keep looping the animation.

5. Test the movie.

    In the Flash Player window, the ovalMc instance goes through the same motions that you created for the Star symbol in the first task in this section, even though there's only one single keyframe in this FLA.

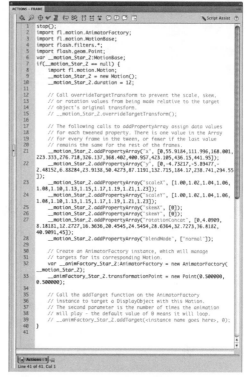

Figure 15.42 The code derived from a motion tween is filled with comment lines to help identify what's happening. These comments may seem daunting to those unfamiliar with ActionScript, but don't worry. You just need to pay attention to the final line of comments. That comment line contains one bit of code you need to add to the script to target your movie clip on the Stage.

✔ Tips

■ When working with a script created from a motion tween, you might prefer to keep that last comment line for future reference. Copy all but the initial slashes of the line, insert a new blank line as the penultimate line of the script, and paste the code there. You can modify the copy and still refer back to the comment in its original form (**Figure 15.43**).

■ When you copy the motion of a motion tween and set it up to loop, the scripted animation loops endlessly (or the number of times specified), even if the Timeline it is on is stopped. If you want the animation to pause on startup, or you want to have a button that stops it, you need a little workaround. Place an instance of

the symbol to be animated and the code in a separate movie-clip symbol named, for example, OvalAnimated. In the main Timeline, create two keyframes: label the first Static and the second Animated. Place an instance of the Oval symbol in the Static frame (this simulates pausing the animated oval) and add a stop(); action at this frame. Place an instance of the OvalAnimated movie-clip symbol in the Animated frame. Use the techniques from "Modifying and Extending Button Scripts," earlier in this chapter, to create a Stop button that displays the Static frame and a Play button that displays the Animated frame. Advanced scripters can also control the animation directly with ActionScript code.

continues on next page

    └─ *Remove slashes*   └─ *Add instance name*

Figure 15.43 To apply the actions to your movie-clip instance, delete the initial slashes that cause Flash to treat the text as a comment. Then change <instance name goes here> to the name of your movie-clip instance.

- When you copy a classic tween, you may paste the script created by the Copy Motion As ActionScript 3.0 command, and then discover you entered the wrong instance name in the Prompt dialog. You don't have to go back and do the whole copying procedure again. In the toolbar above the Script pane, click the Find button (the magnifying-glass icon). A standard search-and-replace dialog opens. Simply replace the incorrect instance name with the correct one in the pasted script.

- The script created by the Copy Motion As ActionScript 3.0 command can look quite complicated to a novice scripter, but don't be intimidated. If you prefer not to get involved in complex scripting just yet, there's nothing you need to do to the script besides what you learned in the preceding task. If you want to change the ActionScript-generated animation, you can always change the original Timeline animation and repeat the copy motion–paste process. For this reason, it's always a good idea to set up a system for collaboration between graphic designer and scripter. Hold on to your original Flash documents with Timeline animation until you know the project is complete.

USING NON-FLASH GRAPHICS

16

Adobe Flash CS4 Professional's drawing tools are powerful and flexible, but you may prefer the tools offered by another vector graphics program—Adobe Illustrator or Adobe FreeHand, for example. Or you may want to use artwork created in Adobe Photoshop or include scanned photos or other bitmaps in your Flash document. Fortunately, you can import vector art and bitmapped graphics through the Clipboard or the Import command. You can also drag and drop items from Photoshop CS4, Illustrator CS4, and FreeHand versions 7–11 (MX), directly into Flash.

Flash has two import commands: Import to Stage and Import to Library. The two work similarly. Some import dialogs offer slightly different options depending on which command you choose. The tasks in this chapter use Import to Stage.

This chapter teaches the basics of the import process via tasks for importing bitmaps and Adobe Photoshop files. To learn about importing files from Adobe Illustrator, Fireworks, and FreeHand, please check out the companion Web site to this book (for details, see "Artwork, Scripts, and More," on page xviii in the introduction to this book.

What Graphics Formats Does Flash Import?

Flash imports a variety of bitmapped and vector-graphic file formats. Flash CS4 can import the following types of files: Adobe Illustrator version 10 or earlier, Adobe Photoshop, AutoCAD DXF, Bitmap (BMP), Enhanced Windows Metafile (EMF, only on Windows), Adobe FreeHand versions 7–11 (MX), FutureSplash Player (SPL), GIF and animated GIF, JPEG, PNG, Flash Player 6/7, and Windows Metafile (WMF). If you have QuickTime 4 or later installed on your system together with Flash CS4, you can also import the following file formats: MacPaint (PNTG), PICT (as a bitmap on Windows), QuickTime Image (QTIF), Silicon Graphics Image (SGI), TGA, and TIFF.

Importing Bitmaps

No matter what type of non-Flash artwork you wish to import, the first steps of the import process are the same. For simple bitmaps, the import commands bring the artwork directly into Flash.

To import bitmaps:

1. In a Flash document, choose File > Import > Import to Stage.

   The Import dialog appears (**Figure 16.1**).

   When you choose Import to Stage, Flash imports the file into your document, stores a master bitmap asset in the library, and places an instance of the bitmap on the Stage in the current keyframe of the active layer (**Figure 16.2**).

2. From the Enable (Mac) or Files of Type (Windows) menu, choose the format of the file you want to import.

3. Navigate to the file on your system.

4. Select the file.

5. Click Import (Mac) or Open (Windows). The bitmap is now available in the Library and on the Stage.

✔ Tips

■ In step 1 of this task, you could choose File > Import > Import to Library. The Import to Library command places assets in the library but skips placing an instance of the asset on the Stage.

■ You can edit an imported bitmap in any installed bitmap-editing program. Select the bitmap in the Library panel, Control-click (Mac) or right-click (Windows) the bitmap icon, and choose Edit With from the contextual menu. In the window that opens, navigate to an editing program and click Open. Edit and save the bitmap; Flash updates it in the library.

Figure 16.1 Bring graphics created in other applications into your Flash document through the Import dialog.

Figure 16.2 When you import a bitmap to the Stage, Flash stores a master copy of the bitmap in the library.

Figure 16.3 When you import one file in a series of numbered files (top), Flash asks whether you want to import the whole series (bottom).

Preview mode shows images in keyframes

Series of bitmaps added to the library

Figure 16.4 When Flash imports a numbered series of files, it places each one in a separate keyframe in the Timeline of the current document.

To import a series of graphics files:

1. Follow steps 1–5 of the preceding task. In step 2, choose the appropriate format, and navigate to the first file in the series.

   The series must be in a single folder, and the filenames must differ only by a number at the end—for example, bounce1, bounce2, and bounce3. If these conditions are met, a dialog appears, asking if you want to import a series of sequential images (**Figure 16.3**).

2. In the dialog, click Yes.

   Flash places each image in a separate keyframe in the active layer (**Figure 16.4**).

Import to Library vs. Import to Stage

When you import files, you choose to import to the Stage or library. When importing to the Stage, Flash places the items on the Stage, and re-creates any layer hierarchy in the main Timeline of the document. Imported content also goes in the library.

When importing to the library, Flash places the content in the library; but for Photoshop, Illustrator, and Fireworks PNG files, Flash also creates a movie-clip or graphic symbol that contains the content. Flash places the imported content on the symbol's Stage, and re-creates the layer hierarchy in the symbol's Timeline.

Some dialogs present slightly different choices when you choose Import to Library than when you choose Import to Stage. For example, when you import Illustrator and Photoshop files to the library, you can't opt to place objects at their original position or set the Stage size.

IMPORTING BITMAPS

Importing Photoshop Files

When you import content from Photoshop, Flash automatically imports according to your Preferences settings. Using the Import command opens the PSD Import dialog, where you can view and change the settings for individual layers.

To set import preferences for Photoshop (PSD) files:

1. From the Flash (Mac) or Edit (Windows) menu, choose Preferences.

   The Preferences dialog appears.

2. In the Category list, choose PSD File Importer.

   Options for importing PSD files appear on the right side of the dialog (**Figure 16.5**).

3. To set options for importing image layers (**Figure 16.6**), do one of the following:

   ▲ To retain as much of an image layer's opacity and applied blend modes as Flash can handle, select the "Bitmap images with editable layer styles" radio button.

   ▲ To replicate the look of the image layer most faithfully, select the Flattened Bitmap Images radio button. When this radio button is selected, to have Flash create both a bitmap and a movie clip containing the bitmap, select the Create Movie Clips check box.

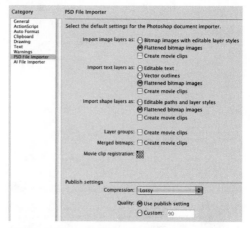

Figure 16.5 Choosing PSD File Importer from the Category list in the Preferences dialog gives you access to options for importing PSD files.

Figure 16.6 You have two choices for importing PSD image layers. If you choose to import them with editable layer styles (top), Flash automatically creates movie-clip symbols to hold the imported layers and applies appropriate Flash blend modes to the symbol instance. If you import image layers as bitmaps (bottom), you can choose to create movie clips to hold them, or import only the bitmaps.

Figure 16.7 You have three options for importing PSD text: as editable text fields (top), as editable shapes (middle), and as bitmaps (bottom). If you choose to import text as editable shapes, Flash automatically creates movie clips to hold them.

Figure 16.8 When you import PSD shape layers as editable paths (top), Flash automatically places the paths inside a movie-clip symbol. When you import shape layers as bitmaps (bottom), you can choose whether or not to have Flash place them in movie clips by selecting the Create Movie Clips check box.

Figure 16.9 When you import PSD layer groups, you can have Flash place them inside movie clips.

Figure 16.10 If you choose to merge PSD layers for import, you can have Flash place the merged layers inside movie clips.

4. To set options for importing text layers (**Figure 16.7**), do any of the following:
   - ▲ To import text in fully editable static text fields, select the Editable Text radio button.
   - ▲ To import text as editable shapes, select the Vector Outlines radio button.
   - ▲ To import text as bitmaps, select the Flattened Bitmap Images radio button.
   - ▲ To have Flash place the editable text or flattened bitmap inside a movie-clip symbol on import, select the Create Movie Clips check box.

5. To set options for importing shape layers (**Figure 16.8**), do one of the following:
   - ▲ To import an editable shape that retains as much of its opacity and applied blend modes as Flash can handle, select the "Editable paths and layer styles" radio button.
   - ▲ To replicate the look of the shape most faithfully, select the Flattened Bitmap Images radio button. When this radio button is selected, to have Flash place the bitmap inside a movie-clip symbol, select the Create Movie Clips check box.

6. To convert grouped layers to movie clips, in the Layer Groups section, select the Create Movie Clips check box (**Figure 16.9**).

7. To convert any merged layers to movie clips, in the Merged Bitmaps section, select the Create Movie Clips check box (**Figure 16.10**). (For more on merging layers, see the next task, "To import content from PSD files.")

continues on next page

8. To set the registration point for any movie-clip symbols created during the import process, in the Movie Clip Registration section, click one of the nine squares in the registration model (**Figure 16.11**).

By default, Flash assigns the same registration point to all movie clips created during import. You can override this setting for individual movie clips in the PSD Import dialog. To learn more about the registration point and symbols, see Chapter 7.

9. In the Publish Settings section (**Figure 16.12**), choose one of the following from the Compression pop-up menu:

▲ To retain all image data for imported PSD items when publishing your Flash file, choose Lossless. Flash applies Lossless compression when creating the SWF file for playback. Lossless compression creates the highest-quality images, but also creates larger file sizes. To learn more about publishing, see Chapter 18.

or

▲ To apply JPEG compression to imported PSD items during publishing, choose Lossy. Select the Use Publish Setting radio button to apply the JPEG quality currently specified in Publish Settings, or select the Custom radio button and enter a value between 0 and 100 to override the JPEG quality. Higher values retain more image data, creating better-looking images but larger files.

10. Click OK to confirm the current Preferences settings and close the dialog.

Figure 16.11 In the Preferences dialog's PSD Importer category, clicking one of the nine squares in the symbol-registration model sets the default registration point for movie-clip symbols imported from PSD files.

Figure 16.12 The Compression pop-up menu lets you choose which compression method Flash applies during publishing. Lossless compression (top) preserves all the image data. Lossy compression (bottom) lets you determine how much data is lost.

Layers pane   *Options pane*

Figure 16.13 The Layers pane, on the left in the PSD Import dialog, displays a scrolling list of content available for import. When you select an item in the list, its settings appear in the Options pane, on the right in the dialog. General import settings appear in the lower half of the dialog.

Figure 16.14 The lower portion of the PSD Import dialog offers settings that apply to the entire imported content. You can choose how Flash deals with the PSD file's layer structure (A), how to position the imported objects on the Stage (B), and whether or not to resize the Stage to match the dimensions of the PSD file (C).

To import content from PSD files:

1. Follow steps 1–5 of the first task in the preceding section, "Importing Bitmaps." In step 2, choose Photoshop as the format, and navigate to the file you want to import.

   After you click the Import (Mac) or Open (Windows) button, the PSD Import dialog appears (**Figure 16.13**).

2. To set import options that apply to the whole document, in the lower portion of the PSD Import dialog (**Figure 16.14**), do any of the following:

   ▲ From the Convert Layers To pop-up menu, choose a conversion method. To re-create the PSD file's layer structure as Timeline layers, choose Flash Layers. To convert the PSD layers to keyframes, choose Keyframes.

   ▲ To have Flash place the items on the Stage at their original *x*- and *y*-coordinates, select the "Place layers at original position" check box. Otherwise, Flash centers imported layers on the Stage (the imported items will retain their positions relative to one another).

   ▲ To resize the Stage of your Flash document to match the dimensions of the PSD file, select the "Set Stage size to same size as Photoshop canvas" check box.

continues on next page

A Note About Photoshop Adjustment Layers

Flash has no equivalent to Photoshop's adjustment layers. If a selected layer has an adjustment layer and you want to maintain the visual effect, import the selected layer as a bitmap. Otherwise, Flash ignores the adjustment layer on import.

483

3. To identify layers for import, in the Layers pane, select the check box to the left of each item you want to import; deselect the check box next to any items you don't want to import (**Figure 16.15**).

If the PSD file contains layer groups, the Layers pane displays them hierarchically. Click the triangle to the left of the group name to expand or collapse the set. To select (or deselect) the check boxes of all the layers in a group, select (or deselect) the check box to the left of the group name.

4. To merge layers for import, in the Layers pane, Shift-click the name of each layer you want to combine, then click the Merge Layers button (**Figure 16.16**).

Flash creates a new layer in the Layers pane with a default name of Merged Bitmap. The individual layers are listed hierarchically beneath the Merged Bitmap layer. Flash combines the items on the merged layers and imports them as a bitmap.

Figure 16.15 in the Layers pane, selected check boxes indicate items you want to import.

Figure 16.16 To merge layers for import, in the Layers pane, shift-click the name of each layer you want to combine (left), then click the Merge Layers button. Flash combines the layers. Original layers appear hierarchically beneath the merged layer (right).

Enter instance name

Select registration point for this movie clip

Figure 16.17 Selecting an item in the Layers pane gives you access to its import settings in the Options pane. Whenever the item can be imported as a movie clip, Flash displays an Instance Name field and a Registration model. Choosing a new registration point for an individual movie clip overrides the default registration-point location currently set in Preferences. The new registration point applies only to the movie clip created from the selected item in the Layers pane.

Figure 16.18 When you use the Import to Stage command, Flash imports all the items selected in the Layers pane and places them on the Stage (top). (Here, import options were set to re-create the PSD layers in the Flash Timeline.) Flash adds a folder to the library to hold the assets created by importing the PSD files (bottom).

5. To override PSD Import Preference settings for individual layers, click the layer name to select it in the Layers pane and choose new settings in the Options pane (**Figure 16.17**).

6. After selecting the layers that you want to import and adjusting the import settings as desired, click OK.

Flash imports all the selected items, places them on the Stage, and places the associated assets in the library (**Figure 16.18**).

✔ Tips

- If the source PSD file contains *layer comps* (a layer-management feature for quickly viewing various combinations of visible and hidden layers), a Select Photoshop Layer Comp pop-up menu appears at the top of the PSD Import dialog. When you select a comp version from the menu, Flash automatically selects the check boxes of the visible layers in that version and deselects the check boxes of layers that are hidden.

- You can Shift-click to select multiple contiguous PSD layers; the settings you choose in the right-hand pane apply to all the selected items.

- You can rename the layers during import. In the Layers pane, double-click the name of a layer to activate its text field; enter a new name, and press Enter to confirm the name. When Flash creates the layers and assets, it uses the new name.

ADDING SOUND AND VIDEO

Adobe Flash CS4 Professional enables you to incorporate sound and video in your projects to give your audience a full multimedia experience. Sound in Flash can be an ongoing background element or a synchronized element that matches a particular piece of action—say, a slapping sound that accompanies a pair of hands clapping. To add a sound, you import a sound-clip file to the library and then place an instance of the sound on the Stage. To add video, you have a couple of options: you can import the video data and embed it into the Flash Timeline, or you can add a special component that displays external video files. Advanced scripters can use ActionScript to add and control sounds during playback or to display encoded video files as streaming video in their Flash creations. (The scripting techniques, however, are beyond the scope of a *Visual Quickstart Guide*.) In all cases, the video data must be encoded in a format that's compatible with Flash; for embedded video, the file must be in FLV (Flash video) format. You can use Adobe Media Encoder CS4 (AME), which comes with Flash and is installed by default, to encode video files in an appropriate format.

While Flash lets you carry out limited sound-editing tasks, Flash has no video-editing capabilities. AME does let you perform simple video edits as part of the encoding process.

What Sound Formats Does Flash Import?

Flash deals only with *sampled sounds*—those that have been recorded digitally or converted to digital format. Flash imports files in AIFF format for the Mac OS and files in WAV format for Windows. For both platforms, Flash imports files in MP3 format and ASND format (a sound file format created by Adobe Soundbooth CS4). In addition, with the combination of Flash CS4 and QuickTime 4 (or later versions), users on both platforms can import QuickTime movies containing just sounds and Sun AU files; Mac users can import WAV, Sound Designer II, and System 7 sounds; and Windows users can import AIFF sounds. Any sounds you import or copy into a Flash document reside in the file's library.

Importing Sounds

The procedure for importing sounds is similar to that for importing bitmaps or other artwork. You use either of these commands: File > Import > Import to Stage or File > Import > Import to Library. Both commands bring the sound file into the library for the current document. Neither actually places the sound, however. You must drag a copy of the sound from the Library panel to the Stage to make the sound available for assignment to a keyframe.

To import a sound file:

1. Open the file to which you want to add sounds.

2. Choose File > Import > Import to Stage or press ⌘-R (Mac) or Ctrl-R (Windows) (**Figure 17.1**).

   You can also choose File > Import > Import to Library. The standard file-import dialog appears (**Figure 17.2**).

3. From the Enable pop-up menu (Mac) or the Files of Type pop-up menu (Windows), choose the format of the sound file you want to import.

   Choose All Sound Formats to see files in any sound format.

4. Navigate to the sound file on your system.

5. Select the file.

Figure 17.1 Choose File > Import > Import to Stage (or Import to Library) to bring sounds into your Flash document.

Choose file type

Figure 17.2 The Import dialog lets you import sound files into Flash. Choose a sound-file type that is appropriate for your platform from the pop-up menu of file types. You can also choose to see all sound formats.

— Play

Figure 17.3 Flash keeps sound files in the library. You can see the waveform for a selected sound in the preview window. Click the Play button to hear the sound.

6. Click Import (Mac) or Open (Windows).

Flash imports the sound file you selected, placing it in the library. When you select the sound in the library, the sound's waveform appears in the preview window (**Figure 17.3**). Sound files can be quite large; as sounds import, a dialog named Working appears, showing a progress bar. You can stop the import by clicking the Stop (Mac) or Cancel (Windows) button in the dialog.

✔ Tips

■ Despite the fact that one command choice is "Import to Stage," when you work with sounds, all imported assets wind up in the library. You must drag an instance of a sound clip to the Stage yourself to place it in a keyframe initially. Once the sound has been placed, you can assign it to other keyframes via the Property inspector.

■ You can hear a sound without placing it in a movie. Select the sound in the Library panel. Flash displays the waveform in the preview window. To hear the sound, click the Play button in the preview window.

IMPORTING SOUNDS

Flashy Sounds

Flash CS4 comes with a common library of sound effects that you can use in your Flash movies. To access these sounds, choose Window > Common Libraries > Sounds. Flash opens a library containing 186 sounds. You use these sound assets just as you'd use sounds you imported to a document. Drag the sound asset from the Sounds common library to the Stage of your Flash document (see the next section, "Adding Sounds to Frames").

Adding Sounds to Frames

You can assign a sound to a keyframe the same way you place a symbol or bitmap: by selecting the keyframe and then dragging a copy of the sound from an open Library panel (either that document's or another's) to the Stage. You can also assign any sound that resides in a document's library to a selected keyframe in that document by choosing the sound from the Sound pop-up menu in the Sound section of the Frame Property inspector.

To assign a sound to a keyframe:

1. Open a Flash document to which you want to add sound.

   The Ping-Pong animation you created in Chapter 12 makes a good practice file. The document contains a motion tween in which a ball connects with a paddle at four position keyframes. Adding sound can heighten the reality of that contact: You can make the sound realistic (say, a small *thwock*) or make it humorous, if the sound is unexpected (a *boing*, for example).

2. Add a new layer for the sounds in your document, name it Sound, and set its Layer Height Property to 200% (**Figure 17.4**).

   For details on how to set up a sound layer, see the sidebar "Organizing Sounds."

3. In the Timeline, select the Sound layer, and add keyframes at frames 5, 10, 15, and 20.

   These four keyframes match the position keyframes in which the ball hits one of the paddles in the motion tweens that make up the animation (**Figure 17.5**).

Figure 17.4 It's a good idea to enlarge sound layers to make viewing sound waves easier. Double-click the layer icon in the Timeline to access the Layer Properties dialog, then choose 200% or 300% for layer height.

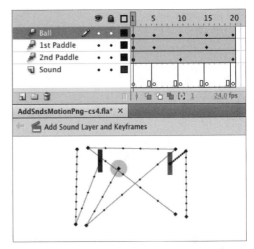

Figure 17.5 Create a separate layer for the sounds in your movie. In that layer, add a keyframe at each place where you want a sound to occur. Here, the keyframes in the Sound layer correspond to the position keyframes in the tween spans where the ball makes contact with a paddle.

Figure 17.6 After you've imported a sound, it appears in the Library panel. Select the sound, and drag it to a keyframe.

Sound-symbol outline

Waveform of the sound assigned to keyframe 5

Figure 17.7 When you drag a sound from the Library panel to the Stage, you see the symbol outline (top). A sound has no visible presence on the Stage, but Flash displays the sound's waveform in a keyframe span in the Timeline (bottom).

4. Import the sound you want to hear when the paddle connects with the ball.

5. In the Timeline, select keyframe 5 of the Sound layer.

This is the first frame in which the ball and paddle connect.

6. Access the Library panel, and select your sound (**Figure 17.6**).

Its waveform appears in the preview window.

7. Drag a copy of the sound from the Library panel to the Stage.

Although sounds have no visible presence on the Stage, you must drag the sound copy to the Stage. As you drag the sound, you see the outline of a box on the Stage. When you release the mouse button, Flash puts the sound in the selected keyframe and displays the waveform in that keyframe and any in-between frames associated with it (**Figure 17.7**).

8. In the Timeline, select keyframe 10 of the Sound layer.

This is the second frame in which the ball and paddle connect.

9. Access the Frame Property inspector.

continues on next page

10. In the Sound section, from the Name pop-up menu, choose your sound.

All the sounds in the document's library are available from the menu (**Figure 17.8**). You don't have to drag a copy of the sound to the Stage each time you want to turn on that sound in a keyframe.

For now, leave the other Sound settings alone. You'll learn more about them in later tasks.

11. Repeat steps 6 and 7 (or 8, 9, and 10) for keyframes 15 and 20.

After adding the sound to the Sound layer's four keyframes, you're ready to play the movie and check out the sounds (**Figure 17.9**). As each paddle strikes the ball, Flash plays the assigned sound, adding a level of realism to this simple Ping-Pong animation.

✔ Tip

- Flash CS4's common library of sounds (see the sidebar "Flashy Sounds") contains a nice sound effect for this task. It's called Sports Ball Ping Pong Ball Hit Table Single01.mp3.

Figure 17.8 In the Sound section of the Frame Property inspector, the Name pop-up menu lists all the sounds that are in the library of the current document. From this menu, you can choose a sound that you want to assign to the keyframe that's selected in the Timeline.

Figure 17.9 For each spot in the movie where a sound should occur, add a sound to a keyframe in the Sound layer. A condensed image of the sound's waveform appears in the keyframe span. Within a single keyframe, you won't see much of the waveform; in keyframe 20, for example, just the initial line is visible.

ADDING SOUNDS TO FRAMES *(side margin)*

The Pitfall of Sounds in Tween Spans

Flash lets you place a sound in the tween span of a motion tween; the sound plays just as it does when you place it in a keyframe span as the exercises in this chapter have you do, with one important exception: After you place a sound in a tween span, you cannot remove the sound from that tween span. When you select the tween span, the Property inspector displays properties of the motion tween, but Sound is not one of them. Even if you select just the initial keyframe of the span, you'll see properties for the motion tween, but nothing for sound. You can *change* the span's sound by dragging a new sound to the tween span. The only way to return the tween span to a state where it has no sound is to delete the sound from the library entirely (not a good solution if you've used the sound elsewhere in your movie).

Organizing Sounds

Nothing prevents you from placing sounds in layers that contain other content, but your document will be easier to handle—and sounds will be easier to find for updating and editing—if you always put sounds in separate layers reserved for a soundtrack. Placing a sound in a motion-tween span can cause special headaches (see the sidebar "The Pitfall of Sounds in Tween Spans"). Here are some tips for working with layers for sounds:

◆ Name layers as a reminder of their content. For detailed instructions on working with layers, see Chapter 6.

◆ Place all the sound layers either at the bottom of the Timeline or at the top, so you can find them easily. The position of layers in the stacking order has no effect on the playback of sounds in the movie.

◆ Create a layer folder for sounds. Flash Player 8–10 can handle up to 32 sounds playing at one time; earlier Flash Player versions can handle up to eight simultaneous sounds. (You'll learn about publishing for Flash Player in Chapter 18.) If you put each sound on a separate layer, that's a lot to track. If you'll be working with lots of sound layers, create a layer folder and name it SoundTracks. Placing all the sound layers in the SoundTracks folder makes it easier to work with the sounds (**Figure 17.10**)

◆ Increase the height for sound layers to make it easier to see the waveform (a graphic image of the sound) for that layer. Choose Modify > Timeline > Layer Properties (or double-click the layer icon of the selected layer) to access the Layer Properties dialog. From the Layer Height pop-up menu, choose 200% or 300% to make the layer taller. Click OK.

◆ After you've placed sounds in a layer, lock the layer—to prevent yourself from adding graphics to it accidentally—by clicking the bullet in the Lock column.

◆ To avoid adding sounds to the wrong layer, Option-click (Mac) or Alt-click (Windows) the sound layer you want to work with. Flash locks all other layers.

Figure 17.10 It's best to keep sounds in separate layers from the graphics and actions in your movie. To organize multiple sound layers, place them in a separate layer folder. Increase the layer height for sound layers to make more room for the waveforms.

Adding Sounds to Buttons

Auditory feedback helps people who view your Flash creation interact with buttons correctly. For buttons that look like real-world buttons, adding a click sound to the Down frame provides a more realistic feel. For more fanciful buttons or ones disguised as part of the scenery of your movie, adding sound to the Over frame lets users know they've discovered a hot spot.

To enhance buttons with auditory feedback:

1. Open a Flash document containing a button symbol to which you want to add sound.

   (To learn about working with button symbols, see Chapter 14.)

2. Open the file's Library panel (choose Window > Library), and select the button symbol you want to modify.

3. From the library's panel menu, choose Edit (**Figure 17.11**).

   Flash opens the button in symbol-editing mode.

4. In the button symbol's Timeline, add a new layer (click the New Layer button), and name it Sound.

5. In the Sound layer, select the Over and Down frames, Control-click (Mac) or right-click (Windows), and choose Convert to Blank Keyframes (**Figure 17.12**).

Figure 17.11 To edit a symbol, you can select it in the Library panel and choose Edit from the panel menu.

Figure 17.12 Add a new layer for the sounds in a button symbol. In that layer, create keyframes for the button states where you plan to assign sounds.

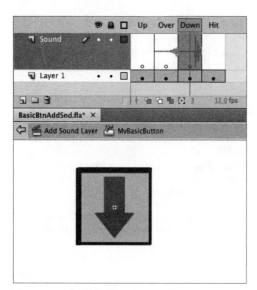

Figure 17.13 Flash displays the waveform of the assigned sound in the keyframe. Unlike movie Timelines, button-symbol Timelines have no in-between frames that can contain part of the waveform. Increasing the layer height for a button symbol's Sound layer enlarges any waveforms in the button's frames, letting you see more detail.

6. Using the techniques described in "Adding Sounds to Frames," earlier in this chapter, assign a sound to the Over frame and a different sound to the Down frame.

Flash displays as much of the waveform as possible in each frame. When you add sounds to buttons, it makes sense to increase the height of the layer that contains sounds (**Figure 17.13**). Make sure that the sound's Sync property is set to Event (the default) in the Sound section of the Frame Property inspector. (You'll learn more about setting the Sync property in the next section.)

7. Return to document-editing mode.

Every instance of the button symbol in the document now has sounds attached.

8. To hear the buttons in action, choose Control > Enable Simple Buttons.

When you move the pointer over the button, Flash plays the sound you assigned to the Over frame. When you click the button, you hear the sound you assigned to the Down frame.

✔ Tip

- The most common frames to use for button feedback are the Over and Down frames, but you can add sounds to any of the button symbol's frames. Sounds added to the Up frame play when the pointer rolls out of the active button area. Sounds added to the Hit frame play when you release the mouse button within the active button area.

Using Event Sounds

One of the parameters available in the Sound section of the Frame Property inspector is Sync. Sync determines the way Flash synchronizes the sounds in your movie. Sync has four settings: Event, Start, Stop, and Stream. The default is Event.

Event sounds play independently of the main Timeline. Flash starts an event sound at a keyframe in a movie; the event sound plays until Flash reaches the end of the sound clip or encounters an instruction to stop playing that sound or all sounds. Long event sounds can continue to play after the playhead reaches the last frame in the movie. If your movie loops, every time the playhead passes a frame with an event sound, Flash starts another instance of that sound playing.

To understand how synchronization works, it's helpful to work in a file that has identifying text in keyframes.

To set up a file for testing sounds:

1. Create a 20-frame, three-layer Flash document.

2. Label the layers Objects, Sound 1, and Sound 2.

3. In all layers, insert keyframes into 5, 10, 15, and 20 (frame 1 has a keyframe by default).

4. In the Objects layer, place identifying text on the Stage for each keyframe.

5. Import several sounds of different lengths into the file's library.

   This example uses a 15.8-second sound clip of a musical-scale passage, a water drop sound, a melodic passage, and some rhythm sounds.

6. Save the document as a template for use throughout this chapter, and name it SoundSyncMaster (**Figure 17.14**).

Figure 17.14 After setting up a testing file for use in this chapter, choose File > Save As Template to access the Save As Template dialog. Save the file as SoundSyncMaster. Be sure to close the template document after creating it. For detailed instructions on saving documents as templates, see Chapter 1.

Independent Sounds vs. Synchronized Sounds

Unsynchronized sound clips play independently of the frames in a movie and can even continue playing after the playhead reaches the last frame in the movie. Flash starts these *event sounds* at a specific frame, but thereafter, event sounds play without relation to specific frames. On one viewer's computer, the sound may play over ten frames; on a slower setup, the sound may finish when only five frames have appeared.

Flash can also synchronize entire sound clips with specific frames. Flash breaks these *stream sounds* or *streaming sounds* into smaller pieces and attaches each piece to a specific frame. For streaming sounds, Flash forces the animation to keep up with the sounds. On slower setups, Flash draws fewer frames so important actions and sounds stay together.

Figure 17.15 Select the keyframe to which you want to assign a sound. Settings that you create in the Sound section of the Frame Property inspector are applied to the selected keyframe.

Figure 17.16 In the Sound section of the Frame Property inspector, choose a sound from the Name pop-up menu.

Figure 17.17 From the Sync pop-up menu, choose Event to make the assigned sound start in the selected keyframe and play to the end of the sound, without synchronizing to any subsequent frames of the movie.

To make an assigned sound an event sound:

1. Open a new document using the SoundSyncMaster template you created in the preceding task.

2. In the Timeline, select keyframe 5 of the Sound 1 layer (**Figure 17.15**).

3. In the Sound section of the Frame Property inspector, from the Name pop-up menu, choose a long sound, such as the 15.8-second sound named Scale.AIFF (**Figure 17.16**).

4. From the Sync pop-up menu, choose Event (**Figure 17.17**).

   The Scale.AIFF sound is assigned to keyframe 5 of the Sound 1 layer.

5. Position the playhead in keyframe 1, and play your movie (choose Control > Play).

   In a movie that has a standard frame rate of 24 frames per second (fps), the 15.8-second Scale sound continues to play after the playhead reaches the last frame of the movie.

✔ Tip

■ To understand better how Flash handles event sounds, choose Control > Loop Playback. Now play the movie again, and let it loop through a couple of times. Each time the playhead enters keyframe 5, Flash starts another instance of the Scale sound, and you begin to hear not one set of notes going up the scale, but a cacophony of bad harmonies. When you stop the playback, each sound instance plays out until its end—an effect sort of like people singing a round.

USING EVENT SOUNDS

To play overlapping instances of the same sound:

1. Using the file you created in the preceding task, to assign a sound to a later point in the movie's Timeline, do either of the following:

   ▲ Select keyframe 15 of the Sound 1 layer.

   ▲ Select keyframe 15 of the Sound 2 layer.

   Because Flash starts a new instance of an event sound even if that sound is already playing, you have the choice of adding a second instance to the same layer as the first or adding it to a different layer.

2. In the Sound section of the Frame Property inspector, from the Name pop-up menu, choose the same sound (Scale.AIFF).

3. From the Sync pop-up menu, choose Event.

   The Scale.AIFF sound is assigned to keyframe 15 of whichever layer you chose (**Figure 17.18**).

4. Position the playhead in keyframe 1, and play your movie one time.

   When the playhead reaches keyframe 5, the Scale.AIFF sound starts. When the playhead reaches keyframe 15, another instance of the Scale.AIFF sound starts, and the two sounds play together (you hear two voices). When the first instance ends, you again hear only one voice. Within a single layer, each frame can contain only one sound. To make Flash begin playing different sounds at the same point in a movie, you must put the sounds in separate layers.

5. Save this file for use in a later task; name it OverlapSnds.fla.

Figure 17.18 You can add a second instance of your sound and make it play on top of the first. Event sounds play independent of the main Timeline, so you're free to add the second sound to the same layer as the first (top). Alternatively, you can add the second sound to its own layer (bottom).

Figure 17.19 To make two different sounds begin playing simultaneously, you must put each sound in a different layer in a keyframe at the same spot in the Timeline—for example, keyframe 5.

✔ Tip

- All the information required to play an event sound lives in the keyframe to which you assigned that sound. When you play the movie, Flash pauses at that keyframe until all the information has downloaded. It's best to reserve event syncing for short sound clips; otherwise, your movie may be interrupted by long pauses for downloading sounds.

To start different sounds simultaneously:

1. Open a new document using the SoundSyncMaster template you created earlier in this chapter.

2. In the Timeline, select keyframe 5 of the Sound 1 layer.

3. In the Sound section of the Frame Property inspector, from the Name pop-up menu, choose the first sound (here, Scale.AIFF).

4. From the Sync pop-up menu, choose Event.

5. In the Timeline, select keyframe 5 of the Sound 2 layer.

6. In the Sound section of the Frame Property inspector, from the Name pop-up menu, choose a different sound (here, Melody.AIFF).

   You can also import a new sound to your movie's library, or open the Sounds common library or the Library panel of another movie containing the sound you want to use, and then drag a copy of the sound to the Stage.

   Flash places the waveform for the second sound in keyframe 5 of the Sound 2 layer (**Figure 17.19**).

7. In the Sound section of the Frame Property inspector, from the Sync pop-up menu, choose Event.

8. Position the playhead in keyframe 1, and play your movie one time.

   When the playhead reaches keyframe 5, Flash starts playing the Scale.AIFF and Melody.AIFF sounds simultaneously.

Using Start Sounds

Start sounds behave just like event sounds, with one important difference: Flash doesn't play a new instance of a start sound if that sound is already playing.

To set an assigned sound's Sync parameter to Start:

1. Open OverlapSnds.fla, the file you created in "To play overlapping instances of the same sound," earlier in this chapter.

   One instance of the Scale.AIFF sound is in keyframe 5; another is in keyframe 15, in the Sound 1 or Sound 2 layer, depending on what you did in the earlier task.

2. In the Timeline, select keyframe 15 containing Scale.AIFF (**Figure 17.20**).

3. In the Sound section of the Frame Property inspector, from the Sync pop-up menu, choose Start (**Figure 17.21**).

4. Position the playhead in keyframe 1, and play your movie one time.

   When the playhead reaches keyframe 5, the Scale.AIFF sound starts. When the playhead reaches keyframe 15, nothing changes; you continue to hear just one voice as the Scale.AIFF sound continues playing. When a sound is playing and Flash encounters another instance of the same sound, the Sync setting determines whether Flash plays that sound. When Sync is set to Start, Flash doesn't play another instance of the sound.

✔ Tip

■ To avoid playing multiple instances of a sound when a movie loops, set the sound's Sync property to Start. If the sound is playing when the movie starts again, Flash adds no new sound. If the sound is done, Flash restarts the sound again when the playhead enters a keyframe containing the sound.

Figure 17.20 To change a sound's Sync setting, first select the keyframe that contains the sound.

Figure 17.21 To prevent Flash from playing another instance of a sound if that sound is already playing, choose Start from the Sync pop-up menu in the Sound section of the Frame Property inspector.

Figure 17.22 To make Flash force a sound to synchronize with a specific frame of your movie, choose Stream from the Sync pop-up menu in the Sound section of the Frame Property inspector.

The Mystery of Streaming Sound

When you choose Stream as the Sync setting for a sound, Flash divides that sound clip into smaller subclips and embeds them in individual frames. The movie's frame rate determines the subclips' size. In a movie with a frame rate of 10 frames per second (fps), for example, Flash divides streaming sounds into subclips that are a tenth of a second long. For every 10 frames, Flash plays 1 second of the sound.

Flash synchronizes the start of each sub-clip with a specific frame of the movie. If the sound plays back faster than the computer can draw frames, Flash sacrifices some visuals (skips drawing some frames of the animation) so that sound and images match up as closely as possible. Setting a sound's Sync property to Stream ensures, for example, that you hear the door slam when you see it swing shut—not a few seconds before. If the discrepancy between sound-playback speed and frame-drawing speed is big enough, however, those dropped frames make the movie look jerky, just as it would if you set a low frame rate to begin with.

Using Stream Sounds

Stream sounds are specifically geared for playback over the Web. When Sync is set to Stream, Flash breaks a sound into smaller sound clips. Flash synchronizes these subclips with specific frames of the movie—as many frames as are required to play the sound. Flash stops streaming sounds when playback reaches either a new keyframe in the sound's layer or an instruction to stop playing that specific sound or all sounds.

Unlike event sounds, which must download fully before they can play, stream sounds can start playing after a few frames have downloaded. This situation makes streaming the best choice for long sounds, especially if you'll be delivering your movie over the Web.

To make an assigned sound a stream sound:

1. Open a new document using the SoundSyncMaster template you created earlier in this chapter.

2. In the Timeline, in the Sound 1 layer, remove keyframe status from keyframe 10 (select it and choose Modify > Timeline > Clear Keyframe).

3. In the Timeline, in the Sound 1 layer, select keyframe 5.

4. In the Sound section of the Frame Property inspector, from the Name pop-up menu, choose a long sound (here, Scale.AIFF).

5. From the Sync pop-up menu, choose Stream (**Figure 17.22**).

continues on next page

6. To see how the sound fits into the available time in your movie, in the Sound section of the Frame Property inspector, click the Edit Sound Envelope button (the pencil icon).

The Edit Envelope dialog appears.

At 15.8 seconds, the Scale.AIFF sound is too long to play completely in the frames between keyframe 5 and keyframe 15. When Sync is set to Stream, Flash plays only as much of the sound as can fit in the frames that are available to it—in this case, slightly less than a half second. In the Edit Envelope dialog, a vertical line indicates where Flash truncates this instance of the sound (**Figure 17.23**).

7. To close the Edit Envelope dialog, click OK or Cancel.

The truncated waveform appears in the keyframe span (**Figure 17.24**).

8. Position the playhead in keyframe 1, and play your movie to hear the sound in action.

When the playhead reaches keyframe 5, the Scale.AIFF sound starts. When the playhead reaches keyframe 15, the keyframe span ends, and Flash stops playback of the Scale.AIFF sound.

9. Choose Control > Loop Playback, and then play the movie to hear the sound in looping mode.

Flash repeats the same snippet of sound, stopping it each time the playhead reaches keyframe 15.

✔ Tip

■ You can hear streaming sounds play as you drag the playhead through the Timeline (a technique called *scrubbing*). As the playhead moves over the waveform, you can see how the images and sounds fit together. You can then add or delete frames to better synchronize the sounds with the images onscreen.

Sound will stop playing here

Figure 17.23 When you set a sound's Sync to Stream, you can check how much of the sound will play, given the number of in-between frames there are for the sound to play in. In the Sound section of the Frame Property inspector, click the Edit Sound Envelope button (top) to open the Edit Envelope dialog (bottom). The sound-editing window displays a sound's full waveform in relation to time or to frame numbers.

Figure 17.24 There is time enough in the 9-frame keyframe span to play only the first note of the Scale sound. Flash displays just that much of the full 15.8-second waveform in the Timeline.

The Rhythm sound

The Melody sound

After adding blank keyframe

Figure 17.25 Inserting a new keyframe cuts off your view of the preceding sound's waveform in the Timeline. If the sound is an event sound, however, it continues playing even when the playhead moves past the keyframe.

Figure 17.26 To stop a sound's playback at a specific point in a movie, create and then select the keyframe where the sound should stop. In the Sound section of the Frame Property inspector, from the Name pop-up menu, choose the sound you want to stop. From the Sync pop-up menu, choose Stop. Here, the Stop instruction refers to the Rhythm sound.

Stopping Sounds

Although event sounds normally play to the end, you can force them to stop at a specific keyframe. To issue an instruction to stop a specific sound, set that sound's Sync property to Stop.

To stop playback of a sound:

1. Create a new single-layer 15-frame Flash document with two fairly long event sounds (at least 2 or 3 seconds each); place one sound in keyframe 1 and the other in keyframe 5.

   In this example, keyframe 1 contains the sound Rhythm.AIFF, and keyframe 5 contains the sound Melody.AIFF. Make sure that Sync is set to Event for both sounds.

2. In the Timeline, at frame 8, insert a new blank keyframe (**Figure 17.25**).

   The blank keyframe cuts off the waveform in the Timeline, but on playback, both event sounds continue to play after the playhead reaches keyframe 8.

3. Select keyframe 8.

4. In the Sound section of the Frame Property inspector, from the Name pop-up menu, choose Rhythm.AIFF.

5. From the Sync pop-up menu, choose Stop (**Figure 17.26**).

   Flash uses this instruction to stop playback of the Rhythm.AIFF sound at keyframe 8.

continues on next page

Flash places a small square in the middle of keyframe 8 in the Timeline to indicate that the frame contains a stop-sound instruction (**Figure 17.27**).

6. Position the playhead in keyframe 1, and play your movie to hear the sounds in action.

    The Rhythm.AIFF sound starts immediately; Melody.AIFF kicks in at keyframe 5. When the playhead reaches keyframe 8, Rhythm.AIFF cuts out, but Melody.AIFF plays on even after the playhead reaches the end of the movie.

Sync is set to Stop for this keyframe

Figure 17.27 In the Timeline, a small square in the middle of a keyframe indicates the presence of the stop-sound instruction.

✔ Tips

■ The Stop setting and the sound that it stops can be in different layers. The Stop setting stops playback of all instances of the specified sound that are currently playing in any layer.

■ To stop only one instance of a sound, set the Sync parameter of that instance to Stream; then, in the layer containing that instance, put a blank keyframe in the frame where you want that instance of the sound to stop.

Using Buttons to Control Sounds

In this chapter, you learn to use sounds two ways. You create user-friendly buttons with audio feedback by adding sounds to keyframes in button symbols. You create sound tracks or sound effects for animation by adding and removing sound instances directly in the Timeline during authoring. A third way to work with sound is to use ActionScript (AS) to control sounds during playback—loading, playing, and stopping sounds as needed at runtime. For AS 2.0, Flash provides a set of Behaviors for common sound-related tasks. Behaviors attach scripts directly to sound-control objects (button symbols, button components, or movie clips). You can use Behaviors to set up buttons that load and play a specific sound, that replay a loaded sound, or that stop all event sounds that are currently playing whether they were loaded with AS or placed in the Timeline during authoring. For AS 3.0, you must script any sound-control objects yourself. You can create frame scripts that target sound-control objects and carry out the same types of sound-control tasks as the AS 2.0 Behaviors. With either version of ActionScript, when setting up buttons to control sounds you must set the sound's Linkage properties. Scripting sounds is a complex task, beyond the scope of a *Visual Quickstart Guide*. To learn about creating basic frame scripts in ActionScript 3.0, see Chapter 15.

Editing Sounds

Flash lets you make limited changes in each instance of a sound in the Edit Envelope dialog. You can change the start point and end point of the sound (that is, cut a piece off the beginning or end of the waveform) and adjust the sound's volume.

Flash offers six predefined volume edits: Left Channel, Right Channel, Fade Left to Right, Fade Right to Left, Fade In, and Fade Out. These sound-editing templates create common sound effects, such as making a sound grow gradually louder (Fade In) or softer (Fade Out), or (for stereo sounds) making the sound move from one speaker channel to the other.

In addition to changing a sound's volume, you can make a sound shorter by instructing Flash to remove sound data from the beginning of the waveform, the end, or both.

To assign packaged volume effects:

1. Open a new document, and add a sound track.

   Add a layer named Sounds, and place a sound in keyframe 1 of that layer. For this task, use the sound Animal Dog Bark 26.mp3 from the Sounds common library. This sound clip is a recording of a dog that barks three times. If you like, add more defined frames to the Sounds layer to see more of the sound's waveform in the Timeline.

2. In the Timeline, select keyframe 1 of the Sounds layer.

3. In the Sound section of the Frame Property inspector, click the Edit Sound Envelope button (the pencil icon).

   The Edit Envelope dialog appears, with a sound-editing window showing the waveform of the sound from keyframe 1 (**Figure 17.28**).

   continues on next page

Figure 17.28 Flash lets you perform simple sound editing—for length and volume—in the Edit Envelope dialog.

4. In the Edit Envelope dialog, click the Frames button.

The sound-editing window can measure the length of the sound in seconds or in frames. Clicking the filmstrip icon in the lower-right corner of the window sets the units to frames; clicking the clock icon sets the units to seconds.

5. From the Effect pop-up menu, choose Fade In (**Figure 17.29**).

Flash adjusts the sound envelope (**Figure 17.30**). When the envelope line is at the top of the sound-editing window, Flash plays 100 percent of the available sound. When the envelope line is at the bottom of the window, Flash plays 0 percent of the available sound.

6. Click the Play button to hear the sound with its fade-in effect.

The barking starts soft and grows louder.

7. Click OK.

Flash returns you to document-editing mode.

✔ Tip

■ If you don't need to look at your sound's waveform, you can bypass the Edit Envelope dialog. Just choose an effect from the Effect pop-up menu in the Sound section of the Frame Property inspector.

Figure 17.29 The Effect pop-up menu in the Edit Envelope dialog offers six templates for common sound effects that deal with volume. Choose Fade In to make the sound start soft and grow in volume.

Figure 17.30 The Fade In effect brings the sound's envelope down to 0 percent (the bottom of the sound-editing window) at the start of the sound and quickly raises it to 100 percent (the top of the sound-editing window).

EDITING SOUNDS

Figure 17.31 To edit the volume of a sound yourself, from the Effect pop-up menu in the Edit Envelope dialog, choose Custom.

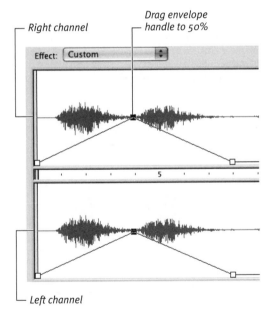

Figure 17.32 Click the waveform in the sound-editing window to add a handle. Drag the handle to adjust the sound envelope. You can make the sound envelope the same or different for both channels. For monaural sounds, both waveforms are identical.

To customize volume effects:

1. Follow steps 1–3 in the preceding task.

2. From the Effect pop-up menu in the Edit Envelope dialog, choose Custom (**Figure 17.31**).

3. In the sound-editing window, drag the square envelope handles that appear at the beginning of the sound in both channels down to 0 percent.

4. In the right channel (the top section of the window), click the waveform at three places to set a different level for different parts of the sound.

   For this example, click the waveform at frames 4, 8, and 12. Flash adds envelope handles so both channels have four handles. Divide the sound roughly into thirds.

5. In the right-channel window, drag the second handle up to the 50 percent volume level (**Figure 17.32**).

6. Repeat step 5 for the left channel.

7. In both channels, drag the third handle to the 50 percent level and the fourth handle to the 100 percent level.

   You can use as many as eight handles to create a variety of volume changes within one sound.

8. Click the Play button to hear the sound with its fade-in effect.

   Flash fades in the dog's first bark, plays the second bark at half volume, and plays the last bark at full volume.

9. Click OK.

✔ Tip

■ To remove unwanted envelope handles, drag them out of the sound-editing window.

To edit sounds for length:

1. Using the movie you created in the preceding task, select keyframe 1.

2. To access the Edit Envelope dialog, in the Sound section of the Frame Property inspector, click the Edit Sound Envelope button.

3. In the sound-editing window, drag the time-out control (the second bar in the "Timeline" between the two channels) to the end of the sound where the wave-form begins to go flat (**Figure 17.33**). Flash shortens the sound in both channels (**Figure 17.34**).

4. Click OK.

   Flash returns you to document-editing mode. Now the waveform of the entire sound is visible in the keyframe span in the Timeline (**Figure 17.35**).

✔ Tip

■ To remove dead air from the beginning of a sound, drag the time-in control. Flash places a light gray background behind the initial portion of the sound's waveform to indicate that it won't play.

Figure 17.33 Flash lets you trim the beginning and end of a sound in the Edit Envelope dialog's sound-editing window. Here, dragging the time-out control clips off the end of the sound where the wave's amplitude is smaller, almost a flat line. (The small amplitude indicates a very soft sound or silence.)

Figure 17.34 After you reposition the time-out control, the new, shorter waveform appears in the Edit Envelope dialog's sound-editing window.

Figure 17.35 The original sound is too long to fit completely within the keyframe span in the Timeline. After you shorten the sound, the shorter wave fits completely in the keyframe span.

Adding Video to Flash

The process for adding video to Flash is similar to the process for adding sound. You start by choosing the Import Video command. This command accesses Flash's Video Import Wizard. The wizard asks you to locate an encoded video file and choose how you want to deliver the video. You can embed the video data to make it part of the FLA file during authoring; after you publish your movie for playback, the embedded video data becomes part of the SWF file (see Chapter 18). Alternatively, you can create a link to an encoded video file and use a component to display the video data at runtime. The Video Import Wizard ensures that the video data you select is encoded correctly. The wizard then imports the data or makes the appropriate link to it. The precise steps vary somewhat depending on the delivery method you choose.

Importing Video for Streaming or Progressive Download

Flash can stream video over the Web or deliver video as a progressive download. Both methods allow you to work with larger amounts of video data and avoid delays in playback while video data downloads to the end user's system. To deploy the video as streaming or progressive download, you must use a playback component to link to the video data in an external file. Flash Player displays the video inside the component at runtime.

About Encoding Video for Flash

Flash's Video Import Wizard can only handle files that have already been encoded in a Flash-compatible format (FLV and F4V are examples). When you choose to import for embedding, the wizard only allows files in FLV format. Flash includes a stand-alone video encoder—Adobe Media Encoder CS4 (AME)—that lets you encode video data in the appropriate formats to work with Flash. AME lets you encode multiple files in batches. You create a list of files, then choose encoding options for video- and audio-compression, add filters, create cue points, and perform basic edits (cropping and resizing). Not sure if your video file is in a Flash-compatible format? Try importing it with the wizard. If the data is not encoded appropriately, the wizard notifies you. You can open up AME quickly by clicking the Launch Adobe Media button on the Select Video page of the wizard.

ADDING VIDEO TO FLASH

About the Video Import Wizard

Flash CS4's Video Import Wizard walks you through the process of importing video clips for use in Flash. The clips must already be encoded in a format that works with Flash, such as FLV (Flash video) or F4V. (F4V is a subset of the H.264 video-compression specification developed by the standards group known as the JVT [Joint Video Team]. Most video files encoded as MPEG-4—such as video podcasts in your iTunes library—qualify as F4V.)

The biggest decision you have to make when using the wizard is how you want to deliver the video data to your viewers. You can embed the video data into the Flash document, or keep the data in an external file and display the video via a special Flash element—the FLVPlayback component.

Embedded video adds to the size of a published Flash movie, which may have negative effect on your end users' experience as they wait for enough data to download to start viewing. Video displayed using the FLVPlayback component doesn't add to the size of the published movie. How long users must wait to see the video depends on whether you use progressive or streaming video and on the particulars of each user's computer setup.

You can have video displayed with the FLVPlayback component download progressively from a Web server. In this method, Flash downloads the entire video file. You can start watching data as it downloads, but if download speed is slow you may catch up to the downloaded video and have to wait for more to reach your system to continue watching. You can't skip ahead to start downloading at a different section of the video.

You can have Flash stream video displayed with the FLVPlayback component, either from a Flash Video Streaming Service or from your own server using Flash Media Server. For streaming, Flash divides the video data into small segments. The video can start playing as soon as a few segments have downloaded. The server continues to download video data while the end user watches. Users can skip around to different segments of the video easily. Streaming video is also more efficient for longer videos; if users only watch a portion of the video, they don't need to download the whole thing. And the video streams don't wind up in the user's cache. To use streaming video, you must have access to a Flash Media Server, have a Flash Video Streaming Service account with your ISP, or use a dedicated streaming service, such as Limelight Networks.

In addition, Flash can deploy video for use with mobile devices.

Figure 17.36 Choose File > Import > Import Video to open Flash's Video Import Wizard.

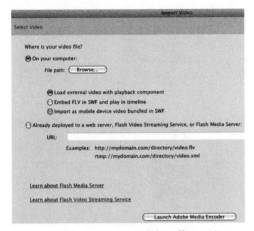

Figure 17.37 The Import Video dialog offers options for displaying encoded video in your Flash movie. The first step is locating the video file you want to display.

To import video for display in a playback component:

1. In a new Flash document, or a new layer, create a blank keyframe where you want the video to start playing.

   It's best to create a separate layer for the video component that Flash will add at the end of this task. Keeping the component on a separate layer helps you organize the Timeline and avoids the problem of inadvertently placing the component into a motion-tween span, which would require replacing the current tween target with the playback component.

2. To begin the import process, with the desired keyframe selected, choose File > Import > Import Video (**Figure 17.36**). The Select Video page of the Import Video dialog appears (**Figure 17.37**).

3. To use a file on your hard drive, select the On Your Computer radio button and click the Browse button in the File Path area (**Figure 17.38**). When the Open dialog appears, navigate to your file, select it, and click the Open button. The Video Import Wizard returns you to the Select Video page and displays the file's path.

   or

   To use a file that is located on a Web server, select the "Already deployed to a Web server" radio button (**Figure 17.39**) and enter the file's address in the URL field.

   continues on next page

Figure 17.38 To locate video on your computer for import, select the On Your Computer radio button, then navigate to the file and select it.

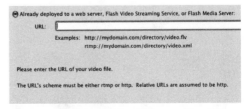

Figure 17.39 To import video that's on an external server, select the "Already deployed to a Web server" radio button and enter the video file's URL.

4. Click Continue (Mac) or Next (Windows). The Skinning page appears (**Figure 17.40**).

5. To create playback controls for end users, from the Skin pop-up menu, choose either of the following:

▲ To create a controller bar that floats on top of the image in the video-display window, choose a skin whose name starts with the words *SkinOver* (**Figure 17.41**).

▲ To create a controller bar that sits beneath the video-display window, choose a skin whose name starts with the words *SkinUnder*.

Minimum width: 330   Minimum height: 60

Skin: SkinOverAll.swf   Color:

URL:

Figure 17.40 In the Skinning page of the Import Video dialog, you can choose a skin that creates user-interface controls for the progressive or streaming video displayed in your Flash movie.

Minimum width: 330   Minimum height: 60

Skin: SkinOverAll.swf   Color:

URL:

    None
    ✓ SkinOverAll.swf
    SkinOverAllNoCaption.swf
    SkinOverAllNoFullNoCaption.swf
    SkinOverAllNoFullscreen.swf
    SkinOverAllNoVolNoCaptionNoFull.swf
    SkinOverPlay.swf
    SkinOverPlayCaption.swf
    SkinOverPlayFullscreen.swf
    SkinOverPlayMute.swf
    SkinOverPlayMuteCaptionFull.swf
    SkinOverPlaySeekCaption.swf
    SkinOverPlaySeekFullscreen.swf
    SkinOverPlaySeekMute.swf
    SkinOverPlaySeekStop.swf
    SkinOverPlayStopSeekCaptionVol.swf
    SkinOverPlayStopSeekFullVol.swf
    SkinOverPlayStopSeekMuteVol.swf
    SkinUnderAll.swf

Figure 17.41 Each skin in the pop-up menu uses a different set of elements to create the controller bar. Skins that contain the word Over get layered on top of the video image; skins that contain the word Under wind up just below the video-display window.

Figure 17.42 The Finish Video Import page of the Import Video dialog provides information about how to work with the video files for publishing. To learn more, select the "After importing video, view video topics in Flash Help" check box.

6. Click Continue (Mac) or Next (Windows).

The Finish Video Import page appears (**Figure 17.42**), describing the assets created by the wizard and giving a brief overview of how to use them (see the sidebar "Final Steps for Using FLVPlayback," later in this chapter).

7. Click Finish.

The Getting Metadata dialog appears. To stop the import process, click the Cancel button. When loading has finished, Flash places an instance of the FLVPlayback component on the Stage in the keyframe you selected. The properties of the instance are already set to point to the source video file and to use the skin you chose in step 5.

✔ Tips

- In step 5, to create a video clip with no controller bar, choose None from the Skin pop-up menu.

- To select a color for the controller bar, in the Video Import dialog's Skinning page, click the Color control and choose a new color from the pop-up swatch set.

- Best practice: Before importing the video, copy the encoded video file to the same folder as the FLA or SWF (or a subfolder in the same folder). The URL Flash creates as the Source parameter (see "Working with the FLVPlayback component," later in this chapter) will be a relative path, ready to be put on a Web server.

Importing Video for Embedding

When you choose to embed a video file, the video data becomes part of the FLA and SWF files. Embedded video must be in FLV format. When you import video for embedding, the Video Import Wizard has an extra page of settings.

To import and embed video:

1. Follow steps 1–3 in the preceding task.

   You only need to select a keyframe if you want Flash to place the video in the Timeline for you.

2. Select the radio button labeled "Embed FLV in SWF and play in Timeline" (**Figure 17.43**).

3. Click Continue (Mac) or Next (Windows).

   The Embedding page of the Import Video dialog appears, with options for working with embedded video clips (**Figure 17.44**).

4. From the Symbol Type pop-up menu (**Figure 17.45**), choose one of the following:

   ▲ **Embedded Video** places the video frames directly into the main Timeline of your movie.

   ▲ **Movie Clip** places the video frames into the Timeline of a movie-clip symbol.

   ▲ **Graphic** places the video frames into the Timeline of an animated graphic symbol.

5. To have Flash automatically place video frames in the Timeline (if you chose Embedded Video in step 4) or place a symbol instance on the Stage (if you chose Movie Clip or Graphic in step 4), select the "Place instance on Stage" check box.

   Upon completing the import process, Flash places the video or symbol instance in the currently selected keyframe.

Figure 17.43 When you choose embedding as the delivery method (top), Flash puts all of the video data into the published SWF file. This method has pluses and minuses, as indicated in the warning text that appears in the dialog when you choose to embed (bottom).

Figure 17.44 You must choose settings for working with the embedded video. You can have Flash place an instance of the video clip on the Stage for you, expand the number of defined frames in the Timeline to display all the frames of the video, and include an audio track.

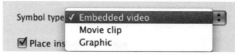

Figure 17.45 The Symbol Type menu in the Embedding page of the Import Video dialog gives you the choice of turning the video clip into an animated graphic symbol or a movie-clip symbol, or placing the frames of the video directly into the main Timeline.

Figure 17.46 With embedded video, you can include the sound track within the video itself or exclude it.

6. If you chose Embedded Video or Graphic in step 4, to have Flash add enough frames to the selected keyframe span in the main Timeline to display all the video's frames, select the "Expand Timeline if needed" check box.

7. To include an audio track, select the Include Audio check box (**Figure 17.46**).

8. Click Continue (Mac) or Next (Windows). The Finish Video Import window appears.

9. Click Finish.
   Flash completes the import process. For details, see step 7 of the preceding task.

✔ Tips

■ When you import video for embedding, do not attempt to place it in a tween span; as Flash doesn't allow embedded video in a tween span. Flash places the video clip (and movie-clip or graphic symbol if you chose to create one) in the library of your document but places nothing in the Timeline.

■ Warning: Don't change the frame rate of your document (FLA) after you've imported video, as that all but guarantees synch issues during playback. If you must change the frame rate, reimport the video afterwards. It may also be beneficial to encode the video at the same frame rate as the FLA.

ADDING VIDEO TO FLASH

Working with Embedded Video

Depending on the settings you choose when you use the Video Import Wizard to create embedded video clips, Flash places an instance of the clip on the Stage or just places the embedded-video asset in the library. When automatically placing an instance on the Stage, Flash can create enough frames in the Timeline to show the full video, or allow the existing keyframe span to truncate the video. When you place an instance of an embedded clip into the Timeline yourself, you need to create a keyframe span that accommodates as much of the video as you want to show.

To place embedded video clips in the Timeline:

1. Open a Flash document and import the embedded video as described in "Importing Video for Embedding," earlier in this chapter.

   For this task, deselect the "Place instance on Stage" check box in step 5.

2. In the Timeline, select the keyframe in which you want the embedded video to start playing.

   The keyframe must not be part of a motion tween. Flash cannot use an embedded video clip as a tween target.

3. From the Library panel, drag a copy of the embedded video clip to the Stage (**Figure 17.47**).

Figure 17.47 To place embedded video in a Flash movie, drag an instance of the embedded-video clip from the library to the Stage.

Previewing Embedded Video Clips

In Flash's authoring environment, embedded video clips display their images within the keyframe span that contains the clip. You can simply play the movie (choose Control > Play) or move the playhead through the Timeline to view the changing video frames. If the embedded clip has an audio track, however, you must use one of the test modes to preview the sound. You must also use one of the test modes to see the embedded video in context with interactive elements, such as movie clips or scripted buttons.

Figure 17.48 Flash alerts you when you attempt to add embedded video that has more frames than the current keyframe span where you are placing it.

Before adding embedded-video instance

After adding embedded-video instance

Figure 17.49 Layer 3 in this Timeline shows the result of answering Yes in the dialog that warns that the current keyframe span is too short: Flash adds enough frames to display the full 16-frame clip. Layer 2 shows the result for answering No: the existing keyframe span truncates the video.

Unlike movie clips, which play in their own independent Timeline, embedded video clips need to fit their frames into the Timeline of the movie or movie clip containing them. Each time you drag an instance of an embedded video clip to the Stage, if the selected keyframe span contains fewer frames than the clip, a warning dialog asks whether you want to add enough frames to display the entire clip (**Figure 17.48**).

4. To enlarge the keyframe span, click Yes.

Flash adds enough frames to the span to reveal the entire video clip (**Figure 17.49**).

or

To retain the current number of frames in the keyframe span, click No.

Flash places the video clip on the Stage, but the keyframe span cuts off the end of the clip.

The Mystery of Embedded Video

Embedded video clips bear similarities to some Flash symbols, yet embedded video is a unique type of element. Like animated graphic symbols, embedded video clips play within—and must synchronize with—frames in the main movie Timeline. Embedded video clips can contain audio, although if you import the audio as an integrated track, you won't see the sound's waveform in the Timeline. As with any symbol, you place an instance of an embedded-video clip by dragging a copy from the library window to the Stage. The Property Inspector gives you information about selected instances of embedded video clips. You can modify a selected instance of an embedded video clip in many of the ways that you modify other objects in Flash: you can use the free-transform tool, for example, to resize, rotate, or skew the video image. You can't use an embedded video clip as the tween target in a motion tween; you must put the embedded clip inside a Flash movie-clip symbol. In addition, to give an embedded video clip an independent Timeline and to gain the same control over the clip's appearance that you have over movie clips (to be able to change the clip's brightness, tint, or alpha, for example), you must place the embedded video clip inside a Flash movie-clip symbol. You can have Flash's Video Import Wizard create that symbol for you on import.

Working with the FLVPlayback Component

When you use Flash's Video Import Wizard to import video for use with a playback component, the wizard adds a component named FLVPlayback to the library and places an instance of it on the Stage. You can replace the component instance's generic icon with a frame from the video clip, change the source file, and modify the other parameters.

To choose source video for an FLVPlayback instance:

1. Select the FLVPlayback component instance on the Stage.

2. Access the Component Inspector panel.
   If the panel isn't open, choose Window > Component Inspector.

3. Click the Parameters button (Mac) or tab (Windows).
   Parameter settings associated with the component appear in a two-column table (**Figure 17.50**).

4. To choose the video that appears in the video-display window during playback, in the Name column click the Source parameter.
   A search button (a magnifying-glass icon) and text field with the path name of the current source activates in the Value column (**Figure 17.51**).

5. Click the field or the search button.
   The Content Path dialog appears.

6. To identify the source video file (it must be encoded in a Flash-compatible format, such as FLV or F4V), do either of the following:
   ▲ Enter a URL for the source video in the Content Path field (**Figure 17.52**).

Figure 17.50 The Component Inspector panel's Parameters section contains settings for all the parameters of a selected instance of the FLVPlayback component.

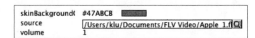

Figure 17.51 Clicking a parameter name activates a field for changing the parameter's value.

Enter URL

Browse to locate file

Figure 17.52 The Content Path dialog lets you identify the video that the FLVPlayback-component instance will display to the end user.

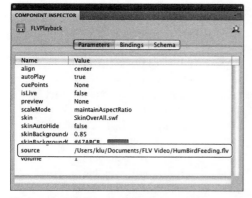

Figure 17.53 The filename in the Value column for the Source parameter of the FLVPlayback component is the file that end users see in the finished movie.

▲ To find the file you want, click the folder icon on the right side of the field. In the Browse for Source File dialog that appears, navigate to the file you want, and click Open. Flash enters the URL in the Content Path dialog.

7. To determine how Flash sizes the FLVPlayback component instance, do either of the following:

▲ To resize the component to fit the source video, select the Match Source Dimensions check box.

▲ To resize the video to fit within the default FLVPlayback component (320 by 240 pixels), deselect the Match Source Dimensions check box.

8. Click OK.

The Getting Metadata progress bar appears. Once it's done, Flash updates the Source parameter with the file name (**Figure 17.53**). Depending on what you chose in step 7, Flash also resizes the FLVPlayback component instance on the Stage. The instance now points to the desired encoded video file.

✔ Tip

■ If the skin you've chosen for the FLVPlayback instance includes a volume-control slider, you can set the starting slider position. Click the value for Volume and enter a new number: 1 sets the slider all the way to the right (full volume); values from 0.9 down to 0.1 set the slider farther to the left (lower volumes); a value of 0 sets the slider all the way to the left (no sound). You can enter values greater than 1, and those values create increasingly louder starting volumes, but the lever for the volume slider disappears. During playback, clicking anywhere in the slider brings the lever back, but end users may find this confusing.

About the FLVPlayback Component

Flash's Video Import Wizard imports encoded video files (such as FLV or F4V files) for use in your Flash movies. When you select the wizard's options to use the video with a playback component, the word *import* is a bit misleading. In fact, the data in the encoded file remains separate from your FLA and SWF files, but the wizard creates a link between your movie and the encoded video file via an element known as the *FLVPlayback component*. During the "import" process, the wizard places the FLVPlayback component in the library of your Flash document, places an instance of the component on the Stage, and sets the instance's source parameter to point to the file with the encoded video data. At runtime, the FLVPlayback component creates a video-display window within your Flash movie, and the video from the encoded source file appears in that window.

Components are a special type of Flash element. (You learned a bit about working with the button component in Chapter 14.) Components contain ActionScript that governs their behavior, but you can modify a component's behavior without actually doing any scripting; you simply change parameters in the Component Inspector panel. ActionScript 3.0 user-interface components such as the button component are not fully compiled. You can modify the graphic elements that make up their look (their *skin*) the same way you'd modify any graphic element. Unlike ActionScript 3.0 user-interface components, the FLVPlayback component is fully compiled; you cannot directly access its skin to modify it. The FLVPlayback component comes with a variety of packaged skins that create a controller bar for the video-display window. You can choose a new controller-bar style by setting the skin parameter for an FLVPlayback component instance. (Flash does allow you to create new skins for the FLVPlayback component, but that's beyond the scope of a *Visual Quickstart Guide*.)

Like other assets, the FLVPlayback component is reusable. To place another video-display window in your movie, drag a new instance of the FLVPlayback component to the Stage, then set its source parameter to point to the encoded video file you want to display. If you want, you can even bypass the Video Import Wizard. Access the Components panel (by choosing Window > Components, for example). Expand the panel's Video folder, then drag an instance of FLVPlayback to your document. The instance's source parameter is blank, but you can set it to point to an encoded video file as described in the task "To choose source video for an FLVPlayback instance."

Figure 17.54 When you position the pointer over the video preview in the Select Preview Frame dialog, a controller bar appears. Drag the slider to select the frame the FLVPlayback instance displays during authoring.

To create an author-time preview for a video component:

1. Follow steps 1–3 in the preceding task.

2. In the Component Inspector, in the Value column, double-click the current Preview parameter, None.

   The Select Preview Frame dialog appears. Depending on the length of the video, you may see the message "Loading. . ." as Flash reads the encoded video file. The preview video plays once through.

3. Position the pointer over the dialog's video-preview window.

   A controller bar appears (**Figure 17.54**).

4. Drag the slider triangle to move to a specific frame of the video.

   Elapsed time appears beneath the preview window. To play the video again, press the Play button.

continues on next page

Animating FLVPlayback Components

The FLVPlayback component has many similarities to a movie-clip symbol. It's an asset that lives in the library, you can modify it using the free-transform tool, you can mask its content using a mask layer, it appears as a static image on the Stage, and it displays its frames only in Flash Player. But there's an important difference: you can't use an FLVPlayback component instance in a motion tween, a classic tween, or an inverse kinematics (IK) armature. Flash lets you set up a tween using the FLVPlayback component instance, but when you test the movie, it becomes clear that the tween doesn't work. The video-display window just sits in its original spot, and none of the changes you set up to animate occurs. The IK bone tool won't let you link FLVPlayback component instances into an armature; if you try, a warning dialog appears.

If you want to move the component's video-display window around the Stage (or create other animated effects) with motion or classic tweening, or create an IK armature out of video clips, first put the FLVPlayback component instance inside a movie-clip symbol. You can then animate the movie-clip symbol instance to get the tween effects you want. (To review the process of creating movie-clip symbols, see Chapter 12; to review classic tweening, see Chapter 9; to review motion tweening see Chapter 11; to review IK animation, see Chapter 13.)

5. With the desired frame of the video showing in the preview window, click OK.

The selected frame appears in the component instance on the Stage, and the preview parameter in the Component Inspector updates to show the elapsed time for that frame (**Figure 17.55**).

✔ Tips

■ Instead of using the FLVPlayback component's prebuilt controller-bar skins, you can use other ActionScript 3.0 video components to create a user interface for controlling video that runs in the FLVPlayback window. Choose None as the skin for the FLVPlayback component instance on the Stage. Access the Components panel and expand the Video folder. You'll see a number of user-interface components: PlayButton, PauseButton, VolumeBar, and so on. Drag an instance of each element you want to use to the Stage. You can position the elements anywhere and modify them as you did with the button component (see Chapter 14).

■ You can change the size of an FLVPlayback component instance on the Stage using the free-transform tool, the Transform or Info panel, or the Position and Size section of the Property inspector. But if you've chosen a controller-bar skin for your video, be careful. The controller bar must be wide enough to hold all the user-interface elements that are part of the skin (the Play, Pause, and Mute button; the volume slider; and so on). If you narrow the component instance too much, the controller bar may stick out over the edges of the video-display window.

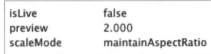

isLive	false
preview	2.000
scaleMode	maintainAspectRatio

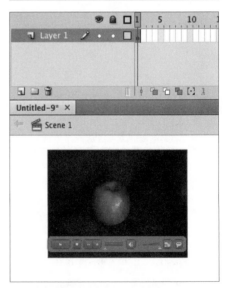

Figure 17.55 By default the FLVPlayback component's Preview parameter is set to None, and it displays a generic icon on the Stage (top). Specifying an elapsed time as the Preview parameter (middle) allows you to see one frame of the video clip during authoring (bottom).

Figure 17.56 Use the Select Skin dialog to change the user controls for video playback.

To change controller-bar skins:

1. Follow steps 1–3 in "To choose source video for an FLVPlayback instance," earlier in this chapter.

2. In the Component Inspector, in the Value column, double-click the current Skin parameter.

   The Select Skin dialog appears, showing the same items as in the Skinning page of the Import Video Wizard (**Figure 17.56**).

3. From the Skin pop-up menu, select a new skin.

   For details, see step 5 of the first task in "Importing Video for Streaming or Progressive Download," earlier in this chapter.

4. If desired, from the Color control, select a new background color for the controller bar.

5. Click OK.

   Flash updates the Skin parameter in the Parameters tab of the Component Inspector and changes the controller bar in the FLVPlayback component instance on the Stage.

THE FLVPLAYBACK COMPONENT

✔ Tips

■ To change the color of an FLVPlayback component's controller bar, select the FLVPlayback component instance on the Stage, access the Component Inspector panel, and click the Parameters button (Mac) or tab (Windows). In the Value column, double-click the hex value or color chip for the SkinBackgroundColor parameter, and choose a new color from the pop-up swatch.

■ You can also create transparency for a controller bar. In the Value column, click the parameter for SkinBackgoundAlpha to activate the parameter's text field. Enter a new value between 1 and 0 (1 equals completely opaque, 0.5 equals 50 percent transparent, and 0 equals fully transparent).

■ With one exception, the changes you make to parameters in the Component Inspector are persistent. Change the skin parameter, and the next time you place an FLVPlayback component instance it will be set to use that skin. The same is true for color, volume, transparency, and other parameters. Only the source parameter changes, to the video you specified in the Video Import Wizard, or to nothing if you place a new component instance yourself.

Final Steps for Using FLVPlayback

When you publish a Flash movie to make it available to your audience, you must place the resulting SWF file on the Web server that hosts your creation. (You'll learn more about publishing in Chapter 18.) When you use the FLVPlayback component to deliver streaming video or progressive-download video, two other files must go on the server: the file containing the encoded video (for example, an FLV file), and a SWF file containing the controller-bar skin (if you use one for your video). When you publish your movie, including whenever you choose Control > Test Movie, Flash places the SWF file of your movie and the SWF file for the controller-bar skin in the folder with your FLA. The encoded video file remains at its original location.

You may publish your movie many times as you test it during the authoring phase. During that phase, all the pathnames Flash uses to locate these required files let you test without problems. Before you publish your movie for final delivery to your audience, make sure that the source parameter for each instance of the FLVPlayback component shows the correct URL for the final location of the source video file on the hosting server. (For details about setting the source parameter, see "To choose source video for an FLVPlayback instance," earlier in this section.)

DELIVERING MOVIES TO YOUR AUDIENCE

When you finish creating graphics, animation, and interactivity in Adobe Flash CS4 Professional, it's time to deliver the goods to your audience. You must publish or export the Flash document (FLA) to create a file in a format for playback. You have several formats to choose among. The one that guarantees viewers will see all your animations and take part in all your movie's interactivity is the Flash Player format (SWF).

When you install Flash CS4, you can also install version 10 of the Flash Player application. You can view SWF files running directly in Flash Player on your computer. Other programs, such as Web browsers, can also use Flash Player to display Flash content.

You can export movies as a series of images in either bitmap format (GIF or PNG files, for example) or vector format (such as Adobe Illustrator files). Another option for movie delivery is a self-playing file called a *projector.* Users double-click the projector file to open and play the movie. And you can print your entire movie or individual frames, should you want to give someone a hard-copy version of the movie (for storyboarding, for example).

Preparing Your Movie for Optimal Playback

When creating movies to show over the Web, you face the issue of quality versus quantity. Higher quality increases file size, leading to longer download times and slower movies. You need to find a balance between the two (see the sidebar "Putting File Size into Perspective"). Things that add to a file's size include bitmaps (especially animated bitmaps), video clips (especially embedded video), sounds, multiple areas of simultaneous animation, embedded fonts, gradients, and the use of separate graphic elements instead of symbols and groups. Flash's simulated streaming helps you find out where your movie is bogging down. The Size Report and Bandwidth Profiler reveal which frames may cause download hang-ups.

To use the Bandwidth Profiler:

1. Open the Flash document that you want to test for playback over the Web.

2. Choose Control > Test Movie (or Test Scene). Flash exports the movie and opens it in Flash Player.

3. From Flash Player's View menu, choose Download Settings, and select the download speed you want to test.

   The menu lists eight speeds, all of which are customizable. To change them, choose View > Download Settings > Customize (**Figure 18.1**). By default, Flash lists five common connection speeds—14.4 Kbps, 28.8 Kbps, 56 Kbps, DSL, and T1—with settings that simulate real-world data-transfer rates. You can see the settings in the Custom Download Settings dialog (**Figure 18.2**). To create a custom setting, enter new values, and then click OK.

Figure 18.1 To create a custom connection speed for simulating playback over the Web, from the test environment's View menu, choose Download Settings > Customize.

Figure 18.2 At its default setting, Flash offers choices for simulating five standard connection speeds. You can change the names and rates for these speeds in the Custom Download Settings dialog.

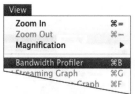

Figure 18.3 To view a graph of the amount of data in each frame, choose View > Bandwidth Profiler when a Flash Player window is open.

Downloads within the set frame rate ⎤
Causes a delay in playback ⎤

Figure 18.4 The Bandwidth Profiler graph at the top of the Flash Player window shows how much data each movie frame contains. Each bar in this version of the graph represents a frame of the movie.

Figure 18.5 In Frame by Frame Graph mode, the height of each bar indicates how much data the frame holds.

4. From Flash Player's View menu, choose Bandwidth Profiler (**Figure 18.3**).

At the top of the Test Movie window, Flash graphs the amount of data that is being transmitted against the movie's Timeline (**Figure 18.4**). The bars represent the number of bytes of data per frame. The bottom line (highlighted in red) represents the amount of data that will safely download fast enough to keep up with the movie's frame rate. Any frame that contains a greater amount of data forces the movie to pause while the data downloads.

To view the contents of each frame separately:

1. From the Flash Player's View menu, choose Frame by Frame Graph, or press ⌘-F (Mac) or Ctrl-F (Windows).

Flash presents a single bar for each frame in the Bandwidth Profiler graph. The numbers along the top of the graph represent frames (**Figure 18.5**). The height of the bar represents the amount of data in that frame.

2. Select a bar.

Specifics about that frame and the movie in general appear in the profile window.

To see how frames stream:

1. From the Flash Player's View menu, choose View > Streaming Graph, or press ⌘-G (Mac) or Ctrl-G (Windows).

   Flash displays the frames as alternating bars of light and dark gray, sized to reflect the time each one takes to download (**Figure 18.6**). The numbers along the top of the streaming graph represent frames as a unit of time based on the frame rate. (In a 10-fps movie, for example, each number represents .1 second.) Where frames contain little data, several bars may appear in a single time unit. Frames that have lots of data may stretch out over several time units.

2. Select a bar.

   Specifics about that frame and the movie in general appear in the profile window (**Figure 18.7**).

Figure 18.6 In Streaming Graph mode, the width of each bar indicates how long the frame takes to download at the given connection speed and frame rate. In this movie, frame 49 contains 6 KBytes of data and takes about 1.3 seconds to download at a frame rate of 10 fps over a 56-Kbps modem.

Frame 26

Frame 44

Figure 18.7 The profile window to the left of the graph displays information about the movie. The State section identifies the selected frame (the frame highlighted in red) and indicates the amount of data in that frame. You can see that frame 26 (top) has 1016 bytes of information, whereas frame 44 (bottom) contains only 50 bytes.

To display a download-progress bar:

◆ With Bandwidth Profiler active, from Flash Player's View menu, choose Simulate Download, or press ⌘-Return (Mac) or Ctrl-Enter (Windows).

As the animation plays in the test window, Flash highlights the numbers of the Timeline in green to show where you are in the download process.

To exit Bandwidth Profiler:

◆ From Flash Player's View menu, choose Bandwidth Profiler again to deselect it.

✔ Tip

■ To get information about the amount of data in each frame in text form, choose Generate Size Report in the Advanced section of the Flash tab of the Publish Settings dialog. During the publishing process, Flash creates a file showing the number of bytes of data in each frame of the movie.

Putting File Size into Perspective

Throughout this book, you've seen notes about techniques that add to file size. You should pay attention to file size and its impact on the end user's experience, but it's also important to keep things in perspective. In Flash's early days, its ability to keep file sizes tiny was a boon to developers who wanted to create rich, interactive Web content that people with slow dial-up connections could enjoy. Today, lots of people have fast Internet connections. The huge popularity of video sites like YouTube, live wildlife Webcams, and streaming TV shows—complete with commercial advertisements—indicate that you need not be overly concerned about adding a few bitmaps, using frame-by-frame animation, even adding sound and video, if that's the best way to convey your message or fulfill your creative goals. If your main target audience is still dialing into the Web using 14-Kbps modems, or you're developing for mobile devices using Adobe Flash Lite, then yes, minimizing file size is a high priority. Otherwise, allow yourself to take advantage of all the Flash techniques that help you create the content you envision.

A Note About Accessibility

As you think about the best ways to deliver Flash movies to your audience, also consider the fact that some members of the audience may have physical conditions that affect the way they interact with your site. As the Web has become more visually interesting, it presents challenges to visually impaired users who want to take advantage of the many resources available.

Our society is becoming more sensitive to the ways in which activities and resources exclude people with disabilities. Web designers need to use Flash to make not only eye-catching Web sites that dazzle with artwork, animation, interactivity, sound, and video, but also sites that convey information to a wide range of people. Remember that some of your users are unable to view or hear a site's content; some may not use a mouse, instead navigating and exploring the site by tabbing to each element in turn.

To address the issue of accessible Web sites, Flash lets you make content available to screen-reading software that uses Microsoft Active Accessibility (MSAA) technology. (At the time Flash CS4 was released, MSAA was available only for Windows and works only with Internet Explorer.) Screen readers provide audio feedback about a variety of elements on a Web site, reading aloud the labels of buttons, for example, or reading the contents of text fields. Through Flash's accessibility features, you can create descriptions of objects for the screen reader; prevent the screen reader from attempting to describe certain objects (such as purely decorative movie clips); and assign keyboard commands that let the user manipulate objects by pressing keys or tabbing through text fields, for example.

Figure 18.8 The Accessibility panel contains settings for making selected objects in your movie available (or unavailable) to screen-reader software.

In addition, Flash CS4 enables you to create accessible video. Flash's FLVPlayback component (see Chapter 17) creates video controllers that respond to keyboard commands and screen readers. The FLVPlaybackCaptioning component supports the World Wide Web consortium's DFXP standard for closed captioning.

The considerations that go into making an effective, accessible site are too numerous and complex to cover in a *Visual QuickStart Guide*. But you can check out the tools for defining accessible objects in the Accessibility panel. Choose Window > Other Panels > Accessibility to open the panel. The accessibility parameters for selected objects appear in the panel (**Figure 18.8**). You can also learn about best practices for accessibility from Adobe's Accessibility Resource Center (http://www.adobe.com/accessibility/).

Figure 18.9 To access the settings for publishing a movie, choose File > Publish Settings.

Figure 18.10 The Formats section of the Publish Settings dialog lets you publish your Flash content in as many as six formats at the same time. A seventh format choice creates an HTML document for displaying the published files in a browser.

Publishing

To make your movie available to the public, you must publish or export it. Flash's Publish function is geared toward presenting material on the Web and creating a range of formats for various viewers. The Export feature has similar settings but creates just one format at a time (see the sidebar "Publishing vs. Exporting").

To set the publishing format:

1. Open the Flash document you want to publish.

2. Choose File > Publish Settings, or press Option-Shift-F12 (Mac) or Ctrl-Shift-F12 (Windows) (**Figure 18.9**).

   The Publish Settings dialog appears. The top of the dialog displays a Current Profile and buttons for working with profiles. If you're working in a new document and have never created a profile, Default is your only option. If you open a file made with a previous version of Flash, the profile name reflects that version. A profile is the compilation of settings for the various publishing options. You can save settings in new profiles. Leave the current profile in place.

3. Click the Formats button (Mac) or tab (Windows) (**Figure 18.10**).

4. Choose one of the seven format options.

   The options are Flash (.swf), HTML (.html), GIF Image (.gif), JPEG Image (.jpg), PNG Image (.png), Windows Projector (.exe), and Macintosh Projector.

5. To set the options for a selected format, select the button (Mac) or tab (Windows) associated with that format (as outlined in separate tasks later in this chapter).

continues on next page

PUBLISHING

6. To save these settings with the current file, click OK.

Flash uses these settings each time you choose the Publish or Publish Preview command for this document. Flash also uses a file's current publish settings when you enter test mode (by choosing Control > Test Movie or Control > Test Scene).

✔ Tip

■ If the Document Property inspector is open, you can access the Publish Settings dialog quickly: in the Publish section, in the Profile area, click the Edit button.

Publishing vs. Exporting

Flash's Publish command uses a document's publish settings to create all the elements needed to display your Flash creation on the Web: a Flash Player (SWF) file, and an HTML file that includes JavaScript. The HTML and JavaScript work together, creating HTML code that displays the SWF (running in Flash Player) in a browser window. The JavaScript can also perform version detection, ensuring that end users have the right version of Flash Player to view your content. The Publish command can also create alternate file formats—GIF, JPEG, and PNG—and the HTML needed to display them in the browser window. Alternate formats let you make some of the animation and interactivity of your site available even to end users who lack the Flash Player plug-in. Finally, the Publishing command can create stand-alone projector files.

Flash's Export Movie command translates a Flash document directly into a single format. In general, the options for exporting to alternate graphics formats—GIF, JPEG, and PNG—are the same as for publishing to those formats. The arrangement of some options differs between the export and publish dialogs, and some formats have more options in the Publish Settings dialog. For example, the Publish Settings dialog offers the choice to remove gradients from GIFs (to keep the file size small), whereas the Export GIF dialog lacks that option. Another difference between publishing and exporting is that while Flash stores the Publish Settings with the FLA file for reuse, you must set export options each time you export a FLA file (even when you re-export the same FLA file to the same format).

Exporting allows a delivery option that's unavailable when publishing: QuickTime. When you export to QuickTime, you lose any interactivity features in your Flash movie. QuickTime export works by playing back the SFW file in Flash Player, then capturing each frame of the animation (including animation generated by ActionScript) and writing it to a frame in a QuickTime MOV file.

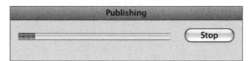

Figure 18.11 Click the Publish button in the Publish Settings dialog (top) or choose File > Publish (bottom) to publish your Flash files.

Figure 18.12 To cancel the publishing process, click the Stop (Mac) or Cancel (Windows) button in the Publishing dialog. If you've published the file before, the dialog may appear only briefly, making it difficult to cancel the operation.

Figure 18.13 The File > Publish Preview submenu displays all the formats selected in the Publish Settings dialog. Flash publishes your movie in the selected format and opens it in your browser.

To publish a movie:

1. Open the Flash file you want to publish.

2. To issue the Publish command, do either of the following:

   ▲ Choose File > Publish Settings.

   The Publish Settings dialog appears. You can follow the steps in the preceding task to set new format options or accept the current settings. Then click the Publish button (**Figure 18.11**).

   ▲ Choose File > Publish, or press Shift-F12.

   The Publishing dialog appears (**Figure 18.12**). Flash uses the publish settings stored with your Flash document, creating a new file for each format selected in the Publish Settings dialog.

✔ Tips

■ By default, Flash places each published file in the same location as the original Flash file. You can choose a new location. In the Formats section of the Publish Settings dialog, click the folder icon to the right of the filename. The Select Publish Destination dialog appears, allowing you to choose a new location for the file.

■ You can open your browser and preview a movie in one step. Choose File > Publish Preview. Flash offers a menu that contains all the formats selected in the Publish Settings dialog (**Figure 18.13**). Choose a format. Flash publishes the file in that format, using the current settings, and opens the movie in a browser window. Note that if you're using Publish Preview to test SWF files that reside on your local system, and your Flash movie links to a URL on the network, you can run into security issues (see the sidebar "A Note About Flash Player 10's Security Settings," later in this chapter).

PUBLISHING

Working with Flash Player Settings

The stand-alone Flash Player is an application file that installs with Flash. The Player opens when you double-click the icon of a SWF file. (From within Flash Player, you can use the File > Open command to open and play SWF files.) To prepare a Flash movie for playing in the stand-alone Player, choose either the Publish or Export command in the Flash editor. The options are basically the same for both commands.

To publish a Flash Player (SWF) file:

1. From an open Flash document, choose File > Publish Settings.

   The Publish Settings dialog appears; choose a base publishing profile, or leave the current setting.

2. Click the Formats button (Mac) or tab (Windows).

3. In the Type section, select Flash (.swf).

   If you wish, type a new name in the File field for the Flash (SWF) file. Be sure to include the .swf extension.

4. Click the Flash button (Mac) or tab (Windows) (**Figure 18.14**).

5. Set Flash options as described in the following tasks.

6. Click Publish.

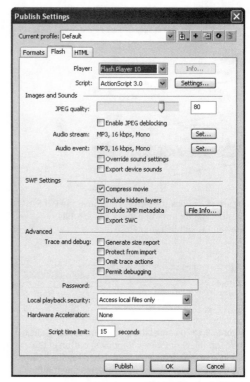

Figure 18.14 The Flash section of the Publish Settings dialog offers options for publishing your Flash movie as a Flash Player (SWF) file.

Figure 18.15 Choose a version of Flash Player to publish to. Publishing to versions earlier than 10 makes some features of Flash CS4 unavailable, but ensures that a wider audience will have the correct player.

To choose a Flash Player version:

◆ In the Flash section of the Publish Settings dialog, from the Player pop-up menu, choose a version of Flash Player (**Figure 18.15**).

Your options are Flash Player 1 (formerly known as FutureSplash Animator) through 10, Adobe AIR 1.1 (a development platform that enables Internet applications to run on an end user's system without an Internet connection), and Flash Lite 1.0, 1.1, 2.0, 2.1, and 3.0 (players that work in devices such as mobile phones). If you publish your file to a Flash Player version earlier than 10, you lose some features specific to Flash CS4.

✔ Tips

■ Before you start scripting with ActionScript, in the Flash section of the Publish Settings dialog, select the earliest version of Flash Player you plan to use to deliver content to your audience. The Actions Toolbox in the Actions panel provides feedback about actions that won't work in the selected player version.

■ When you choose Flash Player 6, 7, 8, 9, or 10, the Compress Movie check box becomes active. Compressing a file that has lots of text or ActionScript helps keep the file size down.

To choose the version of ActionScript used (Flash Player 6–10):

◆ In the Flash section of the Publish Settings dialog, from the Script pop-up menu, choose ActionScript version 1. 0, 2.0, or 3.0 (**Figure 18.16**).

This setting tells Flash which version of the scripting language you've used in your document so the compiler treats the code appropriately. The menu becomes active only when you've chosen Player 6, 7, 8, 9, or 10.

✔ Tips

■ Flash's components rely on ActionScript. It's crucial that the ActionScript version selected in the Publish Settings dialog match the components used in the FLA. If the FLA contains components from one ActionScript version and you publish to another, the components may not work or may not even appear in the published movie.

■ During authoring, the Components panel displays only components that work with the version of ActionScript currently selected in Publish Settings. To have the panel show ActionScript 3.0 components, for example, you must choose ActionScript 3.0 for publishing.

Figure 18.16 ActionScript 1.0, 2.0, and 3.0 present different tasks for the compiler when Flash publishes a SWF file. Be sure to select the version you used (or plan to use) for scripting.

Figure 18.17 To set JPEG compression for any bitmaps in your movie, type a value in the JPEG Quality field or use the slider. A setting of 0 provides the most compression (and the lowest quality, because that compression leads to loss of data); a setting of 100 results in the least compression (the highest quality).

To apply JPEG compression to bitmaps:

◆ In the Flash section of the Publish Settings dialog, in the Images and Sounds area, do either of the following:

▲ Adjust the JPEG Quality slider.

or

▲ Enter a specific value in the JPEG Quality field (**Figure 18.17**).

This setting controls how Flash applies JPEG compression as it exports the bitmaps in your movie.

✔ Tips

■ Flash doesn't apply JPEG compression to GIF images that you've imported into your movie, because Flash defaults to using lossless compression for GIFs.

■ You can set compression for individual bitmaps in the library of your Flash document. Select the bitmap in the Library panel. From the panel menu, choose Properties to access the Bitmap Properties dialog. A Compression pop-up menu offers two choices: Photo (JPEG) and Lossless (PNG/GIF). The Photo option creates lossy compression.

■ When you apply high levels of JPEG compression (low values in the JPEG Quality field), you can wind up with artifacts— areas that look blurry or blocky— in the published images. To smooth out blocky artifacts, select the Enable JPEG Deblocking check box just beneath the JPEG Quality slider.

WORKING WITH FLASH PLAYER SETTINGS

To control compression and sample rate for all movie sounds:

Figure 18.18 You must set the sample rate and compression options for stream sounds and event sounds separately. Click the Set button to access the options for each type of sound.

1. In the Flash section of the Publish Settings dialog, in the Images and Sounds area, for the Audio Stream option (or the Audio Event option), click the Set button (**Figure 18.18**).

   The Sound Settings dialog appears. Flash divides sounds into two types: stream and event (for more details, see Chapter 17). You must set the compression for each type separately, but the process and options are the same for both.

2. From the Compression pop-up menu (**Figure 18.19**), choose one of the following options:

   Disable removes sound from the published file.

   ADPCM compression works best for movies containing mostly short event sounds, such as hand claps or button clicks. (Generally, you'll use this setting in the Audio Event section.) The ADPCM options appear. From the ADPCM Bits pop-up menu, choose one of the four bit rates to determine the degree of compression applied to the sounds (**Figure 18.20**). With the ADPCM setting, you can also set a sample rate and convert stereo sound to mono sound.

Figure 18.19 Choose a compression method from the Compression pop-up menu. Other options appropriate to the selected method appear. Choose Disable to turn off sound.

Sample-Rate Rule of Thumb

Sample rates are measured in kHz or frequency. Recording for music CDs is done at 44 kHz. For multimedia CD-ROMs, 22 kHz is a standard rate. For music clips in Flash movies played on the Web, 11 kHz is often sufficient. For shorter sounds, including spoken words, you may be able to get away with even lower sampling rates.

Figure 18.20 The ADPCM Bits pop-up menu lets you control the amount of compression applied to the sounds in your movie. Choose 2-Bit for the greatest degree of compression (resulting in the lowest-quality sound); choose 5-Bit for the least compression (resulting in the highest-quality sound).

Figure 18.21 With MP3 compression and a bit-rate setting of less than 20 Kbps, Flash converts sounds from stereo to mono. At settings of 20 Kbps and above, you can publish stereo sounds or convert them to mono sounds.

MP3 compression works best for movies containing mostly longer stream sounds. (Generally, you'll use this setting in the Audio Stream section.) The MP3 options appear. From the Bit Rate pop-up menu, choose one of 12 bit rates for the published sounds (**Figure 18.21**). From the Quality pop-up menu, choose Fast when you are testing your movie; choose Medium or Best when you publish for your target audience, as they provide better quality.

Raw omits sound compression. Raw does let you control file size by choosing a sample rate and converting stereo sound to mono.

Speech sets compression for sounds consisting of spoken words. Choose a sample rate from the pop-up menu that appears.

Options for Publishing Digitally Recorded Sounds

As motion pictures are to movement, digital recordings are to sound. Both media capture slices of a continuous event. By playing the captured slices back in order, you re-create the event. In a movie, the slices are frames of film; in a digital recording, they're snippets of sound.

You can think of the recording process as capturing a sound wave by laying a grid over it and copying a piece of the wave at each intersection on the grid. The lines across the horizontal axis are the *sample rate*—how often you capture the sound. The lines up and down the vertical axis are the *bit rate*—how much detail you capture about the sound wave's amplitude. The greater the frequency and bit rate (the finer the mesh of your recording grid), the greater the realism of your recording during playback. This greater realism translates into larger files.

The options in the Images and Sounds section of the Publish Settings dialog give you the flexibility to create different versions of your movie with different sample rates and bit rates without actually changing the sounds embedded in the movie. You might allow yourself larger file sizes and higher-quality sounds for a version being delivered on CD-ROM than for a version being distributed on the Web. As you try different sound options, be sure to listen to your published sounds to determine the best balance between sound quality and file size.

To compress the SWF file (Flash Player 6 –10):

1. In the Flash section of the Publish Settings dialog, from the Player pop-up menu choose Flash Player 6, 7, 8, 9, or 10.

2. In the SWF Settings area of the dialog, select the Compress Movie check box (**Figure 18.22**).

    Compress Movie is an option only when you publish for Flash Player versions 6–10. The setting has no effect on the JPEG-quality and audio-compression settings you chose in the preceding tasks.

To include XMP metadata:

◆ In the Flash section of the Publish Settings dialog, in the SWF Settings area, select the Include XMP Metadata check box (**Figure 18.23**).

Select to compress

Figure 18.22 When you've chosen to publish to Flash Player versions 6–10, you can also choose to compress the movie. Compression helps reduce the file size, especially for text-heavy movies or those with lots of ActionScript.

Figure 18.23 When you select the Include XMP Metadata check box, the published SWF file includes information—such as titles, descriptions, copyright notice—that you've entered into the XMP info dialog.

About XMP File Info

Flash CS4 lets you include XMP (Extensible Metadata Platform) information in your FLA file. Adding XMP data can be helpful when you work collaboratively, sharing the file with others and using multiple Adobe products to create content. You can also include XMP metadata as a part of a published SWF file. You can use XMP metadata to create titles, descriptions, copyright notices, and so on. When you include XMP metadata with a SWF, the data becomes available to Internet search engines for indexing. To create the XMP metadata, during authoring choose File > File Info. The File Info dialog that appears offers 12 categories of information. To choose a category, click its tab at the top of the dialog window. For example, click the Description tab to enter information about your Flash document, including title, author, description, rating, keywords, and copyright notice. Once you've entered information into all the categories you want, click OK. When you select the Include XMP Metadata check box in the Flash section of the Publish Settings dialog, the data you entered into the File Info dialog becomes part of the published SWF file.

Trace and debug: ☑ Generate size report

```
OUTPUT
SpringScene1©copy.swf Movie Report
-----------------------------------
Frame #   Frame Bytes   Total Bytes   Scene
-------   -----------   -----------   -----
    1         4371          4371      Scene 1 (AS 2.0 Classes Export Frame)
    2           22          4393
    3            9          4402
    4            9          4411
                 9          4420
                            4429
```

```
   71
   72        13
   73        13         15136
   74        31         15167

Scene                Shape Bytes   Text Bytes   ActionScriptBytes
-----                -----------   ----------   -----------------
Scene 1                  1661          0               22

Symbol               Shape Bytes   Text Bytes   ActionScriptBytes
------               -----------   ----------   -----------------
Butterflywing            203          0               0
Butterflybody            118          0               0
Antenna1                 108          0               0
Antenna                   94          0               0
Butterfly                215          0               0
drops                    643          0               0
Rain drops                 0          0               0
Leaf 1                   100          0               0
Leaf 3                   138          0               0
Leaf                     115          0               0
Bush trunk               727          0               0
Leafy bush                 0          0               0
rectanglefor rainbowmask  41          0               0
Rainbow                   98          0               0

TweenedShapes  133 bytes

ActionScriptBytes    Location
-----------------    --------
       13            Scene 1:Actions1
        7            Scene 1:Actions2
        2            Scene 1:Actions74

Event Sounds  11KHz Mono 16 kbps MP3

Sound name           Bytes     Format
----------           -----     ------
cricket              6463      11KHz Mono 16 kbps MP3
DRIP1.aif             847      11KHz Mono 16 kbps MP3
```

Figure 18.24 Choose Generate Size Report (top) to have Flash use the Output panel to list the amount of data in your movie (bottom).

Trace and debug: ☑ Generate size report
☑ Protect from import
☐ Omit trace actions
☑ Permit debugging
Password: [   ]

Figure 18.25 Select the Protect from Import check box to prevent viewers from converting a SWF file back into a FLA file.

To list the amount of data in the movie by frame:

◆ In the Flash section of the Publish Settings dialog, in the Advanced area, select the Generate Size Report check box (**Figure 18.24**).

Flash lists the frames of the movie and how much data each frame contains in the Output panel. This data—known as the *Size report* helps you find frames that bog down the movie's playback. You can then optimize or eliminate some of the content in those frames.

✔ Tips

■ In addition to displaying the Size report in the Output panel, Flash creates a text file containing the Size report.

■ The Size report also details how much data is in each symbol used in the movie. Symbols that aren't used appear in the report, but they contain 0 bytes of data.

■ Depending on how you've sized the Output window, and the specific data generated by the Size report, you may see only white space in the Output window. Resize the window or scroll up to view the Size report data.

To protect your work:

◆ In the Flash section of the Publish Settings dialog, in the Advanced area, under Trace and Debug, select the Protect from Import check box (**Figure 18.25**).

This setting prevents viewers from obtaining the SWF file and converting it back to a Flash document (FLA).

✔ Tip

■ You can make the Protect from Import setting selective. Enter a password in the Password field. Only those who enter the correct password can import the SWF file.

To set trace and debug options:

◆ In the Flash section of the Publish Settings dialog, in the Advanced area, under Trace and Debug, select either of the following check boxes:

Omit Trace Actions prevents trace actions from appearing in the Output window during debugging (**Figure 18.26**).

Permit Debugging allows remote debugging of ActionScripts (**Figure 18.27**). You or other users running the debug version of Flash Player can debug a Flash Player (SWF) file as it plays over the Internet.

✔ Tip

■ When the Permit Debugging option is selected, you should always select Protect from Import and enter a password in the Password field (**Figure 18.27**). This password prohibits unauthorized individuals from accessing your script but allows authorized personnel to debug the file remotely.

To control access to local and network files for security:

◆ To determine which types of files the SWF file can copy data from or write data to, in the Flash section of the Publish Settings dialog, in the Advanced section, from the Local Playback Security pop-up menu (**Figure 18.28**), choose either of the following options:

Access Local Files Only. With local-only access, the SWF file can share information with files on the local system where the SWF file resides, but not with files located on the Internet. Local-only access prevents a SWF file from loading XML files from the Internet or posting data from an entry form to the Internet, for example.

Access Network Only. With network-only access, the SWF file can share information only with files located on the Internet, not with local files.

Figure 18.26 When you select the Omit Trace Actions option, the Flash compiler strips all trace actions from the SWF file, allowing you to view only non-trace debugging items in the Output window. Omitting trace actions also reduces file size slightly if your scripts contain lots of trace actions.

Figure 18.27 When you select the Permit Debugging option, you should also select Protect from Import and enter a password to protect movies that are open to remote debugging.

Figure 18.28 Flash CS4 provides security by restricting SWF files from manipulating data on different systems. With Access Local Files Only as the setting, the published SWF file can copy or write data only to files on the local system. With Access Network Only, the SWF file can copy or write data only to files on the Internet and not on the local system.

A Note About Flash Player 10's Security Settings

Flash CS4 and Flash Player versions 8–10 let you create content that uploads and/or downloads files at runtime; this capability gives Flash more power than it had in earlier versions, but with that power comes the potential to do harm. Flash Player versions 8–10 use a security feature that ensures that SWF files can't perform malicious deeds on the systems of your target audience. Flash's default local-security settings prohibit SWF files running locally (on a single computer) from communicating with files being served on the Internet (and vice versa); to allow such communication, you must give Flash Player specific permissions.

When you choose Flash Player version 8, 9, or 10 in Publish Settings, the security model comes into play. When you publish your Flash creation locally before deploying it to a server and you try out the movie in a browser, clicking a button or link in the movie that connects to the Internet may trigger a warning that Flash Player has stopped an operation that might be unsafe.

If the SWF you're testing doesn't need to communicate with both the local system and the Internet, you can solve the problem by changing your Publish Settings. In the Flash section of the Publish Settings dialog, under Local Playback Security, choose Access Network Only. (Note that if you try out your movie using one of the testing modes, the security alert does not appear. In test mode, Flash automatically trusts all local files being accessed.)

If, after changing the Local Playback Security setting, you still get the warning, you need to give your SWF file special permission to communicate with the Internet. When the Adobe Flash Player Security dialog appears (**Figure 18.29**), click the Settings button. Flash opens a browser window and directs you to a page of the Flash Player documentation on the Adobe site (http://www.macromedia.com/support/documentation/en/flashplayer/help/settings_manager04a.html). This page gives you access to the Adobe Flash Player Settings Manager (**Figure 18.30**).

continues on next page

Global Security
Settings tab

Click to add trusted
files and/or folders

Figure 18.29 When a SWF file on a local computer attempts to access a file on the Internet, Flash Player 10 won't allow it to, unless you've set the proper security settings. You'll see a warning dialog to alert you to the fact that your settings don't allow this communication.

Figure 18.30 The Global Security Settings tab of the Adobe Flash Player Settings Manager lets you create a list of trusted files and/or folders for Flash Player 10 security. Any SWF files in locations covered by this list can communicate with Internet files.

A Note About Flash Player 10's Security Settings *continued*

Use the Global Security Settings tab of the manager to create a list of trusted items. Flash Player always allows SWF files from the Global Security Settings list to communicate with the Internet, even if they're being run locally. Use the Edit Locations pop-up menu to add individual SWF files or folders to the trusted list or remove them from the list (**Figure 18.31**). If you'll be doing lots of this type of testing, it makes sense to set up a special Trusted folder where you keep only your own SWF files you need to test. Don't allow Flash Player to trust folders on your system that might include SWF files downloaded from other sources. Such files have the potential to do something dangerous, such as copying information from your system and sending it to an outside location.

Figure 18.31 Click the Edit Locations pop-up menu to manage a list of trusted files (left). Click Add Location to open a window (middle) where you can add a new file or folder to a trusted list. If you opened the Global Security Settings Manager by clicking the Settings button of the security warning dialog (Figure 18.30), the window's Tip field shows the path name for the file you were working on. Copy and paste that name to the Trusted field (or use a Browse button to find a file); click Confirm to add the trusted file to the trusted list (right).

Advanced Sound Handling

Flash applies the sound-compression settings in the Publish Settings dialog to all sound assets that have no specific settings of their own. By assigning higher quality to some sounds, you can keep file size reasonable and have high-quality sound where needed.

To set compression options for sounds individually, select a sound asset in the Library panel; then click the Properties button (the *i* icon) at the bottom of the panel or choose Properties from the panel menu. The Sound Properties dialog appears. Its Compression pop-up menu gives you access to the same sound-export settings you find in the settings for Audio in the Images and Sounds area of the Flash section of the Publish Settings dialog.

If you apply individual sound-export settings to some sound assets, Flash uses those settings for those sounds when you publish the movie. For all other sounds in the movie, Flash uses the current sound settings in the Publish Settings dialog.

You can force Flash to ignore the individual sound settings and publish all sounds with the sound-export settings currently selected in the Publish Settings dialog. In the Images and Sounds area of the Flash section of the Publish Settings dialog, select the Override Sound Settings check box. You might use this feature to make a lower-quality Web version of a movie you created for CD-ROM.

Figure 18.32 The HTML section of the Publish Settings dialog contains options for displaying your Flash movie in the browser window.

Publishing HTML for Flash Player Files

An *HTML document* is a master set of instructions that tells a browser how to display Web content. The Publish function of Flash creates an HTML document that tells the browser how to display the published files for your document (these files can be in SWF, GIF, JPEG, and/or PNG format—whatever you choose in the Formats section of the Publish Settings dialog). The Publish command creates the required HTML by filling in blanks in a template document. Flash comes with ten templates; you can also create your own.

To publish HTML for displaying a Flash file:

1. In the Flash document you want to publish for the Web, choose File > Publish Settings.

    The Publish Settings dialog appears; choose a new publishing profile, or leave the current setting.

2. Click the Formats button (Mac) or tab (Windows).

3. In the Type section, select the HTML (.html) check box.

    When you choose HTML, Flash automatically selects the Flash check box (.swf) as well.

4. Click the HTML button (Mac) or tab (Windows) (**Figure 18.32**).

    The options for displaying your Flash movie in the browser window appear in the dialog. When you publish the current file, Flash feeds your choices into the appropriate HTML tags and parameters in the template of your choice.

To create HTML for Flash only:

◆ From the Template pop-up menu, choose Flash Only (**Figure 18.33**).

This template is the simplest one. It uses HTML to display your Flash content for viewers who are properly equipped with the Flash Player version that you select in the Flash section of the Publish Settings dialog. To allow viewers to install or upgrade their Flash Player, select "Detect Flash Player Version" below. Flash fills in the version based on your current setting in the Flash settings. (Other template choices create HTML that performs other tasks; for example, the Image Map template creates HTML that displays alternate images or files when the viewer lacks the proper Flash Player plug-in.)

✔ Tip

■ If you can't remember what one of the included HTML templates does, select it from the Template pop-up menu in the HTML tab of the Publish Settings dialog, and then click the Info button next to the menu. Flash displays a brief description, including instructions about choosing alternate formats, if necessary.

Figure 18.33 Choose Flash Only (A) as the template when you want to create HTML for displaying only a Flash movie with no other options for alternate images. Click the Info button (B) to see a description of what the template does (C).

A Background of a Different Color

The default HTML template automatically sets the background color of your Web page to the background color of your movie. If you want to use a different color, try creating a modified template. Open the default template, and save a copy with a new name. In the first line of code—$TTFlash Only—change the title to something like $TTFlash Only (BlackBackground), so Flash recognizes and adds the template to the Template menu. In the tag <BODY bgcolor="$BG">, replace $BG with the HTML code for a specific hex color (000000 for a black background, for example). Be sure to place the new template in Flash's HTML folder inside the Configuration folder (for more details about locating this folder, see the sidebar "The Mystery of the Configuration Folder," in Chapter 1).

The Mystery of HTML Templates

The traditional HTML codes (called *tags*) required for displaying a SWF file in a browser window are `<object>` for Internet Explorer (Windows) and `<embed>` for other browsers. (In addition, Flash can use the `<img>` tag to display a file in another format, such as a JPEG image or an animated GIF.)

Flash's Publish command works hand in hand with HTML templates—which are fill-in-the-blank recipes—and JavaScript to define the parameters of the `<object>` and `<embed>` tags. These parameters include the width and height of the movie window, the quality of the images (the amount of antialiasing to provide), and the way the movie window aligns with the browser window.

Each option and parameter in the HTML section of the Publish Settings dialog has an equivalent template variable. The *template variable* is a code word that starts with the dollar sign (\$). When you choose an option in the Publish Settings dialog, Flash enters your choice as an HTML tag that replaces the variable in the template document. If you set the width of your movie as 500 pixels in the Publish Settings dialog for HTML, for example, Flash replaces the template variable for width (`$WI`) with the proper coding to display the movie in a window 500 pixels wide. To get a bit more technical, the template variables are actually parameters in a JavaScript function. When you publish, Flash creates an HTML file that calls the JavaScript function to write out the `<object>` and `<embed>` tags dynamically at runtime.

Flash's HTML templates contain coding not only for displaying your Flash movie, but also for showing the JPEG, GIF, or PNG version of your movie that you want to make available to viewers who don't have the proper browser player to view Flash.

During the publishing process, Flash saves a copy of the HTML template for your movie, giving it the name of your movie file and adding whatever extension the template file has. (The template files that come with Flash use the extension .html, for example.) You can go into a template file as you would any other text file and modify the HTML coding.

You can extend the Publish command's capacity for creating HTML documents by setting up your own HTML templates. To be available to Flash's template menu, the HTML file must include a title (use the code `$TT`). The HTML file must be inside the HTML folder, which lives in the Configuration Folder. For more details on locating this folder, see the sidebar "The Mystery of the Configuration Folder," in Chapter 1.

To set the dimensions of the movie-display window:

◆ To set the width and height of the rectangle that displays your movie in the browser, from the Dimensions pop-up menu in the HTML section of the Publish Settings dialog (**Figure 18.34**), choose one of the following options:

Match Movie uses the movie's dimensions (specified in the Document Properties dialog).

Pixels lets you specify new dimensions. Type the new values in the Width and Height fields.

Percent lets you specify the dimensions as a percentage of the browser window's dimensions. Type a value between 1 and 100 in the Width and Height fields.

Figure 18.34 Choose a method for sizing the movie-display window (the window in which a browser displays your Flash movie).

Fitting Movies into Browser Windows

When you publish HTML for displaying movies in a Web page, think in terms of three windows:

◆ The *browser window* contains the entire Web page.

◆ Within the browser window is a *movie-display* window (created by the JavaScript script and/or by the HTML <object>, <embed>, and <img> tags) where the Flash Player plug-in displays a Flash movie.

◆ Inside the movie-display window is the actual *movie window,* which corresponds to the Stage of your Flash document.

Each of the three windows has its own dimensions, and you need to tell Flash where to put the windows and how to handle them if, for example, their aspect ratios differ, or if a user resizes the browser window. To instruct browsers on how to deal with these three windows, choose settings in the HTML section of the Publish Settings dialog. When you define a movie-display window with a different width or height from the original Flash document, you must tell Flash how to scale the movie to fit in that window.

Figure 18.35 The scale method tells Flash how to fit the Flash movie inside the movie-display window that you define. You need to set the scale only if you define a movie-display window with different dimensions from those of the movie itself—as a percentage of the browser width and height, for example.

Dimensions:
Match Movie
Scale: No Scale

Dimensions:
100 by 50 pixels
Scale: No Border

Dimensions:
100 by 50 pixels
Scale: Exact Fit

Figure 18.36 This 300-by-300–pixel movie looks quite different in the various dimension-and-scale combinations. The movie-display window's dimensions and the scale setting are identified in the examples above. (Here the browser background has been set to black to make the movie-display window visible.)

To scale the movie to fit a movie-display window:

◆ From the Scale pop-up menu (**Figure 18.35**), choose one of the following options:

Default (Show All) keeps the movie's original aspect ratio (width to height) and resizes the movie so that it fits completely within the newly specified rectangle (**Figure 18.36**). Be aware that the resized movie may not fill the new rectangle: gaps may appear on the sides or at the top and bottom.

No Border keeps the movie's original aspect ratio and resizes the movie so the whole new rectangle is filled with it. Some of the movie may slop over the edges and be cropped.

Exact Fit changes the movie's height and width to the new specifications, even if it involves changing the aspect ratio and distorting the image.

No Scale keeps the movie at a constant size. Resizing the browser window can crop the image.

✔ Tip

■ If you define the movie-display window as 100 percent of the width and height of the browser window, in some browser versions, no matter how large your viewer makes the browser window, a scroll bar always appears. Setting the width and height to 95 percent (or lower) ensures that all viewers will be able to enlarge the browser window enough to eliminate the scroll bar.

PUBLISHING HTML FOR FLASH PLAYER FILES

To control placement of the movie window in the movie-display window:

◆ To align the movie window within the movie-display window, in the Flash Alignment section of the HTML tab of the Publish Settings dialog, do either of the following:

▲ From the Horizontal pop-up menu, choose Left, Center, or Right.

or

▲ From the Vertical pop-up menu, choose Top, Center, or Bottom.

Flash positions the movie within the movie-display window (**Figure 18.37**).

To set playback options:

◆ In the Playback area of the HTML section of the Publish Settings dialog, select any of the following options (**Figure 18.38**):

Paused at Start makes users begin the movie manually (by clicking a button or by choosing Play from the contextual menu).

Loop makes the movie start over when it reaches the last frame.

Display Menu creates a contextual menu with playback options available to users.

Device Font speeds playback on Windows systems. The Device Font option allows Windows systems to substitute aliased system fonts for fonts that aren't installed on the user's system. This substitution takes place only in static text blocks where you've enabled device fonts during the authoring phase.

Horizontal: Right; Vertical: Center

Horizontal: Left; Vertical: Center

Figure 18.37 The Flash Alignment section's Horizontal and Vertical pop-up menus let you position your movie within the movie-display window when the dimensions of that window differ from those of the movie. Compare the results of two different settings for this 300-by-300–pixel movie set inside a 200-by-100–pixel display window (with Scale set to Default). The light gray rectangle is the display window, which automatically fills with the same color as your movie's background.

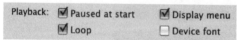

Figure 18.38 The HTML section of the Publish Settings dialog gives you options for controlling playback. You control whether the movie starts playing immediately in the browser window, or if it's in a paused state waiting for user input to start; whether the movie loops, or plays through just once; and whether users can control playback from the contextual menu. For Windows machines, you can improve playback speed by activating device fonts.

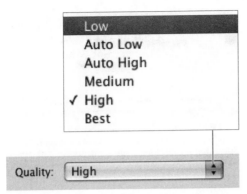

Figure 18.39 The Quality setting for publishing HTML balances image quality against playback speed in a published movie.

To control antialiasing and smoothing:

◆ From the Quality pop-up menu in the HTML section of the Publish Settings dialog (**Figure 18.39**), choose one of the following options:

Low. Flash keeps antialiasing off.

Auto Low. Flash starts playback with antialiasing off; but if it finds that the viewer's computer and connection can handle antialiasing while keeping the movie's specified frame rate, Flash turns antialiasing on.

Auto High. Flash turns antialiasing on to start, and turns it off if playback drops below the movie's specified frame rate.

Medium. Taking the middle ground, Flash forgoes bitmap smoothing but does some antialiasing.

High. Flash uses antialiasing on everything but smooths bitmaps only if there is no animation.

Best. Flash keeps antialiasing on and smooths all bitmaps.

Printing from Flash Player

By default, choosing Print from the Flash Player contextual menu prints every frame in the movie. You can restrict printing to certain keyframes by labeling them as printable in the original Flash document. To define a keyframe as printable, select it; and in the Label section of the Frame Property inspector, from the Type menu, choose Name; in the Name field, enter #p (it must be a lowercase letter *p*). For the contextual menu to be available in Flash Player, you need to set the playback options in the HTML section of the Publish Settings dialog to Display Menu (see "Publishing HTML for Flash Player Files," earlier in this chapter). To disable printing from Flash Player, select any keyframe in your Flash document, and in the Label section of the Frame Property inspector, with Type set to Name, in the Name field enter !#p. When you publish the file, the Print option is disabled in Flash Player's contextual menu.

To control transparency:

◆ From the Window Mode pop-up menu, choose one of the following options (**Figure 18.40**):

   Window plays the Flash movie window in a separate movie-display window within the Web page.

   Opaque Windowless plays the Flash movie window directly in the browser window.

   Transparent Windowless plays the Flash movie window directly in the browser window.

Figure 18.40 For viewers of your Flash movie who use qualified browsers, you can create a transparency effect that reveals Web-page elements beneath any transparent areas of the movie. In the HTML tab of the Publish Settings dialog, set Window Mode to Transparent Windowless.

To see warnings about missing alternate content:

◆ At the bottom of the HTML section of the Publish Settings dialog, select the Show Warning Messages check box if you want Flash to notify you if the currently selected template creates tags to display alternate content—a GIF file, for example—but you've neglected to select the appropriate format in the Formats section of the Publish Settings dialog.

More About Window Modes

In Window mode, the movie-display window blocks elements of the Web page on layers below the Flash movie and often blocks (or interferes with) elements above the movie-display window as well. Window mode gives Flash complete control of the window-display area of the screen and therefore results in the best performance. In Opaque Windowless mode, elements of the Web page that lie above the Flash movie do appear. Elements of the Web page that lie below the Flash movie do not appear. The Transparent Windowless setting allows elements of the Web page to show through any areas of your Flash movie that don't contain objects. This setting may slow the playback of your animation. In addition, keyboard commands may behave differently in Opaque Windowless and Transparent Windowless modes, and some browsers may have problems aligning the hit areas of buttons. Be sure to allow more time for testing when you use these modes.

Only certain browsers (and certain versions of Flash Player) support the ability to create transparent backgrounds for published SWF content. The earliest versions of Flash Player that support the Transparent Windowless setting are 6.0.65.0 (Windows) and 6.0.67.0 (Mac).

Using Alternate Image Formats

Most end users will have access to the Flash Player plug-in required to view your Flash content, but some may not. You can make at least part of your site available to them by providing alternate image files for their browsers to display. If you're using Flash animation for a simple Web banner, for example, you can use an animated GIF to re-create that banner for viewers who lack the Flash plug-in. Flash can publish alternate GIF, JPEG, and PNG. Of course, you need a file with the proper HTML coding to direct the viewer's browser to display the alternate file. The HTML Template named Image Map assists you in creating the necessary HTML file, as does Flash's version-detection feature (see "Using Version Detection," later in this chapter).

Although each image format has its own set of publishing options, the basic methods for publishing the alternate formats are the same. This task walks you through the settings for GIF files.

About the Image Map Template

If your Flash file contains button symbols using ActionScript 2.0 to link to URLs, you can convert that content to an *image map*—a GIF (or PNG or JPEG) file containing hot spots that link to other sites. To have Flash create an image map whose hot spots coincide with your Flash button symbols, choose HTML as well as GIF (or PNG or JPEG) in the Formats section of the Publish Settings dialog. From the Template pop-up menu in the HTML section of the dialog, choose Image Map. Click Publish. Although Flash creates a SWF file whenever you publish HTML format files, the Image Map template creates an HTML file that tells browsers to display the GIF (or PNG or JPG) file and not the SWF. When the browser displays the image map, viewers see your graphic content, and the buttons seem live because they're active links. (Note that the Image Map template creates hot spots only from button symbols, not button components or movie clips acting as buttons. And the button symbol must use the ActionScript 2.0 action getURL. Flash can't create image maps from button symbols targeted by ActionScript 3.0.)

To publish GIF files:

1. Open the Flash document, and choose File > Publish Settings.

   The Publish Setting dialog appears; choose a new publishing profile, or leave the current setting.

2. In the Formats section of the dialog, choose GIF Image (.gif).

3. In the GIF section of the dialog (**Figure 18.41**), set GIF options as described in the following tasks.

4. Click Publish.

To set the dimensions of the GIF image:

◆ In the Dimensions area of the GIF section of the Publish Settings dialog (**Figure 18.42**), do either of the following:

▲ To create a new size for the published GIF image, deselect Match Movie and enter values in the Width and Height fields.

   or

▲ To keep the GIF images the same size as the original Flash movie, select Match Movie.

To create static or animated GIFs:

◆ In the Playback area of the GIF section of the Publish Settings dialog (**Figure 18.43**), select either of the following options:

Static creates a static GIF.

Animated creates an animated GIF. The animation settings become active. To make the animation run repeatedly, select Loop Continuously. To repeat the animation a set number of times, select Repeat and enter a number in the Repeat field. Flash exports all the frames of the movie as an animated GIF.

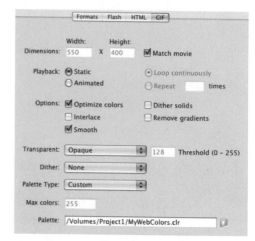

Figure 18.41 Click the GIF button (Mac) or tab (Windows) of the Publish Settings dialog to access the options for creating a static or animated GIF for your alternate image.

Figure 18.42 Deselect Match Movie to enter the dimensions you want the published GIF image to have, or select Match Movie to use the movie's dimensions as those of your GIF image.

Figure 18.43 To preserve the motion of your Flash movie (though not the sound or interactivity) for viewers who lack the Flash Player plug-in, select the Animated radio button under Playback in the GIF section of the Publish Settings dialog.

Figure 18.44 Assigning the frame label #Static tells Flash to use that frame for static GIF files.

Figure 18.45 The Options settings in the GIF section of the Publish Settings dialog help you limit the amount of time your viewers spend looking at a blank screen, waiting for an image to appear. (The Remove Gradients option is available only in the Publish Settings dialog, not in the Export GIF dialog.)

✔ Tip

- By default, when creating a static GIF, Flash uses the first frame of your movie. To use another frame, create a keyframe at the desired frame number, select it, and access the Frame Property inspector. In the Label section, from the Type menu, choose Name; in the Name field, enter the frame label #Static (**Figure 18.44**).

To balance size, download speed, and appearance:

◆ In the Options area of the GIF section of the Publish Settings dialog, select any of the following options (**Figure 18.45**):

Optimize Colors removes any unused colors from the GIF file's color table.

Interlace makes the GIF appear quickly at low resolution and come into focus as the download continues. (The Interlace option should be used only for static GIFs.)

Smooth makes Flash use antialiasing to smooth bitmaps for your animated GIF. Deselecting Smooth reduces the size of the file.

Dither Solids applies the dither method selected in the Dither menu to solids as well as gradients and bitmapped images.

Remove Gradients reduces file size by converting gradient fills to solid fills. (Flash uses the first color in the gradient as the solid fill color.)

To control colors that aren't in the current color palette:

1. From the Dither pop-up menu in the GIF section of the Publish Settings dialog, choose one of the following options (**Figure 18.46**):

   None replaces the missing color with the closest match from the current palette.

   Ordered simulates the missing color by applying a regular pattern of colors from the current palette.

   Diffusion simulates the missing color by applying a random pattern of colors from the Web 216 palette. (You must also choose Web 216 as your Palette Type in step 2 for Diffusion to work.)

2. From the Palette Type pop-up menu, choose a color table for use with this GIF (**Figure 18.47**).

   Your choices are Web 216 (the standard 216 Web-safe colors), Adaptive (only colors used in your document; 256 colors maximum), Web Snap Adaptive (a modified Adaptive palette, substituting Web-safe colors for any near matches to colors in the document that aren't Web safe), and Custom (the color table specified in step 4).

3. If you chose Adaptive or Web Snap Adaptive as the Palette Type, in the Max Colors field, type the number of colors you want to use.

   This option lets you further limit the size of the color table available for the GIF and thus reduce file size.

4. If you chose Custom as the Palette Type, load the custom palette (**Figure 18.48**).

   Click the Browse button (the folder icon). The Open dialog appears; navigate to the custom palette file, select it, and click Open.

Figure 18.46 The GIF format has three options for dithering colors that aren't included in the current color table.

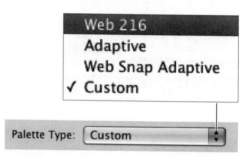

Figure 18.47 Choose a palette that optimizes colors for the published GIF image. You can create custom palettes or use the Web-safe or adaptive palettes provided by Flash.

Browse button ⏊

Figure 18.48 When you choose Custom from the Palette Type pop-up menu, you must enter the palette file's path in the Palette field. Click the Browse button (the folder icon) to open a dialog for locating the file.

Figure 18.49 To get automatic version detection when you publish your Flash document, you must select Flash Player 4 or later from the Player pop-up menu in the Flash section of the Publish Settings dialog.

Using Version Detection

The Flash Player plug-in is widely distributed, but not everyone has the latest player version installed. To make sure your audience has the right player for viewing your Flash content, use one of the three templates that create HTML that performs version detection (see the sidebar "About Version Detection").

To detect the viewer's Flash Player version:

1. In an open Flash document, choose File > Publish Settings.

   The Publish Settings dialog appears; choose a new publishing profile, or leave the current setting.

2. Click the Flash button (Mac) or tab (Windows) in the dialog.

   The settings for Publishing SWF files appear.

3. From the Player pop-up menu, choose Flash Player version 4 or later (**Figure 18.49**).

4. Click the HTML button (Mac) or tab (Windows) in the dialog.

5. From the Template menu, choose Flash Only, Flash HTTPS, or Flash Only–Allow Full Screen.

   These are the only included templates that automatically create version-detection code for you.

continues on next page

USING VERSION DETECTION

6. Select the Detect Flash Version check box.

If you want to detect specific revisions to the Flash Player, enter them in the fields for minor and incremental revisions (**Figure 18.50**).

7. To confirm your settings, click OK.

When you publish a document using version detection, Flash creates an HTML file that displays the SWF file in a browser window; this HTML file also contains JavaScript coding for detecting the Flash Player version on the end user's system.

Minor revision ⎤

Incremental revision ⎤

Figure 18.50 When you select the Detect Flash Version check box, the fields for minor and incremental revision numbers become active. Enter the precise version numbers that your end user will need to view your Flash content.

About Version Detection

Version detection is the process of verifying what version of Flash Player is running on a viewer's system. Three of the HTML templates that come with Flash CS4—Flash Only, Flash Only–Allow Full Screen, and Flash HTTPS—create the coding necessary to carry out one form of version detection. If an end user tries to view your Flash content from a system that has the required player, the browser displays your content. If Flash Player is missing or the version number is too low, the browser displays a Web page containing a link to Adobe's Web site where the correct player can be downloaded. (If you use the Flash HTTPS template, the browser sends the user to an Adobe HTTPS site to download the player.)

Flash's other HTML templates don't carry out version detection. The Image Map template is specifically designed to create HTML that doesn't require Flash Player; therefore, version detection is unnecessary. The remaining templates use JavaScript that conflicts with the JavaScript used by Flash Only, Flash Only–Allow Full Screen, and Flash HTTPS (the script that embeds the SWF file in the HTML). If you want to use one of these templates, you can still get help with version detection from the Publishing command, but you must create an additional short FLA that directs users to your main Flash content. Publish the short FLA using one of the HTML templates that does version detection. If your viewers have the right player version, the short SWF sends them directly to your main content. If they lack the right version, they get directed to the Web site to download the current Flash Player first.

INDEX